Weathering the Storm

Weathering the Storm

Working-Class Families from the
Industrial Revolution to the Fertility Decline

◆

WALLY SECCOMBE

VERSO

London · New York

First published by Verso 1993
© Verso 1993
All rights reserved

Verso
UK: 6 Meard Street, London W1V 3HR
USA: 29 West 35th Street, New York, NY 10001-2291

Verso is the imprint of New Left Books

ISBN 0-86091-333-3

British Library Cataloguing in Publication Data
A catalogue record for this book is available from the British Library

Library of Congress Cataloging-in-Publication Data
A catalog record for this book is available from the Library of Congress

Typeset in Monotype Bembo by NorthStar, San Francisco, Calif.
Printed in Great Britain by Bookcraft (Bath) Ltd

Contents

Acknowledgements

This work and its precursor were originally conceived as a single volume; the patient assistance of all those whom I happily acknowledged at the outset of *A Millennium of Family Change* ought to be seconded here; their knowledge was certainly confined to the preindustrial era, nor did they refrain from acquainting me with their views concerning the arguments I have offered here. A special thanks to those who commented on specific parts of 'the second half': George Alter, Ida Blom, Ian Davey, Anna Davin, Bob Davis, Nancy Folbre, John Gillis, John Knodel, David Levine, David Livingstone, Kate Lynch, Angela Miles, Pavla Miller, Louise Tilly and Susan Watkins. I have very much appreciated the forebearance, encouragement and intellectual stimulus of June Corman, David Livingstone and Meg Luxton while I took time away from our work on the Hamilton Families study to wrap this up. My heartfelt thanks to Steven Hiatt and Lucy Morton at Verso, who have shepherded both volumes to print with patience, pride, and attention to detail.

To Helena Wehrstein, my deepest love. Ten years ago I solemnly swore that I'd give birth to this text before the arrival of our child. I kept my promise, as it turned out, but only because our joint endeavour took a little longer to come to fruition than we had planned. It is only fitting, then, to dedicate this work to Linnea – her exuberant hugs give courage to face the future.

Preface

This book is a sequel to *A Millennium of Family Change: Feudalism to Capitalism in Northwestern Europe*, where I outlined, in broad strokes, the development of peasant families through the Middle Ages, and the subsequent transformation of family forms during the early modern era as the ranks of the proletariat swelled. That text concluded with a discussion of the population boom immediately preceding the Industrial Revolution, which, I argued, was unleashed by the mass circumvention of a set of land-based constraints on marriage and family formation that for centuries had been pivotal to the slow-growth equilibrium of the *ancien régime*.

The subsequent development of industrial capitalism in the nineteenth century, from dispersed manufacture to centralized machinofacture, entailed a number of far-reaching changes in prevailing patterns of capital accumulation, labour-power utilization, demographic reproduction, and working-class family life. By the First World War the urban proletariat had assumed its modern form, and 'the traditional family', as we think of it today, had taken shape. In this book, I shall endeavour to provide a condensed sketch of these changes unfolding unevenly across Northwestern Europe, bringing the story to a close with a discussion of the initial phase of working-class fertility decline in the early twentieth century.

While the two texts are closely linked, *Weathering the Storm* has been designed to stand on its own, intelligible without reference to its predecessor. The chapters proceed as follows. First, a number of theoretical clarifications are made in order to situate working-class family forms in the capitalist mode of production. The historical account begins (or resumes, for readers of the prior text) in the second chapter, with a survey of urban working-class families struggling to survive in the midst of 'the first Industrial Revolution'. The mixed and transitional nature of the social relations of workplaces and households is highlighted during this stage. The third chapter examines the inherent

1

limits of capital's extensive mode of consuming labour-power in the first phase of industrialization and the response of urban working-class families to these strains. The forces inducing conversion to a more intensive regime in the latter half of the nineteenth century are then indicated. Changing family forms during the 'second Industrial Revolution' are examined in the fourth chapter, where the consolidation of modern industry went hand in hand with the crystallization of the male-breadwinner wage norm, the advent of compulsory schooling, and the stabilization of working-class family life. The fifth chapter takes up the struggle of working-class couples to limit their fertility in the first three decades of the twentieth century. This is the last revolution in family relations I wish to address, and in some respects the most far-reaching. Finally, by way of conclusion, we shall consider how 'the long view' of family history might inform contemporary discussions of 'the crisis of the family', as we approach the twenty-first century.

The theoretical framework employed in the development of both studies was elaborated in the first chapter of *A Millennium of Family Change*, and needs only the briefest summary here. In response to feminist criticisms of 'sex-blind' marxism, I have sought to open up historical materialism's central theoretical category – mode of production – so as to include family forms at the heart of the construct. A mode of production is defined conventionally as a set of productive forces mobilized within a given ensemble of relations of production. The problem is that this forces/relations combination has been taken to refer exclusively to the production of material goods; the production of people and their labour-power has been omitted. Yet this is primarily what families do: they people societies, restoring their members' energies and replacing worn-out labourers with the 'fresh blood' of youth. The exclusion of labour-power's daily and generational reproduction from the conception of modes of production has made it almost impossible to see producer families, as labour teams, pumping the life-blood through socioeconomic systems. In orthodox marxist models, 'the family' is assigned to the superstructure and domestic subsistence is treated, one-sidedly, as a process of consumption. To situate families in modes of production, we need to invert this perspective, analysing goods production as a process of labour-power's consumption, while seeing the domestic consumption of food and shelter as a process of labour-power's production. This is the vantage point adopted here. Most domestic work is done by women, which places them, much more than men, at the centre of labour-power's production. In marginalizing the labours of birthing, childcare, meal preparation and housework, mainstream marxism has effectively displaced women's core contribution to the production of life; the masculine bias of the traditional framework is manifest.

All societies must establish an overall relation between the schedule of labour-power's exhaustion and its demographic replacement through the medium of its domestic groups. The ways this relation is regulated and upset furnish important insights into the core dynamics of the society in question. For whole periods, producer families may inadvertently align the demographic regime with the labour demands of the socioeconomic system by flexibly adjusting the ratio of hands to mouths in their own households. At other times, their family-formation strategies come into conflict with the labour requisites of the system as a whole. Inefficiencies accumulate; if unresolved, they lead eventually to stagnation and crisis.

Prevailing modes of production facilitate the reproduction of certain family forms, while impeding the development of alternatives. In class-divided modes of production, the ways in which ruling classes harness and consume labour-power limit the ways in which labouring classes are able to form families and reproduce themselves from generation to generation. Conversely, the ways in which the men and women of labouring classes mate, procreate and socialize the young condition the evolution of the mode of production in which they toil, above all because families shape people's capacities for work, compliance and struggle.

In order to recognize the deeply reciprocal nature of this equilibration, and to gauge its resilience or vulnerability, we must eschew structural-functionalist models in which the prevailing mode of production determines, in a full or sufficient sense, the familial reproduction of its labouring class. No *telos* may be imputed to the socioeconomic system as a whole. The family-formation strategies of subordinate classes respond to their own subsistence imperatives; they must never be treated as if producers, by balancing the dependency ratio of their households, were striving to reproduce the present mode of production or to satisfy the demands of their masters. Producer classes (to paraphrase Marx) make their own families, but they do so in conditions that are not of their own making. My concern is to clarify the dynamic interplay between capitalist constraints and proletarian choice: on the one hand, the shifting demands imposed upon working-class families, most crucially by the ways capital harnesses and consumes their members' labour-power; and on the other hand, their own creative response to the exigencies of urban survival, industrial labour discipline, and fluctuating family fortunes in labour markets and in markets for consumer goods.

The historical survey undertaken here is designed to explore the potential utility of this revised paradigm for marxist inquiry. The author's commitment to historical materialism, however, in no sense privileges readers who would share it; the book ought to be of interest to a much broader readership. Certainly the great majority of historians whose research I have drawn upon are not marxists. Whatever the book's deficiencies, its broad survey could never have been attempted had I not taken the liberty of standing on their formidable shoulders to peer a little further down the dimly lit pathways of family history. The sociologist who surveys the daily lives of common folk in the past owes an enormous debt to the countless historians who have built the empirical foundations of the knowledge he or she interprets; I hasten to acknowledge it. As to the validity of this particular overview, readers will decide for themselves whether it achieves the author's objective: to enhance our understanding of decisive shifts in family forms as they develop in the long run.

In so far as we are currently living through a period of far-reaching change in the prevailing family form, it seems apposite to examine past watersheds. Yet most family historians are poorly equipped to illuminate transitions, since their studies have tended to foreground aspects of continuity while downplaying elements of change. Following Peter Laslett's lead, the scholarly consensus holds that the small nuclear family prevailed in pre-industrial times and underwent no profound or lasting changes in the transition to industrial capitalism. That thesis was countered in some detail in *Millennium*, where I endeavoured to show how changes in the mode of production transformed the structure of the family economy in the transition from feudalism to capitalism. The same conceptual approach will be utilized in this text, where alterations in working-class family life during the nineteenth century will be correlated with transformations in the capitalist mode of production during the first and second Industrial Revolutions.

1

Working-Class Family Forms in the Capitalist Mode of Production

By way of introduction, five related theoretical issues require clarification. In the first place, the sphere of private households must be explicitly situated within the capitalist mode of production. Second, the fetishism of the wage form will be discussed: what are its implications for unpaid domestic labour? Third, we shall examine the relation between the male breadwinner's domestic prerogatives and women's subordination in the labour force. Fourth, we need to clarify the dynamic interplay between the capitalist demand for labour-power and its proletarian supply, mediated through the labour market. Finally, we ask: does capitalism give rise to a particular form of the family among the working class, and if so, what is its nature?

In standard marxist accounts of class formation under capitalism, all eyes are riveted on the workplace, while households and neighbourhoods remain peripheral to the field of vision. Marxist sociologists and social historians have recently broken with this blinkered view of class relations, yet the full inclusion of households has yet to be adequately theorized at the level of the mode of production.[1] This is what I shall endeavour to do here.

Capitalism is distinguished from all prior modes of production in history by the fact that labour-power assumes for the labourers themselves the generalized form of a commodity. Private capital consumes labour-power, indispensable to its existence, but does not produce it. Proletarians do, on their own time and in their own households. They cannot live without working for wages; but they cannot work for wages without living in definite places outside the sphere of capitalist production where they restore their capacity to work and raise the next generation, their eventual replacements in the labour force. A balanced, comprehensive account of the proletariat must analyse the social relations within which this class lives and labours at both locations, and their changing relationship with one another. In the sphere of capitalist production, proletarian labour-power is consumed and its monetary recompense, the wage, is

5

generated. At home, the means of subsistence are consumed and the capacity to work again tomorrow and in the next generation is produced. Capitalists consume labour-power under the competitive imperative of maximizing labour's output while minimizing the payment necessary to sustain its productivity. From the employers' standpoint, workers rest at home in order to be able to return to work. The wage-earners' interests are diametrically opposed: they toil for wages in order to live independently. While optimizing residential comforts for themselves and their families, workers try to limit their exertion on capital's behalf. The historic struggles of the labour movement for a shorter work-week and higher pay manifest a striving for autonomy, strengthening workers' living independence from capital on their own time and in their own households.

The private residence is the home-base of workers' independence from capital. It may be as meagre as a rented room in a boarding-house, retainable by means of payment from next week's wage; or it may be as comfortable and relatively secure as a detached house on private land owned outright. But a private domicile is a prerequisite of stable proletarian existence. Homeless vagrants soon cease to be able to sell their labour-power in a durable fashion, sinking beneath the proletarian condition and forming a wasted underclass. With the separation of residence from place of employment, workers normally no longer live with, or on the property of, their employers. In their private lives away from work, they cease to come under the latter's legal jurisdiction and moral authority. With the severance of paternalist ties, proletarians are free to act as renters and purchasers of accommodation on their own behalf. Food, clothing and shelter all assume a commodity form under capitalism (as befits a system of generalized commodity production). Housing stock is rented and sold in free-standing units on a legally open market. The bourgeois conception of freedom, based in private property and possessive individualism, sustains a vigorous assertion of private domicile rights for individuals and family groups who are paying their own way.[2] The freedoms associated with private property in the means of *production* could hardly be expected to have much appeal for those who are excluded from substantial property claims in productive enterprise unless this prerogative were linked with a symmetrical right to private ownership in the means of *subsistence*. But this is not simply a matter of ideological congruence. The private production of housing furnishes key vehicles of capital accumulation: the builder's profit, the landlord's rent and the banker's mortgage.

Given a choice, wage-earners have consistently demonstrated a willingness to exercise their market prerogatives, establishing independent households whenever they can afford to. And no wonder. To possess one's own domicile maximizes a person's autonomy from parents, employers and state authorities. If it is clear why proletarians would *prefer* to live independently, what *enables* them to do so? Can employers not furnish lodgings for their workers, inducing them to reside therein? In some circumstances, of course, they do. Firms are obliged to provide accommodation to attract workers to remote sites such as mines and lumber camps where housing stock is absent or grossly inadequate and there is no municipal infrastructure. Frequently this is a temporary arrangement, but in other circumstances (particularly in mining districts) employers may erect durable dwellings to attract and retain a more settled workforce. If high labour turnover is a major concern, employers may find it in their interest to supply workers and their families with cheap rental accommodation and company stores, involving them in a web of commercial and community relationships that are employment-dependent, making it difficult to leave. Yet legally free labourers will accept such paternalist conditions only so long as independent alternatives are not readily available. Effective demand for untied accommodation has generally been sufficient to attract private builders, real-estate speculators and landlords prepared to offer workers an alternative to their employers' dwellings. While always present, company housing has seldom been a widespread residential form. In the case of 'public' housing leased by state agencies, tenants remain in effective possession of their domiciles so long as they pay the rent on time, just as they do with private landlords.[3]

The Fetishism of the Wage Form and the Concealment of Domestic Labour

Because the household has been marginalized in orthodox marxist accounts of capitalism, the labour of its daily maintenance has tended to disappear altogether. This occlusion has figured centrally in feminist criticisms of 'sex-blind marxism'.[4] Ironically, domestic labour is shrouded by 'the fetishism of the wage form', the mysteries of which Marx originally unravelled in a justly renowned section of *Capital*.[5] It was his paradigm case of the more general phenomenon of commodity fetishism: the way in which the myriad exchange of commodities and money in the marketplace obscures the underlying relations between people in the 'hidden abode of production'.[6] The wage appears as a payment for labour performed, when in reality it is a payment for labour-power. The common-sense confusion of labour with labour-power disguises the source of profit in the unpaid labour-time workers toil for free in capitalist production. This familiar analysis constitutes a brilliant first step; but it blows only part of the wage form's cover. It overlooks that domestic production, the other half of the proletarian condition, which the wage both underwrites and conceals. For the household, too, is a 'hidden abode', obscured by the deceptive appearance of capitalist relations and also, unfortunately, by orthodox

7

marxism's tunnel vision riveted on 'the point of production'.

Once wage labour becomes the dominant form of labour in society, the various meanings of 'work' are reordered. Gradually, the pre-eminent usage of the word becomes an abbreviation for 'paid work', and the unpaid labour of homemakers is cast into the shadows – out of speech, out of mind. Since no wage is paid for this work, it is difficult to take it seriously as 'real work'. Domestic labour appears as a natural service, a simple act of caring, a labour of love, with all the attendant mystification this entails. Since the homemaker's housekeeping allowance enters the household in her husband's pocket, 'there is no money remuneration for the mother's task, no guarantee of her maintenance while she performs it and … no consequential relationship … between the quantity and quality of her product and the quantity and quality of the tools she has at her disposal.'[7] This hiatus is a largely overlooked facet of capitalism's irrationality and waste.

The fetishism of the wage form comes into its own with the full development of capitalism. A number of related changes integral to the process of proletarianization laid the groundwork for the wage's deceptive appearance. The key change was the gradual disjunction of capitalist production relations from proletarian subsistence relations:

■ the spatial separation of the workplace from the household and the subsequent decline of various forms of commodity production in and around the household;

■ the decline of subcontracting arrangements and family hiring, so that the great majority of wage workers were now hired and fired individually and paid in person for their work;

■ the severance of all remaining paternalist strings to the sphere of subsistence, so that employers no longer had any direct jurisdiction over the lives of their employees off the job;

■ the complete monetization of the wage, so that workers received nothing but their paycheques in exchange for their labour-power.

When the relations of proletarian subsistence and capitalist production have been disentangled, the wage form presents a Janus face, looking forward towards the site of capitalist production and backward towards the domestic site of proletarian subsistence. General conceptions of a fair wage spontaneously embrace both façades. The notion of a 'fair day's pay for an honest day's work' – still a bedrock value in contract bargaining – expresses the production side: a sense of personal worth on the job and just recompense for work done. On the subsistence side, the ideal of a 'living wage' is articulated: an income sufficient to feed and clothe oneself and one's dependants at some minimal standard of decency to which the respectable members of a working-class community have become accustomed. Ideologically, these two conceptions are complementary; but the dominant pole within the discourse is the production side, for it is this term that defines what happens at the capitalist site as 'production' (that is, worthy of a wage) and what happens in the household as 'consumption' (therefore unpaid).

From the standpoint of the working class, it is important to reverse the optic. Labour-power is *consumed* in the workplace; at home it is *produced* apart from capital. Wages fund the latter production. This perception is suppressed in the wage form, which appears as a payment for labour performed in capitalist production during a definite time period, and nothing else. The worker who does this work 'earns' the wage. (Let us assume, for the moment, that our worker is male and his family's main breadwinner.) On payday, he takes possession of his paycheque; it is his by right, and no one else's. By virtue of this entitlement, he can spend it as he wishes, subject only to the impersonal constraint that he must spend it in such a way that he is fit to return to work for his employer tomorrow. Any responsibility that he may have to provide for his family is an additional obligation of citizenship, not particular to wage-earners and in no sense intrinsic to the wage form. For in a developed capitalist context, this is a payment made to an individual who is hired and fired as an individual; family circumstances do not enter into it.

Nothing in the wage form takes account of the family household as a pooling-sharing unit whose members are jointly involved in a collective effort to make ends meet. The fact that the wage paid to one employee is spent raising a family while another lives alone is beyond the scope of the employer's active concern. Unlike the slave-owner, who may benefit from the proliferation of his labour force, the capitalist reaps no advantage from his workers' progeny. Their upbringing makes no contribution to the accumulation of his capital, and he lacks any incentive to make special provisions for female employees who are pregnant or nursing. As they shift their energies from commodity production to family reproduction, he finds them increasingly 'unproductive' and hence dispensable.

The coverage of the wage fund is thus highly variable. The stock marxist assertion that 'wages fund the reproduction of labour-power' begs the question: '*whose* labour-power'? Do wages simply cover the personal maintenance of the present labour force or do they fund, in addition, the private costs of its eventual replacement by the next generation? There is nothing in the wage form that resolves the matter. The purpose of the wage payment from the employers' standpoint is to ensure that workers reappear tomorrow, ready, able and willing to work once again. At a cost-cutting minimum, capitalists must pay out in wages only the replacement price of the labour-power they consume daily. Whether wages fund more than this is determined by the bargaining power of labour and capital in the context of the state's employment policies. Wages will tend to sink towards the floor of daily maintenance whenever unemployed labour is plentiful, workers are unorganized, on-the-job training costs are low, and minimum-wage provisions are weak or absent.[8] In the early stages of industrialization, these conditions prevailed across Northwestern Europe. Rock-bottom wages and long working days gradually wore down the urban workforce, while 'fresh blood' from the countryside made up the difference. In subsequent stages of industrialization, trade unions forced employers to hike the take-home pay of adult men well above the daily costs of their personal maintenance, so that families could be raised in many union households with little or no income required from other sources. In the households of unorganized workers, however, the primary breadwinner's earnings fell far short of family sufficiency. In these cases, the wife's earnings were essential, and children had to seek employment as soon as they were legally eligible, paying for their own upkeep while living with their parents.

Men's Domestic Prerogatives and Women's Subordination in the Labour Market

A key factor in women's overall position in any society is the relative ease with which infant-care can be combined with other labours, ensuring that women are not excluded from the crucial arenas of goods production and politics. Are women to be penalized for their natural capacity to bear children and nurture them at the breast? Under capitalism, the answer is clear. 'It is the ultimate alienation of our society that the ability to give birth has been transformed into a liability.'[9] No compensatory exaltation of the glories of motherhood can eradicate this socially structured disadvantage. Mothers have been stuck in increasingly privatized households with near-exclusive responsibility for infant- and childcare.

At the dawn of the industrial era, married women already had a well-defined responsibility for what we now call domestic labour: household maintenance, meal preparation, and the home-based care of infants and young children. In most forms of joint family enterprise, these responsibilities were an embedded part of women's overall workload. Wives normally combined domestic labour with the production of foodstuffs and handicrafts for use and sale. The total burden was a heavy one, but at least the two components of women's labour were fairly compatible with one another. A mother could interrupt spinning or gardening to feed her baby and stoke the fire beneath the cooking pots. She often enjoyed the company and assistance of a daughter or

10

domestic servant. With the separation of residence from workplace, it became much more difficult and dangerous to combine employment with the care of infants and young children. This was not only because workplaces were at a distance from residences, but perhaps more importantly because capitalist work discipline made it practically impossible for mothers to halt work on an impromptu basis to care for infants.

In so far as a married man is assumed to be his family's primary breadwinner while his wife is viewed as the natural homemaker, their partnership works to his advantage in the following ways:

■ Since it is his wage and he collects it, he may take his spending money off the top before it enters the common pool for housekeeping. This advantage is subject to great abuse: drinking the paycheque, concealing overtime and pay increases from one's wife and spending the difference, and so on.

■ Since it is his money that purchases consumer durables, he owns them. Homeownership is particularly important in this regard.

■ Since the value of the breadwinner's labour-power is the household's paramount financial consideration, it is advisable that any scarcity in the provision of food or clothing be assumed by his wife and children. So he is served most of the meat in the family diet, for example, as was common in the nineteenth century, where two standards of living prevailed in working-class families.[10]

■ By bringing home his paycheque regularly and reliably, the husband is seen to do his part. The rest is up to his wife; at best, he helps her out around the house. For him the household is a place of rest and leisure away from work, while for her it remains primarily a worksite. Industrial work entails a sharp separation of work and leisure, on and off the job. The consoling promise of uninterrupted work-time is uninterrupted leisure-time once the shift is over. This sustains a breadwinner ideology which legitimates male abstention from domestic labour.

■ As a cohabiting couple, the primary breadwinner and the homemaker are functionally interdependent; but in the event of desertion, death or divorce, *her* economic dependency stands exposed. While separation often plummets women into poverty, it tends to raise men's living standards.

The point is not that all working-class husbands are uncaring bastards who exploit these advantages to the hilt. While some men drink their paycheques and leave their wives in desperate straits, others bring their pay home without

11

fail, handing it over in full to their wives.[11] Regardless of whether men exercise such prerogatives with selfishness or consideration, they have nevertheless been available to primary breadwinners whose wives have had little or no independent income.

Mirroring this domestic inequality is the stratification of the labour force, where women are pervasively streamed into a few 'female' occupations, while being excluded or grossly underrepresented in most others. This division of labour is stereotyped; while men predominate, almost exclusively, in heavy industry, women tend to be concentrated in jobs which replicate some aspect of their traditional domestic labour (as teachers, nurses, maids, cleaners, seamstresses, secretaries, and so on).[12] Since women are streamed away from the higher income occupations, they typically receive much less pay than men. Wage disparity between the sexes did not originate with capitalism, but every modern capitalist society has perpetuated it. Despite various forms of pay-equity legislation passed into law by governments (in response to intense feminist pressure and over the vigorous objections of private employers), all national labour markets in the Western world continue to register male–female wage ratios on the order of three to two.[13] It seems unlikely that this immense wellspring of profit and hierarchical stability could be uprooted without shaking the foundations of bourgeois societies.

These, then, are the twin pillars of male dominance in capitalist economies: the domestic prerogatives accruing to men as primary breadwinners, and the occupational subordination and inferior pay of women in the paid labour force. What is their causal interconnection? We can address this question by developing polar arguments; both are based on one-way models mediated by the labour market. In the first (labour-supply) hypothesis, the household is conceived as the primary site of male dominance, and workplace inequality is held to be an effect of domestic patriarchy. The second (employer-demand) argument inverts the causal logic, postulating a capitalist rationale for maintaining gender hierarchy in employment, and finding that this inequality tends to perpetuate male dominance at home. We shall consider each model in turn.

A *labour-supply thesis* begins by identifying a male power drive within marriage (or in unofficial partnerships of lengthy cohabitation). We find that men have a rational interest in maintaining their primacy as breadwinners, since an attractive bundle of prerogatives accrues to the earner of the family's main income: an independent source of spending money, homeownership, pension security in old age, and the customary right to be served at home while abstaining from domestic labour. In this argument, women's inferior position in the labour force is derived from their domestic subordination. Saddled with the bulk of their family's domestic responsibilities, women are at a competitive disadvantage in the labour market. Their working hours must fit with their husbands' and children's schedules so they can prepare family meals and care for the kids. In order to cope with the double day of labour, women are inclined to take part-time work at places of employment close to home; such jobs typically pay less. During their childbearing years, when their earning power would otherwise reach its peak, childcare responsibilities often remove women from the labour force altogether; at the very least, these duties curtail their availability for many kinds of employment. Such constraints result in much greater employment discontinuity than men typically experience. And interruptions prove costly to women's lifetime earnings curve, through loss of seniority, fewer opportunities for skill upgrading and on-the-job training, and so on. Subsidized in part by their husbands' wages, women have lower wage thresholds than men; they will accept jobs the latter refuse. Recognizing these patterns, employers take advantage of them. If they can attract female labour at lower pay, they have no reason to pay them at the going male rate.

Now let us reverse the logic, considering an *employer-demand model*, in which causal forces flow through the labour market in the opposite direction. The initial premise here is that sexist discrimination profits employers under most circumstances. They benefit from women's cheap labour, the gendered division of their labour forces, and the sense of status conferred on male employees at all levels who are ranked above women in their departments. By sex-streaming in hiring, promotion and the organization of work-teams, managers take advantage of prevailing patterns of authority and deference in society; by 'naturalizing' the firm's chain of command, they raise the overall productivity of their labour forces. Since men do not take direction well from women or work with enthusiasm under their supervision, an employer who promoted women to positions of authority over men in a non-discriminatory way would normally be acting against his interest as a profit-maximizer.[14] Segregating co-workers by sex reduces sexual diversions and tension, while promoting the age-old tactic of divide and conquer, making it unlikely that workers will be able to set aside gender divisions to unite against management. The second part of the argument is that pervasive inequality in the labour force conditions the division of labour in wage-earning households. Male/female pay differentials make it rational from a couple's standpoint to prioritize his employment career over hers. When childcare is required at home, it is more economical for the household as a unit for the wife to leave work while he retains his present job and seniority or pursues better employment opportunities elsewhere. In short, if women are paid less than men and have fewer opportunities for advancement in employment, there is bound to be a rational recognition of the labour market's bias among wage-earning couples who must manage the awkward combination of paid and unpaid work in the allocation of their total labour-time.

The foregoing are two apparently polar explanations for the interrelation of gender inequality in households and in the paid labour force. While the first thesis sees domestic patriarchy constricting women's participation in the labour force, the second model identifies the profit drive, having harnessed gender divisions historically, as perpetuating the male breadwinner/dependent home-maker division of labour between spouses. I see no compelling reason to choose between these models; elements of both may be combined, postulating reciprocal forms of reinforcement, structuring a tenacious and durable com-plementarity.

But a word of caution is in order here: the symbiosis between capitalism and patriarchy is not devoid of contradiction. The persistent need of most working-class families for supplementary income has often unsettled the male-breadwinner arrangement. When men's real wages decline or their employ-ment is interrupted, married women may seek employment outside their homes in great numbers. In this context, they may be increasingly inclined to press their husbands to take more responsibility for housework and childcare, as the latter's patriarchal prerogatives weaken. There is, in short, no fixed or eternal relationship between labour-market inequality under capitalism and the male breadwinner/dependent homemaker division of labour between spouses. This conjugal convention was forged in the course of great struggles in the nineteenth century. As we shall see, it was not the prevailing norm among proletarians in the eighteenth century, and it has once again ceased to be so today. Consequently, we need to go beyond the general analysis of the wage form and the household–workplace antagonism offered thus far to make a historically specific examination of the ways the male-breadwinner norm was constructed. This will be done in Chapter 4.

Labour-Power: Proletarian Supply and Capitalist Demand

The relationship between labour-power's consumption and its demographic replacement is an absolutely critical one in all modes of production. Under feudalism, there was a tight connection between seigneurial exploitation and peasant demography mediated through marriage and inheritance. This matrix was broken up in the transition to capitalism, as surplus extraction was separ-ated from the site of domestic reproduction. In its place, a much looser form of equilibration took shape, mediated by markets for labour-power and hous-ing and a quasi-market in prospective marriage partners. The upshot has been a labour-supply dynamic exhibiting a wide margin of *autonomy* from the underlying rate of demographic replacement, and a persistent tendency to generate a labour *surplus* relative to employer demand.[15] What is the structural basis of this unusually 'loose' equilibration?

Unlike the slave-owner, the capitalist does not have his capital tied up in the person of his workers. This is the peculiar virtue of free labour as far as he

14

is concerned. He can run his present workers into the ground, if he can get away with it, and then replace them with fresh ones, while never having to pay for their rehabilitation or sell their deteriorated labour-power on the market. To be rid of them, he merely ceases to rehire them. The responsibility to re-establish the value of their labour-power with another employer falls 'naturally' on the shoulders of the workers themselves. The only economic deterrent the employer incurs in replacing workers is the recruitment and on-the-job training costs of new ones. These expenses, while not inconsiderable when labour turnover is high, have been held in check by the provision of publicly funded schooling and by deskilling trends in certain sectors of the labour force. Thus, while the idling of slaves is at the expense of the master, the idling of wage workers is primarily at their own expense. Once the reserve army of the unemployed is constituted, labour flows through the capitalist economy with an ease which is unique to this mode of production. The absence of an enduring responsibility of private employers to their employees liberates capital to move about at will, take risks, and accumulate. Free labour makes for freewheeling capital.[16]

Labourers are engaged and discharged in a largely unpredictable fashion, according to the rhythms of the business cycle, the course of technological change, and the successes and failures of firms in competition with one another. The restless movement of capital in search of higher profits recomposes the labour force continuously. Typically, the process is marked by pervasive job insecurity, periodic bouts of unemployment, high labour turnover, frequent relocation, and the outmoding of yesterday's skills by new training requisites and employer demands. The remarkable responsiveness of proletarians to the anarchic movements of capital has been achieved through a process that Marx termed 'labour's abstraction'.[17] With the development of mass labour markets where impersonal hiring became the norm, employers were increasingly inclined to select 'general labourers' to do whatever needed doing on a week-to-week basis, reducing their reliance on workers with specialized skills recruited to work at particular tasks. The demise of traditional forms of apprenticeship training meant that most workers could no longer restrict themselves to a single trade or life-time occupation.

Proletarians have played an active role in fostering the job versatility and high labour turnover typical of dynamic capitalist societies. As industrial work became more fragmented, repetitive and noxious, the compensation for 'unskilled' workers was that they were increasingly free to move about, trying their hands at different jobs as an antidote to boredom and stupefaction. Unable to persuade their employers to sponsor a change, they provided variety for themselves by seeking work elsewhere. Quit rates have exceeded lay-offs and firings in all but the deepest periods of depression. In the long run, the typical proletarian adaption to alienated labour and the vagaries of the labour market has been to acquire a general industrial literacy, with broad work experience and a willingness to try one's hand at almost anything. To be able to pick up new skills fairly quickly on the job has become the characteristic form of proletarian competence, gradually displacing the specialized skills and narrow training of traditional craftsmen.[18]

The mobility of private capital is predicated on the malleability of the proletariat as manifest in the labour and housing markets; the key to this protean capacity is the working-class family. Responding to fluctuations in the business cycle and irregularity in the primary breadwinner's income, proletarian families have adapted accordingly, obtaining supplementary income from a wide variety of sources to 'make ends meet'. One key variable in this regard is the age of youth's inauguration into full-time employment, which has fluctuated widely: from the physically premature ages of eight or ten in the midst of the Industrial Revolution to overly ripe post-adolescence today. Similarly, proletarians have displayed a remarkable ability to fit their family groups to the available housing stock: doubling up, sleeping in cellars and attics, taking in lodgers, partitioning rooms, building extensions to dwellings, and so on.

While there are almost as many strategies for making ends meet as there are working-class families, there is none the less an underlying consistency in the subsistence rationale of proletarian families over time. They have typically been inclined to supply just enough labour-power to employers to cover their present subsistence costs, while using wage increases to raise their immediate living standards. The strains of combining wage work with domestic labour have generally sufficed to deter them from toiling additional hours, while the aggregate labour supply has been sufficient to keep wages down to a level where they have been unable to accumulate enough capital to go into business for themselves.[19] Under this rationale, the higher the wage rate of the primary earner and the steadier his employment, the less income other family members are compelled to provide. In periods when men's real wages have risen, working-class families have tended to diminish the employment commitment of supplementary earners. Conversely, when men's wages have fallen or their employment has been curtailed, families have increased the involvement of other earners. In the nineteenth century, children supplied the bulk of supplementary earnings, while in the twentieth century wives have.

In addition to the working class's own malleability in adapting its subsistence needs to the vagaries of the labour market, the state has been compelled to supplement and rationalize the private wage under pressure from the labour movement and left-wing parties. This has been accomplished through the direct state provision of schooling and a range of transfer payments based upon legally specified criteria of entitlement: old age pensions, baby bonuses, unemployment and health insurance, injured workman's compensation and welfare. These payments have been called 'the social wage', which conveniently highlights the inadequacy of the private wage. The term is misleading, however, since state transfer payments do not take the form of a wage, nor are they part of a market contract.[20] Since the mid nineteenth century, this portion of the value of labour-power has displayed a long-run tendency to rise. The trend appears to be endemic to capitalism, due to the radical deficiencies of the wage form as a means of funding the long-term reproduction of labour-power.[21]

The persistent tendency of the labour supply to exceed demand while wage rates fail to decline towards a point of equilibrium which would clear the market is a real conundrum for bourgeois economists. Most conceive of all markets in the same highly stylized paradigm, failing to make an adequate analysis of specific conditions on both sides of the labour market. On the supply side, neo-classical theory postulates that rational suppliers of a given commodity will respond to market gluts by cutting back on production as surplus inventories build up. If proletarian households were little firms they would indeed behave in this fashion, but they are not. The insistent 'push' of subsistence needs, with bedrock minima, not the 'pull' of market opportunities for profit, induces household groups and individuals to offer their labour-power to an employer. Unemployment and falling real wages typically impel an *increase* in labour supply, as families strive to offset the losses of their primary earners by offering more of their members' labour-power for sale. Wages beneath the subsistence costs of individual workers may attract those – such as wives and children – whose upkeep is being partially covered by the main breadwinner's income.

On the demand side of the market, employers have furnished their own long-term antidote to labour scarcity and rising wages, as Marx pointed out.[22] As full employment is approached and labour strengthens its bargaining power, wages tend to rise; in response, capitalists are competitively driven to adopt labour-saving technologies in order to keep their costs down and control their payrolls. While pruning their labour forces, firms expand their productive capacity. The demand for labour thus lags behind the pace of capital accumulation under the prevailing mode of technological change.

The upshot of these dynamics working on both sides of the labour market is that while the supply of labour tends to grow in response to expanding employer demand and rising real wages, it does not fall to a similar extent in the face of slumping demand and declining real wages. In the face of cyclical demand fluctuations, labour supply increases in a ratchet-like fashion. The reserve army of labour is insulated from underlying population trends. It follows that there can be no market-driven equilibrium between labour demand and underlying rates of population growth. We may discern forms of congruence between dominant patterns of labour-power utilization on the one hand and family formation on the other; I shall endeavour to identify such alignments in the following chapters. But these accommodations were historically forged, not determined (in a sufficient sense) by the dynamic regularities of capital accumulation. This is because the relationship between capitalist labour demand and working-class proliferation is deeply mediated by non-capitalist mechanisms: mate selection and marriage; coital norms and contraceptive practices; the parental valuation of children; the provisions of the welfare state; and international migration patterns.

Capitalism and the Nuclear Form of the Working-Class Family

Does capitalism give rise to a particular family form amongst the wage-earning populace? Given the variety of causal effects entailed here, the question is best addressed in three parts: What family form(s), if any, does capitalism: (a) preclude and obstruct; (b) admit and incorporate; (c) nurture and stabilize?

As a mode of production, capitalism actively deters the formation of any family cycle (such as the stem and joint families) based on generational continuity in the means of production. Since proletarians are divorced from all forms of productive property that might be passed on from parents to their children, their family cycle is necessarily discontinuous. Inheritance remains perfectly legal, and working people do bequeath nominal forms of wealth, but for those without an ownership claim in productive property, this act has no substantial impact on parent–child relations. When capitalists won the unfettered right to hire and fire workers at will, selecting them individually without reference to family background, community standing or a father's trade, working-class parents lost control over the transition to adulthood. Proletarian youth had no alternative but to seek jobs on their own initiative, hoping to be hired 'on their merits'. As well as jobs, youth were free to secure their own residential accommodation and prospective marriage partners. The latter two prerogatives were pragmatically dependent upon the former. Once the wage form was fully individuated (as a payment to a person who was entitled to spend it as he or she saw fit), there was nothing to prevent proletarian youth from leaving home as soon as they secured full-time jobs, proceeding to marry whomever they wished whenever they could afford to. Over time, these patterns became increasingly commonplace. In effect, capitalism severed the family cycle at the point of transition from family of birth to procreative family. Proletarians, in their great majority, could sustain no family form except the nuclear, two-generation, version. (I am not implying that they were barred from augmenting the household's nucleus with boarders and kin. But we are here concerned with the form of the family *cycle*, and for proletarians, generational renewal is necessarily discontinuous.)

Despite the breach that capitalism forged in the family cycle, the bonds of familial obligation between adult children and their parents have remained surprisingly vigorous throughout the modern era. Even though the hiring prerogative rests incontestably with the employer, parents often manage to assist their children in obtaining their first jobs, and kin networks remain a vital resource in the labour market. Parental influence lingers on in mate selection, and young marrieds, in establishing their own households, often strive to remain close to their parents. Regardless of where they live, most young adults keep in fairly regular contact with their parents and provide them with at least modest forms of support in old age. Yet these connections, remarkable in their own right, receive no structural support from capitalism as a mode of production, with the result that they have been eroded over time. In so far as they have been preserved at all, it has been through the tenacious commitment of people working against the grain of the system.

Having blocked other types of family formation, capitalism admits the nuclear form: private wages sustain autonomous household groups wherein proletarians are free to bear and raise children. But does the capitalist mode of production positively nurture this form? I think not. Capitalism's fundamental deficiency in this regard resides in the wage form and the lack of employment security. As previously discussed, the wage makes no special provision for the maintenance of a family group. It fails to recognize or reward childbearing, building in no means of recouping the costs of childcare, nor of inducing adult children to support their elderly parents. Instead, the wage engenders an individualist incentive for workers, as subsistence optimizers, to form temporary liaisons in accordance with the episodic nature of employment and its freely terminable contract. This militates against enduring family formation, costly childbearing, life-long marital fidelity, and unquestioned kin loyalty. The economic insecurity and restless mobility fostered by capitalism make it difficult to keep families together and ensure their residential permanence, particularly among the lower strata of the working class. Markets of all sorts 'reduce individuals to abstractions, anonymous buyers and sellers whose claims upon one another are determined only by their capacity to pay'.[23] The very nature of commercial contracts – temporally limited and readily terminable – render the life-long marital pledge 'till death do us part' a historical anachronism. Capitalist social relations encourage easier divorce and serial monogamy in the long run, but do not determine these marital norms in a strong or sufficient sense.

It remains for other bastions of the capitalist order – churches, schools and state welfare agencies – actively to promote family life while discrediting alternative domestic arrangements. Bourgeois ideologues of all stripes are perennially alarmed about a 'crisis of the family', warning of its vulnerability and possible disintegration.[24] Defying all such prognostications, the nuclear family form has proved extremely resilient. Prophesying its imminent demise, alarmists have repeatedly exaggerated its fragility. In doing so, conservative pundits have none the less registered a visceral awareness of the ways in which the unfettered economic system they champion undermines the family form they hold sacred. Victorian-era conservatives, less impressed with the wonders of *laissez-faire* capitalism, were prepared to acknowledge this antagonism. Modern-day conservatives prefer to blame the family's ills on sexual permissiveness, moral degeneracy and creeping welfare socialism.[25]

2

Changing Family Forms
in the First Industrial Revolution

As the nineteenth century opened, the majority of producer households in Northwestern Europe were at least partly proletarian: they had to secure wage income in order to subsist. Most, however, were far from being fully proletarian. Their members took part-time and seasonal employment, devoting the rest of their labour-time to their own tiny plots, knitting frames, and other domestic means of production. The sources of their subsistence were typically varied, fluctuating from season to season. They were still inclined to treat wage work as a temporary necessity, while clinging tenaciously to alternative livelihoods. For the most part, the proletarian populace lived in rural and smalltown settings, with at least a marginal attachment to the land or some form of income derived from agriculture.[1]

By 1914, all this had changed. The great majority of wage-earning households had taken up residence in cities or large towns and were unable to extract very much (if anything) from the soil, nor were their members employed in agriculture or cottage industries. Most were divested of all productive property and thus had to rely almost exclusively on wage income to make ends meet. Primary breadwinners could expect to remain in wage work for the rest of their working lives. However much they might aspire to work for themselves, they none the less had to seek continuous employment in full-time jobs on a year-round basis.[2] Working-class families were now forced to define their options *within* the labour market, instead of allocating their labour-power *between* wage work and other productive pursuits, as their predecessors had done. In this text, we are concerned with the movement of working-class families from partial to full proletarian existence. In the process, markets increasingly mediated the turnover of the family cycle and the passage of youth to full adulthood. Upon its completion:

■ Adolescents were no longer sent into service or set up in a trade by their

21

parents, but were now compelled to obtain their own jobs in an open *labour market*.

■ Through the development of a *housing market*, rented accommodation was increasingly available to young people to live in 'on their own', without the paternalist strings of supervisory guardians.

■ Working-class youth could date, pair off, court and make nuptial decisions independently. Mate selection occurred through (what might loosely be termed) a *marriage market*.

Before investigating changing family forms, we need to situate these developments in their socioeconomic context. Since our attention will focus on cities, we should recall the rural backdrop against which the urban drama was played out. In many respects, the real miracle of the Industrial Revolution occurred in the countryside. Through a century of unprecedented urban growth, the rural economy managed both to feed the masses and to people the cities – a double-barrelled supply feat. On the first front, agricultural productivity rose sufficiently to permit a massive reduction in the proportion of the total labour force active in food production, while at the same time keeping the supply of basic foodstuffs more or less abreast of soaring demand, so that food prices did not go through the roof and strangle industrialization. Just as impressively, on the second front, the rural zones generated a prolific excess of births over deaths while simultaneously detaching labourers *en masse* from their last remaining footholds on the land, creating a seemingly inexhaustible pool of dispossessed labourers who flooded the cities in their millions, seeking jobs, marriage partners and housing. Until the 1870s, roughly four-fifths of the growth of the cities of Northwestern Europe was due to inflow from the surrounding countryside. Many cities would not have grown at all without newcomers. The largest part of the rural exodus stemmed from the landpoor and landless ranks of the proletariat; less often did the sons and daughters of established peasants become first-generation urban wage-earners.

The Industrial Revolution

The industrialization of Western Europe is now understood to have proceeded in a much more gradual and piecemeal way than had formerly been supposed. The annual rise in gross national product did not exceed 2 per cent in any country of Western Europe before 1880, and in France it was very much slower.[3] Even for England, which was far ahead at the beginning of the process, impressions of economic growth in the first half-century, from 1780 to

1830, have been scaled back.[4] The inaugural flourish of steam engines and mechanized textile mills is now considered to be a prelude to industrial acceleration, rather than constituting a bona fide takeoff in the way that earlier scholars (from Smith and Marx to Rostow and Landes) had envisioned. More attention has been focused on the middle four decades of the nineteenth century, on the initial phase of the iron and railway boom, as the 'first Industrial Revolution' got rolling on the continent; yet the inchoate and fragmentary growth of the Western European economy in this period has also been underlined. These revisions, in turn, have set the stage for much greater emphasis on 'the second Industrial Revolution' in the latter decades of the century. This was the era when factories displaced workshops *en masse* across the urban landscape, and concentrated machinofacture finally replaced dispersed manufacture in most types of commodity production.

Some economic historians have questioned whether it is appropriate to speak of the Industrial *Revolution* at all, in reference to a process that is now perceived to have been graduated and continuous.[5] I think, however, that we ought to retain the term. For what has been cut down to size is a prior *perception* of change, of a sudden and all-encompassing rupture.[6] Once the 'big bang' model is set aside, we are still confronted with the global *reality* that nineteenth-century industrialization constituted a momentous and irreversible turning-point relative to all previous forms of socioeconomic development. Taking the long view of history, it demands to be recognized as a watershed, regardless of the overall pace of change (which none the less accelerated very substantially from 1800 to 1914).

The significance of the Industrial Revolution for marxist accounts is that it was during this period that capitalism came into its own as a mode of production, spawning a technology – powered machinery – and a form of mass production – the factory system – that were particularly suited to its prodigious self-expansion. With the spread of industries based on the serial production of standardized goods, a new form of profit-making dynamized capital accumulation, becoming the inner mainspring of the system's subsequent growth.[7] The decisive advance in industrial profit-making lay in the sphere of production. In modern industry, capital's profit imperative (competitively enforced) was to cut the costs of producing standard commodities in order to lower their price and sell more of them, raising the rate of return through an extension of the market to the mass of wage-earning households. This was a logic of mass production: of lengthy production runs attaining economies of scale; of a vast subdivision of the labour process with greater co-ordination under tighter supervision; and, stemming from these advances, a reduction of per unit costs by means of a sharp rise in productivity, thereby augmenting profits without having to raise the profit margin on each unit sold.[8]

Having argued for retaining the term, one must acknowledge that the way the Industrial Revolution has been discussed in the past, dating back to Marx himself, has been misleading in many ways. There has been a fixation on the leading edge of change – on coal mines, ironworks and textile mills. Extrapolating from vanguard trends, marxist accounts have tended to project an image of 'Modern Industry' (as Marx termed it) across the entire economy, as if the generalization of new technologies had swept up every sector in its wake and the competitive displacement of prior forms of production was implacable and thorough.[9] Yet what is striking about the first Industrial Revolution, relative to the second, is the limited application of steam power, the halting pace of technological diffusion, and the resulting narrowness of its base, confined initially to textiles (most notably cottons), and then to the metal industries and engineering. In a whole range of consumer-goods industries – footwear, leather, glass, ceramics, woodwork and food processing – the advances of the first stage were almost entirely organizational in nature.[10] Even in England, the spread of mechanized production and the factory system in the first half of the nineteenth century was extremely limited, involving a small fraction of the proletariat. In 1851, less than a quarter of the waged labour force in non-agricultural occupations were employed in mechanized workplaces; the rest were toiling in traditional workshops or at home. At this time, factory workers comprised barely 5 per cent of the total population in England, 3 per cent in France, and were a minuscule component of the labouring classes in Germany.[11]

Marxist emphasis on the competitive displacement of pre-factory workplaces has been similarly premature. A few lines of domestic industry were overwhelmed by superior factory competition early on. English handloom weavers, numbering 200,000 in 1810, were squeezed unmercifully in the next forty years, dwindling to 40,000 by 1851. A similar, though less severe, trajectory of decline was traced by framework knitters. But these occupations were exceptional. Most traditional lines of handwork, done in households and small workshops, expanded in the first three-quarters of the nineteenth century, many to an enormous degree. In part, the growth of sweatshops and domestic outwork occurred in traditional trades where mechanized industry had made no headway. But in many more cases, small-scale forms of commodity production burgeoned as direct spin-offs from factory production: sawmills spawned carpentry shops; sugar refineries, home-made sweets; iron furnaces, backyard smithies; textile mills, hand-sewn finishing work; and so on.[12] Mass production at centralized workplaces did appropriate most of this work eventually, competitively displacing outwork, which went into decline in most trades in the late nineteenth and early twentieth centuries. But in the short and medium term, the effects of industrialization were highly stimulating to small workshops and home-based production.[13] Consequently, the average size of workforces in the first stage of industrialization was modest: in England and

Wales in 1851, the vast majority of employers reported having fewer than twenty employees.[14] On the continent at mid century, the mean size of production units was even smaller. Outside of cotton mills, ironworks and coal mines, the typical industrial establishment was a workshop.

Shifting our attention from the leading edge of industrialization to the main course of its spread, fixing our sights on more typical proletarian experiences, we come to concentrate, in the early stages of the process, on:

- workshops and small factories rather than the few large establishments of several hundred workers;

- backbreaking manual labour, rather than machine-tending (still a minority experience);

- face-to-face relations between workers and masters imbued with a paternalistic sense of deference and obligation, rather than the impersonal contractual authority of modern management;

- subcontracting arrangements with lump-sum wages calculated on a piece-rate basis, instead of the anonymous market hiring of unrelated individuals paid an hourly wage.

If the revised perspective scales down the importance of powered machinery and the largest workplaces in the Industrial Revolution, it would be a big mistake to 'overcorrect' the earlier view, ignoring the pervasive influence of new technologies and the factory system on the broader pattern of labour-power's exploitation by capital. In the first place, there is no doubt that within factories, the working day was prolonged and intensified as labour exertion was harnessed to the pace of machines. 'The new gas-illuminated, steam-driven mills were oblivious alike to darkness, Saint Monday, and the vagaries of the weather.'[15] It is true that primitive spinning machines were forever breaking down, and could be unobtrusively sabotaged if workers were desperate for a break, but in comparison with prior forms of labour compulsion they none the less facilitated a real escalation in the demands employers were able to place upon legally free labourers.

More importantly, work discipline in manufacturing had pervasive effects on related labour processes conducted elsewhere. Because so many domestic producers and workshops were directly tied in as adjuncts to manufacturing processes that were centred on powered machinery and a regulated industrial work-pace, their own exertions were accelerated: delivery dates were tightened, raw materials and finished products were standardized, and quality was more strictly monitored.[16] As the competition of factory goods spread, piece rates for outwork declined, and domestic workers had to intensify their labour to make up the difference.

The rhythm of wage work was gradually regularized and intensified throughout the nineteenth century. The tightening up of daily shift schedules stemmed in part from escalating investments in fixed plant and machinery, and the rising production costs of unscheduled interruption and idled machines. Here, employers were primarily concerned with the insouciant work habits of operatives and unskilled factory hands. Taking aim at higher levels of the labour force, managers sought to eradicate the capacity of skilled craftsmen and engineers to set their own work-pace and control their immediate work environment, though they did not have much success in this respect until very late in the century. The state's role in repressing pre-industrial work rhythms and imposing capitalist time discipline should not be overlooked. In Germany, for example, 'from the late eighteenth century to the 1860s, [state and local authorities] probably contributed more than the employers to suppressing Saint Monday, to forbidding large demonstrative funerals, feasts, and parades.'[17]

Labour historians have highlighted the pervasive resistance of workers to the enforcement of industrial time-discipline.[18] First-generation factory workers drew upon a traditional sense of the integration of life and labour to defend their informal prerogatives: to walk about and chat up their mates; stretch out midday breaks to two hours; adjourn to the pub when their specific task was done; take Mondays off whenever the spirit moved them; and observe a wide array of holiday festivals. The transition from what Marx had termed 'the formal to the real subsumption of labour by capital' was by no means completed in the first stage.[19] In the face of this intransigence, capitalists tackled the problem from the outside in, as it were. They first strove to enforce a basic punctuality around the perimeter of the working day, insisting that workers show up at the designated starting time, that their midday break not drag into the afternoon, and Monday absenteeism be curtailed. On this front, they made considerable headway in the early phase of industrialization. Where they were unable to prevail at this stage was in wresting control from workers over the interior of the labour process: in the detailed ways in which work was organized and tasks performed, in regularizing the rhythm of work and quickening the pace. Here the employers' progress was modest and workers were largely able to defend their autonomy; management's conquest of the interior domain would have to await the second stage. As it was, the victory of employers on punctuality, with the active assistance of state authorities, extended the exertions of labour on behalf of capital very substantially. The outcome of the struggle may be observed in four time planes: the working day, the week, annually, and over the lifespan.

On a *daily* basis, employers gradually succeeded in curtailing impromptu breaks and tightening up starting times and shift schedules. In many industries, they also managed to lengthen the working day. In Germany, the normal day was stretched from thirteen hours in the eighteenth century to fourteen hours in the nineteenth, peaking in the 1850–70 period. Shifts in the early textile mills in Rouen, Lille and Mulhouse were extended to roughly fourteen hours, and this had indirect effects on the rural cottage and urban workshop economies, widespread in France. In England, the working day of mill-hands was certainly prolonged, but beyond their ranks it does not appear that a general extension occurred.[20]

On a *weekly* basis, capitalists became increasingly intolerant of the traditional Saint Monday absenteeism; in the 1850s and 1860s, English employers managed to suppress it, often compensating with Saturday half-days, though elsewhere the customary Monday absence persisted in many trades (particularly where workers toiled on Sundays) until the early twentieth century.[21] The average work-week in England was roughly sixty hours at mid century; it was longer on the continent, peaking at about seventy hours in France and Germany in 1850–70. While lengthening the work-week of many workers, the advent of machinofacture thus spelled long bouts of unemployment for many others.

Perhaps the greatest axis of labour extension during the Industrial Revolution was on an *annual* basis. The Bank of England, setting commercial trends for the pioneering industrial nation, closed for forty-seven holidays in 1761, but had cut down to four by 1834.[22] Seasonal variations in labour exertion were greatly reduced as the bulk of the labour force shifted from agriculture to industry, while simultaneously, the growing amplitude of the business cycle generated a new form of unevenness in labour deployment that plagues capitalist economies to this day. The length of the working year rose on one estimate from 2,500 hours in 1750 to 3,000 hours a century later, due primarily to the decrease in seasonal unemployment and the replacement of domestic workers by factory hands. Young and Wilmott reckon that regularly employed workers increased their total labour-time by 13 per cent between 1750 and 1850, to occupy an astounding 75 per cent of their waking hours by the latter date.[23]

From the perspective of people's *lifespan*, as well, there appears to have been an increasing workload in the first phase of industrialization, with an intensification of pre-adolescent child labour, and at the other end of the life-course, less provision for retirement in old age than there had been in the early modern era. Along the four axes, taken together, there was clearly a considerable increase in the average exertion required by proletarian households.

In addition to these objective measures of labour-power's consumption, the cultural dimension of proletarian deterioration merits consideration. Factory workers in particular felt that they had lost independence by relinquishing control over their own time. Labourers had always worked hard over long hours; but in an earlier era they could interrupt their work for a drink or a chat with a neighbour and leave when their task was done. Now, in capitalist industries, 'the greatest hardship was the awful regularity of time-keeping.'[24] Workers had to arrive for work on time or risk being shut out, docked pay, or fired. Even in order to relieve themselves, workers were now expected to ask their overseer for permission to take a break. Not surprisingly, they felt demeaned.

Furthermore, the status of early industrial proletarians among the labouring population as a whole was extremely low. Recruited from the ranks of the poorest strata, they were desperate for work and in no position to resist; many were coerced.

> Early entrepreneurs, looking for docile labour of a new kind, turned easily to unfree labour, both [in Britain] and on the Continent. ... There were few areas of the country in which modern industries, particularly in textiles, if carried on in large buildings, were not associated with prisons, workhouses, and orphanages.[25]

In France, the early textile employers were legally permitted to recruit 'enfants assistés' from orphanages, subject them to military discipline and forcibly retain them until they were twenty-one. They also relied on religious orders to provide cloistered accommodation in convent-like establishments for their female employees. Exploiting the Master and Servant Law and other draconian codes, British employers often hired on long-term contracts, such as the miner's bond, which indentured labour for a year or more.[26]

While the necessity of going to work for another highlighted people's dependency, many none the less found that they could retain a measure of autonomy from the employers' supervision within the sphere of production. Multitiered subcontracting arrangements placed an array of intermediaries between capital and labour, blurring class polarity, subdividing authority, and delegating the supervision of the labour process to piece-masters. The familial dimension of subcontracting will be discussed at length below. Here it is sufficient to note that these arrangements proliferated in the first stage of industrialization, fundamentally because capitalists lacked the technical knowledge and organizational capacity to manage production directly.[27] Production skills were largely confined to the labouring classes, broadly conceived, and they gave workers with specialized or scarce skills the power to insist upon a degree of self-direction in the labour process that wage labourers fifty years later would envy and fight to preserve.

The Separation of Workplaces from Households:
Effects on the Family Wage Economy

Gradually, by fits and starts, proletarianization disentangled the social relations of capitalist production from the domestic relations of workers' families. A continuously rising proportion of wage-earners went to work in places that were entirely separate from their homes. Even small workshops increasingly stood on their own; if they were connected with anyone's household, it was much more likely to be the employer's or his agent's than that of one of the employees. This uncoupling was not begun in the nineteenth century, nor was it completed by its close; none the less, capitalism made great strides in sundering the two spheres, especially in the century's latter decades. There were several processes at work.

■ In one sector after another, industrialists centralized production at a single site, terminating contracts for finishing work that had formerly been completed in workers' homes. Consequently, there was a massive rise in employment offered in locations entirely separate from residences.

■ Independent worker-proprietors were driven out of business by competition from capitalist firms and forced to seek employment outside the home.

■ Masters and apprentices were increasingly disposed, each for their own reasons, to end the traditional practice of young workers-in-training living under their masters' roof. In the second half of the century, journeymen and apprentices sought their own accommodation.[28]

■ When the owners of small workshops and stores saw their businesses prosper and took on additional employees beyond the members of their own families, they were inclined to separate their households entirely from the enterprise, moving one or other to a new location. Thus, even in the case of small-scale businesses, domestic and commercial space were increasingly divorced.

■ As the century wore on, the average distance between residence and workplace lengthened. The biggest change came in the last decade of the century with the advent of the electric tram. Increasingly, workers who could afford the fares opted to live much further away from their place of employment than had formerly been feasible. The rise of mass transit thus furthered the spatial segregation of the urban landscape into distinct industrial, commercial and residential districts (see Chapter 4).

■ The spatial separation of workplaces from households had its temporal correlate: the gradual emergence of a sharper delineation between work- and leisure-time, and a clearer sense of being on and off the job. Though workplace relations remained steeped in paternalist deference throughout the century, proletarians increasingly insisted upon freedom from the boss's authority and influence on 'their own time' away from work.

While the process of separation was inexorable in the long run, labouring families did not suffer it placidly. The divorce of the workplace from the household was widely 'regarded as a calamity'.[29] Labourers felt that the family work-team toiling at home maintained a degree of independence from op- pressive capitalist control that full proletarians forfeited.[30] Women in the Co- ventry silk trade, it was reported, 'all liked the freedom from control which the ribbon loom affords them'.[31] In many trades, workers refused the higher wages available in factories in order to cling to their domestic independence. A contemporary observer of French handloom weavers noted that they

> consented to the biggest wage cuts rather than change the locale of their work. The reason they are attached to it is that they carry out their work under their own roof, beside their relatives and also more or less when they feel like it. They have an insuperable horror of the barracks-room called 'common workshop', and would rather give up their trade altogether than submit to factory enrollment.[32]

In the struggle against full proletarianization, artisan leaders painted an idyllic picture of the independent family enterprise. The husband and wife toiled in perfect complementarity: 'without their union nothing is complete, moral, durable or possible.'[33] This vision was counterposed to a pitiful picture of the proletarian family disrupted by the poverty of its existence, with parents exploiting their own children prematurely, sending unprotected daughters to work in morally perilous environments, and so on. The artisans saw them- selves as self-employed masters, even when they were not. Their resistance to full proletarianization undoubtedly impeded the development of working-class consciousness and solidarity. Given the insular basis of this loyalty, 'the family tended to absorb anger, disappointment, frustration and aggression, diverting these feelings from being channeled into collective actions.'[34]

The increasing separation of paid work from the home did not entail the abrupt demise of familial relations of production.[35] In an important sense, working-class families were still an integral team, in what Tilly and Scott have termed the family wage economy.[36] The wages of adult men, even when they were able-bodied and living with their families (as often they were not), were rarely sufficient to provide for their families' needs. The gravest deficiency of the male breadwinner's income stemmed from the chronic irregularity of employment: the marked seasonality of outdoor trades, the prevalence of casual labour, and periodic bouts of unemployment during recessions. Low rates of pay were a subsidiary problem.[37] Consequently, it was imperative that other members of the family supplement the primary breadwinner's income. The poorer a family was, the greater this ancillary portion was likely to be.

The blend of incomes required to cover costs varied over the family cycle. Each phase placed different resources within the grasp of proletarian families and made different demands upon them. In the first stage of industrial capitalism, the turns of the wheel of economic fortune could be very sharp indeed, passing from one phase of the cycle to the next.[38]

- When working-class couples began serious courting, they generally made an effort to accumulate a modest saving fund for marriage; both partners were normally employed. After the wedding, women would sometimes continue working outside the home until 'confinement'. Since first births were likely to follow within a year of nuptials, this phase of employment tended to be brief. The initial phase from marriage to first birth was a relatively comfortable one.

- Once women began childbearing, it was virtually impossible for them to work outside the home. Even though most continued to do various forms of homework for pay, their earning power was bound to be drastically curtailed. The only mitigating factor was that the male breadwinner's wages normally rose throughout his twenties and early thirties. At best, his income gain would offset her loss. In the meantime, the household's costs were rising, with a growing number of children at home, still too young to work. This phase of the cycle placed great strain on family resources; for many, it was a time of dire poverty and bare survival.[39]

- In the nineteenth century, the lifetime earnings curve of working-class men peaked early, beginning to descend in their late thirties.[40] As the househead's income waned, the eldest children would reach an employable age and be sent out to work immediately. By age eight to ten, employed children could offset the costs of their own upkeep; thenceforth, they became indispensable contributors.[41] By the time two or three children were working, it was not unusual for them to bring home half the family's income or more. Living standards would rise appreciably.

- At this point, the greatest imponderable was the temporal sequence of children leaving home and ceasing to contribute income while their parents retired and died. Since the mean age of parents at last birth was around forty, and children normally remained at home into their twenties, it was likely that at least one parent would die before the youngest surviving child had grown up and left home. Consequently, there was not a lengthy 'empty-nest' phase of the domestic cycle after the last child had moved out and parents were left to cope on their own. It was probably just as well. In the absence of pension funds (with the partial and inadequate exception of Friendly Society benefits) the elderly sank rapidly into abject poverty. Many widows went to live with their married children.

Women's Employment Patterns

Women constituted a very substantial minority of the paid labour force in the nineteenth century, though it is difficult to determine its precise size, since the censuses of the time tend to underreport women's remunerated homework. In France around 1840, roughly 29 per cent of the industrial labour force was female; in Britain in 1851, about a third; and the rate in Germany in 1882 was also calculated at 29 per cent.[42] While sectoral patterns fluctuated somewhat, the overall ratio (of one woman to two or three men) remained remarkably stable throughout the century.

The great bulk of employed women worked then, as they do today, in a few sectors. In Britain in 1851, 37 per cent of all working females toiled as (non-farm) domestic servants; the second-largest employment was needlework. Both were almost exclusively female domains. The cotton industry was the third- and agriculture the fourth-largest employer of females; these sectors were more integrated. Seventy-two per cent of all employed females worked in these four occupations.[43] The occupational configuration in Germany and France was much the same, except for the larger proportion of the entire labour force in agriculture.[44] The sex segregation of the labour force tended to become more pronounced as child labour was curtailed.[45]

Women earned about 60 per cent of men's hourly or piece *rate*, but their total *incomes* were considerably less, since a greater proportion of female wage-earners worked part-time. These gross disparities hardly changed at all between 1750 and 1914.[46] Evidently, the Industrial Revolution did very little to disturb traditional pay differentials between the sexes in Western Europe.

Who were the females working in sweatshops and factories? The great majority of them were poor, young and single. Young women were typically employed as members of a family labour-team, reflecting intense concern for the safety and moral propriety of 'working girls' (as they were called) toiling in close proximity to unrelated men, unless close kin or trusted friends of the family were present. Rarely did women seek employment 'on their own', or take jobs in capitalist workplaces 'without protection': that is, completely beyond the purview of a kin-based network. There was, in other words, a strong patriarchal aversion to their full proletarianization.

With the exception of the uppermost skilled trades, proletarians bore a deeply ingrained sense of family members as contributors to a joint production unit. At an early stage of industrialization, the status of men as householders did not rest on male-breadwinner pride and the attainment and control of the family's primary wage. Consequently, the initial response of proletarians to women working for wages was overwhelmingly positive. It was widely re-marked that no working man 'but a fool would take a wife whose bread must be earned solely by his labour and will contribute nothing towards it herself'.[47] With the spread of the factory system, working men complained that it took remunerative work away from women at home.

> Many of the journeymen, particularly among the weavers, objected strongly to the growth of a system which deprived them of the assistance of their wives and children, and it was afterwards one of the bitterest complaints against the factory system that by it women and children were deprived of employment which they could carry on in the home. ... So accustomed were they to the idea of a family wage and the financial contribution of women and children, that the substitution of an individual wage and the responsibility of the father for the entire support of his family were changes which at first were neither welcomed nor under-stood.[48]

Here, then, was a conception of the family wage economy and an attitude to women's employment, articulated by proletarians of both sexes in the early nineteenth century, strikingly at odds with the conception of the male-bread-winner wage and a vigorous opposition to women's employment which came to prevail later in the century.[49] We will explore this critical shift in Chapter 4.

While most girls and young single women of the labouring poor took jobs outside the home, relatively few married women did. Can we develop a rea-sonable estimate of how large this minority was? The 1901 census for England and Wales is the first to distinguish between married and single women's la-bour-force participation; the rate for married women was 13 per cent (declin-ing slightly in 1911 and 1921). We are therefore forced to hazard rough guesses about nineteenth-century patterns, where there are sharp disagree-ments.[50] I can find no evidence pointing to significantly higher employment rates for married women in Victorian Britain, and the age-specific data for women indicate very little change in the four decades from 1881 to 1921.[51] Data from continental Europe appear to be similar. In Caroll Wright's 1889 sample of working-class households, 10 per cent of married women from con-tinental Europe reported an independent income.[52] The German census of 1907 indicates that less than a quarter of employed women were married, except in agriculture, where more than four in ten were.[53] The proportion of women making any income was much higher. Censuses radically underestimate the home-based component, since enumerators did not ask – or were unable to detect – every woman who took in a boarder, did some homework for a piece rate, and so on. But I am concerned here with those leaving their households daily to work for pay. In nineteenth-century cities, probably no more than one in ten married women (omitting widows) did so.

The separation of residence from workplace made it much more difficult and dangerous than it had formerly been to combine employment with the care of infants and young children. This was not only because workplaces were at some distance from residences, but perhaps more important because capitalist work discipline and uninterrupted machine pace made it practically impossible for mothers to halt work on an impromptu basis to care for infants. Employers generally found it cheaper to replace pregnant and breastfeeding women than to make provision for them. If fathers had been more involved with infant- and childcare, the constraint on married women's extra-domestic wage work would not have been so severe. As it was, the employment rates of married women outside their homes remained very low. There were exceptions: widows, women separated from their husbands, and the wives of disabled or unemployed men often had no choice but to return to work, particularly if their children were not old enough to be regularly employed.[54] In many mill towns, a significant minority of the female workforce was married. An adequate recognition of these minority practices must not obscure our vision of the main trend.[55] The great majority of women left work shortly before marriage or soon after, and most never went back. While 'tying the knot' fortified men's commitment to steady employment, it had the opposite effect on women, ending their regular participation in the paid labour force so long as their husbands remained employed. Consequently, a young woman's future class position and living standard were much more dependent on her choice of a marriage partner than on her present employment and job training.[56] 'The departure from industry into marriage was a logical completely expected pattern, for the job had been endurable in large measure because it was known to be temporary.'[57]

This does not mean that working-class women ceased thenceforth to generate any income for their families. There were many more opportunities to do so at home in the nineteenth century than there are today, and it appears that most women did earn income by baking bread for sale, taking in a boarder, doing needlework for a merchant, and so on. But the money they could make working at home was a fraction of their earning potential elsewhere. They forfeited the difference to remain at home, adopting forms of remunerative work that were compatible with their primary homemaking duties as wives and mothers.

By all accounts, most women were relieved to be able to quit work in order to concentrate their energies on raising a family, even though many missed the companionship of workmates and their own wage income.[58] Given the extremely exhausting and debilitating nature of 'the double day of labour', such an attitude is perfectly understandable. We ought to avoid the pitfalls of modernist projection, imputing a 'cultural backwardness' to the homemaker option in the nineteenth century. Wage work was rarely an avenue of female advancement in the Victorian era; whenever women were stuck with a formidable domestic workload, external employment was more likely to lead to their debilitation. For all those who could afford to leave regular wage work when they took on the massive job of continuous childbearing and family maintenance, the decision represented an elementary defence of their own health, longevity and well-being, to say nothing of their children.

Child Labour and Familial Relations of Production

Think of the Industrial Revolution, and one conjures visions of children toiling in 'dark Satanic mills'. In pre-industrial Europe, of course, children had worked from an early age in the family economy. Industrial capitalism did not inaugurate the use of child labour, but it did transform the context of the practice, which was now located in specialized, non-domestic sites, with children toiling under the ultimate authority of employers who were not their kin. The result was a greater intensity of work, extending over daily periods of twelve to fourteen hours, with fewer breaks and diversions than children had enjoyed while 'helping out' in the fields or in their parents' cottages. In short, this was a more voracious consumption of youthful labour-power, sapping people's energy and debilitating their health. While it would be misleading to present an idyllic picture of pre-industrial child labour, one must avoid the opposite error of minimizing the deterioration in children's working conditions in the transition from fields and cottages to workshops and factories.[59]

By raising the value of children's labour, the Industrial Revolution transformed the family economy of proletarians. Since employed children constituted a major financial asset to the families of industrial workers, parents sought to keep them living at home as long as possible. Contrast this to the situation of agricultural labourers, where remunerative work for children was frequently scarce; fearing that the expanding brood would 'eat us out of house and home', rural parents often tried to move their children out into service or an apprenticeship as they reached puberty.

In the first stage of industrial capitalism, young people comprised a substantial minority of the labour force; in France in 1841, 12 per cent of the industrial labour force were under sixteen; in Belgium in 1846, 21 per cent were under seventeen.[60] Hidden behind these figures is a vast array of children working in the informal economy who never came to the census-takers' attention: children who assisted their parents at home as outworkers, ran errands, carried father's dinner to the pithead, hawked papers and sweets on the streets, did odd jobs for local retailers, begged, hustled, scavenged, bartered and stole. In the official economy, the largest numbers of children were employed in textiles, the needle trades (mostly in domestic settings) and in agriculture. Over half the English cotton factory labour force in 1816 were under eighteen; in French textile mills in the mid 1840s, 15 per cent of the labour force were under sixteen.[61] The sex ratio among the child labour force varied from sector to sector: girls predominated in textiles and boys in agriculture. Overall, youth was much less segregated by sex than the adult labour force, and the numbers of employed males and females under fifteen were roughly equal. Wherever youth of either sex were found in large numbers, women were also employed.

From the employers' standpoint, children were recruited because they were small, docile and relatively cheap. Many of the early textile machines were specially adapted to children's physiques. James McNish informed the Parliamentary Committee of 1831:

> They can only be of a certain size and under a certain age; they have to go under the threads to wipe down the machinery; if they are too large they break the threads and destroy the work. ... As the machinery is at present constructed, only children nine to eleven can do the work as it ought to be done.[62]

It is important to distinguish between the employment patterns of young children and adolescents. The widespread use of pre-pubescent children outside their homes occurred briefly during an early phase of capitalist industrialization, beginning with the initial spread of cotton mills, predominating in the textile sector, and peaking within a few decades. Many employers were already reducing the numbers of young children working in their mills before the practice was legally curtailed.[63] While the labour force in English textile mills almost doubled between 1835 and 1856, the number of children under thirteen employed declined.[64] Adolescents, on the other hand, were widely employed throughout the nineteenth century. Even after the introduction of compulsory schooling in the century's latter decades, it was customary for working-class youth to leave school at the minimum legal age to go to work; their labour-force participation rates did not decline significantly before the First World War. Long after extra-domestic child labour had been phased out, the earnings of youth remained an indispensable source of family income.

In the first stage of industrialization, most children were 'put to work' by their parents or guardians. They did not obtain their own jobs, had no effective choice of employers, and frequently did not even receive their own wages. They were far from being in a fully proletarian condition. Fathers were obliged to arrange for their children's occupations, ensuring the safety of daughters in well-supervised settings and establishing sons in trades if they could afford to do so. Agreements between parents and artisan masters had traditionally been set out in a written contract. The young apprentice lived in the master's house and came directly under his domestic authority; the latter was responsible not only for the lad's vocational training but also for his physical and spiritual well-being. During the nineteenth century, the bonds of apprenticeship were loosened; contracts were more often arranged verbally, their average duration was shortened, and masters relaxed, and subsequently relinquished, their supervision of apprentices outside the workshop. 'The arrangement and successful supervision of an apprenticeship was much the most important contribution a father could make to his son's future prosperity.'[65] As for daughters, very few were apprenticed. 'Parents did not want to "waste" money and time training a daughter who they hoped would make a good marriage and soon be out of the work force.'[66] The provision of apprenticeship opportunities to sons effectively extended a father's authority, and inhibited working-class youth from venturing out on their own, for 'if the child left home before the age of apprenticeship, he almost certainly abandoned any hope of a skilled profession later in life, and if he walked out of his apprenticeship, he might also have to sever ties with his parents.'[67] There seems to have been a tacit agreement between fathers and sons: the latter would reside at home, work hard, and hand over their wages loyally to parents; in return, fathers would secure their entry into a trade.

The classic model for this relationship was the master craftsman, training his son in his own shop, which the lad would eventually take over. In this case, the transmission was buttressed by ownership in (or effective possession of) the means of production – a form of inheritance. Yet even as craftsmen were gradually divested of any productive property to pass on and turned into wage-earners, they clung to the tradition of father–son continuity in a trade; it gave their life-work meaning in relation to their children's future. For their part, capitalists vigorously resisted the notion that tradesmen had any right to secure the succession of sons to their vocation, insisting on their own unfettered hiring prerogative. Informally, however, they were normally prepared to hire kin and satisfy family aspirations.[68] The persistence of fairly high levels of patrilineal continuity in the skilled trades long after formal apprenticeship and subcontracting had declined seems remarkable at first glance, considering the pervasive encroachment of capitalist hiring prerogatives on the traditional processes of occupational induction.[69] Evidently, employers were inclined to go along with the informal recruitment of next of kin, finding that it was useful from their standpoint in circumventing the anonymity of the labour market. This form of familial continuity was complemented by trade endogamy, which remained commonplace in the nineteenth century: 'Acquaintanceship, friendship, love, marriage – all took place within the framework of the trade.'[70]

Measured against the values embodied in this tradition, fathers who lacked a trade or had seen their skills and occupational niches outmoded by technological change had to settle for second best, placing sons in other trades if they could afford entry papers and apprenticeship fees. Failing that, they had very little to offer their sons, save to wish them well as they sought work on the casual labour market. Paternal default embittered both generations, diminishing the authority of fathers in their own eyes and in those of their children.[71] In the case of daughters, by contrast, few parents had clear occupational goals in mind for them, and no one expected parents to provide vocational training. Parents sought only to ensure that their daughters laboured in a well-supervised setting, sheltered from the moral dangers of anonymous sex-mixing.[72]

Among the great mass of the labouring poor, where the prerogative of devolving one's occupation from father to son scarcely existed, parents secured children's employment and maintained control over their wages through subcontracting arrangements. As mentioned, wherever children and young women worked outside their homes, they tended to be employed within kin-based networks. Subcontracting was a crucial vehicle for the redeployment of familial relations in capitalist workplaces. While the arrangement varied widely between industries, subcontracting none the less had a discernible coherence, based on the conjunction of three elements: (a) capitalists hired masters to head up labour-teams and the latter recruited children or adolescents to work for them; (b) managers left masters to organize the team's work, to supervise and discipline its members; and (c) employers paid contractors a piece rate for their group's total output. After paying helpers or parents (but not their own children), masters pocketed the difference. These three elements – a collective mode of recruitment, an autonomous form of labour-team organization, and a lump-sum wage form – were strongly correlated with one another, though not invariably conjoined. Later on, as subcontracting declined, all three facets of the relation tended to disintegrate concomitantly. Due to the intermediate position of the contractor and the multitiered nature of the relationships of authority, subcontracting practices impeded the emergence of a clear class polarization between labour and capital.

How prevalent was subcontracting in the first stage of industrial capitalism? J. H. Clapham first demonstrated that the practice was extremely common in Britain, and recent evidence indicates that it was just as important in France.[73] Wherever children formed a significant part of the labour force, subcontracting was widespread; most children were hired by masters, not directly by employers.[74] The arrangement has been most widely studied in textile factories. The 1834 English Factory Commission estimated that half the children working in 225 cotton mills in Lancashire, Cheshire and Derbyshire were employed by operatives.[75] In French textile mills, Villermé estimated that the children recruited by their fathers or mothers formed from a tenth to a half of all young workers employed in these workplaces, and Tilly and Scott are of the view that 'the practice of parents hiring out their own children prevailed.'[76] Subcontracting was also commonplace in pottery, quarrying, mining, iron-smelting, and building.[77]

> Capitalism, in its early stages, expands, and to some extent operates, not so much by directly subordinating large bodies of workers to employers, but by subcontracting exploitation and management. ... In the early nineteenth century ... all grades except the lowest labourers contain men and women who have some sort of 'profit incentive'.[78]

Contrary to the impression conveyed in earlier studies, recent work has shown that most of the children toiling as the assistants of piece-masters were not working for their parents.[79] A great many were 'pauper apprentices' sent to mills and mines by orphanages, religious Orders and state agencies; others were the children of the contractors' friends and neighbours, or had older siblings working on site. As mentioned, masters normally preferred to recruit their own children, above all because they did not have to be paid. But they were not always available – many were too young – and it appears that the normal duration of employment for children in cotton mills, for example, was quite brief. Furthermore, parents often found it best to disperse their children in several workplaces as a hedge against unemployment.[80] It would be a mistake, then, simply to equate subcontracting with the maintenance of family-based labour-teams in industry. The family workshop was not transplanted all at once into the early factories. While striving to preserve their labour-teams intact, parents were rarely able to do so when employment moved to the factories.[81] Yet internal subcontracting could often be combined with outwork, as workers took home piecework to be finished by wives with the assistance of young children; in this way, they extended the family as a productive unit between spheres.

Even when family members had been hired separately in a formal sense, kin connections played a decisive role in shaping the recruitment process and the social relations of the workplace.

> The family, and wider kin networks, acquired growing significance ... as migration increased. Newspapers and journals were used to some extent for white-collar and skilled-labour recruitment ... but their highly localized nature limited their appeal. ... Kin and friends, in contrast to advertisements, could provide information on real, as distinct from nominal, working conditions.[82]

Employers were inclined to cast kin-hiring in a paternalist light, as a special favour to loyal workers. Yet they had their own compelling reasons for hiring next of kin. In the first place, they sought to circumvent the anonymity of labour markets in an era prior to school certificates, employment records and personnel offices. If employers ignored the friendship and kin networks of their workers, they found that they had very little information to guide them in hiring. Second, the preservation of kin relations in their labour forces furnished workers with a strong sense of obligation to one another, thus keeping labour turnover within manageable limits. Third, managers relied heavily on paternal authority in the early factories to keep children and youth in line.[83] By asserting their right to hire anyone, employers put in their debt workers who were anxious to obtain a job for a family member. Only on the basis of the demonstrated diligence of the present employees would managers consider acceding to requests to hire kin. Newcomers were then under pressure to vindicate the employer's choice, proving that the sponsor's recommendation had been justified. Since family members normally had to live with one another at home, pressure for conformity on the job could be very intense.

Familial relations were a two-edged sword, however, as employers soon came to realize. The other side of patriarchal discipline and a stabilizing sense of kin obligation was a feeling of protectiveness and defensive solidarity which could give rise to tenacious forms of resistance against the encroachments of managerial authority.[84] Family members chafed at the exercise of arbitrary power by foremen and managers against their kin. Fathers who were ready to discipline their own children on the shop floor were not prepared to allow overseers to do so, usurping their authority. The management of a labour force thick with kin ties was thus a complicated and delicate operation, requiring insight and sophistication – qualities in short supply among early industrial managers. With the curtailment of child labour in the second half of the nineteenth century, the familial form of subcontracting gradually declined. The reasons for its demise will be examined in Chapter 4.

Housing in the Midst of the Urban Onrush

The European population almost doubled between 1800 and 1910, while the continent's cities expanded sixfold. The population of England and Wales quadrupled over the same period, while their urban areas expanded 9.5 times. In the first half of this massive and historically unprecedented urbanization, cities grew almost entirely by means of in-migration. In England, the influx began to assume torrential proportions in the first two decades of the nineteenth century; the flood was not restricted to short bursts, nor to a few cities. From 1801 to 1851, manufacturing centres grew at an average pace of 2.4 per cent per annum, while the rate in mining and hardware cities was 2.3 per cent.[85] On the continent the urban onrush came later, accelerating sharply in the 1840s with growth rates generally on the same order of magnitude as in English cities, except in France, where the pace was more sedate in most centres.[86] During decades of peak growth, the construction of new housing stock did not keep pace with the urban flood-tide. Antwerp's population doubled between 1797 and 1856, but its number of dwellings grew by a mere 30 per cent; Paris spurted 25 per cent in the decade 1817–27, while 10 per cent more dwellings were built; Berlin grew by 80,000 in the 1830s, yet only 8,920 dwellings were built; while the Viennese population swelled 42 per cent from 1827 to 1847, but the city's housing stock increased only 12 per cent. Similar figures could be cited for other cities. In England as a whole, the excess of families over dwellings swelled from 321,000 in 1801 to 790,000 by 1871.[87] At some point in the nineteenth century, 'nearly every large town in western and central Europe faced a growing discrepancy between supply and demand.'[88] The problem was compounded by the fact that both urbanization and house-building were strongly cyclical phenomena, frequently out of phase with one another. To cite an extreme case: in the 1850s, the population of Paris increased 20 per cent in five years, while the number of dwelling-places actually declined due to an ambitious street-widening programme.[89]

The housing crisis was particularly acute at the lower end of the market in accommodation for the labouring poor. The squeeze had both a spatial and an economic aspect. As propertyless immigrants flooded into the cities looking for work, they necessarily sought housing within ready walking distance of work-places where they had the best prospects of being hired. As a contemporary observer noted, 'the crowding arises from the fact of the desire of the working population to be "near their bread" as they express it.'[90] Newcomers were thus packed into areas immediately adjacent to the districts of the most rapid industrial expansion. It was not unusual for such districts to double their population in a decade. The result was a double-barrelled blow to working-class residents. In the first place, they were hit with skyrocketing costs for accommodation. Homeownership was out of the question for the vast majority, who were compelled to rent. As urban growth accelerated, residential rents boomed across Western Europe: they shot up 60 per cent in Ghent between 1800 and 1860; in Brussels, they doubled during the same period; in Paris, rents rose by half between 1835 and 1870, and in Berlin they jumped 24 per cent between 1830 and 1847.[91] Under these circumstances, housing costs in the inner cities claimed a rising portion of the average working-class family budget – roughly a fifth. The poorer families were, the larger was the portion that went to the landlord.[92] To help pay the rent, families 'huddled' together – doubled up, sublet, and took in boarders. Jammed quarters resulted. Every available nook and cranny was filled – courts, pantries, garrets and cellars. In a poor parish of Liverpool in 1841, a quarter of the population was crammed into courts, and 9 per cent lived in cellars with an average of three persons per cellar. In Preston at mid-century, 23 per cent of family groups shared a dwelling with others. One-fifth of Berlin households contained a lodger in 1861, and half of all dwellings in the city were based on a single heatable room. In the same year, 34 per cent of houses in the whole of Scotland were one-room affairs.[93] The correlate of overcrowding was overbuilding. Every available square foot of private land had to be built upon. In back-to-backs and multiple-storey tenements, dwellings were packed in like sardines, with many rooms having no ventilation or outdoor windows. In Liverpool's Exchange Ward, parallel rows of dwellings were accessed by courts as narrow as six feet; only five of two hundred courts had openings at either end. In Glasgow as a whole, only 542 of 3,000 courts had entrances wider than ten feet.[94] The really 'dark and Satanic' sites of the Industrial Revolution were the dwellings of the poor; the textile mills were well lit and ventilated by comparison.

A deteriorating ratio of rent to income was by no means universal in the towns and cities of Western Europe, but overcrowding was none the less widespread. While horror stories from the worst cities abound, it is difficult to assess the overall extent of the problem. Yet it is clear that in many cities domestic density worsened during the initial phase of rapid population influx. In Antwerp, there were 4.9 persons per house in 1797 and 6.8 in 1830; in Brussels, 7.2 persons in 1829 and 9.7 by 1846; in Liverpool, 6.1 in 1811 and 7.3 by 1851. Dwelling density was higher in London at the end of the century than it had been at the beginning.[95] The upshot was that the younger generation very often paid more money for less elbow room than their parents had enjoyed. In other cities, the trend improved slightly in the first stage of industrialization, so that the aggregate picture is one of stagnation. In England and Wales as a whole, there were roughly 5.5 persons per dwelling at each census from 1801 to 1851, but crowding was denser in urban working-class districts.[96] The true extent of working-class overcrowding is masked by such figures, for two reasons. Neither landlords nor tenants had any interest in disclosing the amount of subletting taking place, and housing inspectors generally shunned unannounced night visits as hazardous to life and limb. Second, the persons-per-dwelling measure takes no account of the average size of the quarters, and in slum neighbourhoods rooms were smaller than in the wealthier parts of town. In Glasgow in 1861, where the standard room was perhaps 10–12 feet square, 34 per cent of city inhabitants lived in one-room households and another 39 per cent in two rooms. In many cities on the continent, residents were even more jammed: in Brussels in 1846, 45 per cent of families were packed into one room. In 1890, over 40 per cent of the population of Dresden, Berlin and Breslau still lived in dwellings with only one heatable room.[97] In these circumstances, it was impossible to maintain a sense of privacy between families, much less within them. 'Neighbours shared hallways, sculleries, and toilets, and might have to walk through each other's rooms routinely to reach the shared facilities.'[98]

Compounding the problem of overcrowding was the woeful condition of waste disposal, contaminated land beneath cellar floors, an absence of indoor drains, open sewers, poor street drainage, and the resulting pollution of water sources. Outdoor privies were grossly inadequate, breeding-grounds for insect infestation and the spread of contagious diseases. In working-class districts, the ratio of toilets to households was often one to five or more. These conditions lay at the heart of high urban death rates, with life expectancy five to ten years shorter than in rural areas. In new industrial towns and old cities alike, proletarian districts were ecological disaster zones. Contagious diseases swept through them like invisible typhoons. Epidemic waves of typhoid fever and cholera were commonplace in the first half of the nineteenth century. Urban death rates did not abate until real improvements began to be made in waste disposal and municipal water supplies in the second half of the century.[99] Overcrowded housing conditions were lethal. In Glasgow, the mortality rate of families living in one or two rooms was two and a half times the rate of those living in five or more rooms.[100]

The reports of Villermé in France (1840), Chadwick in Britain (1842) and Huber in Germany (1845) broadened the focus of public alarm concerning 'the social question' from sweatshops and factories to proletarian neighbourhoods and dwellings. The dreadful housing conditions of the labouring classes – a scandal that would haunt the bourgeois conscience for the rest of the century – had finally been thrust on to the political agenda. While the cholera epidemic of the 1840s shocked the public, the primary object of middle-class anguish was not the mortality of the poor but their morality, or rather lack of same. The conventional wisdom of the propertied classes was that overcrowded dwellings were corrupting working-class family life by making it impossible to live modestly. They cited a lack of family privacy, the impropriety of live-in boarders, the close-quartered mingling of the sexes, the sharing of beds. 'If human beings are crowded together', Reverend Montgomery warned, 'moral corruption takes place, as certainly as fermentation or putrefaction in a heap of organic matter.'[101] By this reasoning, domestic privacy was the *sine qua non* of sexual morality. When personal privacy was physically impossible, moral corruption was sure to follow. The poor were held to be 'gregarious and public' by nature, but when overcrowding became extreme, Lord Shaftesbury was convinced, 'every instinct of personal or sexual decency is stifled.' 'It is impossible', he intoned, 'to exaggerate the physical and moral evils that result.' Slum housing conditions were considered breeding-grounds for casual concubinage, pre-marital promiscuity and incest. The latter vice was a matter of acute concern; Shaftesbury insisted that it was 'frightfully common' in the poorest districts of London. While we have no way of knowing whether incest was increasing in this era, bourgeois Victorians were certainly convinced that it was.[102]

Given the rate at which masses of rural folk poured into the cities as the pace of industrialization accelerated, it is surprising that the urban housing crisis was not worse. A great deal of housing was built, and to focus exclusively on the decades of shortfall in the fastest growing cities is one-sided, for the crisis cannot be conveyed simply in numerical terms. There were two major problems with the housing that was built. In the first place, construction was skewed towards the middle and upper end of the market, where homeowner-ship was a possibility and, failing that, higher rents were affordable. Secondly, the vast majority of inexpensive new housing was of wretched quality – erected in haste by small undercapitalized contractors who threw up shacks and tenements on tiny undrained lots, without plans, in the absence of munici-pal housing standards, using cheap materials and employing unskilled and often casual labourers. George Goodwin (editor of *The Builder* and an ardent hous-ing reformer) observed:

> See the mode in which thousands of houses … are commenced; without any excavation; the basement floor of thin, gaping boards placed within six inches of the damp ground; with slight walls of ill-burnt bricks and muddy mortar, sucking up the moisture … ill-made drains, untapped, pouring forth bad air; and you scarcely need more causes for a low state of health.[103]

The structural fault underlying the entire industry was the parasitic nature of ground rent in dense urban milieus, with competition from alternative in-dustrial and commercial uses driving up the price of coveted residential real estate. Since demand for housing was concentrated within ready walking dis-tance of the city's major worksites, this constriction exacerbated the competi-tive squeeze. When the value of prime land rose way above the value of the housing stock resident upon it, landlords hiked rents or forced mass evictions, paving the way for bulldozing forms of 'slum clearance' that subtracted affor-dable housing from the market, often without replacing it. Evicted families tended to move only a short distance in order to remain in the vicinity, placing further pressure on inner-city housing stock. As the price of land inflated and interest rates rose, capital was sucked from house-builders on the supply side, while exorbitant rents were extracted from tenants on the demand side, the funds of both flowing into the pockets of unproductive middlemen – bankers, landlords and speculators. The medical officer of Hampstead went to the heart of the matter:

> To get the house built something more is needed. The capitalist, often the owner of the land, now comes forward with loans, to enable a class of small builders to undertake the work. These builders, for the most part men with little or no means, but with a certain knowledge and experience, have to build the houses and to support themselves and their families during the period in which the loans can be made to last. … But if the builder is not to fail, it follows that he must go to the cheapest market for the materials. His bricks will be porous, his

timber 'shaky', his mortar deficient in lime, his plaster destitute of hair, his woodwork and joinery of the most unsatisfactory kind, and his sanitary appliances of the cheapest quality.[104]

Women's Domestic Work and the Household as a Workplace

In stating that most women 'left work' when they married, I hardly meant to imply that they ceased working and became ladies of leisure! There in the background, if we care to look, is a vast labour force hard at work: cleaning, sweeping, shopping, cooking, sewing, washing and, amidst everything else, caring for children. Before the fertility decline (which came in the early twentieth century for most working-class couples), women spent perhaps four-fifths of their years from marriage to menopause either pregnant or breastfeeding. In the course of their reproductive careers, most suffered internal injuries or illnesses in childbearing, often permanently debilitating. Perhaps 6 per cent would die in childbed. Mothers had the grievous misfortune of losing 15 to 20 per cent of their infants within the first year (for poor women it was probably one in four); these deaths tended to hasten the arrival of the next infant. Within a few days of giving birth, they rose from 'confinement' to resume their domestic chores. Keep these brute facts in mind as we look at the homemakers' daily labour, for the domestic labour process cannot be understood unless its integration with women's reproductive work is appreciated.

The irony of saying that women 'left work' upon marrying is that in reality they worked many more hours at home in a week than their husbands did elsewhere, even when the latter were regularly employed (toiling roughly sixty hours per week in the mid nineteenth century). Women rose before their husbands in the morning to feed the baby, light the fire, make breakfast and see their husbands off to work. At the other end of a long day, after men's work was done, women cooked dinner, washed up, put the children to bed, and made and mended clothes by candlelight. On the Sabbath, when men (and the Lord) rested, women prepared Sunday dinner, the most ambitious meal of the week, with meat to roast if the family could afford it.[105] Like their sisters of an earlier era, urban working-class homemakers in the nineteenth century remained domestic generalists; they combined a great variety of tasks in the course of a day: interrupting one thing to do another, keeping one eye on a toddler and the other on a boiling pot. Leisure, in the sense of uninterrupted time away from work, was practically non-existent for proletarian homemakers. Yet they snatched moments of respite during the day, stopping for a brief chat with a neighbour on the front step or at the corner store. Unlike their menfolk, who were beginning to segment their daily lives into continuous stretches of work and leisure, homemakers were still involved in a

45

task-oriented labour process. Only a few events in the day, such as breakfast and dinner, entailed producing to a time deadline; other tasks were juggled, traded off and combined, being made to fit the rest of the time available for their completion. Marie Catherine recalled: 'Mama tended to housecleaning, scoured the floor, scraped the table with a shard of glass, threw fresh sawdust on the tiles, boiled potatoes and at the same time prepared the shuttle bobbins that we would use the next day.'[106]

The homemaker's workplace in the mid nineteenth century was a rented hovel of one or two rooms, with perhaps six or seven people per household. The dwelling was dark, dank, poorly ventilated and sooty. Daylight scarcely penetrated the interior of the residence; glass windows were small and sparse; poorer dwellings often had none. Artificial light was furnished by burning rushes, candles, tallow and, later, kerosene or paraffin lamps. Gas lamps, much brighter and cleaner burning, did not become common in working-class homes until the turn of the century.[107] Oil lamps and candles did not cast much light, were smoky and had to be frequently tended and trimmed. They were also extremely dangerous: 65 per cent of all London fires between 1833 and 1849 were attributed to accidents with candles.[108] In such a primitive environment, meeting the most basic needs was a constant effort. Heat was supplied by burning wood, peat or coal in a fireplace with a crude interior chimney; fuel had to be fetched, and the fire lit and stoked. Starting the fire by striking flint against iron to produce a spark was a major chore, particularly in the dark on a cold winter morning. The task was eased considerably in the second half of the century when friction matches became widely available. The main form of cooking was boiling pots hung over an open fire; baking and spit-roasting were also accomplished in this fashion. Cast-iron stoves were luxury items not widely available to working-class households in the nineteenth century. Gas stoves, introduced in the 1880s, did not appear in working-class homes until the twentieth century.[109]

Without indoor plumbing, water had to be fetched in tubs and basins filled from a water pipe on the street or from vats on a horse-drawn cart. In many towns there was an insufficient supply, with the pipes flowing only a few hours a day. Women and children were often compelled to queue and wait 'in foul weather or in fine, carrying pails through muddy and uneven streets, an endless round of drudgery, day in and day out'.[110] To gain some appreciation of the nature of domestic labour under such circumstances, let us briefly consider one major task: doing the laundry. Buckets of water would have to be fetched and brought to the house. Women in rural areas found it easier to carry the laundry to the water source, a nearby stream, pond or well, but homemakers in densely packed urban neighbourhoods typically lacked the space to do laundry outdoors. When the tub had been filled, a cleaning agent was added to the water, frequently stale urine (for its ammonia content) or lye. Commercial soaps were widely available by mid century, but they were expensive and required hot water to be effective; many homemakers economized by using a mixture of lye and soap.[111] A wash, a boiling and a rinse might use up to fifty gallons (400 pounds) of water, which had to be hauled back and forth from the outdoor tap to the flat. 'Rubbing, wringing and lifting water-laden clothes … wearied women's arms and wrists and exposed them to caustic substances.'[112] To launder a family's linen, the entire process of washing, rinsing, starching and drying would need to be repeated several times. At each stage, waste water had to be hauled back outdoors and dumped, and fresh water collected. A mill-hand's wife in Huntingdon in the 1870s described the travail in these terms:

> You had to be as strong as a man to lift the great wooden wash tubs, allus full o' suds, to keep 'em binged [soaked], even without the weight of the wet clothes; and then you had to lift the great iron pot, full of water, on and off the pot hook over a hot turf fire, and drag the wet washing in a clothes basket to the line down the garden, and put it in and out again, perhaps four or five times if it were a wet day.[113]

A survey of London working-class households in the 1840s indicated that women rarely finished the weekly wash in less than two days, and the job often extended into a third.[114] Not surprisingly, homemakers ranked it high on the list of most loathed chores. One of their chief frustrations was to see freshly cleaned clothes, hung out to dry, collecting a layer of soot. Since the labouring poor often lacked a change of clothes, proletarian women were constrained to repeat the ordeal more frequently than upper-class women, who assigned female servants to the task wherever they were present. Even a single cold-water tap and a drain in each dwelling would have greatly eased the labour of doing the laundry (as well as cooking and cleaning); yet indoor plumbing was a rarity in working-class households until the latter decades of the century.[115]

Caught in an economic backwater, her labour devalued and unpaid, the urban working-class homemaker toiled in a pre-industrial workplace. Archaeologists of some future society, excavating the ruins of these squalid tenements, might be excused for thinking that they had stumbled into a perverse timewarp. For here were clustered dwellings, standing at or near the centre of a bustling new economy, that were utterly devoid of the modern technology of that economy. The homemaker was equipped with tools – pots, mops, brooms, buckets, rushlights, flint and tongs – that had not changed for centuries; hand-tools of the crudest variety, requiring unassisted muscle-power.

In districts of pervasive dust, grime and filth, house-proud women struggled against all odds to keep their households 'clean and decent'. What could this mean under the circumstances? Obviously, standards of hygiene and cleanliness varied widely – not only across classes, but within the working class between

47

'respectable' and 'rough' neighbourhoods. John Wesley had declared that 'cleanliness was next to Godliness', and masses of proletarian women were convinced of it. In the 'better' districts, housewives 'kept up appearances', exerting considerable peer pressure to ensure that their households presented a clean exterior to the world. The older women of the neighbourhood tended to pronounce judgement: 'Aye, she hangs out a lovely washing', or 'She's hangin oot her grey things', the latter comment boardering on ostracism. 'Even offhand comments of slatternly housekeeping could be devastating.'[116] Such rigorous standards extended well down into the heart of the industrial working class. 'Oh, that Lancashire cleanliness!' Harry Pollit recalled of his own childhood in the mill town of Droylsden in the 1890s. 'That cleaning of the front steps and flags! That scrubbing down of the back-yard! ... Those brass candlesticks that had to be polished until you could see your face in them!'[117] This was not merely a question of presenting a well-groomed exterior to the world. The personal value of cleanliness was almost universally acknowledged in the nineteenth century. Very few people remained absolutely indifferent to filth and squalor; they sought to optimize their own bodily comfort and sense of well-being: 'Poor families whose members often literally had no change of clothing, willingly retired naked to bed while their clothes were washed.'[118] As the century progressed, more and more proletarians became aware of the importance of domestic hygiene in averting the spread of contagious diseases. It was not only middle-class reformers and public health inspectors who believed that it was every housewife's duty to do what she could, within the limits of her family's resources, to keep her children 'decent' and her household clean and neat. The vast majority of working-class women struggled to meet their own standards, which were of course very different from the norms that middle-class observers sought to impose upon them.

How much help did homemakers receive from other family members as they strove to keep the house clean, their infants alive, and the primary bread-winner from going to work hungry? It appears that women were increasingly carrying the domestic burden on their own in the nineteenth century. To be sure, children of both sexes had tasks to perform, and girls in particular could be expected to help out regularly around the house; many did a great deal.[119] Loane recounts that in one home she visited, 'the girl of twelve goes to bed at seven in order to rise at five and get her father's breakfast; she then prepares breakfast for the others, and cuts and packs the school dinners.'[120] Older girls did much of the 'minding' of their younger siblings, as they had in the past.[121] Yet daughters who were not at home could be of no direct assistance, and a great many of them worked all day long elsewhere: in middle-class homes as domestics, and in factories and sweatshops. Husbands were not much help. Even when their work-day was over, men evidently did less to assist their wives at home in the nineteenth century than they had in previous centuries.[122] Although the gradual intensification of the working day in most sectors of industry must have contributed to male neglect, their abstention was not simply due to exhaustion. As a rule, men spent very little time at home beyond eating and sleeping, preferring to pass the time after work with male friends in pubs and clubs.[123] Those who involved themselves in housework were widely considered to be eccentric or effeminate:

> In Northampton, working-class men did not even do minor chores such as fetching coal, chopping firewood or carrying dustbins out to the pavement. In Salford, likewise, men proved their virility by avoiding anything that was considered women's work. If, on occasion, they had to lend a hand ... they locked the doors first so that the neighbours would not see. Those husbands who were caught in the act of scrubbing a floor, washing, or cooking were apt to be called derisive names such as 'mop rag' or 'diddy man'.[124]

This increasingly rigid demarcation of male and female spheres of responsibility and jurisdiction was certainly a far cry from the rather fluid, pragmatically adaptive allocation of tasks between spouses in eighteenth century proto-industrial cottages.[125] The spatial segregation of spheres was closely bound up with the sharpening temporal delineation of work and leisure for men; the more continuous and unrelenting work-time became for men, the more they resented any incursion on their leisure-time. At its inaugural congress in 1866, the International Workingmen's Association (the First International) took up the struggle for the eight-hour day. Their slogan was 'les trois huits': eight hours of work, eight hours of leisure and eight hours of sleep. In their eight hours of leisure, working men, even their socialist vanguard, were not thinking of doing much work at home. The hardening of sex segregation, particularly notable in the latter half of the nineteenth century, is intimately bound up with the consolidation of the male-breadwinner wage norm; I will return to this topic in Chapter 4.

Working-Class Marriage Informalized

In the first volume of this study (*A Millennium of Family Change*), we saw how rural proletarianization undermined the control that parents, village communities and churches had traditionally exercised over the processes of conjugal union: courtship, betrothal, first coitus, the timing of the wedding, the inauguration of childbearing, and the setting up of a new household. Young people seized the initiative in all these areas, their actions increasingly governed by the balance of market forces as they sought jobs, unsupervised accommodation and eligible marriage partners. The widely recognized index of this revolution in the mode of family formation (and hence in the form of the family cycle) was the rise of childbirth outside marriage from 1750 to 1850, concentrated among proletarians.

Almost all pre-marital sex in the early modern era had been predicated upon expressed marital intent. Sex for single women was 'marriage-oriented', undertaken to catch a husband, to demonstrate fecundity, or to celebrate the impending union. Very few single women were so incautious as to welcome a man's sexual advances without first securing a solemn promise to wed.[126] There is no evidence that the rise in pre-marital childbirth in the late eighteenth century entailed a pervasive neglect of this safeguard; undoubtedly a higher proportion of single women were sexually active, but for the vast majority, trothplight remained the essential prerequisite. In this context, 'illegitimacy was not the rejection of marriage but rather its failure to take place.'[127] Why did women's nuptial plans increasingly go awry? In answering this question, it is useful to distinguish between three broad categories of marital default which tend to be fostered by somewhat distinct social conditions. First, in some cases, nuptial plans were thwarted by the refusal of Church and state authorities to marry people who lacked property and standing in the local community. In other cases, suitors deserted, leaving pregnant fiancées in the lurch. Finally, some couples chose to defer nuptials and live together in the meantime. The first variant, thwarted marriage, was most prevalent in peasant communities in the initial throes of proletarianization: marriage was still tied to land inheritance, and places on the land were growing scarce; local employment was strictly controlled, and the authorities refused to marry paupers and newcomers so as to inhibit the growth of the indigent population. There was a rash of such legislation in the early nineteenth century, peaking in the 1830s. State laws and local ordinances combined to require couples who wished to marry to satisfy certain requirements, such as demonstrating permanent residence in the parish and presenting evidence of property-holding or secure employment therein. In Germany, such laws undoubtedly 'made marriage between persons from different communities difficult and narrowed the range of economic opportunities open to those wanting to establish a family.'[128] In Britain, where the process of proletarianization was much further advanced, the levels of residential transience and urban anonymity were such as to render legal restriction largely nugatory.[129]

Suitor desertion, by contrast, became widespread in the midst of full-fledged proletarianization. As land inheritance and dotal exchange declined, the betrothal promise became less secure. Heightened labour turnover and high rates of mobility for single men, the increasingly impersonal nature of hiring workers and renting them accommodation – these conditions made it easy for men to be on their way when they learnt that a female companion was pregnant. Many were already on the road by the time the discovery was made.[130] Paternal desertion appears to have been a major factor in the rise of 'illegitimate' childbirth after 1750. In six German villages in the first half of the eighteenth century, the couple eventually married in two-thirds of first births conceived out of wedlock; a century later, just over half did.[131]

The third variant, informal cohabitation, became increasingly common as the burgeoning proletarian population migrated *en masse* to the cities.[132] Social historians have noted the rise of informal cohabitation in the early nineteenth century in many industrializing regions of Northwestern Europe; while this trend is unevenly spread, it is evident that common-law unions were a fairly general phenomenon of the period. In England and Wales at the end of the Napoleonic Wars, Gillis estimates that possibly a fifth of the population lived at one time or another in common-law unions, 'most no doubt as a prelude to marriage, but also some as a substitute for it'.[133] In Paris in the 1830s and 1840s, Chevalier has calculated that

> a population of some 100,000 to 110,000 lived in illicit unions with a degree of stability which ... should not be confounded with casual sexual relations. ... Almost all such unions were working-class ... [and] the illegitimacy statistics show ... that this was a working-class custom.[134]

Living tally (as the English dubbed it) was generally marked by a secular and public ritual, such as stepping over a broomstick or exchanging vows before friends. While it was not a legal union, such an arrangement involved more than casual cohabitation. A 'tally bargain' was an informal contract, based on mutual consent, typically entailing a modicum of affection and regard, and in the event of offspring, explicitly recognizing paternal obligation to mother and child.[135]

Consensual unions were most prevalent amongst groups who, for various reasons, found it difficult to marry. Newcomers to the city, particularly those who had moved far away from the parental home or were immigrants from another country, frequently cohabited unofficially. The practice also tended to run in occupations. In the textile centre of Mulhouse, weavers constituted almost one-third of the town's male cohabitants; in Bezons (eight miles north-west of Paris), over 40 per cent of the town's female cohabitants were factory 'girls'.[136] Casual unions seem to have been particularly common among itinerant workers such as navvies and sailors, and casual labourers – rag-pickers, chimney sweeps, dust collectors, and the like. Mayhew noted a marked hostility to marriage amongst London costermongers, who informed him that they resented lining the parson's pocket; he estimated that only 10 per cent of costermonger couples living together were legally married.[137] Informal unions gradually declined in the second half of the nineteenth century, yet in Bezons, working-class cohabitation before marriage was still 'extremely widespread, perhaps not much short of universal' in the 1890s. Similarly, in working-class districts of London in the late nineteenth century, a very high proportion of couples gave the same address on their marriage certificates.[138]

Casual cohabitation alarmed the propertied classes, being taken as a sure sign of incipient radicalism and defiant secularism. A report to the Assemblée Nationale in 1849 declared: 'We must extirpate this system of regularized concubinage, which forms only households and not marriages, and which is even more threatening to society because it constitutes an organization of the proletariat.'[139] The irony of such alarm is that the cohabitation of parents and their eventual marriage furnished a far more favourable context for infants born to single women than absent and neglectful fathers; in the latter case, infants were frequently abandoned. Is there any way to estimate the proportions of each? In Mulhouse, a father was officially recognized in more than half of all illegitimate births, this proportion peaking in late 1830s. And in the six German villages mentioned above, a rising proportion of all births out of wedlock were subsequently legitimized by the marriage of women to men recognized as fathers at the time of birth. Of course, it had always been the case that the majority of pregnancies conceived out of wedlock had been followed by the parents' marriage; this in itself was not new. But in the early modern context, nuptials almost invariably occurred before the birth; in the nineteenth century, a much higher proportion took place afterwards.[140]

The increasing propensity of proletarians to defer marriage while living together and bearing children was but one facet of the larger process of informalizing working-class marriage. Among those who legally wed, more and more couples reduced the formalities to obtaining a marriage licence, thus avoiding the publicity of a church wedding with the calling of the banns. The licence, which was not cheap, had traditionally been the preserve of the rich, but with the suppression of clandestine marriage, more and more proletarians made use of it to evade 'the chaffing of neighbours'. In parts of Wales, the Midlands and the North of England, one marriage in four was by licence. An observer in Stepney noted that 'poor people have a great desire to marry secretly', and if they wished to have a church wedding, they often went to the next parish to arrange it.[141] Among proletarians, the ceremony itself was scaled down and simplified. The big wedding of peasant custom, associated with substantial property exchange and laden with community rites, was replaced by 'the little wedding', a plainer and more limpid ceremony conducted before a small circle of family and friends. Much of the symbolic conflict, ambivalence and resolution endemic to the big wedding's community involvement was curtailed or eliminated. The bride was no longer fetched from the home of her reluctant parents, but met the groom at the church door. Post-nuptial obstructions and threshold rites were dispensed with or appeared as quaint relics, perfunctorily repeated. The honeymoon faded, as most proletarians returned to work the next day. With the value of the parental dowry slashed, compensation was sought in the form of gifts from friends and neighbours solicited as part of the wedding invitation. For those who could afford neither a marriage licence nor the pastor's fee, secular rites of self-marriage were available in the cultural repertoire of most communities. Before friends, and parents if they approved, couples exchanged vows and rings, or stepped over a broomstick at the front door of their abode. Together with the secularization of marriage rites, informal divorce proceedings were popularized, such as the wife sale and brief ceremonies of annulment (jumping backwards over the broomstick, returning rings, and so on).[142]

The spread of conjugal informality, ignoring Church requisites, did not amount to a mass repudiation of 'sacred matrimony', much less its cultural foundation in heterosexual monogamy. Certainly there was a swelling anticlerical sentiment in proletarian milieus, and 'nonconformity was rising everywhere that the squire and the parson were not firmly in control.'[143] Militant secularists – Owenite radicals, Painite freethinkers and early feminists – openly defied Church strictures, flaunting their nonconformist principles in celebrating consensual unions. Many socialist papers proclaimed free unions to be morally superior to bourgeois marriage. Yet the self-conscious rebels were a small minority, clustered in the upper artisanal ranks of the labouring classes. The great bulk of consensual cohabitants were poor and more inclined to religious indifference than to fervent sacrilege. They explained to Church visitors that they had not wed because they could not afford to buy a suit for the occasion, obtain a licence, or pay the parson's fee. For semi-literate folk, the written formalities were discomfiting; often, they found them too bothersome to complete. Most cohabitants, especially women, were quick to add that they would prefer to be married, and intended to 'tie the knot' when they felt able to do so properly.

Yet it would be equally mistaken to attribute their religious indifference simply to the exigencies of poverty. The poor had been destitute long before common-law unions became a proletarian custom. The investigators found (to their chagrin) that most couples were unabashed about being unmarried or raising children out of wedlock. Men in particular resisted any insinuation that they were 'living in sin'. Both men and women exhibited a casual attitude to formal marriage, were not acutely concerned with the approbation of their social superiors, and preferred to do things their own way. Opening the front door of her tiny abode to the local pastor, a poor woman beckoned him to step inside quickly lest he be seen calling 'on the likes of us'. More worried about his reputation than her own, she readily admitted that she and her mate were living tally. 'But we are very happy', she assured him. 'I does my duty to him and he – well, there is not a better man on earth than my Tom.'[144] Several investigators noted that 'living tally' was especially prevalent in the rougher proletarian districts, where the practice was not subject to serious stigma. A French inspector complained,

They know very well that an illicit union is contrary to the precepts of morality and the customs of society. ... [But] if you represent to them the impropriety of an illicit union as a deterrent, they will quote in reply many examples among their own comrades; these examples ought, in their opinion, to acquit them of the reproach of immorality because it applies to too many people.[145]

At root, the revolution in the mode of family formation in this era stemmed from rapidly accelerating proletarianization in the midst of the Industrial Revolution and mass migration to the cities. Initially, this process undermined the parental, Church and community structures that had traditionally regulated entry to marriage; subsequently, proletarianization completely overran the land-based structures of the *ancien régime*. The authorities reacted to the surge of youthful initiative, labour transience and market anonymity by tightening state and parish regulations so as to limit the capacity of 'masterless men' and women to marry at will. These moves threw up barriers to marriage, even as proletarianization was making it easier for young people to select mates, begin childbearing, and set up their own households. But what the Industrial Revolution tore asunder, the Church and state could not keep together. Large numbers of young adults 'jumped the gun', inverting the proper sequence of marriage, household formation, and childbearing. For young men, the move can be seen as a partial emancipation from the rule of the father backed by community elders; for young women, the new freedoms bore attendant risks, increasing their vulnerability to men of their own generation.

'A Crisis of the Working-Class Family'?

During the 1840s, middle-class reformers became increasingly alarmed about the squalor of working-class life. Discerning ominous signs of disintegration and revolt in the making – the uprisings of 1848 soon confirmed their worst fears – they did not hesitate to castigate the ostrich-like insouciance of their peers, 'the propertied and ruling classes [who] labour under the dangerous conceit that there is no basis for the social question, [behaving] as if it were possible to distance oneself from the whole issue.'[146] Reformers grappled with 'the social question' on a number of fronts, from child labour and factory working conditions to drink, hygiene, infant-care and housing. Well-publicized exposures of horrific conditions in all these areas set off a chain reaction, galvanizing widespread fear and conscience-stricken anguish amongst the prosperous, provoking heated debate as to causes and remedies, and sparking the creation of reform associations which lobbied for government action. Reformers assessed the gravity of all social problems by one decisive criterion – their impact on working-class family life. They strove to keep the proletarian family intact; rehabilitate the man at its head in order to rekindle the family's proper respect for his leadership and authority; and revive a domestic culture of civility and 'family feeling' amongst the poor by eradicating the causes of despair, dissipation and debauchery. In essence, they diagnosed the problem as a spiritual one: 'the improvement of the moral conditions of the poorer classes and their preservation from misleading and incendiary tendencies' (namely, socialism and anarchism). If 'the evil is at bottom a moral disorder', Jules Simon reasoned, '[then] moral reform will inevitably follow domestic reform, because the influence of family life is irresistible.'[147]

Middle-class observers were haunted by the perception that working-class families, suffering the strains of rapid and anarchic industrialization, were about to disintegrate.[148] There was a pervasive fear that industrial capitalism had corroded family ties, unleashing an atomistic individualism that rendered the propertyless masses impulsive, insensate and depraved. The prognosis was grim:

> The plague that devours society is the destruction of family feeling and paternal authority. We must ... attack this problem to prevent the decomposition of the family.[149]

> Domestic life and domestic discipline must soon be at an end; society will consist of individuals no longer grouped in families; so early is the separation of husband and wife, of parents and children.[150]

These fears were based in large part on the impact of proletarianization (that is, of propertylessness) on masses of poor people.

> To conceive of property without the family – the family without property is impossible. ... [Without heritable property] there is no family, and the poor man is proof. ... His children disperse, succeeding generations forget their names. ... Ask a poor man about his genealogy and he'll think you're kidding.[151]

Beyond a vague angst fuelled by the visceral fear of impending social breakdown, middle-class moralists pointed to a number of specific maladies that were thought to be widespread among proletarian families. Overcrowded housing was a prime concern, giving rise to all manner of debauchery: 'fathers, mothers, daughters and sons live together pell mell ... their souls atrophy and their habits become corrupted.'[152] For the German reformer Victor Hubor, terrible housing conditions were 'nineteen twentieths of all evil. ... For many thousands of families, the "home" of which we are so proud has no meaning. The man who contrives to exist [in such a way] with his wife and children cannot lay claim to be head of the family; he is simply the biggest pig in the sty.'[153] A closely related concern was demographic: the well-being of the working class was imperilled by a crisis of reproduction. Citing horrendous infant mortality statistics in proletarian districts (particularly textile regions, where married women were employed outside their homes), observers doubted that women would be able to go on reproducing the species if their labour burdens were not relieved. As far as 'the labour question' was concerned, parents were accused of exploiting their children unmercifully through subcontracting arrangements. Critics were not opposed to child labour, but they did take strenuous exception to factory work, which they held to be morally degrading for children.[154]

If subcontracting was pernicious, so was its obverse – free wage labour. When women and children were hired as individuals and paid their own wage, the hierarchies of gender and generation were threatened. Free wage labour in anonymous factory settings was 'overturning all the bases of paternal authority', imperilling the family as a keystone of social order.[155] Several sources of independent wage income would subject families to centrifugal forces: 'The family income is not earned by a common head, nor does it flow from a common source. ... A law of self-preservation takes over from the force of habit and affection.'[156] Once children gained their own wage, they would pay no heed to their parents' wishes. The underlying fear, explicitly enunciated by Le Play, was that once family discipline and paternal respect were enervated, the younger generation would lose respect for *all* authority.[157] Women working outside their homes were unable to socialize their children properly, virtually ensuring puerile disregard:

> The employment of women at once breaks up the family; for when the wife spends twelve or thirteen hours every day in the mill, and the husband works the same length of time there or elsewhere, what becomes of the children? They grow up like wild weeds; they are put out to nurse for a shilling or eighteenpence a week, and how they are treated may be imagined.[158]

Furthermore, bourgeois Victorians were convinced, the problem extended through adolescence into young adulthood. Youth were leaving home precipitately, many living independently of any custodial supervision, and (as unprecedented illegitimacy rates indicated) indulging in sex before making serious undertakings to marry. They were then marrying prematurely, without seeking parental approval and before accumulating sufficient resources to establish proper households. Even worse, vast legions were not bothering to wed at all! These insouciant types were 'living in sin' as common-law cohabitants. Even when they did properly wed, proletarians had no respect for monogamy. 'The chastity of marriage is little known among them', Peter Gaskell believed, 'husband and wife sin equally and a habitual indifference to sexual rights is generated which adds one other item to the destruction of domestic habits.' Women were held to be in rebellion 'against the duties and functions of childbearing and home-keeping'.[159] Their continued employment outside the home after marriage was undermining male househeadship. If a man had the misfortune to be laid off, the couple's 'natural' roles would become inverted; marital chaos would surely ensue.

Middle-class anguish and moral outrage were widespread; with subtle variations, the same basic themes can be found in the public discourse of Britain, France and Germany during the first phase of industrialization.[160] Pundits and politicians arrayed across the political spectrum (from Marx and Engels on the left through liberal reformers like Lord Ashley in the centre to conservative Catholic moralists such as Count de Villeneuve-Bargemont on the right) were all convinced that unless drastic measures were taken, the breakdown of the working-class family was imminent. In Germany, as elsewhere, 'right and left converged in condemning the predominant [family] form within the working class as "unstable" and therefore undesirable.'[161] It is true that they allocated blame for the crisis in very different directions, and Marx and Engels broke with the rest by welcoming the dissolution of the traditional family (placing them squarely at odds with conservatives and with most of the labour movement as well).[162] But substantive perceptions of the crisis ran along very similar lines. The consensus was capped by the founding fathers of family sociology, Frederic Le Play in France and Wilhelm Heinrich Riehl in Germany, who concurred with the general content and tenor of this analysis and tried to document it empirically. They drew a sharp contrast between the incipient disorder of urban proletarian families and the organic solidarity of peasant and proto-industrial families where, under the robust guidance of the patriarch, a sense of natural hierarchy and familial respect was instilled in children and successfully reproduced from generation to generation.[163]

From the standpoint of the propertied classes, what was the answer to the crisis of the working-class family? The only way to buttress familial order amongst the propertyless was to reinstate a clear sense of male househeadship by encouraging the formation of a male-breadwinner family wage norm. As a conservative Reichstag deputy from the Ruhr area remarked:

> A happy family is the best reward for a worker; the feeling that he is working to support his wife and offspring gives him encouragement in his work; and in his family he finds peace and contentment. But such is only the case when the wife can devote herself to the family. If she is out of the house the whole day, then the house becomes dirty and untidy; the husband cannot get a proper meal … and this is not conducive to the creation of a feeling of contentment within the family.[164]

With the benefit of hindsight and a century of historical research, what do we make of this analysis? Since the early 1970s, historians of the family have rejected the conventional view that working-class families in the midst of the Industrial Revolution were truncated, fragmented, enervated and poised on the brink of disintegration.[165] Beginning with Michael Anderson's pathbreaking examination of mid-century Preston households (published in 1971), one study after another has found that urban households in Western Europe (and North America) had grown larger and more complex in the first phase of industrialization.[166] This evidence is sufficiently strong to merit a general characterization: in the first stage of industrialization, the typical working-class family form was an augmented nuclear family; in Germany, the same phenomenon has been dubbed the 'half-open family'.[167]

This finding, which overturned conventional widsom, has been taken to mean that proletarian families, far from being in crisis in the Industrial Revolution, were actually robust and surprisingly free from strain:

> The initial reaction to industrialization is neither attenuation and decline nor mere persistence, but an upsurge of kinship solidarity and heightened commitment. The kinship unit is larger, co-operation within it has been intensified and extended.[168]

The increment of proletarian *households* is here read as a sign of *family* strength. According to the new orthodoxy, the alarm of middle-class contemporaries was groundless and self-induced, a hysterical projection based in large measure on a lament for the passing of the patriarchal peasant family, which (as Laslett first argued) was also based on a fantastic misperception, imagined as an extended (stem) family when in reality it had been nuclear all along.[169] The nineteenth-century pundits and family sociologists had evidently got both the 'before' and 'after' pictures all wrong. In the new version of Western family history, the advent of industrial capitalism and the concomitant process of proletarianization did not alter the structure of the family in any fundamental way; consequently, the process of adjustment to socioeconomic change was not nearly so profound or fraught with the disintegrative risks of maladjustment as Victorian observers had imagined. The modest augmentation of households in the nineteenth century was attributable to an increasing availability of potential kin cohabitants – or, in a different version, to unprecedented levels of migration to the cities. This, then, is the indictment of the old orthodoxy by the new.

In my view, Laslett, Wall, Anderson, Hareven and their colleagues have 'overcorrected' the prior account, discarding well-grounded elements of the previous understanding. It is thus necessary to sift the wheat from the chaff in both accounts. Turning now to consider the merits and deficiencies of the Victorian account from my own perspective, it is first of all necessary to distinguish (though we can never wholly separate) the cultural values and political agendas of contemporary observers from the substantive claims made as to real trends in working-class family life. While the former are interesting as a study in the history of ideas, it is the latter that merit consideration here.

Certainly the ideological perspectives of most of these observers were pernicious; the reactionary lament for times past, for a romanticized depiction of patriarchal peasant families living happily on the land; the class condescension of moralists who saw in the divergence of the proletarian masses from the norms of their social superiors only displays of disorder and depravity, as if working people were incapable of developing their own norms of conduct in circumstances of secular nonconformity.[170] All this, from our vantage point, is thoroughly odious. But what of the substantive claims?

The fundamental idea underlying the Victorian analysis was that industrial capitalism had revolutionized the lives and family structures of the proletarian populace; the propertied classes feared that this transformation would tear working-class families apart. Some placed the emphasis on industrialization, focusing in particular on the strains of women's extra-domestic employment after marriage. Others looked more at capitalism, and hence proletarianization, with particular attention to the way that the divorce of masses of people from property rights in the means of production subverted the rule of the father and undermined the basis for stable lifelong marriage. The analysis of Le Play and his followers underlined the basic structural difference between property-based peasant families and propertyless proletarian families. These are entirely valid insights. It is a shame that they have been submerged by the recent revisions of Western family history, based on the nuclear family continuity thesis.[171]

Despite the current consensus that working-class living standards rose very substantially during the Industrial Revolution, I am of the view that the demographic concerns of nineteenth-century observers were also well founded. There is ample evidence of women labouring under severe strain, resulting in appallingly high rates of infant carnage. (This grim situation will be examined in Chapter 3.) In view of capitalism's corrosive effect on family relations (above all, the tendency of the private wage system and commodity consumption to promote individual interest at the expense of the family group), the pervasive anxiety of bourgeois Victorians seems fully warranted from the standpoint of their own conservative interests. As a mode of production and exchange, capitalism offered no support to the nuclear family. Proletarianization had severed the patriarchal order from its traditional property roots and shaken both the gender and the generational axes of family hierarchy. It would take some time before the tendons of domestic patriarchy could be regrafted on to the bones of the private wage system by means of the hardening cast of the male-breadwinner norm. In the meantime, other bastions of the bourgeois order, Church and state, entered the breach to bolster the family as a conservative kin ideal, ensuring that it remained common to all social classes. This is precisely what the reformists of the day were calling for.[172]

If these are valid elements in the assessment of contemporaries, where did they go awry? Much of the Victorian alarm about working-class family disintegration stemmed from a perception that a great many married women were toiling outside their homes, and that an absolute majority would in the near future. The empirical premiss of this prognosis was erroneous. Wives were not flocking into mills, mines and sweatshops in vast numbers. The great majority of women working in these places were single, and most of the rest were widowed. Nor was it to be the wave of the future (at least in the short and medium term).[173] The rate of married women's extra-domestic employment in the nineteenth century seldom exceeded 10 per cent, except in a few textile regions on which public attention was riveted. The spectre of conjugal role reversal – of redundant men becoming househusbands while their wives earned the family income – was thus largely a phantom, though none the less influential in the drive to consolidate the male-breadwinner wage norm (and in this context, a subject to which we shall return in Chapter 4).

In their hostility towards all forms of proletarian nonconformity, bourgeois Victorians exaggerated the danger of family disintegration. They were unable to perceive or predict the tenacity with which working people would stick by kin through thick and thin, developing their own sense of family loyalty and conjugal propriety while displaying a casual attitude to religious norms and legality concerning marriage. Modern social historians have shown how working-class families weathered the Industrial Revolution by fortifying group interdependence and relying on kin networks in order to migrate to the cities and to obtain support within them, especially in times of family crisis. In stressing family resilience, they have corrected the earlier view which mistook class independence and secular nonconformity for dissipation and disorder. On this ground, their critique of the earlier interpretation is salient.

Obsessed with co-residence patterns, the new family historians have paid insufficient attention to marriage, and to the conduct of courtship and wedding rituals as a window on the ways communities construe conjugal relations. John Gillis's magnificent study of British marriages, *For Better, For Worse*, together with the work of Jean-Louis Flandrin, Martine Segalen and Katherine Lynch on France, changes the map of Western European family history as inscribed by Peter Laslett and the Cambridge Group. There is a world of difference between peasant mate selection and wedding rituals (with invigilated courtship, parental involvement, betrothal and dowry, marital bargaining and the big wedding) and their proletarian counterparts. If marital customs are to be taken seriously in family history and not trivialized as cultural window-dressing, then the message of these studies is clear: they point to a basic divergence in the mode of family formation between peasants and proletarians.

The Augmentation of Nuclear Families

In the work of scholars such as Goode and Parsons, family history was recast in the mould of modernization theory.[174] From the first generation of family sociologists, they retained the basic notion of a discontinuity between extended families based on the land and nuclear families in modern cities. Under the impetus of industrialization and urbanization, households became smaller and their composition exclusively nuclear. This dichotomous perspective remained the prevailing view of Western family history until the early 1970s. The new work encapsulated in *Household and Family in Past Time* (1972) overturned the conventional wisdom of Western family history. If early modern households turned out to be smaller and simpler than expected, nineteenth-century urban households were larger and more complex. Not only was the earlier thesis of progressive nuclearization disconfirmed, but a shift had apparently occurred in the opposite direction. It was a startling finding, exploding the prevailing paradigm.

Modernization theory had postulated a basic 'fit' between the nuclear family and the industrial economy; empirical studies now indicated that the posited connection did not exist – at least for the initial phase of industrialization. The anomaly was tacitly resolved by retreating to a 'relative autonomy' position: 'the family' was evidently an endogenously reproduced institution, able to insulate itself from momentous transformations taking place in the underlying demographic and economic systems. This conclusion flowed ineluctably from the thesis of nuclear continuity; how else can we explain domestic perdurance in the face of societal change? Rather than return to first principles and rethink the relationship between socioeconomic transformation and familial reproduction from the ground up, it was easier to take the path of least resistance, concluding that the previously postulated fit was much looser than had been formerly supposed, dressing it up in 'cultural lags', 'traditional adaptations', and so forth.[175] It seems preferable to plough tougher ground, theorizing the relationship of family forms to the capitalist mode of production, and then presenting a historically grounded account of the interaction of socioeconomic and familial change in the development of capitalism.

How is the augmentation of nuclear family households in the initial phase of industrialization to be explained in a mode-of-production framework? To address this question, let us begin by examining the empirical phenomenon in some detail. Studies indicate that the build-up in urban household size and complexity stemmed from three changes: (a) children remaining in their parents' households longer than they had in the early modern era, in most cases until marriage; (b) a rising incidence of unrelated lodgers, living in and paying rent while working elsewhere; and (c) an increase in the co-residence of non-nuclear kin, accounting for the rise in household complexity. Let us consider each of these elements in turn.

Offspring: In the early modern era, it was a normal experience for children to leave the parental home around the time of puberty or shortly thereafter, entering service or becoming live-in apprentices. As agricultural service declined and craft associations gradually lost control over the recruitment and training of youth, opportunities waned for the placement of young adults in the households of their social superiors to work and train therein. Increasing numbers of youth lived at home throughout adolescence and well into their twenties. Evidence of this trend is broad. In the industrial town of Preston, 79 per cent of males aged fifteen to nineteen were living at home in 1851, while in small villages surrounding Lancashire, only 56 per cent were at home.[176] In four rapidly industrializing towns in the Lille district of Northern France, two-thirds to three-quarters of 20- to 24-year-old men were found to be residing in their parents' homes in 1861, and a majority of women of the same age. In the Roubaix area, 'parents and children lived together longer in the textile city than in agricultural and weaving villages.'[177]

Since children's wages represented an indispensable component in the proletarian family's income, it is easy to see why parents were keen to keep their children at home as long as possible. The reasons for their evident success in this regard are not so clear, given that they lacked the carrot and stick of substantial property inheritance. Why did the great majority of proletarian youth remain under their parents' roofs, subject to their domestic authority, until marriage? Was it merely out of a sense of familial loyalty? Reading autobiographical accounts, one cannot doubt that a powerful sense of devotion to parents, particularly to mothers, motivated vast numbers of working-class youth.[178] Recalling a proud moment as a boy, one man recounts: 'Even now, while writing, I feel the self-importance which animated me when, after my first whole week's work, I marched into the house and tendered to my mother half a crown.'[179] A French girl exclaimed: 'What happiness when I have earned my first money to place it in my mother's hands and say to her, "Yours, maman. It isn't much but it will help you."'[180] Yet this deep sense of familial reciprocity, of pride in being able to contribute to the family in gratitude for what one had received as a young child, cannot have been a sufficient cause, particularly as youth grew older and looked increasingly towards their own futures. Other factors staunched the flow of youth from their parents' homes.

In the initial phase of industrialization, many children working in mills, mines and sweatshops did not receive their own wages; these went directly to their parents or guardians. Their economic dependency remained complete. When youth did obtain their own pay (as the two cited above evidently did), the great majority living at home appear to have handed it over to their parents. Young men, following in their fathers' footsteps, would often retain a modest 'pocket allowance', but the earnings of sons under fourteen and

62

daughters of all ages were normally remitted in their entirety.[181] The individuation of the wage form certainly strengthened the bargaining power of young
earners within families, but it was not sufficient to sponsor a mass exodus of
youth. Many more youths were *paid* as individuals than were *hired* in this
capacity. Beyond casual day labour, jobs could be very difficult to obtain for
youth out on their own. As public sentiment hardened against child labour,
employers insisted on parental approval before hiring minors. Even after formal apprenticeship programmes had broken down, fathers were still instrumental in securing entry-level jobs for their sons in skilled trades. If boys
left home precipitately, they risked burning their bridges to respectable and
higher paying occupations. Above all, the extremely low level of wages for
young people inhibited their departure from the family household; their earnings would not readily support an independent existence. When they were
living at home, children did not have to pay for their mothers' unpaid services;
when they moved out, these provisions became expensive.[182] Even when
young people could afford a lodger's rent, the custodians of boarding-houses
and private householders were frequently reluctant to take them in (particularly young women) without the explicit agreement of parents or guardians.
While secure lodgings were generally necessary to obtain employment, the
continuous income of a steady job was essential to pay the rent. The interdependence of employment and accommodation was so tight that even a short
spell of joblessness compelled youth living on their own to return home. A
great many must have stayed with their parents because of the sheer insecurity
of leaving.

Lodgers: The decline of farm service and live-in apprenticeship subtracted
large numbers of unrelated individuals from family households; swelling numbers of lodgers offset the loss. If we treat this simply as a question of household
composition (in the Cambridge Group's typology), then not much changed:
the number of non-kin 'others' remained roughly the same. But in economic
terms the two situations were very different, generating opposite resource
flows. Servants and apprentices contributed *labour* to the household in exchange for some form of remuneration; lodgers contributed *income* to the
household, while increasing the homemaker's workload. The reversal of the
labour/money exchange was an integral facet of proletarianization: the separation of the household from the means of production and the need to obtain
outside income to ensure its ongoing maintenance.

How prevalent were lodgers in the nineteenth century? Studies of English
towns indicate that 15 to 25 per cent of households contained lodgers at any
point in time; in German cities, it was roughly 10 to 20 per cent. While most
estimates have thus far been developed for a single census date, it appears that
the incidence of lodgers living in private households peaked at some time in
the latter half of the century, declining thereafter as municipalities and private

associations moved to provide more specialized facilities for casual lodgers.[183] Estimates of 10 to 20 per cent may lead us to underestimate the prevalence of the phenomenon, unless two factors are borne in mind. The incidence was usually higher in working-class districts than in middle-class areas, while the ranges cited above are based on entire cities.[184] Second, a much greater proportion of households would have taken in lodgers over the course of the family cycle than did so at a given point in time. We can reasonably conclude that it was a normal, though by no means universal, experience for working-class families to live in close quarters with a series of unrelated residents for varying lengths of time.

The practice of renting space to boarders in already overcrowded dwellings varied with women's employment status and the phase of the family cycle.[185] Particularly for women stuck at home caring for young children, taking in lodgers was a major means of earning money; their entry often coincided with women's withdrawal from the paid labour force.[186] When several children were working, the need for a boarder's income eased and fewer were taken in. Later on when offspring left, making space available, elderly couples and widows frequently resumed the practice; subletting could be a crucial source of income for older people when other sources dwindled.[187] Taking in lodgers was thus a flexible adjustment in the family economy, altering household composition to counteract unfavourable shifts in the family's dependency ratio.

Who were these boarders, and why did they seek out this form of accommodation? In the main, they appear to have been single men in their late teens and twenties who were new to the area. Most, presumably, would have come from rural areas and smaller towns and lacked close kin in the city. They needed some form of inexpensive accommodation within walking distance of their workplaces. Frequent job changes required residential transience. Live-in lodging was well suited to these ends. The prevalence of lodging does not mean that single people were completely indifferent to domestic privacy and felt no desire to have 'a room of one's own'. They were certainly in no position to cultivate the desire for privacy in bedrooms and washrooms that has become the norm in the twentieth century, but those who could afford to live in private quarters generally did so. The great attraction of lodging was its price: living in was much cheaper than a small flat, a room with a private entrance, or a hotel room.

Other kin: The Cambridge Group's studies have demonstrated that the households of early modern villagers were overwhelmingly simple (that is, nuclear) in composition. In the course of industrialization, however, households became more complex. Where only eleven relatives had been resident in one hundred English households between 1650 and 1749, eighteen were in 1821 and thirty-two by 1851.[188] If we focus on the proletarian component, the change is even more striking: the proportion of 'labourer' and 'pauper' households with non-nuclear kin rises from 8 per cent in the early modern era to 17 per cent in 1851.[189] Who were these kin? Most were either the parents or grandchildren of the household and his wife, extending the co-resident group vertically across three generations. Horizontal extension to siblings, while not rare, occurred in about a fifth of all cases.[190] Despite its degree of co-resident extension, the family cycle of nineteenth-century proletarians was overwhelmingly nuclear, with households typically being established by the younger generation around the time of marriage, and funded through income acquired independently of parental property and wealth. Vertical extension most often occurred when widows came to live in their children's households. In the early modern era, by contrast, the greater part of vertical extension had been attributable to young adults marrying into their parents' households.[191]

The predominantly vertical axis of co-resident extension highlights the acute problems of maintaining a viable balance between wage-earners and consumers in the household over the course of the family cycle prior to the development of the modern welfare state. The private wage form makes no provision for meeting unpredictable household emergencies precipitated by unemployment, sickness, disabling injury, desertion or death. Such crises were extremely common in the nineteenth century. Consider the most severe emergency, the death of a parent: half of all children who lived to the age of five would lose a parent by the time they were twenty-one; one in four would be orphaned by that age.[192] For propertyless families renting residential space, the sudden loss of the primary breadwinner's earnings or the death of the homemaker broke up the household, requiring the immediate placement of orphans and motherless children, and the taking-in of destitute widows. When these types of misfortune befell peasant families and others with a viable means of production beneath their feet, the co-resident group was usually reconstituted on site, by means of a *centripetal* process of replacement. But for employment-dependent proletarians, whose labour mobility was high and residential location limited by place of employment, these types of crises more often compelled the *centrifugal* movement of dependants, the very young and the elderly, to stay elsewhere, typically in the households of close kin. But why parents or children; why not siblings more often? Vertical extension is based upon the parent–child bond, the strongest link in the chain of lifelong kin obligation. To take in a mother when one's father passed away, or a grandchild when one's daughter died in childbirth, was the most 'natural' affirmation of blood ties. In times of life-crises, most people turned to their parents or children, whenever they were available. Mother–daughter bonds were especially important. Young women with illegitimate children remained at home, while older women whose husbands had died or deserted them often returned to live with their daughters. Both these situations would raise the level of complex households as reported in censuses. The taking-in of widows appears to have been very common. In Preston in 1851, over 80 per cent of women aged sixty-five and over lived with their children.[193] Nor were widows simply dependants, unproductive consumers:

> A woman's domestic skills made her less of a burden to her offspring ... charring, taking in sewing, knitting, child-minding, hawking, ... acting as 'takers' or 'runners' to the pawnshop ... being a linchpin of the street network and taking a hand in everything that happened, from births to funerals.[194]

It is no surprise to find that bilateral kin networks listed slightly in a matrilocal direction. In Preston, Anderson found that 57 per cent of married children who lived with parents resided with the wife's; 66 per cent of widows living with their married children were resident in their daughters' households; and 65 per cent of women who lived with a married sibling resided with their sisters.[195]

What accounts for the widespread increase in extended co-residence in the first phase of industrialization? In a ground-breaking use of computer-assisted micro-simulation modelling, Steven Ruggles has demonstrated that earlier marriage and the abatement of adult mortality in the nineteenth century increased the availability of relevant kin, making it possible for families who were so inclined to take in unattached kin.[196] He argues that their propensity to do so reflects a continuity in the stem family ideal persisting from the early modern era. The increase in co-resident complexity is thus explained by the demographically improved chances of realizing the traditional ideal. For the most part, this is a compelling argument; there is no doubt that residential arrangements are constrained by the availability of relevant kin, and that demographic rates are principal determinants of availability. I take exception to equating *stem* co-residence (where a child marries into the parental household) with the vertical extension of a *nuclear* household (where a parent comes to live with a married child). From a cyclical standpoint, these are very different structures. Regrettably, Ruggles has accepted the co-residence paradigm of the Cambridge Group, while faulting their methodology and casting doubt on their principal findings.

The difficulty for Ruggles's account – or indeed for any explanation of residence pattern which posits the underlying operation of a familial ideal – is to distinguish between preference and obligation. An elderly woman is taken into her married daughter's home: is this because the young couple are striving to fulfil an extended family ideal, or because they find the alternatives unacceptable and are not prepared to see her homeless and destitute? This is not simply a question concerning motives, however interesting that question is in its own terms. When the primary form of evidence we have before us is data on household composition (as is so often the case), the way we interpret change over time has major implications for causal reasoning in family history, in this case for our understanding of the increasing complexity of households in the nineteenth century. A 'preference account' sees demographic and socio-economic constraints acting to *subtract* people from the optimal household, thus comprehending an increase in complexity over time as the result of the relaxation of these constraints, permitting people to live closer to their ideals. An 'obligation account' sees increasing complexity resulting from the *addition* of unattached extras who were not part of the ideal family but were increasingly numerous and forced upon the nuclear group by the absence of viable alternatives. While Ruggles persuasively argues that demographic availability is a primary factor underlying the change, he simply assumes that it works through preference, thus fulfilling an ideal, and ignoring the possibility that augmentation may have come about through a strong sense of kin obligation. My own view is that the latter was probably operating in the bulk of cases, particularly in poor households, placing considerable strain on family relations.

Whatever the co-residence preference was, there is evidence that immigrants to the cities settled in the same districts as their kin.[197] Wherever employment was relatively stable and proletarians were able to settle down in one locale for extended periods, kin networks soon grew thick on the ground and played a vital role in family life. Towards the end of the nineteenth century, residential mobility diminished and city neighbourhoods became more settled. (We will examine this phenomenon in Chapter 4.) Dating and courtship were more likely to proceed on a local basis. When offspring moved out of their parents' home, many made an effort to rent a dwelling in the neighbourhood and were often successful in doing so.[198] The development of ethnic concentrations in specific urban neighbourhoods was based in large measure on migrating to the same locale as one's family and friends and the consequent build-up of extended kin networks in residential proximity. Neighbouring kin were especially important to women caring for young children at home; grandmothers and sisters could often be called upon to mind children while mothers went out to shop or to work. In a study of German working women, 60 per cent of children whose mothers were factory workers were cared for by relatives, usually their grandparents.[199] In the absence of kin support, the mobility of homemakers was severely impaired. The supposition that children grew up in nuclear households, where parents were their only meaningful adult role models, is clearly inadequate. In most working-class neighbourhoods, other adult kin were likely to be present, either living in the child's household for varying periods of time or else residing nearby and visiting frequently.[200]

Having discussed particular reasons for the co-resident augmentation of the nuclear family group by unrelated lodgers and other kin, I want now to situate this family form within the broad development of the capitalist mode of production at this stage. The overarching context is the massive centralization of the means of production. For our purposes, two dimensions of this process were crucial: (a) the separation of labour from capital, competitively displacing independent domestic enterprises, furthering the separation of households from workplaces; and (b) the spatial centralization of commodity production in new industrial towns and pre-existing cities, and the centralization of job formation there. The upshot of these factors was the massive migration of propertyless and underemployed labourers into urban areas and the rapid growth of proletarian populations there.

We have already discussed the chain reaction which then ensued: population influx overwhelmed the existing housing stock; new housing starts failed to keep pace with population growth and acute housing shortages arose; dwellings became more crowded as every nook and cranny was made into residential space; households 'doubled up', the elderly moved in with their children, and families took in boarders to help defray rising rents. If these trends were sufficiently widespread, then the underlying reason for the augmentation of nuclear family households with lodgers and the doubling up of two families in single quarters was probably the space/rent squeeze. Overcrowding became so acute that it is impossible to tell what the working-class co-resident ideal was. All one can infer from the widespread practices of subletting and taking in lodgers is that proletarian families found these tolerable arrangements under the circumstances, practical ways to defray the rent.

The taking in of unattached kin, by contrast, was not likely to be advantageous to the family group in its struggle to make ends meet, although elderly mothers certainly made themselves more useful around the house than fathers did.[201] Here a strong sense of obligation to one's next of kin, particularly to one's parents or children, was evident in a context where many more of these people were hovering around as unattached and needy individuals than had been the case in earlier periods. Many authors have argued that the augmentation of the household was a 'mechanism of self-help', cushioning families against economic shocks and helping them survive crisis situations.[202] As the foregoing discussion indicates, I find this argument valid, but let us be clear about the limits of 'pragmatic adaptation' as a response to overcrowding in explaining nuclear augmentation. Such pressures furnish a necessary condition; they by no means constitute a sufficient one. While overcrowding severely restricted families, it did not dictate how they lived in the space they had.[203] There is more than one way to live in cramped quarters. We need to know much more than we currently do about the interior partitioning of dwelling-space before we can assess familial sensibilities concerning the relationship between family members and other residents. Certainly the periodic presence of other kin is indicative of much more than pragmatic necessity; it registers the strength and defensive resilience of kin bonds in coping with the vulnerability of propertyless dependants, young and old alike. We may never know if most families genuinely welcomed the arrival of relatives on the doorstep, or took them in simply out of a sense of duty. They probably considered it a mixed blessing. We can infer, however, that most did not slam the door in their faces, and Janssens's study indicates that kin normally stayed longer than a few months.[204]

3

Strains in the Extensive Reproduction of Labour-Power

The debate over the living standards of English workers during the Industrial Revolution has enjoyed a remarkable longevity, subject neither to decisive scholarly verdict nor to the laws of discursive entropy. Yet in the contest's seventh decade, the optimists – those who have argued that proletarian living standards improved in this period – have clearly gained the upper hand. In recent years, several weighty statistical contributions have ostensibly demonstrated that real wages rose very substantially from 1820 on.[1] The pessimists' case has been repeatedly pummelled in scholarly journals without consequential rejoinder. After a long and stimulating run, the show appears ready to close its doors and fade into history. But the optimists are undaunted. With a paucity of opponents in sight, they have taken to playing the devil's advocate with their own findings, setting up pessimistic objections and then knocking them down.[2] This is great sport; predictably, the good guys invariably win. It may be folly to spit into the teeth of the prevailing wind, but I cannot resist trying.[3]

There are four major problems with the way the latest version of the new and improved English wage series has been constructed by Lindert and Williamson, and particularly with the way in which they infer an enhanced living standard from their reconstructed series. First, the optimists do not make allowances for the process of proletarianization. They treat eighteenth- and nineteenth-century wage-earners as if they all relied to the same degree – that is, entirely – upon money wages to obtain the means of subsistence. But over time, proletarian families experienced a diminishing capacity to supplement wage income with productive domestic work – gardening, baking, and production for barter and sale in the local neighbourhood. The extent of this supplementation in the late eighteenth century, especially for rural workers, should not be underestimated. Its gradual loss in the nineteenth century, as an increasing proportion of the proletariat took up residence in dense urban milieus, meant that money wages had to cover more. As productive alternatives to wage-earning grew sparser in the local economy, bouts of unemployment became tougher to withstand. A higher wage was necessary to obtain the equivalent subsistence provision.

Second, the optimists remain fixated on adult male wages, and take no account of the changing capacity of women and children to supplement the primary breadwinner's wage. It might be argued that there was an increase in the degree of income supplementation from secondary earners in the first half of the nineteenth century, and therefore that taking serious account of this factor would strengthen their case. I remain sceptical: the separation of proletarian households from most forms of productive enterprise weakened the earning power of married women. An increase in the contribution of children may have offset this loss, but this is an open question. In any event, the argument for taking serious account of other family earners – to engender realism in modelling the family economy – stands on its merits, regardless of the impact of doing so on the results achieved.

Third, the optimists have ignored evidence that wage-earners worked more in 1850 than their predecessors did a century earlier. As mentioned, the number of working days per year was extended considerably between 1750 and 1850, and seasonal unemployment diminished. There are also indications, difficult to estimate or quantify, that industrial workers, under tighter supervision, were forced to work harder and more continuously than agricultural labourers or cottage producers. The combined effect of this extension and intensification of labour would have been to reduce the time away from work and leave workers more exhausted. How much leisure was an extra hour's pay worth to those with precious little time for rest and recuperation? A greater energy drain at work would require a higher caloric intake to maintain the previous level of vitality; higher real wages would be necessary simply to avoid regression.

Fourth, the optimists' calculation of the cost of living fails to take adequate account of the deteriorating relationship between urban housing and rent. Labourers appear to have spent a greater proportion of their income on rent in 1850 than they had a century earlier. In the wake of mass influx to the cities, acute housing shortages resulted in escalating rents, overcrowding and doubling up. To put a roof over their heads, even a small and leaky one, many proletarian families were forced to pay more for less; money wages needed to rise very substantially merely to maintain an existing housing standard. In short, the rising 'real wages' detected by Lindert and Williamson after 1820 were probably necessary to prevent the living standards of labouring families from serious deterioration.

The optimists' principal mistake is their fixation on real wage trends in abstraction from other aspects of workers' living standards. The debate needs to be recast to bring the concept of 'living standards' into adequate relation

with the environment in which workers lived and toiled. Neo-classical economists gesture in this direction by introducing what they term (in the obtuse
discourse that is their stock-in-trade) 'urban disamenities'. Noting that urban
wages were higher than rural rates, they treat the difference as the employers'
'bribe' which persuaded dispossessed country labourers, coming to work in
cities, to give up five years of their lives and risk the loss of future progeny to
make another shilling a week. By this logic, the fact that they did migrate to
the cities in their millions proves, *ex post facto*, that urban/rural wage differentials were more than sufficient to compensate labourers and their families for
the sacrifices made in moving from 'sweet Auburn' to noxious Sheffield. Since
(we are assured) the migrants came of their own free will, it is tantamount to
second-guessing *them* to question the assumptions underlying this form of neo-
classical reasoning.[4]

I want to recast the debate and broaden its scope to make a general argument concerning the reproduction of the labour force in Northwestern Europe in the first stage of industrial capitalism. Instead of asking: 'What
happened to real wages in the Industrial Revolution?' we ought to ask: 'What
happened to the *relationship between* working and living conditions?' – or, in
marxist terms, between the ways in which capital *consumed* labour-power and
the residential circumstances of its proletarian *reproduction*. Further, we need to
be more specific concerning different strata of the burgeoning proletariat, since
they did not all suffer the same fate. So let us ask: 'For which sectors of the
working class did this relationship improve or worsen?' My argument, in
simple terms, is that the bottom half of the urban working class (semi-skilled
and unskilled manual labourers, commonly known as the labouring poor)
were overworked and underprovisioned to such an extent that they were unable to maintain the vitality of their labour-power over the course of several
generations. Few optimists would disagree that the common labourers were
being treated unfairly in a moral sense. Their own studies have shown that the
distribution of income and wealth was becoming more unequal in this period,
both between classes and within the working class.[5] But I am making a more
ambitious claim: that in an objective sense, more energy was being sucked out
of common labourers by capital than they could durably restore in their
leisure-time, given the level of their wages and the quality of their residential
environment.[6]

My argument is that the vitality, health and stamina of the urban proletariat
was gradually depleted in the first stage of industrialization. Labourers were
washed up at an early age and their children were sickly and frail. Growing up
in conditions of residential squalor, people were put to work by the age of
eight or ten and used up by forty, incapable of working energetically at demanding physical labour for twelve hours a day, five and a half days a week,
year after year. No matter; they could be replaced by young rural recruits. The

lifetime earnings curve of proletarian men, peaking in their thirties and dwindling thereafter, bears mute testament to their premature exhaustion.[7]

The families of the labouring poor were caught in a vicious cycle. By
sucking up child labour while holding down adult wages, capital promoted
high fertility. In order to furnish more offspring as future contributors to the
family economy, parents had to curtail their investment in each child. This
procreative regime was particularly hard on women, who had to combine
productive and reproductive labour. Poor women picked up at home whatever remunerative work they could scrounge. Housework also took its toll.
Too often, they were forced to rise from childbed prematurely to shop, cook
and do the laundry, debilitating themselves and losing infants in the process.[8]
Observers feared that women's double burden 'in the long run ... would
undermine the reproductive capacity of the working class and produce a
generation of weak, feeble, and disabled men and women.'[9] Recent research
on historical trends in birth weights and stillbirth rates indicates that this concern was well founded: in the first phase of intensive urban industrialization,
some deterioration is evident.[10] Where mothers with young children had to
work outside the home and lacked the time to breastfeed, infant and child
mortality was extraordinarily high. In the French textile town of Mulhouse,
450 infants in 1,000 were lost by their fifth year.[11] This is roughly on a par
with the worst rates in early modern France. With a high proportion of infants
dying, much maternal care was wasted; mothers were numbed and demor-
alized by the losses. In most historical periods, females in all age groups have
enjoyed longer life expectancy than males, but during early industrialization
women often had higher mortality rates through their childbearing years. This
was the case in France and Germany, though not in Britain.[12] Maternal mortality in the strict sense does not account for the excess, but the travails of
combining continuous childbearing and infant nurture with various forms of
industrial work almost certainly do. At the other end of the life-course, acute
strain was evident as well. Very few working-class families could afford to
support the elderly on their own; they too had to find something to do to earn
their keep.

A multiple-earner strategy enabled the families of the labouring poor to
survive, but its impact on the working class as a whole was disastrous. It
flooded the market with easily replaceable labour and kept wages low, perpetuating the very conditions that had engendered the response in the first place.
In these circumstances, wages funded merely the *daily replacement costs* of labour-power, not the full *generational reproduction costs*; the difference was reaped
by capitalists as profit. Vast sectors of industrial capital were dependent upon
the replacement of worn-out urban labourers with 'fresh blood' from the
countryside. This was a form of 'primitive accumulation' – an immense value
appropriation from the periphery to the centre. Since state social expenditures

on health, welfare and education were minimal in this period, the indigenous reproduction of the urban working class, beneath its upper artisanal strata, was jeopardized in the long run.

Contemporaries were certainly aware of the problem. Charles Booth observed that 'the second generation of Londoners is of lower physique and has less power of persistent work than the first.' In his view, it was 'the result of conditions of life in great towns ... that muscular strength and energy got gradually used up.'[13] 'How is it', John Simons wondered in his report of 1862, 'that in much of our best national industry, the workman, by reason of his work, loses a considerable part of his life?'[14] Both Chadwick in Britain and Villermé in France placed the primary responsibility for the urban proletariat's excess mortality on poverty and domestic squalor, not on debilitating working conditions.[15] Yet the main point should not be to disaggregate the end-result, attributing a certain portion of the damage to various factors, but to recognize that their *combination* was lethal.

The health of industrial workers was considered to be 'vastly inferior' to that of peasants. Factory operatives were repeatedly described in inspectors' reports as 'a degenerate race – human beings stunted, enfeebled, and depraved – men and women that were not to be aged – children that were never to be healthy adults.'[16] These are subjective impressions; what of objective measures? Instead of making a host of assumptions in constructing real wage series, are there more direct ways to compare living standards between groups and over time? Mortality rates are considered to be valid indices of general health, provided the subpopulations being compared have similar age structures.[17] Since there are reasonably reliable mortality statistics for the major states of Northwestern Europe in the nineteenth century, they furnish an important empirical check on the argument being advanced here. In the first half of the century, the crude death rates of most cities improved only marginally or not at all, and some regressed amidst rapid population influx during the peak phase of a city's initial industrialization. In Glasgow, for example, the crude death rate in 1821–4 was 24.8; by 1845–9, it had soared to 39.8.[18] For urban Britain as a whole, mortality worsened slightly in these decades. Urban residents had a shorter life expectancy than country-dwellers. The inhabitants of Manchester and Liverpool in 1861 could expect to live less than thirty years, while in Devon life expectancy was over fifty.[19] The crude death rate in Stockholm at mid century was twice that of rural Sweden.[20] While these may be extreme contrasts, the consistency of the urban/rural differential is striking, with death rates in the cities averaging roughly 20 to 25 per cent above those of agricultural districts in the first half of the century. The disparity appears to have widened in the initial phase of rapid industrialization, as rural longevity improved considerably while urban levels stagnated. 'Until 1870, the mortality decline in Northwestern Europe was essentially a rural phenomenon.'[21]

Since most newcomers to the cities were young adults about to marry and begin childbearing, migration boosted urban birth rates. Even with this stimulus, the net balance between births and deaths was only weakly positive in the first half of the nineteenth century. If migration-related effects are subtracted, most cities would have registered an excess of deaths over births. In absolute terms many did, growing entirely by in-migration. The endogenous growth rates of French cities were particularly feeble, owing to France's declining birth rate. Ninety-four per cent of Marseille's growth from 1821 to 1872 was by immigration.[22] In aggregate terms, the urban balance in France finally turned positive at mid century, but many industrial centres were still registering negative reproduction rates in the 1890s.[23] In other countries, the balance turned positive at some time before 1850. But several major cities lagged: Amsterdam began to grow endogenously at mid century, and Stockholm a decade later.[24] Overall, then, the considerable population expansion experienced by cities across Northwestern Europe in the first phase of industrialization was almost entirely due to a massive and accelerating net inflow. As one observer noted: 'Large industrial cities would lose their working populations in a short time unless they continuously received healthy recruits ... from the surrounding countryside.'[25]

The strongest determinant of a city's mortality rate was not its size, mean income per capita, nor the nature of its economy, but population density.[26] The more tightly people were packed residentially, the more susceptible they were to lethal air- and waterborne diseases. The density factor applies within cities as well; the most crowded slums were generally the hardest hit.[27] The crude death rate in the worst districts of Liverpool in 1841 (Vauxhaul and St Paul's) exceeded the city's best neighbourhoods (Rodney Street and Abercromby) by 54 per cent.[28] It is often said that lethal pandemics 'do not discriminate' between rich and poor, but this is a complacent myth; in the real world, where social inequality matters, the poor and overcrowded are more exposed. In a four-month period at the height of the cholera epidemic of 1832, the disease claimed one person in three in the poorest *arrondissements* of Paris, but only one in nineteen in the richest. In the 1849 crisis, 17 per cent of Londoners died in the poorest boroughs, but only 2 per cent in the wealthiest.[29] It was infant and child mortality in the cities, even more so than in the countryside, that kept death rates elevated. Infants born in cities died at over twice the rate of their rural counterparts. In Sheffield, Manchester and Leeds around 1840, half of all newborn infants died before reaching their fifth birthday.[30] While the evidence for early modern urban mortality is sketchier, it is unlikely that infant carnage was as severe. In four London parishes in the midst of a miserable seventeenth century, 61 per cent of infants survived to age five. In a weighted mean of French parishes (where death rates were high by early modern standards), 63 per cent lived to age five between 1740 and 1790.[31]

When class differentials in life expectancy are combined with the urban/rural disparities just discussed, the full magnitude of the industrial proletariat's dissipation is evident. In Manchester in 1837, 'mechanics, labourers and their families' had a life expectancy of seventeen years, while 'professional persons and gentry and their families' lived an average of thirty-eight years. Was Manchester far worse than other English industrial centres? It does not appear to have been. In Leeds, the life expectancy of labourers was nineteen years; in Liverpool, fifteen; and in Bethnal Green, sixteen. In Sheffield two decades later, the situation had improved for every class, but disparities between classes had narrowed only slightly: professional and managerial men lived forty-seven years on average, while male manual workers lived twenty-eight.[32] The general trend on the continent was for class differentials in mortality to increase in the first phase of industrialization. Among Parisians, there was a greater difference in life chances between rich and poor in 1850 than in 1816. By mid century, the poorest *arrondissement* had a death rate almost twice the level of the richest. Across Germany (where rapid industrialization came later) mortality disparities peaked in the decades from 1860 to 1880, diminishing thereafter.[33]

Throughout the nineteenth century, a great deal of the overall class divergence was due to the drastic inequality in the life-chances of infants in their first year. Infant loss in proletarian families was considerably higher than in upper-class families. In Preston at mid century, 82 per cent of infants born to upper-class parents lived to see their fifth birthdays; among working-class families, only 37 per cent did.[34] In the French textile town of Mulhouse between 1823 and 1834, 69 per cent of the offspring of the town's manufacturers, managers and merchants reached their second birthdays; 44 per cent of those born to spinners survived to age two.[35] While the life-chances of one-year-olds did improve considerably in the nineteenth century, infant mortality did not decrease much, if at all, before 1890.[36] The reason for this age-specific stagnation is bound up with the explosive growth of the urban proletariat. City workers may have earned more pay than rural labourers, but to do so they had no practical alternative but to take up residence within easy walking distance of their places of employment. In circumstances of acute deprivation and overcrowding, the labouring poor paid dearly for the structural primacy of employment over residential location under capitalism.

Throughout their abbreviated lives, industrial proletarians suffered from much poorer health than their class superiors. Contemporary observers insisted that working-class food intake was grossly inadequate in relation to the physical exertion of the manual labourer's workday. Is there any way to check such perceptions? The average height of social groups within a population is considered to be a sensitive measure of 'net nutritional status', the balance between caloric intake and labour exertion, and hence furnishes a much more direct measure of welfare than real-wage indices.[37] Height disparities between classes correspond to the mortality differences just discussed. In the early nineteenth century, upper-class fourteen-year-olds in Britain were twenty centimetres (eight inches) taller than their counterparts from London slums. This staggering discrepancy was gradually reduced over the course of the century.[38] In an 1880 sample of British thirteen-year-olds, upper-class boys were on average 4.2 inches taller than lower-class lads, while upper-class girls towered 5.5 inches over their lower-class counterparts.[39] In the case of US native-born white males, Union army muster rolls indicate a decline in the height of recruits from 1825 to 1840 during the initial phase of American industrialization. Fogel and his colleagues speculate that:

> A decline in height could have resulted because there was an increase in the per capita energy output of these young workers without a corresponding increase in the per capita consumption of calories and nutrients. British investigators of child labour in factories support this hypothesis. Children of a given socioeconomic class who worked in factories were substantially shorter at each age than children of the same class who were not so employed.[40]

Optimists would point out that the deplorable enervation of capitalism's urban underbelly did not originate with the Industrial Revolution. With the possible exception of infant death, the mortality rates of medieval and early modern cities were probably worse; their labour forces were not reproduced endogenously either. This is perfectly true, but it draws a comparison without regard for the growth dynamics of the modes of production in question. In contrast to feudalism's rurally centred and spatially extensive growth, the development of industrial capitalism was primarily urban and centripetal. Under the *ancien régime*, the continuous trickle of the dispossessed to the cities constituted a demographic venting of the system's redundant excrescence; during the nineteenth century, rural–urban migration became the wellspring of capitalism's growth. The immense rural exodus of this century masked an underlying contradiction in the bowels of the new mode of production. Strewn around the sites of its most dynamic growth, capitalism was busy piling up heaps of wasted humanity in teeming slums.

For society as a whole, this mode of consuming labour-power 'extensively' – attracting fresh blood from the periphery and amassing run-down veterans and their frail progeny at the centre – was wasteful and inefficient. Yet it did not initially impair the pace of private capital accumulation. To the contrary: a regime of cheap wages and high labour turnover was undeniably profitable at an early and crude stage of industrialization. As the economy developed, however, it became increasingly problematic from the standpoint of capitalism's enduring metropolitan progress. These strains did not precipitate a capitalist crisis of the sudden volcanic sort that rivets the marxist imagination. Demographic forces tend to operate glacially in their impact on modes of production. In Braudel's terms, they are best understood as structures of 'la longue durée' whose conjunctural effects are oblique and mediated. When misaligned, the modes of labour's production and consumption grind slowly against one another like massive subterranean templates. Surface tremors none the less take their toll; by mid century, the cumulative human debris of extensive reproduction had become evident in the cities. Socially observant members of the propertied classes grew alarmed, especially in the wake of the revolutionary tidal wave of 1848. Animated by a mixture of genuine compassion, condescending paternalism and class fear before the prospect of proletarian revolt, their spokesmen sowed the seeds of public awareness and a sense of urgency that eventually galvanized the reform movements of the late Victorian era.

From the standpoint of capital's long-term development, the problem of proletarian dissipation had two facets. On the *demand* side, low wages limited the purchasing power of the masses, preventing their full participation as consumers in advanced markets for housing, clothing, domestic furnishings and leisure goods. This hampered their immersion in bourgeois culture and slowed the development of mass production in the consumer goods industries. On the *supply* side, employers impeded the long-term development of the labour force by 'underinvesting' in their employees. The problem was not one of numbers. No matter how rapidly capital accumulated and net job formation spurted ahead, there were plenty of warm bodies around, desperately poor and prepared to go anywhere, to try their hand at almost anything, in return for a wage. Paradoxically, this labour-supply windfall was part of the long-term problem, since it induced capital to enforce a cheap labour regime, replacing worn-out 'hands' with reckless abandon. In qualitative terms, however, the vitality, stamina and skills of the indigenous urban labour force were not keeping pace with the development of industry. Employers were actively dismantling a centuries-old mode of intergenerational skill transmission among the labouring classes (based on guild and craft organizations), while state authorities had yet to establish a universal alternative.

For the sake of capitalism's enduring development, it was necessary, sooner or later, to shift gears:

- curtailing the rapacious consumption of labour-power by placing legal restrictions on child labour and the length of the working day;

- making a serious public investment in the schooling of working-class children;

- upgrading the urban infrastructure through investments in roads, public transport, sewers and treated water supplies;

- raising the wages of primary breadwinners considerably, enabling proletarian families to ease their dependency ratio and women to cease childbearing well before menopause, devoting more attention to each child.

Such investments would improve the growth rates and the health of the urban proletariat, gradually diminishing the employers' reliance on attracting fresh blood from the countryside. The conversion from an extensive to an intensive mode of reproducing labour-power was an integral facet of 'the second Industrial Revolution'; its key features will be reviewed in the next chapter.

The bourgeoisie did not bequeath these improvements to the working class as a philanthropic gesture. Changes came about in response to vigorous public campaigns, the development of the trade-union movement, and in 1848, ominous signs of popular insurgence spreading like a brush fire across the continent. Often there was considerable employer resistance to implementing far-reaching changes. The Factory Acts limiting child labour were forced on technologically backward employers who remained addicted to the cheapest forms of labour. It took a long time for most managers to recognize the advantages of a shorter working day.[41] Many needed to be pushed into cutting hours. Although the adjustment often proved painful in the short term, it was very much in the capitalist class's long-term interest. Most employers found it inconceivable that higher wages and shorter hours might actually lower per unit labour costs by raising labour intensity and efficiency in quantum leaps: 'The temptations of a cheap labour economy made employers reluctant to recognize their inefficiency. When it was pointed out to them, many flatly refused to believe their eyes.'[42]

Despite management's resistance, there was nevertheless an inherently capitalist logic in the conversion from an extensive to an intensive mode of consuming and reproducing labour-power. The extensive regime foundered first in technologically dynamic firms as the training costs of labour-power rose and high labour turnover became increasingly costly. In these circumstances, managers began to look for ways to cultivate employee loyalty, reduce quit rates, and staunch the leakage of a firm's best workers to competitors. In the case of child labour, advanced employers saw the writing on the wall, phased out their youngest hands, and then backed government legislation forcing their more retrograde brethren to follow suit.[43] When the most advanced sectors of capital had shifted to an intensive regime, they had every interest in supporting legislation that defended their goods from the competition of cheap-labour firms. At this point, what had formerly been bitterly opposed was now actively promoted by capitalist modernizers. The 1847 Ten Hours Act, for example, was widely regarded by employers at the time as a ruinous interference in their affairs. Shortly after, *The Economist* remarked: 'No-one has any doubt now of the wisdom of those measures.'[44]

4

The Second Industrial Revolution: 1873–1914

The railway boom in the middle decades of the nineteenth century brought the first Industrial Revolution to maturity and laid the groundwork for the second. With the perfection of the locomotive engine, the steam-driven mode of power finally came of age and was quickly adapted for use in a wide range of industries beyond mining and textiles, where it had hitherto been confined. Between 1850 and 1869, steam power capacity in Britain almost trebled, in France quintupled, and in Germany increased tenfold.[1] Rail-building consumed iron, and later steel, in vast quantities, becoming a major stimulus to the development of the iron and steel industry. Britain took the lead in the rush to lay track, beginning with the 'railway mania' of 1835–7, followed by a massive spurt of construction a decade later; by mid century her basic trunk lines were down.[2] Railway technologies were quickly carried to the continent, and by 1860 a primary rail network had been built across western and central Europe. The spread of the system was astonishingly rapid: in 1840, 1,481 kilometres of track were in place across continental Europe; twenty years later, 33,405 kilometres had been laid. From 1860 to 1880 the pace quickened as secondary and local lines filled out national networks.[3] During these decades Germany surpassed Britain as the leading industrial nation of Europe, with major advances in steel-making, hydroelectric power, engineering and chemistry.[4]

As soon as tracks were laid, railways became the cheapest and most efficient way for people to travel between cities and goods to be transported over land. Between 1851 and 1871, the freight tonnage moved by rail increased tenfold.[5] Railways provided a tremendous stimulus to economic development on a number of fronts:

- They eased the supply problems of fast-growing cities, which could be furnished year-round with agricultural produce from a much broader hinterland.

- They freed industrialists from the need to locate their plants close to the sites of iron ore and coal.

- They consolidated national markets and international trade in basic commodities and semi-finished goods, evening out supply and demand across vast areas and fostering more uniform price structures.

- By cutting transportation costs to remote markets, railways rewarded cost-effective production methods, extended the competitive reach of the most technologically advanced companies, and drove out of business inefficient firms with strictly local markets.

These processes, in turn, expanded the international division of labour, stimulated the centralization of capital, quickened the pace of technological diffusion, and furthered the industrial specialization of entire regions.

During the third quarter of the nineteenth century, the stage was set for 'the second Industrial Revolution'. The term refers to a swarm of technological breakthroughs and rapid product developments in steel, chemicals, electricity and gas motors, coming to fruition in the period 1873–1914. The fact that prices fell between 1873 and 1896, 'unevenly, sporadically but inexorably through crisis and boom – an average of about one-third on all commodities' testifies to the leap in productivity that had occurred in the midst of the (mis-named) Great Depression.[6] The second Industrial Revolution cut a much broader swath than the first, transforming the infrastructure of one industry after another, remaking the landscapes of cities and towns. The internationalization of trade and the acceleration of technological diffusion made this stage more synchronous than the first, harmonizing the development of mass consumer markets, national business cycles, and the construction of state infrastructures. Everywhere, local particularisms were undercut. Unevenness was by no means effaced, of course, but divergence increasingly took the form of regional specialization; interdependencies were much more tightly structured by overarching patterns of capital accumulation.

The main changes in capitalist organization during the second Industrial Revolution have been documented by economic historians and do not require extensive reiteration here. But they ought to be briefly discussed, since they shaped the consumption of labour-power in the workplace and the demand for labour in the marketplace. The net effect of these changes was to foster a basic shift by employers from an extensive to an intensive mode of consuming labour-power, based on a reduced work-week, and a quicker, steadier pace of work under closer supervision. Confronting this new production regime, working-class couples had to determine how best to improve their families' living standards and provide for their children's futures. Responding in kind, they forged an intensive family economy: where husbands were designated as primary breadwinners while their wives concentrated on being full-time homemakers; where couples limited fertility, and sent their children to school for longer periods. Before discussing these far-reaching transformations in working-class family norms, we ought to clarify a series of alterations in the relations of capitalist production that occurred during the second Industrial Revolution: changes in technology and enterprise organization, labour supervision, the wage form, and the recruitment and training of workers. These developments completed the centuries-long disengagement of capitalist production relations from proletarian subsistence relations, furthering the specialization of activities in both spheres.

In the first stage of industrial capitalism, machine power had made very limited inroads, principally in textiles and engineering. In the second, mechanization made sweeping advances across a very broad front: in the capital goods sector, with the production of machinery by means of machine tools; and in consumer goods industries, with breakthroughs in food-processing, clothing, glass, ceramics and pharmaceuticals. The new technologies required massive capital investments to set up new plants, renovate old ones and keep abreast of the latest developments. This in turn necessitated a change in the form of the corporation from the privately funded business to the joint-stock company, with the extensive involvement of finance capital. Modern corporations began to undertake their own scientific research in this period, so that the practical application of advances in scientific knowledge to industrial technologies was speeded up, and research agendas were increasingly shaped by the need to solve technical problems and enhance productive efficiency.[7] Major firms also began to apply forms of cost accounting to every phase of the operation: keeping track of inventory, identifying wastage and bottlenecks by means of calibrated machine gauges and recording devices, monitoring the productivity of labour on the shop floor in primitive precursors of 'scientific management', and investigating sales opportunities with crude prototypes of modern market research.[8] A corporate bureaucracy of professional managers grew up, tightening the control of the front office over the shop floor; replacing the ledger book and the untrained clerk with the financial statement and the certified accountant. Towards the end of the period, the overseers' informal hiring process was replaced by personnel departments, application forms and employee records.

Domestic industries that had flourished in the first stage were largely replaced by factory labour in the second. The homeworker had virtually disappeared from the North of England by the 1850s, while outwork held its own in the Midlands and continued to expand in the Southeast in the third quarter of the century. In the 1870s and 1880s, however, 'straw plait and pillow lace were superseded, and hosiery, clothing and footwear followed the basic textile industries into the factory.'[9] By the census of 1901, only 371,000 persons in the whole of England and Wales were counted as working at home (employees and self-employed combined). The decline in Germany was essentially similar, though it lagged slightly due to later industrialization. Outwork peaked in the 1880s, gradually fading thereafter. Its demise in the textile industry was more abrupt: homeworkers comprised 31 per cent of the labour force in 1882, but only 13 per cent by 1907.[10]

As capital was increasingly concentrated in central production sites, the size of the average workplace grew. To be sure, small workshops remained commonplace in traditional industries such as baking, butchering and tailoring; and the sewing machine gave homework a new lease on life. But the main trend was unmistakable. In the last two decades of the nineteenth century, huge mines, foundries and factory complexes grouping several hundred workers at a site became the predominant form of industrial organization across Northwestern Europe.[11] By 1895, an estimated 37 per cent of German workers and 60 per cent of Belgian workers were working for companies with over 50 employees.[12] While the workshop continued to prevail in France, the trend to giantism was especially marked in Germany. In Upper Silesia, 116 coal mines were active in 1856 with 102 miners per site; by 1902, only 63 mines were open, but they employed 1,070 miners on average. Sixty-three ironworks in the same region employed 30 workers apiece in 1852; by 1902, 11 works averaged 310 employees.[13]

The rapid spread of the factory system in the second stage wrought far-reaching changes to the physiognomy of the working class. It was a decisive step in the movement of millions of working people from a partial to a full proletarian existence, completing the separation of workplace from home and rendering family reliance on wage income earned outside the household almost total. With the demise of subcontracting and the decline of outwork, factories revealed and clarified the basic conflict between labour and capital in the sphere of production.[14] They threw unskilled labourers and workers of different trades together at one site, undermining craft sectarianism and permitting the rapid development of inclusive industrial unions. It was no longer tenable to lump labour and capital together as 'the productive classes of industry', over and against the parasites of landed wealth. Now the contest between the working class and the bourgeoisie *within* industry was widely seen as the primary axis of class conflict in society.

The factories of the second stage not only assembled larger workforces, they also inaugurated new forms of production. With advances in precision measurement and machine tooling to fine tolerances, it became possible to fabricate interchangeable machine parts that could be built in one place and assembled elsewhere. Traditional craft methods of nodal construction, with the hand-fitting of individually tailored parts, were gradually replaced by linear flow processes in the serial production of standardized goods, with workers deployed at several connected sites.[15] While the advent of flow processing has been termed 'Fordism', after the first assembly line at the Ford Motor Company, the changeover from nodal to linear production began earlier in metal-work and engineering, with assembly lines appearing in Western Europe after the turn of the century. Flow processes were typically supervised by 'speed and feed men … having nothing else to do but to walk around the shop and see that speeds and feeds … are kept to their proper values'.[16] Beyond the introduction of machinery per se, it was the linking of machines and operators in sequence that enforced a constant and uninterrupted work-pace, binding workers to their stations and making it extremely difficult for them to slow down or rest. Increasingly, workers in these decades feared that they were becoming 'the slaves of machinery'.

The second Industrial Revolution sponsored a major shift towards a briefer and more intense working day. While hardly anyone at the time discussed the change as a quid pro quo, this is in fact what it amounted to: capital obtained a greater work effort while relinquishing twelve- and eleven-hour days; labour won a reduction of hours while submitting to speed-up. In Britain, the shortening of the work-week came in an abrupt step-down. Since mid century, the work-week in industry had hovered at sixty to sixty-five hours. For some time, the labour movement had declared the ten-hour day to be a major objective, but very little progress had been made. Then, in the space of three years from 1871 to 1874, the dam burst. In a conjuncture of full employment, with workers' bargaining power at a peak, the employers and business federations agreed to a cut in hours – at first in industries with strong and rapidly growing unions, and thereafter in one sector after another, forging a new norm of a ten-hour day, establishing a 54- to 56-hour work-week for full-time employees.[17]

With shorter hours came a reorganization of the week: the institutionalization of Saturday half-days and the effective eradication of Monday's customary absenteeism. Under this regime, Saturday afternoons and evenings became the high point of the week as far as male workers were concerned. Workers on the continent had been toiling roughly ten more hours per week than their British counterparts. In the aftermath of the British breakthrough, they too won a series of reductions. In Germany in the 1870s, the typical industrial working day was twelve hours; by the turn of the century, this had been cut by one and a half hours. By 1914, continental workers were roughly in line with the British norm, working a ten-hour day and a week of about fifty-four hours. The next great reduction, to an eight-hour day, was achieved without much delay in the immediate aftermath of the First World War.[18] By 1922, the eight-hour day had been established as a general standard across Western Europe.[19]

Faced with sharp reductions in hours, employers went on the offensive, forcing up the pace of work in one industry after another. They cut back on breaks and policed them more tightly, raised work quotas and speeded up machines, compelling workers to intensify their exertions or risk being sacked. In the first stage, industrial time-discipline had concentrated on punctuality; with that battle largely won, management turned its attention during the Great Depression to the rhythm and quality of work – its steadiness, pace and productivity: 'Devices to measure speed and effort replaced the factory whistle as symbols of industrial labour.'[20] Unions complained that intensified exploitation was causing accidents, leading to physical exhaustion, stress and nervous disorder, but managers were usually able to achieve their objectives. Their success seems attributable to three decisive changes in the relations of production: tighter supervision of the labour process, the break with subcontracting, and changes in the wage form. While these alterations are inextricably related, for expository purposes let us consider each in turn.

As workforces grew in size, older methods of labour supervision based on the personal authority of the family head became outmoded. In traditional industries where women were employed, domestic patriarchy continued to furnish a model for corporate paternalism long after subcontracting died out. Factory overseers tended to be 'fatherly' men, considerably older than the employees they supervised, evoking familial authority in disciplining youthful workers.[21] These patterns of age and gender deference were built into capitalist authority relations on the job; they have persisted in many sectors down to the present day. However, a very different style of authority prevailed in the male bastions of heavy industry. Military and bureaucratic models with vertical chains of command were the only available alternatives for large-scale autocracies; managers adapted them to their particular needs.[22] A central objective in the new drive for increased productivity was to gain greater control over the labour process. By breaking up a production process into simple segments and calculating the costs of each, managers were able to develop more accurate estimates of labour productivity; this gave them the capacity and incentive to control workers' performance in detail.

In the face of employer pressure, workers fought for – and to varying degrees retained – some measure of discretionary leeway in the way they organized and executed the tasks at hand.[23] The more specialized workers' skills were, and the higher their training and replacement costs, the more autonomy they were able to preserve. Skilled workers still knew a great deal about the art of production of which 'scientific' managers remained ignorant. Even when workers were fairly compliant, there were major obstacles to running plants from the top down. Since the right of management to manage was not formally in dispute, the primary axis of the struggle over workers' autonomy was informal: 'The work group endured, not as an explicit mechanism of control, as it had been under [subcontracting], but "as a submerged, impenetrable obstacle to management's sovereignty".'[24] Much of the conflict never became the subject of collective bargaining; this was particularly the case in France, though British unions were more successful in establishing beachheads in contract negotiations, giving a tremendous impetus to the development of the shop stewards' movement.[25] The counter-strategy of managers was to break down complex jobs into their constituent parts, thereby lowering skill requirements, cutting training costs, and gaining greater mastery over the labour process.[26] While mechanization undoubtedly entailed plenty of deskilling, it also generated a demand for new skills and different types of training. The experience gained in running and repairing machines created a new set of indispensable specialists.[27] Furthermore, to the extent that new technologies simplified a great many tasks and shortened the training period required for their competent performance, they enhanced workers' capacity to move about from one job to another within a plant, or to take their skills elsewhere. Many workers changed jobs to acquire new skills, attracted not only by higher pay but also by the prospects of training and advancement in a trade.[28] This type of generalized industrial literacy, quintessentially proletarian, replaced the older form of craft skills and lifetime vocations.

The standard marxist depiction of a loss of *skills* in this period is more accurately described as a loss of *autonomy* in production. The close monitoring of work-flow entailed a more exacting standard of time-keeping and a deeper intrusion into the workers' sphere. Toilets were to be placed "'so that anybody from a distance can see into them" to counter illegal smokes', and one observer noted that 'many large works have a clerk specially for the purpose of booking the time at which men go into and come out of the w.c.'[29] At Siemens, the huge German electrical equipment firm, flexible master–journeymen arrangements were replaced by 'increasingly strict and detailed factory ordinances and sharper surveillance for laxity, theft, and the like'.[30] Such authority structures gave foremen enormous power, which they frequently exercised arbitrarily. Most foremen still hired and fired, set piece rates and assigned work, 'so that many workers believed ... that whether they earned well or not was entirely up to the foreman.'[31] It was as if 'the foreman's will is God's will'.[32] Not surprisingly, foremen provoked workers' ire. Calls for the firing of particularly obnoxious foremen and managers became a more frequent strike demand in this period.[33] In the 1880s, labour papers in the North of France began to refer to factories as prisons and foremen as jailers, printing letters from indignant workers denouncing 'incompetent, tyrannical, fussy and lewd foremen'.[34] Factory girls who rarely complained about working conditions condemned 'foremen who treat us like animals'.[35] Close over-the-shoulder supervision led to high labour turnover, especially among young workers. In Germany, 'disputes with foremen were the most frequent single recorded cause of resignation.'[36] As workforces swelled and serial production became more complex, the traditional foreman's job was subdivided. In place of a single overseer, modern management sprouted rate-fixers, feed-and-speed men, and quality-control inspectors.[37] While this often gave rise to ambiguous jurisdiction and blurred lines of authority, its net effect was to intensify the direct invigilation of labour.

Subcontracting, pervasive in the first stage of industrial development, was the primary means through which kin networks were implanted in the sphere of capitalist production. In the second stage, most employers dispensed with the arrangement. By 1918, G. D. H. Cole observed:

> In most of the coal fields, the butty system has disappeared; the worst forms of the contract system have been driven out from the iron and steel industry; the power of the sub-contractor at the docks is largely gone. In fact, the pure 'contract' system ... has almost ceased to exist in any trade.[38]

The principal deficiency of subcontracting from the employers' standpoint was the way it insulated the labour-team from the direct exercise of managerial authority. At an early and relatively primitive stage of industrialization, when capitalists were in no position to direct the labour process in detail, subcontracting, and the kin relations it congealed, made an indispensable contribution to labour discipline. Yet in the long run, nepotism was inimical to the process of 'labour's abstraction'. Kin-based work-teams generated an unwieldy labour force, difficult to shunt about. Their members had very strong feelings about where, and with whom, they ought to work. They were not readily amenable to being broken up and reallocated to the different departments of a plant. Traditions of parent–child labour socialization died hard. Laying off individual members of a team while retaining their kin could be problematic. With management's representative directly on site, workers no longer hired their own assistants; the foreman or his department supervisor did that. The move to terminate subcontracting and place all workers directly under the foremen's command paralleled the employers' drive to break the workbench autonomy of skilled tradesmen.[39] Attacking different segments of the workforce, both initiatives were designed to increase management's control over the labour process in its detail.

Subcontracting was also eroded by pressures for the individuation of the wage. It was difficult to preserve the lump-sum wage form, paid out directly to piece-masters, when individual earners collected their own pay. Capitalist property forms (as we have seen) legitimate a strong sense of the worker's personal right to his or her own wage. If free proletarians worked alongside the family subordinates of a piece-master's team who were denied the receipt of 'their own' wage, the blatant discrepancy became very difficult to justify in custom or in law. Poverty-stricken parents who depended on setting their children to work from an early age cherished the collective wage form much more than did employers, and often resisted its liquidation. Higher-paid skilled workers who were not caught up in its seductions abhorred subcontracting and fought to end it. In France they succeeded in having it banned in 1848, though legislation, largely unenforced, did not eliminate the practice.[40] Industrial unions, growing rapidly in the 1880s, attacked contracting, associating it with sweating and driving.[41]

Long after subcontracting waned, kin connections were still used to secure jobs wherever adolescents were employed in significant numbers. Such informal selection networks operating on the supply side of the labour market functioned in dynamic tension with the demand side, where capitalists insisted on their right to hire individuals 'on their merits', regardless of their relationship to members of the present workforce. While this was the employers' prerogative, they still found the requests of kin worthy of preferential treatment. In 1869, roughly three sons in four entered their fathers' industries, though by the turn of the century this portion had declined to one in two.[42] A broad survey of British evidence from the late nineteenth and early twentieth centuries indicates that in trades with large workforces, a quarter to a half of workers' fathers had also toiled in the same trade, though not necessarily for the same firm as their children.[43] In Upper Silesia, under conditions of much higher labour mobility, the same patrilineal continuity is evident: more than half the applicants for jobs at the Freidrich foundry from 1895 to 1908 had fathers employed in mining and smelting. In this case, company records reveal an unresolved tension between formal and informal requisites:

> Even when two and sometimes three generations of the same family worked in a particular mine, these workers at times had trouble getting hired, or, once hired, experienced difficulties with their pensions and other fringe benefits. It seems that the whole [paternalist] concept gave way to the exigencies of the daily need for workers and was kept in reserve for pleading a special case.[44]

The gradual decline of father–son occupational continuity in the latter decades of the century probably had more to do with the fading lustre of this career choice for working-class lads than with the refusal of employers to countenance their hiring. We will return to explore this point more fully below.

With the liquidation of subcontracting, workers were hired individually, supervised directly on the shop floor by the employer's agents, and paid individually 'through the office'.[45] The complete monetization of the wage form went hand in hand with its individuation. In early capitalism, at least part of the wage had normally been paid in kind. Whenever workers lived on their master's premises and ate at his table, room and board were part of the wage. Even when they lived apart, workers were often granted the right to take materials away with them when they left the workplace each day: 'the tailors got their cabbage, the shipyard workers their chips, the weavers claimed their "thrums".[46] Capitalists strove to put an end to this practice in the second half of the nineteenth century. What had formerly been taken as a right was now considered theft, and foremen were instructed to be vigilant against pilfering. But the arrangement had been so deeply ingrained in many trades, and understood as a customary right, that the crackdown was met with outrage. Workers perceived an assault upon their person when they 'could be searched at any time to prevent the theft of material ... "without there being any need to give reasons".'[47]

There were other aspects of customary class relations that workers were glad to see the end of and were instrumental in jettisoning. They were generally hostile to live-in arrangements, supervised boarding, the truck system, and company housing, where there were alternatives.[48] As the delegates to a French conference of mechanics put it: 'While we fully appreciate the value of these things, we are partisans of freedom, and we wish to make it clear that we want to run our own lives, and that all we need is the freedom to do so.'[49] The final vestiges of extra-economic coercion were terminated in this period. In Britain, the Master and Servant Laws were abolished, the miner's bond and other long-term labour indentures fell into disuse, and the vicious 1834 Poor Law was moderated in 1867: 'As often as not these legal changes ratified a de facto situation.'[50]

The full monetization of the wage and the dissolution of a web of customary understandings, constraints and prerogatives transformed the terms of contract bargaining. In one industry after another, workers began to perceive and assert their interests within subtly transformed rules of the game.[51] Traditional hierarchies of wage payment for skilled and unskilled labour – customs of pre-industrial origin – gave way before a more fluid market calculus. The overriding principle now became to obtain whatever the market would bear. Concomitantly, solid standards of 'a fair day's work for a fair day's pay' melted away as workers concentrated on limiting their own exploitation, learning how to hold a portion of their labour-power in reserve under the new demands of factory discipline. This represented a higher form of labour alienation. As a French mechanic remarked:

> If we do not produce as much as we could, if we fail to be as careful with the raw materials and our work tools as we could, it is because we have no interest in the boss's prosperity; he pays us as little as he can, we work as little as we can.[52]

In the first stage of industrialization, employers typically assumed that the principal motivation to labour was basic want, and the only way to increase workers' output was to 'drive' them over an extended working day. Prodded by the competitive exigencies of the Great Depression, managers finally became interested in the variability of labour-power and the complexity of the relationship between wages, working conditions and productivity. Able to measure the productivity of labour with a precision that they had previously lacked, employers could refine the wage form as an incentive structure. The first tool in their arsenal was the piece rate, which made a comeback in this period.[53] Only 5 per cent of British engineering workers were paid by the piece in 1886; by 1914, almost half were. Piece rates were particularly effective where foremen were unable to supervise workers closely; in mining, for example, they increased output enormously.

Labour's response to 'the piece' was ambivalent. On the one hand, most unions were at least officially opposed and many, particularly in the skilled trades, fought vigorously in the 1880s and 1890s against its introduction or extension.[54] Opponents argued that piecework was a deceptive mechanism, designed to seduce workers into overwork with the lure of extraordinary pay increments. They observed that the debilitating pace of 'exemplary' rate-busters was soon inflicted on the rest, as foremen insisted that the performance of the quickest revealed that the rest were slacking and that previous quotas were too low. The acceptance of piece rates would therefore trap workers in a vicious cycle, hooking them on short-term increases and then driving them unremittingly in the long run, as income gains proved to be unsustainable. Very often, this is precisely what happened, though in many cases rate-busting acceleration was effectively restrained by informal pressure. A bonus payment, for work done above and beyond a specified quota, was a variant on the piece rate and subject to the same types of abuse. Bonus schemes contributed to industrial accidents and fatalities by presenting a financial incentive to take shortcuts and bend the rules on safety standards in order to work full out for the premium. While drawing the unions' wrath on these grounds, piece rates and bonus schemes were none the less very popular with experienced workers who saw them as opportunities to make far more money than they could under straight-time wages. They argued that 'payment by results' was the only way workers could reap some of the benefits of rising productivity in the midst of rapid technological change; time wages permitted the bosses to appropriate the entire windfall. Piece rates and bonus schemes were so popular among the ranks that many unions were forced to rescind long-standing positions against them. In Germany and Britain, the resistance to piece rates fizzled out around the turn of the century, but lasted somewhat longer in France.

In defence of the rate-busters and those who volunteered for overtime even when their fellow workers were unemployed, can we argue that most were devoted family men, keen to take home more pay to their spouses? Undoubtedly many were, but it is my impression that the motive of most was more often individualist, predicated on masculine consumptionism. The widespread acceptance of pay schemes that combined a stable base rate with variable premiums gained through bonuses and overtime seems to be bound up with the 'allowance system', an increasingly pervasive form of income distribution between spouses. Under this arrangement, male breadwinners handed their wives a fixed sum for the maintenance of the household (often the same amount as their base pay), pocketing the variable residual. If the allowance system was as widespread as I think it was, then the motives of the rate-busters and the overtime workers in going for extraordinary paydays not only displayed a disregard for their workmates, but also showed no great devotion to bettering their families' lot. (The allowance and other wage distribution schemes will be discussed at the end of this chapter.)

The Recruitment and Training of Labour

Throughout the nineteenth and early twentieth centuries, high rates of labour turnover were of great concern to capitalists. Some feared that skilled workers were carrying industrial secrets to their competitors, but the major problems were escalating training costs and the disruptive effects on the labour force of great numbers of workers coming and going. While employers celebrated the freedom to dismiss workers at will, they deplored the way their employees seized upon the converse liberty to 'vote with their feet'. Except in periods of economic depression, there was a great deal more of the latter than the former. Workers had several reasons for job-changing.[55] As mentioned, many fled particularly obnoxious foremen and wretched working conditions. Brighter prospects elsewhere – higher pay, better training, the chance to work with superior tools and safer machinery – were positive inducements to switch. Many workers welcomed a brief vacation of a week or two before returning to the grind. Young men took off in search of variety in employment and a change of scenery, a chance to see different parts of the country before settling down. The rural tramping tradition was here reinvented by urban proletarians.

How high was labour turnover? The conventional rate is calculated as a percentage: the number of workers departing in one year as a proportion of the total labour force employed at the outset. On this measure, annual rates were high, with most sectors ranging from 40 to 70 per cent.[56] Without control for growth, this standard may give an exaggerated impression of flux, since labour forces in most industries were swelling very substantially in this period. A sounder measure is the proportion of workers who departed within a year of being hired. In selected mines in Upper Silesia, 38 per cent did so between 1879 and 1891; this seems to be about average for large enterprises. The distribution of employment duration was (and remains today) markedly bimodal: a high proportion of all departures occurred among those who had worked less than a year: 95 per cent in lead smelting, 75 per cent in coke plants, 75 per cent in iron smelting and 83 per cent in foodstuffs.[57] Most workers who stayed beyond a year settled in for the long haul. It was not unusual for a fifth of the workers in one plant to have been there twenty or more years.[58] Those most inclined to leave in the first year were young, single, untrained and female.[59] Typically, these groups formed a semi-skilled periphery, constantly in flux, loosely assembled around a more durable core of skilled men who were older, married and residing in permanent dwellings near the plant. Short-term workers lived in temporary accommodation – company barracks, commercial hostels and rooming-houses – and came and went with great frequency. The variation in a company's labour force over the course of the business cycle primarily affected these workers. Employers made considerably more effort to keep intact their core complement of trained veterans. For their part, workers were sensitive to the overall balance of supply and demand in the labour market. The two forms of leave-taking thus varied inversely over the business cycle: when the economy was booming and there was full employment, quits peaked while lay-offs and firings ebbed; when business slumped, lay-offs rose but few workers left jobs of their own volition.[60]

In their attempts to reduce quit rates, employers wielded a mixture of sticks and carrots. The most common deterrent was to delay payment of wages a fortnight, and then to refuse to release back pay to those who had left without giving proper notice. Blacklists circulated in some industries identifying the footloose types, but employers rarely mustered the collective discipline necessary to make such schemes bite. Truck systems exploited the trap of indebtedness to the company store to pin down workers. In some fast-developing regions, firms built housing; by 1900, 21 per cent of miners in the Ruhr district were housed in company dwellings, often on long-term leases that were difficult to break.[61] The harder it was for employers to recruit labour, the more inclined they were to undertake paternalist investments.[62]

By way of positive incentives to stay, many employers simply raised wages and improved working conditions in an attempt to make their establishments more attractive than those of their competitors. With the lure of higher wages, employers could screen workers more carefully to weed out the young itinerants and select older men with wives and young children at home. Relatively few would quit when toiling under the full weight of the family-breadwinner obligation. Gradually, employers came to realize that a 'decent living wage', rewarding men's sincere desire to provide adequately for their families, would 'bring out the best in the men and settle them down', reducing labour turnover more effectively than grandiose schemes of corporate paternalism. In this way, employers were able to stabilize and train a labour force of married men with a low turnover, while supplementing the core with a peripheral layer of single workers with a short-term job orientation who were easier to lay off in response to downturns in the business cycle.

Trade unions had their own reasons for discouraging voluntary departures.[63] Rapid turnover of the work force took a heavy toll on labour solidarity and the capacity of unions to defend their members' interests. With workers coming and going every week, the local labour hall often appeared to be an adjunct of the railway station – the venue for a jumble of strangers and fleeting acquaintances – not an environment conducive to nurturing friendship, trust and mutuality. Leaving was an individual response to frequently intolerable working conditions, siphoning frustration and anger away from the body of workers who were in a position to fight collectively to improve the situation.

Although the traditional bonds between artisanal masters, journeymen and apprentices subject to guild regulation were buffeted by early industrial capitalism, they displayed a remarkable resilience, based on the enduring vitality of small workshops and skilled trades. But with the growth of the factory system, artisanal relations underwent a profound metamorphosis – a disintegration on the one hand, and a reincarnation on the other. Guild structures survived until the 1860s in Germany, but 'by the late 1860s the free labour contract had become the rule, and the last remnants of corporate laws had been largely destroyed.'[64] In some sectors, artisans were driven out of business; but in most, they migrated reluctantly to factories, mills and foundries. As the master–journeyman bond gradually evolved into a capitalist employer–employee relationship, masters lost the capacity to regulate the personal lives of their workers, and especially their family-formation strategies. Journeymen began to move out of their masters' homes in droves. Until mid century, nearly all journeymen lived in; by 1867, fewer than three Berlin journeymen in ten did so. The exodus in other German cities lagged slightly, but was not far behind.[65] As a Rhineland master noted, 'the familial relationship between master and journeymen is disappearing.'[66] While the provision of room and board remained common in traditional trades, shop workers grew increasingly hostile to the practice, demanding a purely monetary wage with no strings attached. They wanted to live on their own, be free to socialize with their friends in their own leisure-time, court, marry and have families whenever they wished. With the demise of guild regulation, there was nothing to stop them. The German bakers' union won the abolition of room and board for 4,000 workers in 1905; their demand was a common one at the time, as journeymen's associations were transformed into trade unions.[67]

Traditional apprenticeship arrangements collapsed in the second half of the nineteenth century. In France during the Second Empire, only 14 per cent of workers in industry were designated as apprentices. A survey in 1865 found that 'apprenticeship, defined as receiving one's training in a trade workshop, was virtually nonexistent.' Several factors hastened the demise of this form of job-training. The acceleration of technological change in industry and the concomitant subdivision of tasks rendered the craftsman's specialized skills practically obsolete. The Conseils de Prud'hommes of Paris asked: 'Can one produce a chairmaker from the child whose only work consists of assembling the various parts of a chair which arrive already made up from the provinces or abroad and which have to be dismantled for transport purposes?' Formal apprenticeship had been premissed upon the worker's eventual graduation from apprentice to master. When the incursion of capitalist class relations severed this career transition, the institution reached an impasse: 'the employed could no longer expect to become the employers.' From the masters' standpoint, training was also subject to diminishing returns. Having lost their control over access to a trade, masters complained that apprentices were free to leave prematurely to pursue the job offers of other employers.[68]

The passing of traditional apprenticeship, with its written contract and guild regulation, did not end all forms of apprenticeship. In a bastardized capitalist version, employers who hired young lads promised to provide on-the-job training while paying them a substandard wage. In this case, the employer was not in command of the production skills required in his workplace; he simply instructed one of his more experienced hands to 'take the kid under your wing and teach him the tricks of the trade'. Since there was no agreement between the youth and the assigned trainer, nor any incentive for the latter to share his skills and convey his experience, the arrangement was effectively a cheap labour contract for employers with very little training benefit. Artisans and mechanics frequently sabotaged these charades, fearing the degradation of their skills and the circumvention of their training. The boilermakers explained: 'When a man has spent years in acquiring a perfect knowledge of his trade, such acquisition becomes his own personal capital as much as the gold and silver he carries in his pocket.'[69]

As artisanal skill-training was diluted and occupational induction overturned, the young man's career path of entering his father's trade lost much of its former prestige, security and sense of familial loyalty. Particularly in declining trades, fewer sons followed in their fathers' footsteps. In some cases, 'parents were disheartened by the prospects of their own trade and convinced that apprenticeship had deteriorated anyway. ... [In other instances,] sons were impatient with a training period and eager to earn right away.'[70] It was widely held that the demise of apprenticeship had disrupted the working family: 'It would be desirable to train young people in their father's careers. ... Unfortunately, things do not work out that way in the majority of cases. Sons take a career different from that of their fathers.'[71] So parental career aspirations shifted: 'The hope was not so much to keep the children in specific trades ... as to permit them to enter the more favoured branches of industry.'[72] Increasingly, working-class parents advised their children to get 'a good education'. By the late nineteenth century, this meant staying in school at least until the legal leaving age.[73]

The Rise of Schooling

In the nineteenth century, elementary schools 'for the education of the labouring classes' mushroomed in every city district, small town and village of moderate size.[74] With each passing decade, enrolments climbed and children stayed in school longer. By mid century, two decades before compulsory schooling was introduced in France and Britain, eight boys in ten between the ages of six and fourteen were enrolled in German schools; perhaps six in ten in France and two of three in England and Wales.[75] The majority of working-class children would have been exposed to at least a few years of intermittent schooling before becoming teenagers. Those with no schooling were either very poor or living in remote communities. The children of German workers were enrolled in elementary schools over a period of five or six years on average, their French counterparts over four or five years, English working-class students perhaps one year less.[76] Enrolment, however, is not the same as attendance, and the latter is the better measure (though more difficult to estimate). Bear in mind that both the school day and the academic year were much briefer in the nineteenth century than they are today (the opposite of trends in the working day) and that attendance was very sporadic, with widespread absenteeism at times of peak labour demand in the family economy. In Manchester, for example, only 68 per cent of children enrolled in 1870 attended classes on an average school day, though attendance had risen to 82 per cent by the turn of the century.[77] By 1900, almost all children aged six to twelve were enrolled and attending fairly regularly.

What accounts for the rise of mass schooling? Most analysts have viewed developments from the top down, concentrating on the administrative provision of schools, the regulation of teachers and curriculum by Church and state boards, and the attitudes of political elites (who were divided and ambivalent initially, but gradually became more unified and enthusiastic about the 'civilizing' effects of universal education). From our standpoint, however, it is necessary to shift attention from the supply side to examine instead: (a) the nature of working-class parents' demand for schooling for their children; (b) the growing divergence between a burgeoning proletarian desire for 'self-education' and the form that schooling took, as states forged centrally administered, compulsory systems in the latter decades of the century; and (c) the impact of this increasingly middle-class institution on parent–child relations in working-class families.

Given evidence of widespread student absenteeism in the era of voluntary schools, and of parental resistance after attendance was made compulsory, readers might well ask: What demand? Many scholars have concluded that proletarian parents were at best indifferent, and more often downright hostile, to the education of their children.[78] This interpretation borrows uncritically from the reports of nineteenth-century school reformers who singled out working-class parents as a major stumbling block to educational modernization – their 'utter lack of appreciation of educational work intended for the elevation and mental benefit of their offspring', as one reformer put it. Such a perspective fails to distinguish between parents' resistance to the prevailing *form of schooling* on the one hand, and aspirations for their children's *education* on the other. A one-sided emphasis on proletarian hostility to Church and state schools often obscures the remarkable ardour for education, and particularly for basic literacy skills, displayed by working-class communities all across Western Europe.[79] As David Vincent has noted, 'education was far from being a commodity that was forced upon the working class by outside agencies'; on the contrary, burgeoning working-class enthusiasm for education was a driving force in the development of universal schooling.[80] 'We senden them to school a bit, when we can afford it,' a mother of seven children explained. 'It's a weary thing when people canna read. It's a blessed fine thing to be a good scholar.'[81] The best index of the breadth and depth of the mass desire for education is the vast proliferation of unofficial 'private' schools funded entirely from fees of a few pence a week, willingly paid by working-class parents to provide their children with a brief introduction to basic literacy.[82]

In France, 'one has only to take a closer look at what was going on in the regions to find "clandestine schools" all over the place, flourishing and diverse in form.'[83] In the countryside, itinerant teachers held classes in people's homes, moving from hamlet to hamlet. In towns and cities, unauthorized schools were set up by teachers who offered classes at a more convenient time and place and at lower rates than official schools. In Creuse in 1846, the school inspector reported that workers were '"gathered during the winter, in different places, in the homes of unqualified people, in order to learn to read and write". Summonses, police reports and even convictions were unable to put an end to these unauthorized schools before mid-century.'[84] The proliferation of such establishments demonstrated people's growing appetite for elementary education. 'What better proof could one want of the vitality of the need', ask Furet and Ozouf, 'than the failure of this war on clandestine schools, in spite of the obstinacy of the authorities?'[85] Reflecting this demand, while seeking to politicize it, the radical currents in the workers' movement all included educational objectives in their programmes, often of a far-reaching nature.[86]

Britain witnessed a parallel growth, with private 'venture' and 'dame' schools mushrooming in the first half of the nineteenth century. At their peak, more students were enrolled in these small (mostly one-room, single-teacher) places, supported entirely by fees, than in the 'public' schools, sponsored by the Church-based National and British School Societies. Lacking the public schools' state subsidies (increasing over time), private school fees were typically several times those charged by the approved alternatives (the reverse of the situation in France). If economic constraint had dictated the cheapest course, working-class private schools would never have flourished in Britain. Yet 'a sense of duty and interest induces a large proportion of the working class to make considerable pecuniary sacrifices for the mental cultivation of their off-spring', concluded an 1837 investigation.[87]

When private and public schools competed for students in proletarian districts, most parents demonstrated a strong preference for the former. If financially strapped, they reluctantly moved their children to the nearest subsidized school, but as soon as family income rose, they reverted to private schools. Middle-class reformers held it to be self-evident that the latter were vastly inferior to their publicly funded counterparts – a disgrace to the educational ideals of a civilized society. They found the stubborn preference of working-class parents for their indigenous schools perverse and maddening. It was 'truly astonishing' that the poor were unwilling 'to contribute even a penny in Westminster [to an Infant School] when they used to give fourpence and even sixpence to the most wretched Dame Schools'.[88] The ardent school reformer Kay-Shuttleworth was utterly at a loss to explain to the 1837 Parliamentary Inquiry into the Education of the Poorer Classes why a National School in Manchester stood half empty while seven private-venture schools prospered within five hundred yards of its front door.[89] Two decades later, reporting to the Newcastle Commission, Patrick Cumin was equally baffled by 'a remark-able fact' that in three of the five districts he examined, 'the proportion of children who attend public schools, as compared to those who attend private schools, has actually diminished [from 1851 to 1859].' He regretfully informed the commissioners that 'amongst the mass of the people, I found no great readiness to abandon the private for the public school.'[90]

Buried beneath the denunciatory rhetoric of the inspectors' reports and commission testimony, the reasons why working-class parents preferred the private schools to the middle-class alternative may be dimly discerned. They shed a fascinating light on the constraints of the family economy and the childrearing priorities of working-class parents. Parents experienced an intractable conflict between the desire to provide their children with 'a decent education' for the future and the immediate need to set them to work in order to ease the family's dependency ratio and maintain its living standards. Schools exacted a double price: obviously fees had to be paid but, even more onerous, children's wages and domestic assistance had to be forgone.[91] School records indicate that younger children aged six to ten attended fairly regularly. But as students approached adolescence, with their potential economic contribution rising, attendance slumped; almost all were gone by their fourteenth birthdays.[92] The poorer a family was, the more pressure parents experienced to resolve the bind in favour of the household's immediate needs, removing children from school whenever employment opportunities arose or family living standards deteriorated. There was thus a positive correlation between the wage levels of working men in a community and the effective demand of their families for schooling. The more prosperous layers of the working class sent their children to school for longer periods than the poorest. As real wages rose across the whole breadth of the working class, an increasing proportion of proletarian parents invested in some elementary education for their children. Once the economic constraints of family poverty are taken seriously, one cannot infer that the failure of parents to maintain their children's regular attendance for several consecutive years signified a lack of interest in their education. While blaming the parents, a French school inspector was none the less prepared to concede the point: 'The worker ... understands the advantages of education. But when he is in need, poverty represses his instincts to plan for the future and his paternal ambition, and he falls into thoughtlessness.'[93] Amongst the poor, there was a latent demand for education that became manifest only as real incomes rose. To discern the motives of proletarian parents, we must look at the specific character of the demand that was manifest.

Struggling to make ends meet, parents valued schools that respected the work rhythms of the family economy and did not insist on regular attendance.[94] Mothers expected to be able to call out their children to run messages or mind a younger child at home. Fathers felt within their rights to take their sons along with them when there was extra work to do at the shop and a chance to supplement the family's income. The teachers in fee-paying schools were flexible in this regard, operating as best they could with a student population in constant flux. Most taught for only about twenty hours per week, accepting the fact that in the conflictive relationship between school and work, work came first.[95] The state-subsidized schools, by contrast, were not prepared to countenance this priority; most insisted on regular attendance, and many expelled students whose parents were uncooperative to this end.

Indigenous schools were flexible in other ways as well. They took in very young children when they were accompanied by an older sibling. The need for childcare, apparent in these cases, was particularly acute for mothers who held jobs away from home or toiled as homeworkers for pay. The schools themselves typically had an informal and domestic atmosphere, with teachers living in the same dwelling, very often in the same room, interspersing attention to students with other duties. There was thus an interlacing of domestic and classroom space, paralleling the incomplete separation of living space from workplace in many proletarian households. It was only in the latter decades of the century that the two spheres were completely separated, as the practice of itinerant teachers going from home to home was terminated. Proletarians were not opposed to the creation of separate, single-purpose facilities, but they wanted their schools to be indigenous to the community, which the private-venture schools were. Mothers dropped by unannounced to pick up their children, students came and went at all hours discharging other duties, and schedules were designed to blend in with community activities. Indigenous schools in agricultural districts, for example, were shut down at harvest time.

Teachers set relaxed (that is, realistic) standards of personal cleanliness and did not enforce a dress code.[96] Indignant reformers accused them of having no standards at all, but this is inaccurate. Most encouraged cleanliness and a modicum of neatness (particularly on special occasions) without making a major issue of it. The school uniforms and compulsory haircuts of the religious schools were branded as stigmatizing marks of charity, widely resented by working-class students and parents.[97] Above all, private-school teachers refrained from singling out the scruffy urchins of the poor for inspections and humiliating lectures on cleanliness in front of the class. And they were less likely to beat children, as public-school masters typically did. Parents regarded punishment as their own custodial prerogative, and few were prepared to cede it to other authorities.[98] The teachers in the fee-based schools were 'one of us' – part of the community in a way that middle-class masters never were.[99] Lacking formal training or certification, they depended for their meagre livelihood on parents' support at all times. A sensitivity to parental concerns was thus imperative, and a measure of tact and savvy in navigating the shoals of community conflict was a definite asset.

Working-class parents were prepared to cede teachers only limited jurisdiction over their children's lives. They felt that schools had no business indoctrinating their children with the moral or religious values of the rich, the Church, or the government; it was the parents' responsibility to teach children right from wrong. Basic literacy ought to be taught without the heavy overlay of religious indoctrination that Church schools insisted on.[100] To be taught the catechism and the Lord's Prayer was one thing; for religious parents in particular, memorizing the catechism was important for a child's first communion. But to force youngsters to recite long passages of Scripture while terrorizing them daily with fevered sermons about Sin and Eternal Damnation was beyond the pale as far as proletarian parents were concerned. Private-school teachers respected this distinction; teachers in the state-subsidized Church schools did not. At a working-class meeting in Leeds, a baffled reformer

> asked how it was that, notwithstanding the existence of so many institutions on a public basis, so many parents seemed to prefer the private school. One speaker said strongly, that for his part he thought 'it was because there was too much religion in the aided school' and the remark was very loudly and generally cheered.[101]

The issue of religious indoctrination was one facet of a larger contention over the fundamental purpose of schooling. For the middle- and upper-class proponents of mass education, the main objective of elementary schools was not technical skills-training for modern industry but the moralization of working-class children, who were inclined, in the eyes of their class superiors, to be undisciplined, rude and wilful. Lacking proper socialization in the family, they stood in desperate need of training to instil good manners and correct habits: to teach them to be honest, prompt, industrious, 'God-fearing' and deferential. Above all, they must learn to respect people in authority – parents, clergy, employers, police and magistrates. While this civilizing mission did not concentrate on imparting industrial skills per se, it did focus on the formation of industrial discipline – on inculcating habits of punctuality, diligence and obedience. Yet the educational concerns of the upper classes extended well beyond the workplace. In order to use their new-found liberties wisely, workers needed to exercise self-discipline in their leisure-time; otherwise, they were easily misled. If schools trained children adequately, there was no reason to fear:

> Those unhealthy aspirations to independence which destroy all respect for established organizations ... that rumbling agitation which spreads, for no reason whatever, among little-educated workers, that discontent which comes not from within themselves, but from some leader under whose sway their ignorance places them, those easily-exploited prejudices which education alone can dispel.[102]

These larger ambitions, to 'civilize' the working classes and inoculate their children against subversive ideas, ran smack up against a very substantial working-class resistance based precisely on 'aspirations to independence'. Working-class radicals typically set great store on education because 'when men are better educated they become sensible of the manner in which they have been deprived of the results of their labour.'[103] Yet state-regulated school systems disappointed them bitterly. The paper *Le Socialiste* in France complained that the elementary schools had become nothing more than 'training for subordination', while Wilhelm Liebknecht held that the constant drills in German schools were used 'to deaden the capacity to think. They elevated blind faith – the brother of blind obedience ... to the highest duty, turned free investigation into the work of the devil, and killed all impulse to independent behaviour.'[104] In more prosaic terms, Uriah Heep recalled his numbing experience in a Charity School: 'They taught us all a great deal of 'umbleness – not much else that I know of, from morning to night.'[105]

The fundamental bone of contention was the question of power – who would exercise control over children in the shaping of young minds? Middle-class parents were broadly sympathetic to the values, curriculum and teaching methods employed in their children's education. Consequently, they were more relaxed about the specific bounds of the school's custodial rights, and were prepared to share an overlapped jurisdiction with teachers in order to reinforce one another's authority in the eyes of the children. Working-class parents distrusted the school's ideological influence and thus sought to limit teachers' jurisdiction, narrowing the scope of curriculum and pedagogy.[106] Teachers who felt that they had a mission to civilize the 'lower orders' by educating 'the whole child' were the object of intense parental distrust. Disdainful of working-class culture and defensive about their own efforts, such teachers concluded that most proletarian parents were utterly indifferent to their children's education. This accusation of indifference is rebutted by the evident willingness of parents to pay weekly fees on tight working-class budgets so that their children might be 'properly educated'. From the standpoint of proletarian parents, private fees had the great virtue of making teachers directly accountable to them, evading the control of the public board. As an inspector remarked, 'In these schools, the teachers ... have no one else to please ... their faults and their merits alike arise from a desire to meet the exact demands which the parents make.'[107]

The primary objective of education, as far as working-class parents were concerned, was for their children to learn to read, write and do sums at a rudimentary level. They did not believe that this should take very long, and their main measure of a teacher's worth was the pace at which he or she could convey these skills.[108] If a teacher was minimally competent and the students paid attention, parents felt that most children ought to be basically literate in a few years. Other subjects such as grammar, history and geography were seen as extras; they could be taught if time permitted, but ought not to divert attention from the three Rs. Proletarian parents were no more interested in vocational training, tightly geared to the industrial labour force, than were the educationalists of the propertied classes. They saw the value of basic literacy as useful and empowering – reading would enable youngsters to learn for themselves, and writing would help them to express themselves and communicate with others. We should not impute a revolutionary motive to this aspiration. The purpose was not to change the world, but to participate fully in it on their own terms. As for the ideological baggage that accompanied this core curriculum – the superior values of Christian piety and Western civilization – most working-class parents ignored it, while a class-conscious minority vehemently opposed it.

This, then, was a limited, utilitarian mandate, consistent with the working-class parents' sense of the school's circumscribed jurisdiction. Furthermore, they did not expect that their children would advance beyond elementary school. Far from selling their children short, this was an entirely realistic appraisal of the class-stratified nature of the school system. Elementary schools in working-class districts, public and private, were dead-end institutions, cut off from the bottom rungs of secondary schools in the 'better' parts of town.[109] Barely a trickle of working-class children advanced beyond elementary school, and the vast majority left at, or very soon after, the minimum school-leaving age. In sum, schooling was a short-term investment in basic literacy skills, undertaken by parents who wanted their children to be able to read and write better than they themselves could.

What changes generated this burgeoning demand for schooling as a means to basic literacy? Consider two key factors. First, the development of capitalism tore down older means of child socialization, stimulating the demand for schooling as an alternative. In independent family enterprises, or even in cottage industries, parents had been able to teach their children most of what they needed to know to follow in their footsteps and establish themselves in adult occupations.[110] Fully proletarian parents lost that capacity. Divorced from the means of production, they were largely unable to train their children on the tools and machinery they would eventually be required to use. Even when sons did follow their fathers in a trade, the accelerated pace of technological change typically outmoded the older generation's skills before they had a chance to pass them on. The demise of subcontracting and the consolidation of individuated hiring finished off parent–child teamwork in productive labour. Consumed in work elsewhere, fathers were daily absent from the household; they were in no position to provide on-the-job training for their sons. Daughters were increasingly sent out to work while their mothers remained at home. In these ways, proletarianization disrupted the age-old pattern of early socialization in family settings, where young children had been introduced to adult work-roles through assisting parents of the same sex in daily chores. To compensate for this loss, elementary schooling was differentiated by sex from the outset, with special training for girls in domestic skills. (The gender dimension of the school system will be discussed below.) While the initial effect of industrialization was typically to open up jobs for children and thus to divert them from attending classes, the disruption of family-based training entailed in extra-domestic employment was so severe that as soon as parents could afford it, they strove to send their children to school.

As well as disturbing primary socialization by parents and older siblings, the development of capitalism eroded and devalued the traditional arrangements of secondary socialization, such as apprenticeship and domestic service. The occupational assistance that parents had given their children – placing a son with a master, making arrangements for a daughter's first service contract – either became impossible to fulfil or were subject to diminishing returns. Adapting to the increasingly fluid and impersonal nature of the labour market, working-class parents began to shift training objectives for their children from hands-on experience in a specific trade to 'getting a good education' so that they could obtain 'a decent job' in whatever workplace or trade was hiring when they became teenagers.[111]

Parents hoped that children with a 'good grounding in the three R's' would make out better in the world than they had; they saw education as a means to this end. This is conventionally termed a desire for 'upward mobility', and in a general sense, it is true. But what is the precise nature of this aspiration? For most, it did not entail upward mobility in *class* terms, with children ascending into the ranks of the middle-class. To the contrary, there was a widespread fear that the better-educated children would grow disdainful of parents with little or no formal schooling, 'put on airs', marry above their class, and 'forget where they come from'. The desire for progress through education was much more often (and more realistically) a goal of *generational* advancement within the working class, where parents fervently hoped that their children would enjoy a higher living standard and a more comfortable existence than they had by obtaining better-paying, less debilitating jobs:

> I am a carpenter and my son will probably be a carpenter also. Now, a carpenter who can make staircases gets better wages than a carpenter who does not. To make staircases a man must be able to draw, and therefore, in order to give my son the best chance of getting on, I send him to learn drawing; and what is more, I give a penny a week extra for the purpose.[112]

The prospects of such advancement dignified parental sacrifice and invested alienating labour with a consoling sense of purpose.

The second major impetus behind the burgeoning demand for schooling was the rise of literacy. In the late eighteenth and early nineteenth centuries, the proportion of the population able to sign their names in the marriage register had grown considerably; studies indicate that most signatories were able to read at an elementary level. Many had acquired these skills without the benefit of schooling. Scholars formerly presumed that the spread of elementary schools had resulted directly in the rise of basic literacy. The relationship between the two developments is now understood to have been a rather loose one, with cause and effect frequently inverted, at least in the initial stages.[113] An introduction to basic literacy whetted the appetite of common folk for 'book learning'. As a youngster, the autobiographer John Plummer recalled his 'strange kind of fascination for books; and although I could not read them, yet I would pore for hours over the – to me – mystical letters of the alphabet.' Later on, when he could read, he remembered 'haunting street bookstalls, where I gazed with sad, longing and despairing features on the literary treasures displayed before me, and which the want of a few pence alone precluded me from possessing.'[114]

At the beginning of the nineteenth century, literacy was considered to be a valuable and esteemed skill, but it was not yet taken to be essential.[115] Fifty years later, this evaluation had changed. As the number of people who could read increased, the remaining illiterates, now a minority, were embarrassed and embittered by their disability. Charles Saw recalled his first awareness of class inequity upon seeing another youth reading: 'The sight … forced upon my mind a sense of painful contrast between his position and mine. I felt a sudden, strange sense of wretchedness.'[116] Parents and children shared an intense hunger for literacy. Deeply regretting their own ignorance, illiterate parents were often fanatically devoted to their children's schooling. The wife of a Paris weaver in 1857 'blushes and suffers on account of her ignorance; … accordingly, the couple are determined to give their four children as good an elementary eduation as possible.'[117] In part, this was a practical concern; parents could foresee that the best jobs in the future would require basic literacy. They realized that their children would need to be able to read and write to get on in a world where notification, contract and exchange were now routinely transacted through print.[118] But parents were not thinking solely of employment prospects and material well-being. They also wanted their children to be able to express themselves, to participate and enjoy life to the fullest. To do so, they needed to be able read a newspaper or a good book, and write a letter to a loved one. Since the teaching of these skills was beyond the grasp of most parents, someone else would have to assist their children; increasingly, parents looked to the schools for literacy training. Now, in this second phase, the growth of schooling did play a major role in raising the literacy levels of the labouring classes, spreading a culture 'which endowed the act of reading with a moral as well as a practical significance'.[119] Literacy had become a measure of working-class respectability.

Rates of female literacy had been much lower than male rates in the eighteenth century, but during the nineteenth this gap was gradually closed; by 1913, there was very little difference between the sexes. The rise of mass schooling was undoubtedly an equalizer. Schooling had traditionally been seen as more important for boys, and in most places the enrolment of girls lagged. In France in 1837, for example, 1.6 million boys were enrolled in elementary schools, but only 1.1 million girls.[120] As schooling became more universal, the gap closed, and by the First World War it was virtually eliminated (tracing a similar trajectory to the literacy differential between the sexes). The equalization of school enrolment does not imply, of course, that boys and girls were treated similarly in the classroom.[121] Clear differences in curriculum were manifest from the outset. In Catholic countries, religious instruction figured much more prominently in the training of girls than that of boys; and virtually everywhere boys were assigned more arithmetic, while girls were taught practical domestic skills such as needlework. 'The prevailing assumption among parents and educationalists alike was that girls should be prepared for a role in the home rather than in the wider world.'[122] Working-class parents construed this mandate in practical terms, with a focus on domestic skills, while ruling-class educators, particularly Church leaders, sought to train girls in morality. In

1841, the National Society in Britain declared that the supreme purpose of female education was 'to teach the young women to be sober, to love their husbands, to love their children, to be discreet, chaste keepers at home, obedient to their husbands, that the word of God be not blasphemed.'[123]

Given a pervasive belief that males and females were polar opposites by human nature, there was a general consensus that the best way to train the sexes was in separate institutions. If the funds for building and staffing schools had been unlimited, the result would have been two elementary schools in every district. But since the twin-school ideal was simply too expensive in an era of rapid school expansion, funding limits brought about a progressive result in this case. Within integrated schools, severe space constraints and a scarcity of teachers minimized the degree to which the classroom experience of boys and girls could be differentiated; in practice, the system was far less disparate than educators or parents would have wished. As schools grew in size and became better equipped, the divergence became more pronounced, with the sexes increasingly segregated for particular classes and girls taught a fuller range of domestic skills and an appropriately 'feminine' demeanour.

The prevailing feminine ideal construed extensive classroom exposure to history and geography, for example, as superfluous for girls; many inspectors felt that the 'excessive' pursuit of such knowledge would warp the development of women's true nature. In a comment that was typical of the age, the primary-school inspector in Lille thought that 'education for girls can dispense with the mental exercises which prepare young boys for the struggles and dealings with life.'[124] The saving grace of the elementary schools, however, was that this sexist paternalism was not extended to basic literacy. There was a consensus that girls should learn to read, write and do basic sums, so that as future homemakers they would be able to shop intelligently, keep the family budget in order, read the papers and write a letter. Convinced of the paramount need for literacy, working-class parents objected to girls wasting their time scrubbing school floors, and in some districts complained that sewing classes took up time that could be better spent teaching their daughters to read and write.[125]

The devotion to basic literacy implied a commitment to teaching a common core curriculum at the primary level; its implementation certainly had a progressive impact on gender relations. As well as reducing the literacy gap, integrated schooling strengthened the case for female suffrage and contributed to the breakdown of procreative fatalism, as working-class women became increasingly instrumental in limiting their fertility. The system's impact on entrenched conjugal roles, however, was overwhelmingly conservative. Elementary schools helped to socialize a younger generation of reliable male breadwinners and devoted female homemakers, prepared to sacrifice their interests for the sake of the family. While schools were not germane to the formation of this marital ideal, they made an important contribution to its perpetuation.

The Effects of Compulsory Schooling on Working-Class Families

From its diverse community and parish beginnings in the late eighteenth century, the great movement of mass schooling was gradually taken over and centralized by the state. The legislative introduction of universal schooling (in Britain, through the Elementary Education acts of the 1870s; in France, through the Ferry Laws of 1882) marked a turning-point in the process of institutionalization. As these legal initiatives were effectively implemented in the next two decades, the system emerged in its modern form: constitutionally guaranteed as universal and compulsory; Christian but non-denominational; funded entirely by taxes; staffed by trained and accredited teachers; administered by professional bureaucrats; regulated by elected school boards; and committed to the adoption of standardized timetables, curriculum, textbooks, tests and grade levels.

The consolidation of modern state schooling had far-reaching effects on working-class families. While the new schools did temper the sermonizing moralism of Church schools, they inherited and built upon the latter's multi-tiered, class-ridden structure; in this respect, they were its true offspring. By contrast, the indigenous schools of the working class were displaced. No significant elements of their legacy survived, and the artisanal tradition of self-education withered. This disintegration was not inadvertent: 'It was the aim of the reform to destroy rather than to supplement these institutions.'[126] The phasing out of private fees and the shift to tax-based funding was widely regarded at the time as a great advance for popular education. In fact, it was a Pyrrhic victory. However onerous, the direct payment of fees had ensured a measure of control by parents over the form of schooling to which their children were subjected. When taxes replaced fees as a funding base, working-class communities still paid their way, but they lost the power to determine, or even to influence substantially, the selection of teachers, the curriculum, the academic calendar, school standards and regulations.[127]

The main purpose in passing legislation making attendance compulsory for children of a specified age was to drag an unwilling minority of 'street Arabs' from the 'dangerous classes' into school for the first time.[128] Fearing that there had been a complete breakdown of parental control over young children among the poor, the advocates of coercion often posed the alternatives in apocalyptic terms. Francis Adams of the National Education League considered the debate over compulsory legislation to be the most important that had ever come before the country or the House of Commons: '[Will] the children of the masses be trained in streets, gutters, kennels and hovels, encompassed by misery, vice, dirt, poverty and crime … or in properly appointed and conducted schools?'[129] Spokesmen for the upper layers of the working class did not put the issue in such moralistic terms, but they arrived at a similar conclusion. While striving to preserve the control they had enjoyed over fee-funded schools, they felt that the 'better class of working men had to carry on their backs' the poor, and 'those men who do not understand the value of an education must be made to understand it.' Respectable working-class parents were wary of a mass influx of 'rough and ragged' children, laden with lice and devoid of discipline, into their children's classrooms. Yet they felt that compulsory schooling was needed, and that their 'taxes should be expended on schools instead of on prisons and workhouses.'[130]

Since attendance had been approaching universality in the decades immediately before the introduction of compulsory legislation, the move merely accelerated trends already under way. The new laws did not require attendance for the full school year, and their enforcement was extremely uneven, yet their overall impact was none the less considerable. Forced attendance created hardship for the poorest families, due to the loss of their school-age children's productive contribution. Since children's wages had traditionally gone directly to mothers, they bore the brunt of the blow. By turns belligerent and contrite, mothers faced truant officers at the doorstep and were summoned by school boards to explain their children's absence. The minutes of such meetings 'suggest the extent to which mothers would fight to maintain their traditional power.'[131] Magistrates were initially inclined to accept parents' arguments concerning the need for their children's labour contribution; over time they became less sympathetic, dealing with resistant parents more and more harshly.

When schools compelled working-class children to conform to middle-class standards, they established public benchmarks for an acceptable quality of childcare, stigmatizing parents whose children failed to measure up. School administrators' insistence on enforcing certain standards of cleanliness and neatness exerted enormous pressure on mothers. For most, it meant more work: 'more washing and ironing, bathing and hair-washing, mending and patching and such time-consuming activities as the struggle against head-lice'.[132] The poorest, unable to dress their children 'decently', were forced to withdraw them from school. Parents repeatedly testified in truancy hearings that they wanted their children to be educated, but could not afford to outfit them properly or withstand the loss of their income and assistance around the house.[133] As Mrs Jones, the mother of a truant, pleaded with a London magistrate: 'Please sir, I ain't got no boots to put on 'is feet. My 'usband's been out of work this four months, and I've got six little ones at 'ome.'[134] There is no doubt that parents' resistance against the school authorities was economically induced; overwhelmingly, it was the children of the poverty-stricken who were truant. On the face of it, this was a struggle between parents and the state over the deployment of economic resources. But since the resource in question was the labour-power of their children, the resistance of the poor also involved a struggle to preserve a way of life based on the integrity of the family as a productive unit and the unfettered custodial power of parents over their children.

It was not only the poorest families that were affected by the new regulations. By decreeing a minimum amount of schooling for every child, the state had removed from parents their right to decide how much schooling their children would receive. Regardless of extenuating circumstances, it was now illegal to send them to work. As one opponent remarked, the law 'meddled in household business, its necessities and wants.'[135] By regularizing attendance and extending the number of years children were enrolled, the system compelled working-class families to reverse the priority of work and school. Previously, conflict between the two commitments had been resolved in favour of child labour. Now, school came first. Domestic chores or part-time employment could be undertaken only outside school hours, and a full-time job had to wait until youths reached the minimum leaving age or had passed a 'compulsory standard' exam. The extension of schooling decreased the economic benefits to parents of having children while raising their costs, shifting the incentive structure for childbearing. While this trend had been under way for some time, the enforcement of regular attendance for almost all children by the 1890s reversed wealth flows between the generations. Children ceased to be a form of familial wealth and became instead a net drain on their parents over the life-course.[136] In the next chapter, we shall examine the demographic ramifications of this watershed; here, let us look at its significance for parent–child relations.

By removing from parents the right to allocate their children's labour-power, the state placed the school's authority over and above the family's. The persistent harassment of 'ignorant parents' by school inspectors and civil magistrates reveals a struggle to bring recalcitrant families into line with the new regime. The officers of the state were saying, in effect, 'we will buttress your parental authority only if you knuckle under and align your socializing efforts with ours.' The school's ostensible objective was not to compete with the family but to complement it, not to displace parental authority but to reinforce it. While teachers revered the family in the abstract and told children to respect and obey their parents, the impact of middle-class schooling on the parental authority of working-class adults was often corrosive. The pervasive distrust and frequent hostility that working-class communities exhibited towards teachers and school administrators was well placed; the stature of parents in their children's eyes was being subtly undermined.

As curriculum, testing and grading became increasingly standardized in the twentieth century, students were vertically ranked in competition with one another. School performance, it was widely held, was a reflection on the quality of the family. If students did poorly, the parents were faulted: either they were of inferior 'genetic stock', or they had failed to provide a proper home environment for the child's early development. While disparaging judgements of this sort had always been integral to upper-class condescension concerning their social subordinates, school systems now furnished ostensibly objective tests which 'proved' proletarian inferiority. However much schools praised family values, the inculcation of meritocratic principles embodying the ideology of possessive individualism was deeply antithetical to the collective solidarity of working-class families.

As schools grew larger, students were increasingly segmented into forms and separate classrooms; in response, children's culture became more age-stratified. The rigid hierarchy of school grades, of annual promotion and the stigma of failure, reinforced age hierarchies and the pecking order of the street and play-ground, undercutting more integrated, age-diverse forms of play and friend-ship. The homogeneous age-stratified peer group emerged as a major cultural force, challenging adult authority in general and parental authority in particu-lar. The very fact that parents were legally compelled to send their children to specialized institutions to prepare them for work and citizenship demonstrated parental inadequacy in the fulfilment of these tasks. The institution of a legal school-leaving age, with working-class youth departing in droves to seek full-time jobs, created a modern-day rite of passage. When this giant step towards adulthood was taken, family members were sideline spectators.

As literary skills became universally valued, the hierarchy of esteemed knowledge tilted strongly against the traditional strengths of working-class cul-ture. Schools venerated 'scientific learning' based on the assimilation of textual knowledge remote from the students' life-world, while effectively derogating forms of knowledge based on practical experience transmitted orally through indigenous networks. This reordering of the knowledge hierarchy had inter-generational effects within the working class, discrediting the accumulated wisdom of the community's elders earned by dint of hard work, direct experi-ence and seniority. Schooling separated students from their families and in-volved them in forms of training that were inaccessible to working-class adults. As each generation outstripped their parents in reading, writing and arithmetic, 'book learning' awed and humbled semi-literate adults. The fact that most were keen for their children to learn to read and write, despite the fact that it made them feel stupid by comparison, is a testament to the strength of their motivation to 'do well by their kids' in preparing them for the future. In the meantime, repeated assertions of parental rule, heated rebukes to children who were 'too smart for their own good', could not effectively restore the slowly crumbling edifice of custodial power, once the epistemic foundations of parental credibility had been dislodged. As Max Weber realized, when 'the individual receives his entire education increasingly from outside the home, ... he can no longer regard the household as the bearer of those cultural values in whose service he places himself.'[137] While democrats of all stripes will welcome the attenuation of domestic patriarchy in the wake of universal schooling, democratic socialists can hardly celebrate the subordination of indigenous working-class authority to the centralizing power of the state.

Emergence and Consolidation of the Male-Breadwinner Norm

The male-breadwinner ideal is the notion that the wage earned by a husband ought to be sufficient to support his family without his wife and young children having to work for pay.[138] In the nineteenth century, only the uppermost strata of working men in the skilled trades were able to win high enough wages and sufficiently steady year-round employment to be their families' sole moneymakers. Who would make up the difference in less fortunate families? Usually it was the children, leaving school at an early age (if they attended school at all), taking full-time jobs and turning their wages over to their mothers.[139] The employment of a man's sons and daughters did not undermine his pride as a breadwinner nearly to the same extent as the employment of his spouse. A wife's place was in the home; her husband was something of a disgrace if she had to go out to work.[140]

As a form specific to the class of wage-earners, the male-breadwinner ideal was new, becoming prominent in Britain in the middle decades of the nineteenth century and somewhat later on the continent.[141] But it did not arise *ex nihilo*. The proletarian breadwinner is a modern version of 'the family provider', that venerable figure of masculine pride through the ages. The provisioning onus is an ancient one, a cornerstone of patriarchal ideologies in a great variety of cultures. Fulfilling his obligations to his wife and children, a good provider takes charge of securing the household's subsistence. The conscientious execution of this responsibility (together with the closely related duty to protect the 'weaker' members of the family from physical and moral danger) legitimates his domestic authority as head of the household.[142]

There was nothing novel about the expression of this ideology among all social classes in the nineteenth century. However (for reasons we will explore in a moment), it came to be articulated by male trade unionists in a new form, tying the provisioning ideal directly to the notion of a 'living wage' for men.[143] Proletarians of both sexes became convinced that if a working man was prepared to work steadily, he deserved to earn a wage that would suffice by itself to provide his family with a decent life, according to the standards attained by respectable members of working-class communities. And if a married man was able to earn a living wage, then his wife had no business going out to work; this was the feminine corollary of the masculine wage standard. The male-breadwinner ideal thus affixed a wage-rate benchmark to a division of labour between spouses that was broadly held to be natural, and hence proper, for all classes. In this context, the proletarian definition of a good husband became one who did not abuse his patriarchal prerogatives: a man who held his job on a steady basis and brought his pay home reliably. Once he handed his wife her housekeeping allowance, his family responsibilities were discharged.[144]

As we have seen, this specific version of the provisioning ideal was not prevalent among labouring communities in the eighteenth and early nineteenth centuries. At that time, wives were still considered to be productive members of a family labour-team and there was no general hostility to their gainful employment.[145] Their undeniable contribution to the family economy was reconciled with the ideology of male provision by holding that a man met his obligation by assuming active leadership of the household economy. Making ends meet was a collective endeavour. In so far as the household remained the site of domestic production, there was normally no way to distinguish the working man's contribution from that of other family members.[146]

With the decline in opportunities to generate income while working at home, the conception of the family as a group of co-producers faded rapidly. Wage income ceased to include any part which could be attributed to the wife's domestic labour. The product of her unpaid exertions at home was now solely the labour-power of family members, which was consumed elsewhere. With the deepening fetishism of the individuated wage, this intangible product disappeared from sight, and the wage-earner was credited monetarily.[147] Apparently, men went out to work on their own and earned wages by virtue of their own labour. The increased reliance of the working-class household on money income as the first subsistence resource spelled a deepening reliance of the household's main shopper on its primary wage-earner, not merely to *earn* the money but also to *hand enough of it over* so that she could make ends meet. Spousal *interdependence* assumed the unbalanced form of the housewife's *dependence* upon her husband.

The traditional acceptance of a woman working for pay had been predicated on her subordinate but essential place as a productive member of a family unit. If she could earn money at home, this conception was preserved. When working outside the home, she must do so as a member of a family labour-team (as women generally did in fields, mines and textile factories) to conserve the traditional sense of a woman's place. As family hiring and subcontracting declined, women found it increasingly difficult to obtain these kinds of employment. A rising proportion of those who did work for pay were hired as individuals. They sought jobs outside their homes, competed with men on an open labour market, worked alongside men who were not their kin under the supervision of unrelated males, and took possession of their own wages. These practices were beyond the bounds of patriarchal stricture.[148] They enabled women to achieve a public presence and economic independence that flouted traditional norms of their proper place. When these employment opportunities began to predominate and the more traditional types declined, strong sentiment arose against wage labour for women.

Changes in the form of labour recruitment, supervision and wage payment were not, however, the whole story. It was the direct threat which the widespread employment of women constituted to the job security and wage levels of skilled tradesmen which galvanized the unions into action, and led eventually to the general adoption of the male-breadwinner norm by the labour movement.[149] While the individuation of the wage *form* was an inevitable product of capitalist development, the triumph of the male-breadwinner *norm* was not.[150] Rather, its consolidation was the outcome of a protracted struggle in which the mainstream of the union movement reacted in a narrow exclusionist fashion to the very real threat which the mass employment of women as cheap labour represented to the job security and wage levels of skilled tradesmen. Other responses were possible along integrationist lines; in this case counterfactual speculation is not utterly fanciful. There were minority currents in the labour movements of Britain and France, for example, that pushed unions to take a more progressive stance in combatting divisive gender-based job competition in the labour market, fighting for women's full integration under a programme of equal pay and job access.

In Britain, early fears that industrialization would give work to women and children 'to the exclusion of those who ought to labour – the men' were expressed in discussions of the Factory Bill of 1833.[151] A general sentiment arose that men should have first choice in the labour market; women would have to take whatever jobs were left after men's employment needs had been fulfilled. It was a short step from the prioritization of men's employment rights to arguments for women's exclusion in sectors where their recruitment threatened to undercut men's job security and pay. Brushing against the grain, the Owenite socialists were at the centre of a minority current in the Chartist movement which had a positive attitude to women's employment and sought to help them join or organize unions wherever they were employed.[152] However, the demise of Owenite socialism and the decline of Chartist insurgency by the late 1840s left the labour movement a subdued and conservative force. The notion of a fair wage as the male breadwinner's pay was in ascendancy. In 1851, Henry Mayhew drew the poverty line for 'bare wage sufficiency', distinguishing good wages from bad, as 'a rate of remuneration as will maintain not only the labourer himself while working and when unable to work, but support his family, and admit to the care and education of his children'.[153]

Across Western Europe, unions stiffened their opposition to married women's employment during the latter half of the century. In 1877 the leader of the British Trades Union Congress, Henry Broadhurst, framed the issue in bluntly patriarchal terms. It was the duty of male unionists:

> As men and husbands to use their utmost efforts to bring about a condition of things where wives and daughters would be in their proper sphere at home, instead of being dragged into competition for livelihood against the great and strong men of the world.[154]

In France, where proletarianization was less advanced, the dominant artisanal current in the labour movement, imbued with Proudhon's corporatist perspective, adopted exclusionary tactics. Proudhon was perfectly explicit: women's place was by the hearth in the households of independent producers. The national congresses of craft unions committed themselves to the fulfilment of this ideal in the 1870s.[155] By the First World War, the idea of 'a living wage' sufficient to support a family had become a potent fixture in the labour movement and a primary objective in trade-union bargaining, endorsed by workers' parties throughout the developed capitalist world.

While the male-breadwinner *ideal* had become nearly universal, there was considerable variation within the working class both in the vigour with which it was expressed and the extent to which it was attainable. In textile districts, where married women's employment remained at 20 to 30 per cent throughout the nineteenth century, the male-breadwinner *norm* was never firmly established, and women's work outside the home was not regarded as shameful or deeply embarrassing to their husbands.[156] Yet even here, it was a widely held aspiration for women to stop working outside the home at marriage or soon after.[157] Being able to obtain high enough wages to support one's family became a hallmark of masculine respectability, distinguishing the upper layers of the working class from the labouring poor.[158] German factory inspectors reported that skilled workers 'thought it insulting if their wives were engaged in paid employment outside the household.'[159] Similarly in England, 'a married man whose wife worked, well, you turned up your nose at him. ... If she did go out to work, you never told anybody.'[160]

While the importance of the male-breadwinner ideal for working-class conjugal relations is difficult to overestimate, the norm itself is an elusive cipher, much less substantial than its proponents imagine. The fixing of a universal wage benchmark is an arbitrary abstraction, based on the convenient fiction of a typical family group (for example, 'a living wage for a family of four'). The reality, of course, is that households vary in size and many wage-earners do not support families. Furthermore, the subsistence costs of families fluctuate considerably over the course of the family cycle, according to the number of children living at home, their ages and employment opportunities.

Since income sufficiency is a moving target, the question of what constitutes a living wage remains indeterminate.[161] Employers are thus able to pay lip service to the ideal without coming close to meeting demands for the unions' version of a living wage.

The male-breadwinner wage norm became a compelling construct by the late nineteenth century, despite its vagueness, or perhaps (in part) because of it.[162] The reasons for its enduring attraction are not hard to fathom. In the first place, a 'family wage' was a tremendous source of pride for the working man who was able to bring it home. If his paycheque was 'decent', his family could live decently – self-reliantly, without having to beg or borrow from anyone. The missus could stay home and 'bring the kids up proper'. Such thoughts lent the most noxious jobs a consoling dignity, making the long hours of wear and tear bearable.[163]

Beyond the size of one's paycheque, it has never been easy to derive much satisfaction from alienated labour. Other potential sources of labour pride were limited. Some workers found genuine pleasure in the act of creation; craftsmen, for example, typically took pride in their work. But industrial capitalism systematically divorced product design from production and subdivided tasks to such an extent that this form of job satisfaction, predicated upon an integrated labour process, became relatively rare. Beyond the skilled trades, many working men took pride in the competent performance of tough physical work – the type that 'real men' did, of which females and male office workers were presumably incapable.[164] Pursuing this form of masculine identity was a young buck's game; the lure of heavy manual labour faded quickly as men grew older and the work took its toll on their bodies. For family men, the capacity to earn enough to 'keep the wife and see the kids through school' became the centrepiece of masculine pride in wage labour.

The other major attraction of 'a living wage' was its power as an ideological weapon to wield against employers in the struggle for higher wages. As capitalism submerged all customary standards of 'a fair day's pay' beneath the price-setting rationale of demanding whatever the market would bear, the labour movement fought to preserve a moral dimension in wage bargaining.[165] The 'living wage' became a cornerstone of labour's righteousness. Working men could motivate their demands for higher pay in terms which the propertied classes found morally unassailable. They could say, in effect: 'If we were decently paid, our wives could remain at home and become good homemakers (just like your wives), and our children could stay at school and get a good education (just like your children).' By the values the propertied classes held dear, these were wholly honourable goals; they were nevertheless jeopardized by the anarchic workings of capitalism. In highlighting the discrepancy, unions put employers on the defensive and condemned the operation of the free labour market by the criterion of a higher value – the sanctity of the family – shared by all social classes.[166]

This was a compelling argument within the moral universe of late-Victorian society; it was also resonant within the economic discourse of the marketplace, displaying a suitable flexibility in the way the case could be put.[167] On the one hand, one might argue that only if men were able to win a living wage would their wives and young children be freed from the economic compulsion to submit to capitalist exploitation. On the other hand, reversing cause and effect, one could insist that only if women and children were barred from employment would men's wages ever rise to the level of a living wage and their families be properly supported.[168] This latter argument, far more pernicious from women's standpoint, gained increasing currency in the trade unions over time, legitimating the drive to restrict women's employment.

No voice was to be heard within the workers' movement opposing women's exclusion from a feminist standpoint, contesting the male-breadwinner ideal and the domestic rock upon which it was built – the primacy of women's housekeeping duties and men's abstention from them.[169] The main argument against restricting women's employment was that exclusion ignored the fact that women sought wage labour because their households lacked the steady income of male breadwinners. One of the first suggestions that 'females of any age' should be excluded from factory employment appeared in the *Examiner* in 1832. The 'Female Operatives of Todmorden' replied, putting the case for working women in these terms:

> For thousands of females who are employed in manufactories, who have no legitimate claim on any male relative for employment or support, and who have, through a variety of circumstances, been early thrown on their own resources for a livelihood, what is to become of them? ... [They] have been forced, of necessity, into the manufactories from their total inability to earn a livelihood at home. ... As we are a class of society who will be materially affected by any alteration of the present laws, we put it seriously to you, whether, as you have deprived us of our means of earning our bread, you are not bound to point to a more eligible and suitable employment for us? [170]

The merit of this argument was tacitly acknowledged by exclusionists who exempted single women and spinsters when calling for the phasing out of married women's employment.

Retreating from a positive appreciation of women's productive role in the family economy, women's right to employment was defended as a temporary and exceptional necessity. This position conceded that the optimal situation was for men to earn a living wage so that their wives would not have to work for pay.[171] Even women in the labour movement who were champions of women's employment rights favoured the male-breadwinner arrangement wherever possible, and 'agreed that the withdrawal of female labour would benefit male wages with the additional advantage that working-class homes would be better ordered and managed.'[172] The essential reason for this retreat is not hard to discern. Women who could afford to give up an exhausting and debilitating double day of labour when they married were gratified to be able to do so. Understandably, they became the envy of women who were forced to continue toiling outside the home while raising a family.[173]

If the male-breadwinner ideal commanded near-universal assent, the exclusionist remedy for its absence did not. Even as they defended themselves against the threat of cheap female labour, working men who did not earn enough to be their families' sole breadwinners sought wage work for their spouses. In the 1840s, the male framework knitters of Leicester strove to protect their skilled positions by strictly segregating the textile labour force; but since their families needed supplementary income, they also assumed that their wives would continue to work.[174] In most mining districts of England and Scotland in the same decade, male colliers came to feel that the pits were no place for women and agitated to have them removed. Yet their testimony to the commission examining women and children's work in the mines was 'full of demands for alternative employment and they clearly feared that sole dependence on the male wage would cut their standard of living'.[175] Parisian seamstresses and tailors in the 1840s 'associated women with domesticity, [but] neither defined it as an exclusive role which contradicted the ability or suitability of women for work.'[176] While attitudes hardened against women working in 1860s and 1870s, there was never a consensus on denying women's employment rights in general within the labour movement, the working class, or in society more broadly.[177] For the reality was that the great bulk of the unorganized working poor fell far short of one-wage family sufficiency; supplementary earnings were (and still are) essential. In the 1860s, Jules Simon estimated that only a tenth of Parisian working-class families could have subsisted on the wages of the househead alone. As child labour was curtailed and school attendance lengthened, the family burden of secondary earning fell increasingly on married women.

How could male earnings be raised to the level of family sufficiency? The main thrust of the unions' efforts was not to drive women from industry but to marginalize them, preserving – and if possible increasing – labour market segregation. They did this in a variety of ways: (a) by keeping men's jobs strictly separate from women's through elaborate classification procedures and harassing anyone of either sex who agreed to work on the other side of the line; (b) by upholding rules of all-male apprenticeship and refusing to provide any form of training or assistance that might facilitate gender crossover; and (c) by working to rule or going on strike whenever capitalists attempted to displace men in higher-paid jobs by introducing women into the lower echelons of 'male' trades.[178] This was basically the same way that craft unions responded to the employers' recruitment of other forms of cheap labour, such as children and immigrants. Their *modus operandi* was to control access to a trade, insulating their members from the threat of cheap labour competition in order to negotiate with employers from a position of strength.[179] In return for the consent of employers to curtail access, they offered labour peace on other fronts.

Women were different from other kinds of cheap labour, since their exclusion was bound up with the emotionally explosive issue of the proper division of labour between spouses. Yet male unionists were not waging a crusade against the employment of their own wives, as Heidi Hartmann has maintained.[180] Very few women who worked in industry were the daughters or wives of unionized workmen; if their husbands and fathers had been able to earn a skilled tradesman's wage on a regular basis, they would never have set foot in factories. As members of the same household, both spouses had a substantial stake in their partner's income. Attitudes to women's employment were directly conditioned by this interest, cutting across gender lines. While poor men defended their wives' employment rights, the wives of artisans endorsed attempts to limit female access to their husbands' trades.[181] The drive of craft unions to exclude women from membership and enforce their secondary status in industry thus pitted the higher-paid ranks of the skilled trades against the unorganized labouring poor.

Discussions at union conferences indicate that many men were troubled by exclusionary tactics, since they ran counter to the most elementary principle of labour solidarity: that an injury to one is an injury to all. To support legislated exclusion, they had to be convinced that it was female employment that prevented their members from attaining a living wage. How could such a proposition be persuasively argued? The key to sustaining the case was the notion, commonplace in the nineteenth century, that wages were drawn from a fixed fund regardless of the number of workers hired, and that the appropriate quantity of labour rendered in exchange ought to be fixed as well – the so-called 'lump o' labour'. In 1889, a trade unionist still believed that 'when married women ... become competitors against their own husbands, it requires a man and wife to earn what the man alone would earn if she were not in the shop.'[182] Reasoning thus, many unionists believed that if women would only withdraw, their forgone income would soon be restored by a rise in their husbands' wages. When this conception of how wage rates were determined was supplanted by more dynamic models based on changes in labour productivity and bargaining power, a central pillar of exclusionist ideology was toppled.

The rise of industrial unionism between 1880 and 1914 dealt a second blow to narrow corporatist strategies in the labour movement. As syndicalists gained the upper hand in the CGT in France, displacing the Proudhonist current in the early years of the twentieth century, they advanced a perspective of class integration. 'Syndicalism is a class grouping without distinction of one sex standing against the other for the bosses' profit', the CGT's weekly *La Voix du Peuple* declared. The CGT promised 'to preoccupy itself with propaganda, education and recruitment among working women'.[183] This break with explicitly protectionist strategies did not, however, lead to a discrediting of the male-breadwinner ideal. While a CGT committee pledged to reach out to organize women workers, it did so 'without claiming to be enthusiastic about the entry of women into factory work', and the level of union membership among female employees remained abysmally low.[184] In England, the exemplary 'match girls' strike [of 1888] turned a new leaf in the Trade Union annals', as the labour movement renewed its efforts to organize unskilled workers.[185] The Women's Trade Union League, formed in 1874, was itself transformed by this experience and went on to chalk up some notable victories in the 1890s, organizing small unions of women. Amidst the massive organizing drives of this period, there was a substantial rise in female union membership and several militant strikes by women workers.[186] These successes persuaded male trade-union activists that it was worth reaching out to organize women workers and create genuinely integrated unions. 'Never before', enthused the leaders of the WTUL, had men 'showed themselves more ready and more helpful than they are showing themselves now.' Yet this openness was a fragile, minority expression, soon to be overwhelmed by 'the ill-concealed jealousy and selfishness of male workers' as the threat of male unemployment loomed. By 1913, only 7 per cent of the 5 million women employed in Britain were unionized, almost three-quarters of them in textile unions. The new unionism had done nothing to shake the male-breadwinner norm. It was still common for male union leaders to advise married women 'to stay at home and not do men's work'.[187] This intransigence was evidently successful; married women's labour-force participation in England and Wales did not increase until the 1920s.

The union struggle to win a living wage for men resonated with a growing middle-class concern with the ostensibly deleterious consequences of women's employment for working-class families. The critics levelled several charges which registered alarm at the dissipation of patriarchal power and paternalist protection.[188] Married women were extremely vulnerable to the accusation that they had deserted their duties at home and jeopardized the well-being of their children to 'steal men's jobs' in industry. 'Their houses are therefore comfortless, their husbands driven to the gin shops, their children brought up in squalor, and they themselves thriftless and depraved', raved one moralist.[189] Factory inspector Hawkins insisted that a mother away at work all day was 'quite unable to teach her daughter those attractive qualifications which are to keep their husbands from disreputable associations'. Young factory girls were reputed to be 'nearly ignorant of the art of baking and cooking, and, generally speaking, entirely so of the use of the needle. ... When they come to marry, the wife possesses not the knowledge to enable her to give her husband the common comforts of a home.'[190] Working-class men often expressed similar sentiments. The Short-Time Committee of Manchester claimed that factory women would 'grow up in total ignorance of all the true duties of woman. Home, its cares, and its employments, is woman's true sphere, but these poor things are totally unfitted for [this].'[191]

The direct effect of factory work on women's health through their child-bearing years was a matter of serious concern. As mentioned, abnormally high rates of infant and maternal mortality in the manufacturing districts were attributed to high rates of employment for married women. But even more than their physical well-being, middle-class pundits worried about the morality of 'working girls'. It was the frequent refrain of many that women were toiling at rough work in hot, sweaty environments in close physical proximity to unrelated men. Working women had traditionally done rough, dirty and often dangerous work at home, and no one had worried about their delicacy or morality there. Why a sudden outcry over factory labour? The danger that commentators perceived arose not from the work itself but from the new social relations within which it was being done. Increasingly, factory employment took women away from the protection of their fathers and husbands, fostering extra-familial sex-mixing in anonymous urban settings. This 'unregulated mingling' was widely considered to place single women in 'grave moral danger'; they risked being unsexed and debauched in the process.[192] Factory inspectors in Imperial Germany found it 'self-evident [that] moral outrages occur where both sexes of a raw, often morally depraved class of factory-operatives work in one place, shoulder to shoulder, toe on toe, ... with young girls clad in very skimpy clothing.' Charged by the revised labour code of 1878 with safeguarding the 'health and morals of youth', the inspectors intervened vigorously to segregate the sexes in factories.[193] In France, Villermé was convinced that sexual promiscuity was rampant in textile mills, and blamed manu-facturers for failing to segregate the sexes.[194] These were not solely middle-class concerns. Manchester weavers complained that 'uninformed, un-restrained youth of both sexes mingle – absent from parental vigilance.'[195] Yet segregation of the sexes in the workplace could never solve the entire prob-lem, for large workplaces (textile mills in particular) brought great numbers of working girls together in one place. James McNish, a leader of the spinners' union in Scotland, worried that 'the tendency of bringing so many young women together to such an establishment as this [is] to render them vicious and dissolute and to demoralize them.' Lord Ashley warned that they were 'forming clubs and associations, and are gradually acquiring all those privileges which are the proper portion of the male sex.'[196]

Beyond the perils of the workplace, critics feared that the opportunity to dispose of their own spending money would tempt young women to stray. What would become of factory girls who used their wages to move away from home and live in unsupervised rooming-houses in seamy commercial districts? Surely they would come to no good. A Berlin teacher warned about working girls frequenting smoky dance halls where, after an evening of unchaperoned flirtation, 'many maidens in overheated, sensual states fall victim to passion. Yearly, one hundred and eighty thousand children are born out of wedlock in Germany.'[197] High rates of abortion in the manufacturing districts were often cited as proof that many girls had fallen before 'the plague of libertinage'. Middle-class observers were bothered by the dress and cheeky demeanour of proletarian women. Elise Deutsch, a German youth reformer, noted that 'among these girls cheap decoration, distorted hairdos and some cheap novelty in their toilette replaces concern for the value of the material and solidity of their clothes.'[198] A British factory commissioner complained: 'They often enter the beer shops, call for their pints, and smoke their pipes like men.'[199] It was widely held that wage-earning introduced young women to a lifestyle that would inevitably breed discontent later on when they married and were compelled to settle for a life of unpaid domestic toil. 'There is bred in them', thought Dr Barnardo, 'a spirit of precocious independence which weakens family ties and is highly unfavourable to the growth of domestic virtue.'[200] A German observer was concerned that the factory girl was taking on male attributes, becoming 'enlightened, cold, knowing. Nothing is more alien to her original character, nothing more harmful.'[201] If the risks attendant upon wage-earning were serious enough, what fate lay in store for those who were laid off and unable to find work? Many feared that unemployed girls were resorting to prostitution 'to find in loose living a supplement to their resources and finish by belonging only nominally to the trade they once practised.'[202]

Another liability of female wage-earning, critics charged, was that the practice encouraged men's natural indolence by spreading the household's income base. The breadwinner's obligation to provide a steady family income had a salutary effect on his attitude to work; there must be no let-up on this front.[203] Helen Bosanquet distilled conventional wisdom when she wrote: 'Nothing but the combined rights and responsibilities of family life will ever raise the average man to his full degree of efficiency, and induce him to continue working after he has earned sufficient to meet his personal needs.'[204] The Women's Labour League in Britain 'agreed that women's paid work had a bad effect on the father's willingness to earn.'[205] As far as employers were concerned, the one sure-fire method of reducing high quit rates among footloose workmen was to raise the proportion of the workforce who were married. The conversion of a great many employers to the potential merits of a higher-wage regime was intimately bound up with their growing appreciation of the domesticating effects of fulfilling the male-breadwinner ideal among the regularly employed core of their labour forces.

The business and professional classes increasingly came to see the consolidation of the male-breadwinner norm as the answer to their fears that the working-class family was about to disintegrate. In 1906, Bosanquet posed the same question as her Victorian predecessors had:

> Is it the case that when the Family has no property, or only property of such a nature that each member can, if he will, walk away with his share in his pocket, the Family ceases to be a reality? Or are there other forces and connecting links which preserve its strength, though in another form?

Unlike the Victorians, she was reassured to find 'very strong evidence against the alleged disintegration of the Family.'[206] Bosanquet argued that Le Play's prototype of the inherently unstable proletarian family was a phenomenon of *early* industrialization. It was inevitable that the Industrial Revolution would have 'shaken the Family itself'. Now, in a more mature phase, the family had 'successfully withstood the shocks of change and reorganized itself on another basis'.[207] She noted that working-class children were not leaving home in droves as soon as they collected their first pay, as her Victorian predecessors had feared. Most were staying at home and remitting their wages faithfully to their parents. Furthermore, masses of married women were not going out to work, but 'among the wage-earners at any rate there is an increasing tendency for women to devote themselves more exclusively to the work of housekeeping. ... They expect to have, and they get, the entire management of the family income.'[208] Working-class couples had evidently evolved a stable division of labour, with men, as primary breadwinners, secure at the household's helm, while their wives, as primary care-givers, took their place at the centre of domestic life. Since these were roles for which both sexes were ostensibly 'fitted' by Nature, Bosanquet was confident that their partnership portended a mutually satisfying and enduring complementarity.

The problem was that capitalism kept upsetting the arrangement. Periodically, the mass unemployment of male breadwinners threw the standard division of labour between spouses into turmoil. The more firmly the breadwinner norm was established in a community, the more devastating were the effects of long bouts of unemployment on men's self-respect as house-heads.[209] The low and irregular wages of primary breadwinners were a major source of marital conflict among the labouring poor. Non-support became the principal cause cited by working-class wives seeking separation and divorce in Britain (after this became grounds for divorce in 1886). The 1912 Royal Commission on divorce estimated that 50 to 80 per cent of couples were reconciled when the husband's income improved.[210]

Those infrequent occasions when women became the primary breadwin-

ners while their unemployed husbands kept house riveted the bourgeois imagination, raising the horrifying spectre of conjugal role reversal – 'an inversion
of the order of nature and Providence, a return to a state of barbarism, in
which the woman does the work, while the man looks idly on'.[211] The spectre
of unemployment rubbed a raw nerve in working men's psyches as well. Increasingly, they came to share with middle-class observers a deep revulsion at
the spectre of conjugal role reversal. Whenever unemployment rose sharply,
male hostility intensified towards working women who were 'stealing men's
jobs' in industry.[212]

Just as troubling as involuntary unemployment were the duties men were
compelled to take up at home – women's work. 'It is quite pitiable to see
these poor men taking care of the house and children, and busily engaged in
washing, baking, nursing and preparing the humble repast for the wife who is
wearing her life away toiling in the factory', lamented Lord Ashley. Engels
found it 'easy to imagine the wrath aroused among the working men by this
reversal of all relations within the family, while other social conditions remain
unchanged'.[213] Generating great alarm, the phenomenon gave rise to apocry-
phal tales: a man went to the alehouse, child in arms, and begged his wife to
come home. She replied: 'Not till I have finished my pint.'[214] Engels disclosed
the contents of a letter that told the poignant story of an unemployed man
(Jack) discovered by his mate (Joe) doing housework:

[Joe] found him in a miserable, damp cellar, scarcely furnished ... there sat poor
Jack near the fire and ... mended his wife's stockings with the bodkin; and as
soon as he saw his old friend at the doorpost, he tried to hide them. But Joe ...
had seen it, and said, 'Jack, what the devil art thou doing? Where is the missus?
Why is that thy work?' And poor Jack was ashamed and said, 'No, I know this
is not my work, but my poor missus is i' th' factory; she has to leave by half-past
five and works till eight at night, and then she is so knocked up that she cannot
do aught when she gets home, so I have to do everything for her what I can,
for I have no work, nor had any for more than three years and I shall never
have any more work while I live'; and then he wept a big tear.[215]

After recounting this doleful vignette, Engels waxed as indignant as Joe had
been at this 'insane state of things – this condition which unsexes the man and
takes from the woman all womanliness, without being able to bestow upon the
man true womanliness, or the woman true manliness – this condition which
degrades, in the most shameful way, both sexes and through them, Humanity.'
Engels was under the impression that this type of reversal 'happens very frequently', and claimed that in Manchester alone several hundred men could be
found 'condemned to domestic occupations'.[216] In reality, the vast bulk of adult
women working outside the home had no househusbands to keep the hearth
lit in their absence: they were widowed or had been abandoned.[217]

The other side of the emergent male-breadwinner ideal was a hardening of the notion that the domestic sphere was the domain of the feminine touch. The spatial separation between workplace and home and the temporal division between work and leisure were both deepening in this period, fortifying the conventional sense of men's and women's work as being entirely distinct and non-interchangeable.[218] The feminization of domestic service, heretofore a mixed occupation, reinforced the view that 'real men' would not be caught dead doing 'woman's work' around the house. In Engels's account, poor Jack was ashamed to be discovered by his friend mending. With many men, particularly those toiling at tough physical labour, it became a point of pride that they never lifted a finger to help out at home.[219] As a French worker put it, 'to the man, wood and metals; to the woman, family and cloth'.[220]

Transformations in Working–Class Housing

Wretched housing was a hallmark of urban working-class districts during the initial phase of industrialization, as we have seen. Domestic amenities improved somewhat in the second stage. Until the 1890s, substantial amelioration was mainly confined to prosperous layers of the working class; from that point on, however, better housing was more often enjoyed by the broad mass of proletarian families. Two major forces propelled the advance. First, the price of food and clothing deflated very substantially from 1873 to 1896 in the overproduction phase of the long cycle. As a result, most working families could afford to pay more for accommodation, and did, increasing the proportion of household expenditure allocated to shelter.[221] Rising rents and low vacancy rates stimulated house-building on larger plots. As the construction industry thinned out and became better capitalized, the quality of workmanship and building materials improved.[222] The second factor, probably of greater importance, was the radical overhaul of the urban infrastructure, funded by means of property taxes and a massive expansion of public debt. In addition to legislating and enforcing building codes and public health standards, city councils moved to establish municipal utilities that made provisions for waste disposal and water supply, gas and electricity, roads and tramways. By the early twentieth century, the modernization of basic amenities made cities livable for the working-class populace in a way they had never been before. Let us briefly review these advances.

After decades of worsening overcrowding, residential densities gradually eased. The number of persons per dwelling in Berlin, Frankfurt and Munich declined from around five in the 1860s to four by 1910. In 1861, 34 per cent of Scottish houses had only one room; by 1911, only 13 per cent did. The timing was, of course, dependent on the rhythm of industrialization; in late-developing Duisburg, crowding peaked in 1890, falling sharply thereafter.[223] If working people, on average, spent a larger part of the family budget on housing in 1913 than they had in 1850, they none the less obtained more value for their hard-earned pay than they had at mid century.

Improvements were very unevenly distributed, however. Although the bulk of new housing was built in prosperous districts, most newcomers, being poor, headed for slums where they squeezed into the existing housing stock. In the richest *arrondissements* of Paris from 1878 to 1889, housing starts exceeded population increase by 20 per cent; in the poorest districts, swelling numbers outstripped residential construction by more than 10 per cent. Whenever surges of in-migration coincided with cyclical depression in the building industry (as happened in the early 1870s), crowding worsened, rents soared, and the poor once again paid more for less. In the working-class district of Luisenstadt, Berlin, a higher proportion of dwellings had only one heated room in 1881 than twenty years earlier.[224] Overcrowding in the worst districts persisted in the best of times; from 1891 to 1911, the percentage of the population of England and Wales living in what were deemed to be overcrowded quarters declined only slightly: from 11 to 8 per cent. Proletarians living in great cities paid much higher rents than workers in smaller centres. Rents in London were almost double those in English provincial towns, and the ratio of wages to rent ran heavily in favour of tenants in smaller centres. In 1907, working-class households in Berlin laid out 24 per cent of their income on rent (roughly on a par with London and Paris); in Munich, they spent only 16 per cent.[225]

The greatest improvement in the domestic environment stemmed from a drastic upgrading of the urban infrastructure. While progress on this front was sporadic and piecemeal in the 1850s and 1860s, the forty-year period from 1873 to 1913 constituted, by all previous yardsticks, a great leap forward. Germany got off to a slow start in modernizing its urban infrastructure, but then forged ahead rapidly to surpass Britain by the 1890s. In the four years from 1875 to 1879, the proportion of Berlin households with piped water jumped from 40 to 80 per cent; Munich and Frankfurt were not far behind. By 1910, the homes of 92 per cent of the population of the major German cities (those with more than 100,000 people) were connected to sewers.[226] France lagged behind in all respects. In Paris, the decision to go over to water closets and a central sewer system was stalled for decades and then finally implemented in 1894. Substantial progress was made in the next decade, though by 1904 only 40 per cent of toilets in Paris were connected to sewers; in the working-class ghetto of La Roquette, just one in five were.[227] The public investments undertaken in the latter decades of the nineteenth century were massive, their size unprecedented. Between 1855 and 1913, for instance, the value of British and German waterworks multiplied fifteen to seventeen times. Within this period, the major surge in loans to municipal councils came in the 1870s and 1880s.[228] Except in the field of electricity, the technologies employed in this vast overhaul were not new; why, then, had renovation not been undertaken earlier?

After the cholera epidemics of the 1830s and early 1840s, the lethal effects of open drains, privies and polluted water supplies were widely acknowledged. In France, Villermé's pioneering studies demonstrated beyond reasonable doubt that poverty shortened life expectancy primarily through the medium of domestic deprivation and the infectious contamination of the poorest residential districts.[229] Chadwick's 1842 report revealed that the same basic correlations prevailed in British cities. It was still unclear precisely how diseases such as cholera and typhoid spread. But the types of environment that fostered epidemic dissemination and extraordinarily high rates of infant death were well enough identified to spark calls for regulatory action and major investments in waste disposal and water supply.

At the time these reports were first published and public consciousness was aroused, laissez-faire ideology was so powerful that the role of government intervention was strictly circumscribed. Central parliaments and local councils were able to pass legislation such as the Nuisances Removal Act of 1855 in Britain, which gave authorities the right to order landlords to upgrade dwellings 'unfit for human habitation'. But since the state played no positive role in the construction of housing, the inadvertent effect of such prohibitions was often to subtract dwelling-space from the available stock, exacerbating chronic shortages. In this context, inner-city residents were understandably ambivalent about municipal crackdowns on slum landlords, which often resulted in rent hikes or tenants being ousted from their lodgings without being able to find new quarters in the neighbourhood.[230]

Frequently, the apathy of the poor in the face of clean-up campaigns was interpreted as contentment with their present squalor, and the municipal drive to enforce housing standards would falter. The propertied classes were confident that there was a market solution to every urban ill. Festering cesspools, for instance, simply awaited the entrepreneurial initiative of those who would gather human excrement from the cities and sell it as fertilizer to farmers at great profit. But as urban waste accumulated, fouling city water supplies without attracting private capital, pressure mounted on governments to take remedial action. In 1846, only 5 per cent of municipal districts in Britain possessed their own waterworks; by 1881, 80 per cent did. The big breakthrough came when the Great Depression exposed the folly of government abstention; thenceforth, the prevailing winds of bourgeois opinion shifted decisively in favour of state intervention. Far from ushering in an era of 'municipal socialism', the shift to public provision was a last resort, and a practical solution to a pressing problem:

The propertied and commercial classes capable of influencing council policy realized that it would be in their self-interest to support municipal endeavour. The long-term benefits of a modernized water supply, including reduced fire-risks, lower industrial costs, the enhancement of property values, and a healthier work-force, were sought by the economic elites of manufacturing towns, rather than any kudos gained as a result of famous civil engineering projects.[231]

It was middle-class residents living in relatively clean neighbourhoods who resisted costly municipal initiatives, fearing that their property taxes would skyrocket.

Initially, many city councils simply required all new houses to be outfitted with drains and taps, leaving the established housing stock to fester. Instead of boldly embarking on a complete conversion to underground sewers, they proceeded piecemeal to cap open cesspools and prevent seepage into the surrounding soil, convert privies to the pail system, and regularize waste removal and water delivery. Under torpid leadership, progress was sluggish and extremely uneven. But as the urban reform bandwagon gathered momentum in the 1870s, councils became more aggressive. Those who were intent on rapid modernization voted to require all dwellings to install water closets in a matter of years, took out massive loans to lay a sewer grid, and followed up by offering subsidies to homeowners to defray installation costs. Newcastle proceeded through both these stages, and the pace of its progress appears to be fairly typical of Britain's cities. In the 1840s, only 4 per cent of Newcastle's houses were connected to piped water; by 1883–5, two dwellings in three were; and by 1914, virtually all were.

Late starters often moved quickly, once the political dam burst. Only 26 per cent of Manchester dwellings had water closets in 1899; by 1913, 98 per cent did. Well-publicized mortality differentials between towns were a powerful goad to dilatory councils, since the life expectancy of residents responded quickly to progress in sanitizing waste removal, treating sewage, and decontaminating water supplies. Similarly, the drive to universality was galvanized by reports of extreme mortality differences between districts within a city and even between dwellings on the same block. In Nottingham, the Medical Officer of Health pointed out that typhoid fever was three times as prevalent in houses with privies as in those with pails, and four and a half times as common in houses with pails as in those with water closets.[232]

Life expectancies in England and Wales were seven years longer in 1901 than they had been fifty years earlier; in France, they were nine years longer.[233] While it is impossible to calculate the independent contributions of various factors to this improvement, there is every reason to believe that the overhaul of urban water works and sewage systems was decisive. First, most of the gain in longevity occurred in cities, which closed the gap with rural areas from 1870 on. In 1851–5, life expectancy in the Paris region lagged more than ten years behind the French national average; by 1901–5, this had been cut to four and a half years. Second, a sharp reduction in death by infectious diseases accounted for the bulk of the advance. Of the entire mortality decline in England and Wales (from 1848–54 to 1901), 44 per cent was due to decline in airborne and 33 per cent to water- and foodborne diseases. In Paris, death by water and food-borne diseases fell from 86 (per 10,000 per annum) in 1854–6 to 22 by 1887–9.[234] Statistical analysis demonstrates that the mortality decline in France and England was due to cohort-specific influences rather than period effects; in other words, childhood advantages persisted through life. Preston and Van de Walle conclude:

> Improved water supply and sewage disposal, probably in conjunction with improved nutrition, reduced the incidence of diarrhoeal disease among children (post-infancy) and hence the incidence of other infectious diseases. Together, these factors resulted in improved physical growth and development which ... protect[ed] the cohorts from later death from many causes, infectious and non-infectious alike.[235]

Enhanced nutrition may also have contributed to longer life; it certainly improved people's health. Proletarian diets were still based on bread, potatoes and sugar, with very few dairy products and almost no fresh greens and fruit; they were chronically deficient in iron, calcium and vitamins. However, the quantity of these staples increased substantially, so that by the 1890s the energy level of the working-class diet was much closer to being adequate, with the daily intake of adults exceeding 2,000 kilocalories. One measurable result of improved nutrition was that the mean height of youngsters increased over time: low-income thirteen-year-olds, for example, gained two to three inches from 1880 to 1905.[236] In another index of basic health, the proportion of military recruits failing their physical examinations dropped sharply in these decades (ironically, just as the problem of 'physical deterioration' became the subject of public alarm). While 39 per cent of Parisian day labourers flunked their physicals in 1866, by 1900 less than 15 per cent did.[237]

One sobering note ought to be injected into this picture of substantial progress. In stark contrast to the rest of the age spectrum, infant mortality did not decline until the twentieth century. In 1900, 15 per cent of English babies died before their first birthdays, 16 per cent of French babies, and 23 per cent of German. Furthermore (in Prussia at least), the disparity between social classes in infant death widened between 1877 and 1913.[238]

Changes in Household Technology and Domestic Labour

A second key innovation of the years 1890 to 1913 was the introduction into working-class homes of gas as a cheap energy source, for heating, lighting and cooking. Gas had been used in street lamps and factories since the 1840s, and increasingly in the homes of the prosperous thereafter. Yet the installation costs of piping and fixtures proved prohibitive for working-class consumers, and quarterly billing procedures did not suit household budgeting based on a weekly pay schedule. Gas meters circumvented these obstacles. They were installed free or at a nominal charge, and the customer paid beforehand, a penny at a time for a limited period of use. Slot meters became an overnight success as soon as they were introduced. In the area of London covered by the South Metropolitan Company, over 80,000 meters were installed between 1892 and 1898, the first six years they were available. By 1914, meter-users comprised the majority of the gas companies' customers in Birmingham, Blackburn, Leicester, Liverpool, Newcastle and London. Beginning almost from scratch in 1895, 40 per cent of Berlin households were lit by gas by 1910, and 34 per cent were cooking with gas at that time.[239] The adjustable gas-mantle lamp introduced in the 1890s was much more efficient than earlier jet lamps; the resulting saving made it possible for most working-class households to abandon the dirty and dangerous paraffin lamp, whose sales began to wane in the first decade of the twentieth century. Paraffin lamps persisted, however, as 'the poor man's light' in the slums of large cities and in small towns passed over by gas companies.[240] Households were first lit by electric light bulbs in 1880, and although their superiority was immediately recognized, electrical power was too expensive to offer the gas companies serious competition until the interwar years. In 1913, the domestic use of electricity in Western Europe was still largely confined to the homes of the rich; only 6 per cent of British homes were wired at that date. What is striking in the case of both gas and electricity is the delay between their initial commodification for use by business and state enterprises and their eventual packaging for the domestic use of working people. Despite the very substantial advances of this period, proletarian households remained in a backwater, the last market to be opened in the diffusion of new technologies.[241]

How did all these changes affect domestic labour? There is no doubt that certain tasks – doing the laundry and cooking, for example – became less arduous for those homemakers who enjoyed the benefits of running water, gas stoves, and so on. Newly affordable household items such as linoleum, wall-paper and detergents made houses easier to clean. Yet for every 'new and improved' product available to the homemaker, domestic standards rose concomitantly. Linoleum was much easier to clean than wood or stone, but the kitchen floor now 'needed cleaning' twice a week; indoor taps, drains and new soaps made clothes easier to wash, but the teacher expected Johnny's trousers to be clean every school day. Housewives set higher standards for themselves, but they did so under the powerful sway of family expectations and pressure from middle-class agencies. The advertisers' claims of 'labour-saving' devices for the busy homemaker turned out to be a mirage – an elusive promise receding indefinitely into the future.[242] Every hour saved on one job was taken up with something else that needed doing.

The overall mix of women's work in the home shifted in this period. Production for use withered (or took on the character of a hobby) as food and clothing were increasingly purchased in forms that were ready to use, or in semi-fabricated states that required less time to prepare than they formerly had. With the decline of domestic piecework and the taking-in of lodgers, most women spent less time at home in moneymaking endeavours. On the other hand, the personal service demands of children and husbands increased. It is true that as the birth rate declined, women spent less time in childbirth and breastfed fewer infants; this meant less wear and tear on their bodies over time. One cannot infer from this, however (as Diana Gittins has done), that women spent less time and energy in childcare.[243] As family size shrank, there was a considerable intensification in the care of each child.

In public health campaigns aimed at reducing infant mortality, the child-rearing practices of working-class mothers came under fierce scrutiny. Noting that infant death was much more frequent in proletarian areas than in middle-class neighbourhoods, German inspectors blamed the ignorance and neglect of working-class mothers, holding them responsible for 'injurious health practices and for the numerous deaths of newborn children'. In Britain, a leading health officer declared that the problem of infant death was 'mainly a question of motherhood and ignorance of infant care and management'.[244] Major campaigns were undertaken to save the lives of infants (ignoring the fact that the rate of maternal mortality had not declined as infant death subsided). A central thrust of the effort in Germany, France and Britain was to convince mothers to breastfeed their children and delay weaning them, so that infants could avoid ingesting contaminated water and food. There is no doubt that prolonged breastfeeding reduced intestinal infection and helped preserve infant life; but it was also a considerable drain on undernourished women whose pregnancies followed one another year after year.

In the same period, some recognition of the importance of maternal care for the psychological development of children was fast becoming a shibboleth of 'enlightened' thought. Young children were now thought to require a mother's undivided attention at certain times of the day, and this would entail the partial separation of infant- and childcare from the rest of women's domestic chores. In a complete reversal of the previous half-truth concerning 'maternal instincts', the 'feckless' mothers of the working class were presumed to be entirely ignorant of their children's real needs; they stood in desperate need of education. In France, maternity hospitals sponsored the 'consultations de nourissons' which became a model for the new 'scientifically based' maternal education, dissipating poor women's suspicions and encouraging them to break with customary practices based on 'wives' tales' and community folk wisdom. Twenty-four neighbourhood dispensaries were opened in Paris between 1887 and 1895 to examine babies and to teach working-class mothers the proper hygienic ways to care for them.[245] Babycare centres run by middle-class women's and welfare organizations were set up in the working-class districts of most German cities and towns in the early twentieth century to inform expectant women and the mothers of young infants about healthy and 'rational' childcare practices.[246]

If poor women were often reluctant to visit such centres, then the message would be delivered directly. Proletarian doorsteps were inundated with a daily patrol of health inspectors, charity visitors, public nurses and truant officers. Citing a bewildering array of by-laws and regulations that poor tenants were forever breaking, these intruders force-fed working-class mothers with unsolicited advice on their childrearing and housekeeping practices.[247] The impact of such a guilt-driven programme is difficult to gauge, but it must have been considerable, despite the tenacious independence that proletarian women typically displayed in the face of middle-class remonstration. For these were not simply the free-floating fads of the upper middle class; they were incorporated in a larger programme of 'scientific' reform and brought down from on high by a burgeoning army of rectifiers ('governing and guiding ladies', as Beatrice Webb dubbed the charity brigade). Working in tandem with the schools, they exerted enormous pressure on working-class mothers to intensify the specific labour of childcare.

The personal service that a working man expected of his wife in return for bringing home his pay had traditionally centred on the practical necessities of daily life – preparing his meals, washing his clothes and cleaning up after him. As household technology improved, these duties were also subject to rising standards and demands, but the tasks themselves did not change. Throughout the nineteenth century, most working men had relied on workmates and male friends for companionship and emotional support; the duties of spouses in this respect were minimal. A good wife was 'considerate': she knew her man's domestic likes and dislikes as if they were her own, and she took care to ensure his physical comfort, keeping the children quiet when he was taking his ease. But she was not expected to be his leisure companion or confidante, much less his informal therapist. Around the turn of the century, the focus of leisure-time for men gradually shifted away from workmates towards the home and the neighbourhood. With the rise of entertainments that were couple- and family-oriented, such as music halls and holiday trips to the seaside, the nature of the conjugal partnership began to change.[248] This shift, diffuse and unevenly manifest, did not generate 'companionate marriages' in the modern, middle-class sense of the term; but it did take the husband-care aspect of the housewife's job into new terrain – that of stress management. What did not change in this period was the division of labour between spouses. The involvement of married women in extra-domestic employment remained stable at a very low level from 1890 to 1913 (in England and Wales, there was a slight decline). For their part, men did very little housework or childcare, even in the supplementary form of 'helping out'.

With the upgrading of their households as worksites, were working-class women able to claim a bit of leisure-time for themselves to match the shortening work-days of their menfolk? In a study conducted from 1909 to 1913, Reeves found that domestic work still occupied women's entire waking hours from six o'clock in the morning until ten at night. A Lambeth mother of two recounts what Reeves terms a 'very easy' day, beginning at 6 a.m. ('get up and light fire') and ending at 9.30 ('go to bed'). The longer day of a mother of four began at the pre-dawn hour of 4.30 ('wake husband who has to be at work about five o'clock') and finished at 10 p.m. ('nurse baby and go to bed'). None of the women whose daily timetables were recounted in the study listed any entry indicative of uninterrupted leisure activity for herself. In a few cases, we catch glimpses of leisurely work: 'sew while husband goes to bed. Talk while 'e's doin' it.'[249] Some days of the week were easier than others, of course. Washdays were the toughest; on these days there was little time for anything else. Mondays, on the other hand (in a domestic reiteration of Saint Monday workplace rituals), were 'mother's day', with a small amount of money in hand and a social drink in the pub customary in many neighbourhoods. Certainly women had time to chat with neighbours. However enjoyable these snatches of conversation were, they were also work-related:

> Gossip was the channel through which flowed the goods and help neighbours needed from one another. Indeed, the central female social activity was talk carried out standing in the doorway, in markets, and in shops, at common pumps or in wash-houses, yards, or kitchens.[250]

The Rise of Mass Transit

A third major breakthrough in this period was the provision of electric trams, transforming the daily journey to work for a steadily increasing proportion of the proletariat. Horse-drawn omnibuses (stretch carriages carrying ten or twelve passengers) began appearing in the 1830s, and spread rapidly. But fares were high, rides were slow and routes were few, carrying well-to-do passengers from the railway station to the central business district, for example. In the late 1860s, private companies with government contracts and subsidies laid track and introduced the horse-drawn tram system. Service was begun in Berlin and Hamburg in 1865–6, and in Liverpool in 1868. By the mid 1870s, horse-drawn streetcars were travelling the main thoroughfares of almost every major city of Western and Central Europe. The tram inaugurated the era of urban mass transit, doubling the omnibus's passenger capacity and top speed. Yet the class bias of the service was immediately apparent: routes typically connected middle-class suburbs to the city centre; morning service began well after factory whistles sounded and rush-hour fares were too expensive for daily use by most workers. The primary use of the horse-drawn streetcar by working-class riders was to provide transit for occasional trips to the outskirts of town on a weekend or holiday.

The electrification of streetcars in the 1890s vastly extended urban transit. The new vehicles were cheaper to operate, carried more passengers and ran faster. The start-up costs, however, were considerable – electric generators, motorized tramcars, overhead trolley lines, and relaid track on built-up roadbeds. When private companies operating horse-drawn streetcars proved unwilling to muster these outlays, municipalities took over the service. The results were soon evident:

- a rapid proliferation of lines: a tenfold increase in track length between 1893 and 1898, much of it through working-class neighbourhoods;

- more frequent service and extended timetables attuned to factory shift schedules;

- lower fares, down as much as 60 per cent for special workingmen's rates in fourteen of sixteen British municipalities. Fares were lower in 1903 than they had been under private management.

- a three- to fourfold increase in ridership in two decades.

Ridership in Glasgow jumped from 61 trips per person per annum in 1887 to 271 in 1913; Manchester's rate rose from 38 to 201 in the same period. In twenty-one German cities, the average rate jumped from 39 in 1890 to 137 twenty years later.[251] By the early twentieth century, a substantial and increasing minority of working people were taking trams daily to and from work.[252] What were the effects of the advent of mass transit on working-class life?

In the pedestrian cities of the nineteenth century, the twice-daily trek between home and work placed an outer bound on the distance between the two places, circumscribing the range of feasible movement for either site.

Long working days put a premium on living close to one's work, and as Chadwick noted, working people made 'considerable sacrifices to avoid being driven to a distance from their place of work'. In Halifax at mid century, 37 per cent journeyed less than a quarter of a mile to work, and only 3 per cent went more than a mile.[253] For families that were heavily reliant on the primary breadwinner's income, *his* place of employment set the radius within which they had to reside.[254] If they moved, it was essential to stay within this invisible circumference. If he changed jobs, taking him outside pedestrian range, his family would have to move closer to his new workplace. If other family members wished to obtain employment or to switch jobs, however, they had to take their residential location as a given and confine their search to workplaces within walking distance of home. The greater a person's domestic responsibilities, the tighter was the practical radius of the journey to work. (Compare those who had to return home at noon with others who could be gone all day.)

The time–distance bind of 'secondary' earners restricted women's labour-market participation and undermined their power in wage bargaining. Women do not routinely travel as far away from home as men do in the course of a day's work. This generalization holds across the entire spectrum of human societies from foraging bands to developed industrial states, based on women's near-universal childcare responsibilities. While the advent of mass transit potentially alleviated the disparity, the initial effect was to exacerbate it. While men's average journey to work lengthened considerably, women remained at home and in the neighbourhood. This marked localism was mainly due to an absence of childcare alternatives, but even for single women, low pay made the daily use of public transit an uneconomic proposition.

The creation of systems of mass urban transit that were reliable, affordable, and reasonably convenient did not do away with the journey to work as a temporal constraint, but in trebling and quadrupling the distance one could travel in an hour, it loosened the main breadwinner's spatial bond considerably. The shortening of the work-day in the same period further eased the situation, though for many, the time liberated from the tyranny of work was relinquished to longer commuting times. The spatial relaxation had a number of consequences for urban development and for working-class families. Victorian cities had been gradually moving away from the traditional landscape of small 'cellular units', where manufacturing, retail and residential sites were interspersed and closely packed. As small-scale workshops and outwork declined in importance, urban landscapes became more segregated and specialized by district and block. The major impediment to the spatial differentiation of cities had been the pedestrian journey to work. The advent of mass transit freed cities to spread out in sprawling suburbs located far away from industrial zones of concentrated employment. The growth of huge multi-industry cities fostered residential dispersion; the rise of mass transit hastened the process. Working-class communities were still intensely local, but their 'ingrained parochialism' was broken down.[255] Neighbours were less likely to work at the same place. They would know one another as neighbours, but not as workmates; the two social networks were becoming increasingly distinct. The coming of the electric tram system furthered the protracted process of separating households and neighbourhoods from the sphere of employment.

Mass transit also had a major impact on shopping patterns. Most people still purchased food close to home, but shoppers looking for clothing and home furnishings might now go by tram to specialized retail districts and department stores. The commercial success of retail districts, in turn, took business away from local shops. Residential neighbourhoods became increasingly specialized, losing a measure of self-sufficiency. In the prewar period, these shifts in consumer patterns were largely confined to the upper layers of the working class. It was the middle class and the most prosperous strata of the working class who took advantage of the tram system and moved to suburbs with cleaner air, newer housing and roomier dwellings, several miles from the breadwinner's place of employment. Casually employed labourers could not afford the fares of twice-daily transit to residences remote from their work; they were still stuck in city slums. Urban transit thus widened further the physical and cultural distance between 'respectable' and 'rough' proletarian neighbourhoods.[256]

The Settling of Working-Class Neighbourhoods

Working people moved house often in the nineteenth century. Only 17 per cent of the inhabitants of Preston lived at the same address in 1861 as they had a decade earlier; in Manchester, 18 per cent persisted. These cities appear to be typical.[257] Much of the moving was done by migrants from villages and towns taking up residence for the first time in a city, or travelling from one city to another. Sixty-two per cent of male househeads living in Leeds in 1861 had not been living in the city a decade earlier. In Liverpool ten years later, 71 per cent of househeads were not native-born. Sixty-four per cent of the Parisian population in 1881 were born elsewhere, as were 67 per cent of the residents of Reims, a textile town.[258] Migrants were mainly relegated to the bottom rungs of the labour force and crowded into the poorest parts of town. Urban influx also fostered subsequent moves within cities, as newcomers took up temporary accommodation with relatives or friends before securing their own quarters. The combined effect of all forms of mobility was a remarkable residential transience. In Manchester in 1868, a quarter of residents at specific addresses left within a year and 40 per cent within two years. In Liverpool, 40 per cent were gone a year later, while half had departed within two years. In

Essen in the Ruhr industrial belt at the turn of the century, roughly a third of dwellings were vacated within a year, and half within two years.[259]

Who was most likely to change residence? Young people living as lodgers were extremely peripatetic. While matrimony normally induced another move, thereafter it dampened wanderlust; married couples were inclined to say put, as were the elderly. Tenants were much more transient than homeowners, and workers were three times as likely to move as professionals.[260] The poor were forever moving, displaced by the forced closure of unsanitary buildings, evicted by landlords for failing to meet the rent, or vanished in the night to evade paying rent in arrears:

> We had so many addresses. We couldn't ... pay the rent. We had to keep moving. And we came home from school to find bits and pieces slung out on the road; or passed over the wall to the next bloke to look after.[261]

> I came to London twenty-five years ago [a poor woman informed an East End clergyman] and I have never lived in any room more than two years yet: they always say they want to pull the house down to build dwellings for poor people, but I've never got into one yet.[262]

While proletarians moved often, most did not go very far. Developing strong attachments to local neighbourhoods, they strove mightily to find accommodation close by. In Liverpool at mid century, 12 per cent of intraurban movers took up residence on the same street; a third moved less than a quarter-mile, and 70 per cent less than a mile. In Leeds, 55 per cent of intraurban movers were found to be living within a quarter-mile of the dwelling they had inhabited ten years previously.[263] If these people changed jobs, that too was done within a narrow radius. When a casual labourer was asked by a member of the Select Committee on Artisans' Dwellings why he did not move to the suburbs, he replied, 'I might as well go to America as go to the suburbs.'[264]

Working-class neighbourhoods gradually became more settled around the turn of the century. In 1891, almost 40 per cent of the population in German cities moved house each year; by 1912, less than 30 per cent did. In the 1870s, only 17 per cent of Leicester householders remained at one address for a decade; by 1914, 36 per cent did.[265] What we consider today to be 'traditional working-class communities' – socially tight, generationally persistent, territorially bounded, insular and street-oriented – emerged in the period 1890–1913. These were the 'urban villages' immortalized in Roberts's reconstruction of Salford in the Edwardian era, and in Young and Wilmott's famous study of Bethnal Green in the 1950s. In fact, they exhibited a greater degree of generational persistence than most English villages.[266]

Sinking strong roots in the neighbourhood provided an antidote to urban anonymity and proletarian insecurity. Reeves explained the rationale in 1913:

The people to whom Lambeth is home want to stay in Lambeth. They do not expect to be better off elsewhere, and meantime they are in surroundings they know, and among people who know and respect them. Probably they have relatives near by who would not see them come to grief without making great efforts to help them. Should the man go into hospital or into the workhouse infirmary, extraordinary kindness to the wife and children will be shown by the most stand-off neighbours, in order to keep the little house together until he is well again. A family who have lived for years in one street are recognised up and down the length of that street as people to be helped in time of trouble.[267]

There is no evidence that the desire of working people to remain in (or return to) the neighbourhood of their childhood grew stronger as the century wore on. The gradual settling of proletarian neighbourhoods must therefore be explained by a set of factors that enabled people to fulfil their aspirations in this regard more often than their predecessors had. Five changes seem to be germane:

■ With the demise of many industries that formerly utilized casual labour and a lessening in the seasonality of labour demand, there was a reduction in labour turnover and a regularization of wage income. Lower rates of job-changing cut down work-related residential mobility; steadier income made it easier to plan household budgets and meet the rent.

■ Until 1870, as we have seen, urban growth was dominated by in-migration; thereafter, indigenous growth (an excess of births over deaths) increasingly held sway. As the native-born proportion of the urban population rose, city neighbourhoods gradually accumulated generational depth.

■ With improving health and falling mortality, the incidence of precipitate family break-ups through death, permanent injury or serious illness (always a factor in high mobility) was significantly reduced.

■ While the tram system extended the housing market, making it easier to move away from one's workplace, it also made it easier to stay put when changing jobs. The latter effect seems to have been predominant initially.

■ Improved housing stock, less overcrowding, and a slight increase in home-ownership (still less than 10 per cent for working-class city-dwellers) raised people's level of satisfaction with their present accommodation. Increasing supply and a moderate rise in vacancy rates made it easier to stay in the local area if forced to move.

The long-distance proletarianization that typified the early phases of industrialization – with youth moving away from the village or town of their birth to seek work, accommodation and marriage partners in larger centres – had thinned out kin networks considerably. Studies of rural–urban migration in the nineteenth century have shown that this was not invariably an isolating experience; newcomers to the cities relied on kin networks that were 'stretched' over considerable distances. Nevertheless, it was inevitable that the fastest-growing city districts would be flooded with transients who had relatively few local kin connections. When economic stability and a thriving local economy enabled proletarians to settle down and sink roots in city neighbourhoods, local kin networks and multigenerational ties of friendship between neighbouring families soon multiplied.

The residents of working-class neighbourhoods exhibited a strong tendency to court and marry locally, as country folk traditionally had. In three London parishes around the turn of the century, Ross found that 'parish endogamy was nearly universal, with a majority of marrying couples residing indeed on the same street.'[268] In Huddersfield in 1880, only one marriage in five was conducted with an outsider. Seventy-one per cent of marriages in which both partners lived in town joined people whose parents' homes were less than one kilometre apart; just 4 per cent exceeded three kilometres.[269] While patterns of local endogamy were undoubtedly stronger in inner-city districts than in newer, more diffuse suburbs, it is notable that in Bobigny, a working-class suburb of Paris, 35 per cent of newlyweds chose partners from their own neighbourhood.[270] Wherever feasible, newlyweds strove to live close to their parents. Certainly they preferred to move out and set up their own households; few remained in their parents' household after marrying. But this 'neo-local' norm (in Laslett's terms) was intricately counterbalanced with a 'matrilocal' inclination to remain in the family neighbourhood. In Preston in 1851, 86 per cent of young householders lived within four hundred metres of the parental home.[271] Young brides were particularly keen to stay close to their mothers, since the relationship typically combined practical assistance with emotional support. Lady Bell recounts the story of a recent bride now living in her husband's 'part of town', half a mile from her mother's home. The entrenchment of neighbourhood boundaries created an overwhelming sense of distance between them. 'She was one day found in a flood of tears saying that she missed her mother so dreadfully that she didn't think she could be happy so far away from her.'[272]

The cultural significance of kinship in working-class communities is registered by the frequency with which adults encouraged children to call neighbours 'auntie and uncle'. Informal godparents were also designated, creating a layer of fictive kin. Kin ties provided bridges that broadened a person's social networks; when visiting a relative's home, one met her or his neighbours;

friendships were frequently forged in this way.[273] Yet kin, friends and neighbours were none the less three distinct groups of people, to be treated with
appropriate levels of intimacy and trust. While close friends could be confided
in, neighbours exchanged pleasantries. The elderly woman next door might be
asked to mind a child for an hour, but Mum was called upon when the
mother of a young child was planning to be away for the day. Cups of sugar
were readily passed over the back fence, but a money loan was more discreetly
obtained from a close friend or relative. Such distinctions might be blurred
somewhat in emergencies, and in poor districts more routinely, but they were
never effaced.

Earlier in the nineteenth century, employers and employees had frequently
lived in the same district, close to their workplaces. As small workshops gave
way to larger factories in the latter half of the century, residential segregation
increased. 'Once the elite had separated themselves from the labouring classes,
and the old notions of paternalistic, socially mixed communities had been lost',
urban communities became more homogeneous in class terms.[274] Solidly
proletarian neighbourhoods made a vital contribution to the development of
working-class identity. The common experience of living together on the
same street attenuated the cliquish divisions engendered by trade affiliations
and occupational hierarchy. 'One was working-class, whatever one's job, because one grew up in a neighbourhood that was working-class.'[275] By the same
token, proletarian districts fostered a strong self-awareness of being different
and independent from the propertied classes. The sense of being 'a breed apart'
fuelled an elementary pride in collective self-reliance. This type of class identity has become a much more prevalent feature of proletarian consciousness in
the past century than labour solidarity and opposition to capitalism. Because
marxists have tended to reduce class consciousness to the latter dimension,
pinning their hopes for the class struggle on its spread, the disparity has been a
tough one to face, yet it is not hard to explain from a materialist perspective.
Growing up in neighbourhoods strongly segregated by class is a nearly universal experience for working-class people; by contrast, only a minority of proletarians toil for years in large-scale unionized workplaces, the primary
breeding-ground of class-struggle consciousness.

Residential proximity inevitably entailed countless incidents of social friction, petty animus and status ranking; yet working-class neighbourhoods were
none the less communities of routine co-operation and, when crises struck, of
unsparing generosity. People felt strongly that one ought to come to the assistance of neighbours in an emergency, and they did. In the working-class districts of Antwerp, 'poor people turned to their neighbours when they were ill;
proletarian families shared their food with hungry friends; working women
had no difficulty in finding someone to whom they could entrust their infants
during the day.' As one man recalled his childhood in Vienna at the turn of

the century: 'If people had the impression that someone was really desperate and couldn't pay [the rent] through no fault of their own, then they would go over and hold a collection right away. Twenty or twenty-five women would each chip in a few *Groschen* and that would pay the rent.' A demolition project in East London in the winter of 1905 put several families out in the cold. 'Before the day was out, every one of the twenty or so inhabitants had been taken in by neighbours as poor and crowded as themselves.' Madeline Kerr described very similar patterns of first aid on Liverpool's 'Ship Street', concluding that 'the extent of neighbourliness, especially in times of adversity, cannot be overstressed.'[276] Such gestures of solidarity were based on an implicit assumption of community reciprocity. This was not so much a bilateral calculus of indebtedness (whereby Mabel Jones would owe Mary Smith a favour in return for services rendered); it was more the conviction that 'what goes round, comes round'. Those with a reputation for community involvement and generosity could count on unstinting aid from neighbours in hard times – an invaluable safety-net after the demise of employer paternalism and before the development of the modern welfare state.

To manage family subsistence between paydays, women sustained sharing networks for the routine exchange of goods and services. 'Across hallways, backyards and alleys there was a steady flow of cups of sugar, flour and other necessities. ... The constant borrowing was part of a working-class economy, like the weekly visits to the pawnbroker.'[277] Pawning was primarily a female activity, concealed from husbands to avoid slighting their adequacy as breadwinners. The task was often performed collectively, with one woman delegated 'to collect the pawnable items from each house on Monday mornings and then distribute the tickets to their owners'. In poor districts, 'it was common for neighbours to lend hard-up friends something to pledge if they had run out of articles the pawnbroker would accept.'[278] In contrast with emergency aid offered as an act of neighbourly solidarity, the daily swaps and loans into which people routinely entered were based on a much stricter form of accounting. Repayment was the rule, and 'to be thought of as untrustworthy as a borrower was one of the worst accusations that could be brought against a woman, threatening an important part of her livelihood.' Yet there was substantial flexibility in the currency of exchange: a cup of sugar might be repaid with an hour of childminding; a woman's loan covered by her child's offer to run an errand.[279]

While the practical utility of neighbourhood networks is immediately apparent, their normative function should also be recognized. In the case of the Viennese neighbours cited above, no collection would be taken 'if they got the impression that the woman didn't budget properly. ... They'd say, "You! First set your house in order."'[280] Community networks enforced standards and guarded the neighbourhood's collective reputation. A Battersea autobiographer recalls a verbal slanging match between two neighbours that was about to come to blows when abruptly dispersed by the formidable Mrs Murphy: 'Break it up the lot of yer,' she demanded, 'you're gettin' the street a bad name.' As Ellen Ross has shown, 'neighbourhoods themselves had enormous power to perpetuate their own cultures.' In a respectable neighbourhood, families were under pressure to 'keep up appearances': the exterior of the house had better be immaculate, the front windows curtained, the children well-mannered in adult company, and the husband sober in public. A woman who invited the dustman in for tea on a cold day might find her reputation damaged. While respectable communities cajoled the lax into measuring *up*, collective suasion in rougher districts more often operated to bring social climbers *down* a peg; anyone caught 'putting on airs' was subject to mocking ridicule. Whatever their internal standards, working-class neighbourhoods, both respectable and rough, protected 'their own' against the outside world, being particularly vigilant against the intrusion of the police, government officials, and meddlesome 'do-gooders' seeking their salvation. Miscreants were shielded when the police came looking for them, inspectors bearing summonses were sent to the wrong address, and missionaries were mocked, hooted, and derisively parodied as they made their rounds.[281]

Men's absence for much of the day left the invigilation of community standards largely in women's hands. Their influence in the community at large strengthened their authority in the eyes of their children:

> More often than not it was the 'old queens', grandmothers and older wives, who had the time to exercise real power in family matters. They were the assigned guardians of family morality and delegates to the court of public opinion meeting daily at doorsteps and corner shop, passing perpetual judgment on everyone.[282]

As the kin density and residential persistence of working-class neighbourhoods increased, parents, with the backing of the adult community, began to exercise a degree of authority over adolescents that resembled more the patriarchal power wielded in early modern villages than the parent–child relations of loose-knit urban proletarian communities in the first half of the nineteenth century. A daughter's courtship was closely watched, her chastity valued more highly than her mother's had been; parental approval for a marriage partner was regularly sought, and community pressure was effectively brought to bear, obliging a local lad to 'make an honest woman' of his pregnant girlfriend.[283] One index of the recuperation of patriarchal power was the decline in illegitimacy and common-law cohabitation across Western Europe from the last two decades of the nineteenth century on.[284]

As workplace and residential neighbourhood grew further apart, men found that they had to choose between two increasingly distinct friendship circles.

The social life of young working men still revolved around their workmates who adjourned regularly to the local pub at the end of a shift. Once married, however, men were more inclined to go straight home after work, stepping out after dinner to the neighbourhood pub or club. Getting married and setting up a new household often necessitated a substantial shift in women's social networks as well, particularly if the new residence took them away from families and friends. Both these adjustments could be eased considerably by living close to one's workplace and previous home.

While the play of young children was integrated, adolescents and adults tended to associate mainly with friends of the same sex. The marked segregation of the sexes in daily life was, once again, more reminiscent of the 'sexual geography' of the peasant village than the more heterosocial communities of proto-industrialists and early proletarians.[285] The strong preference for homosocial gatherings could become a source of tension between spouses. A husband's pub mates threatened to soak up a woman's housekeeping allowance, particularly if he were inclined to partake in the collective rituals of 'treating', buying a round of drinks on special occasions. For his part, a man might feel that his wife's involvement with 'the street's gossips' detracted from her attention to his domestic comforts.

There was a delicate balance between involvement in the street life of the urban 'village' and preserving a measure of domestic privacy and family autonomy. Analysing oral history interviews, Frykman and Löfgren note an ambivalence in people's memories of neighbourhood networks:

> People talk about the constant borrowing between housewives and then add: 'but in our family we always kept ourselves to ourselves', or 'we always managed on our own.' To fend for oneself, to be dependent on neither neighbours nor welfare, was an important mark of working-class respectability.[286]

Individuals, of course, were inclined to draw the line between public and private spheres very differently. While gregarious types would think nothing of 'popping in' unannounced, others developed a reputation as 'standoffish', keeping to themselves and displaying a low tolerance for 'idle gossip'. Such reputations adhered to neighbourhoods as well as to individuals. Poor streets were inclined to sustain a very public, street-oriented culture where 'home extended into the street beyond the front door, and mothers sat on the doorstep on warm evenings, not embarrassed to suckle their babies.' In the meantime, the more prosperous blocks became known for quieter and more orderly streets, drawn lace curtains, and more discreet forms of public discourse.[287] Yet across the full spectrum from rough to respectable, working-class neighbourhoods remained oriented to the street and its shops as public gathering-places. As Edna Bold recalled her childhood in a Manchester suburb at the beginning of the twentieth century: 'The "Road" was a social centre where everyone met, stopped, talked, walked.' The street was also the children's playground. 'Working-class children spent only as much time indoors as was absolutely necessary. ... Weather permitting, they spent a large part of their day "on the street".'[288] While mothers endeavoured to keep an eye on them, children enjoyed the run of the streets without close supervision. The lack of constant adult oversight was of great concern to their social superiors, who deplored the way the children of the poor were permitted to 'run wild'.

As the quality of housing improved and overcrowding eased, most working-class families availed themselves of the opportunity to insist on a modicum of domestic privacy. The front door was deliberately closed each time family members went in or out, and a couple's spats were less likely to be conducted in full view of the street. The doorstep became an enforced threshold between public and private domains, and the habit of 'popping in' without an invitation 'just to have a yarn then off out' was discouraged. As standards changed, neighbours entered 'only if we wanted 'em for anything special'.[289] Together with a deepening sense of domestic privacy, the streets themselves were tamed. Their use for trading and buskering, holding fairs, celebrations, dances and football matches was increasingly constrained through municipal by-laws prohibiting cash betting, street trading, assembly and recreation. Police surveillance was designed to disperse large gatherings in the streets and to steer the participants to specialized venues: stadia, parks and dance halls. In 1900, the Reading Trades Council protested: 'The streets are the playground of the poor. ... It will be a sorry day for England when the children of the poor, after being dragooned to school, are dragooned from the streets.'[290]

Household Composition and Domestic Space

The extension of the co-resident family group and the augmentation of households, discussed in Chapter 2, reached its peak between 1850 and 1885.[291] Thereafter, households contracted, as the practice of taking in lodgers declined and fewer families lived with their kin.[292] Subletting rooms and taking in lodgers was never part of a familial ideal; it was a practical way to defray the rent. The willingness to dispense with income from lodgers was a by-product of the rise in real wage income. Inconvenient at the best of times, the practice was no longer felt to be necessary. Yet we ought not to ignore the ideological forces at play in the decline. When couples decided that it was 'no longer worth the bother' to take in lodgers, they were weighing the anticipated income loss against whatever they disliked about the arrangement: increased crowding, extra housework, interpersonal tension, fear of sexual impropriety, loss of status in the community. Clearly, the subjective 'costs' of keeping boarders were rising, as urban reform movements mounted vigorous campaigns against 'the lodger evil'. Reformers had long held that one of the chief blights of overcrowding was an absence of family privacy. They were particularly alarmed by the danger of sexual debauchery between male boarders and daughters. The menace had been identified in the 1840s, when 'the housing question' became a public issue. As overcrowding eased in the latter decades of the century, the municipal reform movement seized on the possibility of eradicating the lodger evil. In Sweden in the 1890s, the lodger system was denounced as 'one of the cancers of working-class life. ... It leads to a moral coarseness and mental savagery that no statistics can reveal.'[293] In Glasgow, live-in lodgers were termed 'a serious social disease', and supervised boarding houses were established to provide an alternative to cohabiting with private families.[294] The campaign against the lodger evil evidently assumed an international character around the turn of the century: the same ominous prognosis, together with proposals to furnish alternative accommodation for young single men, was raised at this time by reformers in Germany, England, Scotland and the United States.[295]

Middle-class observers were also convinced that overcrowded dwellings promoted incest, which was held to be rampant in inner-city slums. Certainly the practice seems to have been less secret in the rougher neighbourhoods. Beatrice Webb recounted that her workmates from the East End of London, though as 'keen-witted and generous-hearted as my own circle of friends, could chaff each other about having babies by their fathers and brothers.'[296] While we have no way of knowing the prevalence of incest in slum neighbourhoods, nor of comparing their rates with more prosperous city districts, the postulated connection between domestic crowding and illicit intimacy seems highly dubious. One might just as plausibly argue the opposite thesis – that the absence of separate bedrooms and indoor privacy would inhibit incest by reducing opportunities and increasing the risks of discovery. Whatever the facts, the cause-and-effect relation was almost certainly a weak one. The thought of several family members sleeping in one bed together fevered the bourgeois imagination, but rather than the sexual debauchery so often portrayed in the scandalized reports of public health inspectors and middle-class reformers, working-class biographers typically recall a repressive sexual climate. Toddlers generally slept with their parents, while the older siblings slept together in a second bed; it was the rare child in a working-class household who had the luxury of sleeping one to a bed. Typically, everyone slept in their underclothes and avoided undressing in front of other family members.

In most families, it appears that poverty and cramped quarters fostered a high degree of control over family interaction indoors, with elaborate routines and codes of behaviour to avoid bedlam. At mealtimes, families observed a strict pecking order as food was served, with the father going first, then the children in descending order by age, and finally the mother. Children who grabbed out of turn would be scolded, cuffed or sent from the table without their supper.[297] Bedtime routines were strictly ordered. Viennese proletarians recall Saturday-evening washing rituals where children were bathed in sequence by age, each child was sent to bed as soon as he or she was out of the tub, and parents took great care to avoid appearing naked before their children. Where physical space was too confined to permit separation, time could be strictly segmented to produce the desired effect. Children were put to bed early, and if they could not sleep they were told to be quiet so that their parents could spend an undisturbed hour together at the end of the day. Despite the close physical proximity, respondents could not recall ever seeing or overhearing their parents making love, and many (females especially) grew up without obtaining the most elementary knowledge concerning sex and reproduction.[298] While the absence of such recollections undoubtedly implies that the adult respondents have selectively forgotten discomforting childhood memories, it also testifies to the social repression exercised by their parents at the time, as manifest in attitudes to nakedness and sexuality.

In a one- or two-room dwelling, there was very little scope for specializing domestic space: cooking and eating, resting and sleeping, all took place 'on top' of one another. The kitchen table served many purposes, packing cases doubled as children's cots, the big copper was a water-heater, a laundry basin and a bathtub rolled into one. The reports of housing investigators furnished many descriptions of such quarters. This one concerns the apartments of Berlin machinists before the First World War:

> A living room and a tiny kitchen: with two adults and three children, that means that everyone sleeps in the same room, all three children in one bed. This is very much the norm in proletarian circles, for the single room of such an apartment has space for, at most, three beds, one sofa, one table, and one wardrobe.[299]

In three- or four-room dwellings, space could be specialized to some degree. In the homes of artisans, where space and layout permitted, the front room was often exempted from daily use and reserved for special occasions such as entertaining visitors at Sunday afternoon tea. The 'parlour', as it was called, was 'a shrine to respectability and domesticity', outfitted with the household's best furniture, adorned with family photographs and heirlooms and the prize possession, a piano, that 'found its way into millions of working-class homes in the last quarter of the [nineteenth] century'. While families endured daily life in the tiny back kitchen – crowded, grimy and profane – the front room stood empty – immaculate, ordered and serene – full of memories, anticipation, dignity and wonder.[300] Kathleen Betterson recalls her parents' Fulham flat: "However crowded we were, we never dreamed of sitting in our one tolerably large room except on special occasions. The "front room", like

145

every other in our street, was sacrosanct.'[301] Middle-class reformers were baffled and chagrined to see such an impractical arrangement flourishing among a class renowned for its down-to-earth pragmatism. The architect Raymond Unwin thought it 'worse than folly to take space from that living room, where it will be used every day and every hour, to form a parlour, where it will be used once or twice a week'.[302] Margery Loane, normally an empathetic observer of proletarian mores, found the pristine sanctity of the front parlour incomprehensible:

> The blinds must not be drawn up because the carpet will fade; the gas must not be lighted because it will blacken the ceiling; the windows must not be opened because the air may tarnish the frame of the looking glass; the chimney must be blocked up, lest the rain should fall and rust the fender. Finally, the door must be locked on the outside.[303]

The parlour was the inspiration of working-class homemakers, forging an inner sanctum against the din, dust and drudgery of daily life.

Wage Distribution Patterns within Families

In the period from 1873 to 1914, working-class families came to depend on the primary breadwinner's income to a greater degree than ever before. Studies of family budgets compiled around the turn of the century consistently place the househead's contribution (where he is present and regularly employed) at 70 to 80 per cent of the total family income.[304] This dependency varied over the family cycle and between strata of the proletariat; the higher a man's pay, the greater was his family's reliance upon him. Yet it seems that among *all* layers of the working class, the male breadwinner's income assumed greater importance in this period. The reasons for this trend are not difficult to discern: a very considerable rise in men's real wages; the curtailment of child labour; and reduced opportunities for women to make money at home.

A deepening reliance on the working man's income meant that the family's fortunes hinged critically upon the division of his wage between his own personal spending money and the housekeeping budget, handled by his wife. This informal distribution occurred on paydays, which were consequently loaded with tension.[305] In a working-class suburb of Paris, an observer noted:

> This day has a very particular atmosphere, a mixture of gaiety and anxiety. ... The housewives wait at the windows or stand in the doorways, and sometimes in their impatience ... one sees them walking toward the factory to meet their husbands. ... In the street voices snarl, in the houses insults fly ... hands are raised, tears flow.[306]

Women's weekly cycle of shopping and pawning revolved around their husbands' pay schedule, as did men's own rounds of the betting shop and pub. By midweek all the money had been spent, and in the last day or two before the next round, essentials were acquired 'on tick'. The timing and location of the employers' payout were pivotal to the subsequent distribution of the wage between spouses and to the homemaker's shopping efficiency. Until the 1870s, most workers were paid at the end of their Saturday shift, an extremely inconvenient time for the shopper who 'was forced to buy either from inferior shops that kept open on Saturday or from the hucksters who sold an inferior commodity at a higher price'.[307] In Black Country mining villages where the butty system still prevailed, wages were doled out in the pub late on Saturday evening. Miners and their wives complained that this 'prevents us from attending the market until near midnight or compels us to be huckstered by small vendors in the neighbourhood where we reside.'[308] With the demise of subcontracting, the site of payment was transferred from the public house to the company office, a move that Mayhew felt would help to diminish intemperance in many trades.[309] The connection between Saturday-night drunkenness and the mode of wage payment became an issue in the temperance battles of the period. In Scotland, the temperance movement won a major victory in 1853 when pubs were forced to close at eleven o'clock. Per capita alcohol consumption declined from then on, and a great many women must have blessed the Saturday closing hour as they set off to market with a greater share of their husbands' pay.[310] Edwin Chadwick suggested that wages ought to be paid on Fridays to strengthen working-class buying power. This norm was instituted in England in the 1870s, making Saturday the week's primary leisure day.[311] Regardless of when payday occurred, housewives much preferred it to be a weekly event, since 'the women will tell you that somehow or other they cannot make the money go so far' on a fortnightly schedule.[312]

Because the distribution of wages within the family is an informal matter that has not been adequately studied, it is impossible to gauge with any precision the prevalence of different patterns of wage allocation. By my reckoning, three broad variants may be distinguished. A significant minority of men came straight home with their pay, handed it over in its entirety to their wives and took back a modest amount for personal needs at their spouses' discretion or by mutual agreement. From women's standpoint, the whole-wage system (as this variant has been called) was exemplary.[313] Men who adhered to it were universally praised as considerate and kind husbands 'who treat marriage as a real partnership, who regard "my wages" as "our wages", and who plan out the expenditure of joint income with their wives'.[314]

Far more common, however, and probably the dominant pattern, was for working men to hand over a housekeeping allowance, generally a fixed sum – 'the minimum on which experience has shown [their wives] can contrive to manage' – keeping whatever was left over for themselves.[315] Strikingly, the allowance was known colloquially as the wife's 'wage', recalling Flora Tristan's adage that the wives of working men were 'proletarians of the proletariat'.[316] The allowance appears to have been set more by prevailing pay norms and community customs than by negotiation between spouses. The arrangement seems to have been closely coupled with the base-rate/bonus system of wage payment; both became prominent in the second stage of industrialization. Normally, the allowance was equal to the smallest wage a regularly employed worker could expect to take home in a week, so that he could deliver it without fail throughout the year. Frequently, this amount accorded with a base rate, allowing men to retain bonuses and overtime pay for themselves. By splitting the wage packet along these lines and treating bonus payments as their personal fund, breadwinners developed an intense interest in pursuing these rewards despite their corrosive impact on labour solidarity and family unity. Men were tempted to keep spouses in the dark as to how much they made in bonuses and overtime so that they could spend these 'extras' as they wished. In her 1907 study of Middlesbrough, Lady Bell found that a third of iron-workers' wives did not know how much their husbands made.[317]

The fixed allowance had the advantage of being a stable arrangement which provided wives with a predictable income to make ends meet. The essence of the provisioning exercise was to adapt the family's collective needs to the size of the allowance – 'to cut the coat to fit the cloth', as homemakers put it. But when the allowance barely covered the regular weekly expenses of food and rent, it was almost impossible to set aside funds for children's boots, new clothes or unexpected medical bills. When extraordinary expenses arose, women had to ask their husbands for additional funds; special purchases thus took the form of 'gifts' from Papa. The alternative was to stint on other items; typically, housewives spent less on food, going short themselves to make up the difference.[318] Perhaps the worst feature of the flat-rate allowance was that it discouraged saving. Men ended up with discretionary cash, but grew accustomed to spending it. Women were more inclined to 'lay some aside'; yet the allowance they received rarely permitted them to do so.

In a third variant, extremely pernicious but not uncommon, the cash wives obtained was an unpredictable and variable residual – the amount left over *after* their husbands had visited the pub or betting shop. It is difficult to gauge the proportion of working men who failed to deliver a regular amount to their wives, forcing the latter to prise it from them. The reports of shocked middle-class contemporaries were undoubtedly selective, focusing unduly on the worst cases and exaggerating the prevalence of the problem. Yet most modern labour historians, displaying a masculine bias, are far too inclined to minimize bread-winner abuse, dismissing such portraits as the moralistic projection of middle-class teetotallers imposing an alien standard on working-class behaviour with no understanding of proletarian leisure culture. Working men who 'drank their pay' caused their wives no end of grief. It was impossible to maintain an orderly household under a random income schedule. Women who were forced to manage the household's finances under such capricious oppression frequently made their feelings known. They needed no prompting from middle-class feminists and temperance crusaders to denounce such men as callous husbands.[319] Men who came home missing 'an undue proportion of their week's wages' risked being attacked by enraged wives.[320]

Women did not condemn the social drinker. They appreciated that their menfolk worked hard for their pay, did not expect them 'to work for nothing', and felt they were entitled to have a round with their mates in the pub.[321] Heavy drinkers, and payday drunks in particular, were another matter. Refusing to wait for irresponsible husbands to return from the pub, wives tried to intercept them on the way there to rescue the family's funds. It was commonplace for women to hover around pub entrances on a Saturday evening, trying to coax or cajole their husbands into calling it a night before the final round. Intimidated by the exclusively masculine nature of the place, they sent sons to fetch fathers home. The bravest or most desperate women ventured inside themselves, attempting to drag their husbands out or to shame them publicly into handing over the remaining cash. Failing that, women emptied their husbands' pockets by stealth as inebriated men slept after returning home from payday benders. When men discovered their loss, they often accused their wives of theft, effectively denying the right of families to secure provision from their wages. Under the circumstances, we are not surprised to find ample evidence in police reports and court records indicating that fights over the distribution of the paycheque frequently came to blows. More domestic violence was perpetrated in the immediate aftermath of payday than at any other time of the week.[322]

What part of their wages did men retain for their own leisure expenses? One British report published in 1850 estimated that working men spent from a third to a half of their earnings on themselves, with lower-paid workers keeping a higher portion.[323] While misappropriation of this order was not rare, it undoubtedly reflected the worst end of the breadwinner spectrum. More reliable estimates indicate that an eighth to a tenth was probably normal. If wives received four-fifths on a regular basis, without having to prise it loose from a drunk, men were not thought to have abused their prerogatives.[324]

The allocation of the breadwinner's wage was of such importance to women that 'the criterion of whether a man is a "good husband" [is] the proportion of his wages which he gives to his wife.'[325] Watching their mothers cope, girls developed a strong sense of a fair division. Opening the account book she kept for her mother, an eleven-year-old girl proudly informed an inspector: 'Mr G's wages was nineteen bob out of that 'e took thruppons for 'es diner witch is not mutch 'e bein' such a 'arty man.'[326] Granted the vast scope for individual difference, which way were the prevailing winds blowing in this period?

Several developments tended to promote breadwinner irresponsibility. While the strengthening of the male-breadwinner norm buttressed the onus to provide, deepening commodity relations generated a host of individualist incentives that undermined the conscientious discharge of this duty. As the last vestiges of corporate paternalism crumbled, workers gained an offsetting sense of freedom from the employers' control of their conduct beyond the factory gates. To earn a wage was to earn the right to spend it as one wished, and this freedom became a cornerstone of the cultural assertion of working-class independence from the propertied classes.[327] Tighter industrial discipline fostered a compensatory hedonism in leisure-time, and shorter working hours gave men more time to exercise it. The leisure axis of proletarian autonomy was predominantly masculine, asserted by working men in 'their own time', often at the expense of wives and children.[328] Bourgeois observers worried that the complete monetization of the wage opened the door to proletarian indiscipline and domestic abuse. In Sismondi's view, the modern working man 'has become accustomed to the fact that he never knows a future beyond next Saturday when he is paid. ... He has too often been led to think about present comforts so as not to be too afraid of the future suffering his wife and children may bear.'[329] Arthur Young preferred the truck system for the same reason: 'An Irishman loves his whiskey as an Englishman does strong beer; but he cannot go to the whiskey house on Saturday night and drink out the support of himself, his wife and his children, not uncommon in the alehouses of England.'[330] As the wage increasingly took the form of a payment to individuals, its subsequent redistribution became a private affair between spouses, widely considered to be 'no one else's business but their own'. This ethic made it more difficult for women to combat its abuse.[331]

On the other hand, labour-market conditions for men improved considerably in the nineteenth century, and these ameliorations fostered family responsibility among primary breadwinners. In the first phase of industrial capitalism, labour markets were characterized by low pay and episodic employment; this combination wreaked havoc on working-class families. Low incomes intensified money conflicts between spouses and saddled homemakers with the excruciating dilemmas of distributing scarcity. The 'rational' way for households to cope with poverty was to impose a rigid discipline on all expenditures, but this objective was persistently subverted by employment interruptions and radical swings in wage income, which disposed breadwinners to celebrate and binge when a pay packet was unusually large. This type of labour market, common in the casual trades, made it extremely difficult for proletarian couples to work out a regular regimen for dividing the main breadwinner's paycheque in ways that both parties found equitable. The family economy of early proletarians was typically based on a rock-bottom floor of subsistence requirements, where income above and beyond the minimum was treated as a temporary windfall.[332] As real wages rose in the last half of the nineteenth century and the cyclical fluctuations of seasonal labour demand diminished, it became easier to establish a viable family budget without emptying the bread-winner's pocket. Community-wide norms of wage distribution began to emerge, whereby wives obtained a regular housekeeping allowance. In York-shire mining communities, for example, women waited on the doorstep for their husbands to return home on paydays. In a ritual called the 'tip-up', men handed over their pay in full view of the street so that neighbours could assure a just exchange.[333] The restriction of drinking hours in pubs and clubs, with evening closing hours, buttressed such norms and was clearly a gain from the homemakers' standpoint.

All sources agree that homemakers possessed day-to-day control of 'the family exchequer', charged with the duty of making ends meet on behalf of the family as a whole. Women had always stood at the centre of the family economy; medieval and early modern peasant women were no strangers to market exchange. None the less, managing the household's finances was a new responsibility for women of the labouring classes. The duty had arisen with the development of the wage economy. It assumed pivotal importance in the nineteenth century, with the full monetization of the wage and the decline of domestic production for use.

Provisioning the household was both onerous and ennobling. On the one hand, housewives shouldered the burden of making ends meet for the entire family: allocating sparse resources between competing demands, suffering in silence to keep the primary breadwinner well fed, going short and pawning the Sunday best. Shopping on a normal working-class budget required enor-mous self-discipline. Without a penny to spare, carelessness or a single impul-sive purchase could sink a family into debt from which it might take months to recover.[334] On the other hand, the role of financial manager lifted wives above the status of menial domestics toiling without pay. Working-class auto-biographers, mostly men, venerated their mothers for service and self-sacrifice in this capacity. Mothers who 'held things together' and 'managed to find us all enough to eat' won their children's undying gratitude and fierce loyalty.[335]

Observers of working-class home life maintained that a woman's house-keeping skills, organization and diligence could make a big difference to her family's living standard. 'Everything depends on her,' insisted Lady Bell, who thought the wife's 'administration of the earnings [just as important as] the husband's steadiness and capacity to earn'.[336] Comparing household budgets in 1893, Henry Higgs noted that good housekeeping could 'turn the balance of comfort in favour of one workman whose wages are much below those of another'.[337] The point was eagerly grasped by the champions of female domesticity, who sought to refute the argument that poor families could not afford to forgo mothers' income until children were old enough to go out to work. They insisted that diligent homemakers could do more to enhance their families' living standards by shopping economically and cooking imaginatively than working women who neglected their domestic duties to earn a second income.[338] The argument *in extremis* was clearly nonsense, but this does not mean that the converse is true – that the quality of domestic labour made very little difference to a family's level of nutrition, hygiene and comfort. The middle-class authors of family budget studies lavished praise upon the working-class housewife who kept her home spotless and her children well turned out, marvelling at how far she stretched a modest working man's income. They were equally fulsome in their scorn for the 'shiftless homemaker with the temperament of a slattern' whose house was a chaotic mess and whose filthy children ran wild in the streets. While such judgements were replete with class abstraction and finger-pointing moralism, the analytical argument remains wholly compelling. A family's living standard was *not* reducible to its income. The quality of domestic labour exerted in converting wages into the means of subsistence made a very considerable difference in the consumable product, whether it was a hot meal, clean clothes or a warm bed.[339]

The division of the breadwinner's pay between his own pocket money and his wife's housekeeping fund was a key determinant of the stability of working-class marriage. Where the allocation was regular and perceived as fair by both parties, the marriage stood on solid ground. Where the dispensation was erratic, the wage misappropriated, or the housewife's demands were deemed unreasonable, bitter recriminations were sure to follow. The basic terms of the provisioning pact were so deeply naturalized as to be taken for granted. The husband's duty was to hold his job on a steady basis and hand the bulk of his pay over to his wife. In a culture of low marital expectations, this was virtually the full extent of his family responsibilities. For her part, the wife was to take the portion he gave her and to 'make it go as far as possible' in providing for the family. Since the arrangement was based on a strict segregation of tasks and spheres of responsibility, it was tacitly agreed that, providing each was discharging his or her duties conscientiously, the other should not 'meddle'. Almost any query could be interpreted as interference. Women took great care not to slight their husbands' adequacy as breadwinners, and bent over backwards to avoid the impression that they were 'driving' their husbands to work in the morning. Men boasted that they never took issue with the way their wives spent the housekeeping allowance.[340] The tacit agreement to 'mind your own business' could be preserved only if both parties felt that the other was upholding his or her end of the bargain. When wives failed to put a hot meal on the table at the end of a shift, men made no secret of the fact that they thought it was 'a poor do', throwing cold dinners in the back of the fireplace. When husbands failed to come straight home on paydays and hand over an amount that was established by custom as a reasonable housekeeping allowance, they were liable to be greeted at the pub door by furious and desperate women demanding the family's share.

Central to the conjugal pact, 'money matters' were thus an extremely sensitive issue between spouses. In the homes of conscientious breadwinners, women went to great lengths to conceal from their husbands how hard it was to get by on the amount of money they provided. "E never knows we go without and I never tells 'im', a woman told Rowntree in his 1902 study, and she was not exceptional. While stinting in silence on their own food intake, poor women hid a 'shameful' reliance on the pawnshop and their own money-making schemes.[341] The issue was so loaded for most men that they looked the other way. Loane thought that 'they are so well aware that they cannot "make the money go round" that they would hand their wages over to a teenage daughter "who knows what her mother used to do" rather than make the attempt.'[342]

Men who broke the silence to question their wives' competence as financial managers delivered a low blow. In *The Ragged-Trousered Philanthropists*, Easton criticizes his wife Ruth for sinking the family into debt, and she bursts into tears: 'I always do the best I can with the money' she sobs. 'I never spend a farthing on myself, but you don't seem to understand how hard it is. I don't care nothing about having to go without things myself, but I can't bear it when you speak to me like you do lately. You seem to blame me for everything.'[343] The men who boasted that they never voiced the slightest criticism of their wives' financial management were undoubtedly moved by a mixture of respect for their spouses' jurisdiction and fear of provoking a bout of bitter recrimination which might arouse pointed questions as to their own employment record and spending habits. Such arguments could so easily degenerate into the hurling of crushing accusations back and forth – wounding slanders that could never really be retracted or forgotten – that most couples tacitly agreed that it was preferable to treat all such topics as off limits, studiously evading them in silence and protective deception.[344]

The strict segregation of duties and spheres of authority between spouses reduced the areas of conflict in working-class marriage, and contained its potentially explosive antagonisms. The arrangement made for a peculiar detachment from the daily cares of one's 'better half' – far removed from the modern ideal of the companionate marriage.[345]

Away at work, the pub or the boxing hall, men construct the parameters of female domestic life not (in most cases) through direct involvement but through the intermittent flow of money resources, often accompanied by the most limited personal contact. 'Dad's chair' by the fire, found in many working-class homes, frequently stood empty – a silent testimony to the place of the *pater familias* in the domestic environment.[346]

Men's studied indifference to their spouses' domestic concerns was reciprocated by wives 'who don't know, when asked, what the man's job is'.[347] Maud Reeves recounted:

> The separation of interests soon begins to show itself. ... He gets accustomed to seeing his wife slave, and she gets accustomed to seeing him appear and disappear on his daily round of work, which gradually appeals less and less to her imagination, till, at thirty, she hardly knows what his duties are – so overwhelmed is she in the flood of her own most absorbing duties and economies.[348]

While homemakers undoubtedly would have liked their husbands to help out more with specific tasks around the house, they valued the autonomy provided by their spouses' disinterest; it gave women a feeling of importance and self-control. This may account for women's willingness to accept their spouses' domestic abstention without making much of an issue of it. In contrast with peasant and proto-industrial spouses, most proletarian wives were out from under close conjugal supervision in their homes. As one man told Margaret Loane: 'If the missus can't have her own way at home, bless us! Where can she have it? Her house is all she's got.'[349]

While father was the ultimate authority figure in most working-class families, he was seldom closely involved in the children's upbringing. 'The fact that sons and daughters alike depend almost solely upon their mother's opinion when in any difficulty', noted Loane, 'makes her ability to advise them of the utmost importance.'[350] We can agree with Berlanstein that mothers were 'the emotional focus of working-class households',[351] but this is not the same as claiming that they held the reins of domestic power. Some social historians have interpreted women's role as financial manager as signifying the de facto operation of a proletarian matriarchy beneath the formal veneer of male househeadship.[352] This view disregards the actual operation of the family economy, where women did not 'control the purse strings' in any meaningful sense. As long as men remained the primary earners, taking initial possession of the family's principal income, women were at their husbands' mercy. The exemplary conduct of the minority of working men who handed over their entire pay does not negate the vulnerability of homemakers to breadwinner abuse. As we have seen, the majority of men were not so munificent; they put their wives on a housekeeping 'wage' and kept back an amount that they themselves determined, making them the only family member who had pocket money to spend on personal needs.

Built into the collective consumption of proletarian households was a clear hierarchy of needs: the primary breadwinner had first call on scarce resources. As a result, two living standards came to prevail within working-class families. Men received the lion's share of the meat in the family diet, for example, while women and children frequently went without.[353] We know from women's own accounts that they were inclined to hide the extent of the discrepancy from their husbands, claiming, when there was not enough to go round, that they felt poorly and had lost their appetite. This was not an irrational form of deference on women's part; it was a matter of economic priority. Maud Reeves explained the reasoning in *Round About a Pound a Week*:

> How is she to keep her husband, the breadwinner, in full efficiency out of the few shillings she can spend on food, and at the same time satisfy the appetites of the children? She decides to feed him sufficiently and to make what is over do for herself and the children. This is not considered and thought-out self-sacrifice on her part. It is the pressure of circumstances. The wage-earner must be fed.[354]

The ranking of the primary breadwinner's needs and desires above the rest of the family's was impressed upon children in rituals of deference when father returned from work. In a Viennese railwayman's family,

> When father came in from work he would open the door, look sternly around the room, and then he would say, 'Water in the washbasin! Food on the table!' Then he would take off his coat and hang up his cap, and then he would wash his hands and ask what had been going on.[355]

At the dinner table, silence was often imposed on children, who were not expected to speak unless spoken to. While on the street, children were permitted to 'run free' and play with exuberance; indoors, in cramped quarters, their movements were strictly controlled and outbursts were stifled. The objective of this stern repression was 'peace and quiet', so that father might rest or sleep without being disturbed. Here too, we find 'the pressure of circumstances'. The family's top priority was to replenish the main breadwinner's labour-power; everyone else's needs were subordinated to that imperative.[356]

5

Starting to Stop:
The Proletarian Fertility Decline

The fertility decline is a fundamental watershed in world history; yet of all the revolutions in the making of the modern world, the reduction of the birth rate by two-thirds must surely be one of the least understood. Research on the decline has been long on quantitative description but disconcertingly short on historical explanation.[1] Great strides have been taken in the study of gender relations in the past two decades, but practically none of it is reflected in demographic theories of fertility regulation, nor in mainstream accounts of the decline. Sexual desire and conjugal power are absent from the standard paradigms: it is as if demographers believed in the Immaculate Conception – for everyone. The fundamental problem with standard models of fertility regulation is that they are begin at the level of the reproductive couple taken as a unified subject. They assume, in other words, the perpetual existence of harmonious needs and aligned interests between husbands and wives with regard to childbearing, sex and contraception. This is unacceptably naive: an adequate theoretical framework must allow for spousal differences in procreative objectives and the means used to achieve them. In this chapter, I will present an account of the fertility decline that is centred on spousal relations and specifically on the changing terms and conditions of marital coitus.

In the latter decades of the nineteenth century, birth rates began to fall all across Northwestern Europe (save in France, where the decline had begun a century earlier). The most striking aspect of the phenomenon was the rapidity of its spread. In the thirty-year span from 1890 to 1920, marital fertility contracted 10 per cent or more in over half the provinces (counties, departments, deaneries, and so on) of Europe.[2] Once under way, the decline proved irreversible, roughly halving the number of children borne per married woman in two generations.

While the adoption of family-limitation behaviour was sweeping, it was not all of a piece. Deliberate birth control was inaugurated by upper-middle-class urban couples; industrial workers and their spouses shortened their childbearing careers decisively a decade or two later.[3] There were very substantial differences between sectors of the working class as well, with married women in textile districts, for example, registering an early decline to relatively low rates (due primarily to high levels of employment outside the home), while couples in mining communities persisted with high fertility well into the twentieth century.[4] Eventually, the small-family norm was generalized across the entire social order, as initial disparity gave way to a subsequent phase of convergence at relatively low rates.[5] During the phase of class divergence, 'the Population Question' came to a political boil, with middle-class women being castigated for selfishly shunning their maternal duty, while poor women were denounced for breeding like rabbits.

The decline was due almost entirely to a reduction in *marital fertility*. Changes in the age and incidence of marriage (which had been the key regulators of the birth rate in Western Europe in the early modern era) made little or no contribution to the descent.[6] Births out of wedlock subsided concomitantly, but this trend accounted for less than 10 per cent of the aggregate contraction. In most regions, the reduction of marital fertility was achieved entirely by means of 'stopping', the deliberate cessation of childbirth prior to menopause. In the rest, stopping accounts for the bulk of the change.[7] Overall, there was no increase in women's age at first birth, nor were intervals between births lengthened. The fertility decline was a historic watershed in two respects: the birth rates of entire societies reached new lows, and the stopping mode of fertility regulation was established as a mass practice for the first time.[8]

How was stopping accomplished? There is evidence that changes in four practices contributed: (a) a rise in the incidence of induced abortion; (b) more frequent resort to coitus interruptus; (c) a decline in coital frequency by deliberate abstention; and (d) increased use of contraceptive devices. Since I shall concentrate on the last three practices in the following discussion, the first ought to be considered briefly. The incidence of induced abortion (relative to live births) rose substantially around the turn of the century.[9] Rates peaked in the 1920s, with German hospitals reporting two to three times as many cases as in the prewar years.[10] In Britain, studies by hospital gynaecological departments and women's clinics estimated that roughly 16 to 20 per cent of pregnancies were deliberately terminated. The Inter-Departmental Commission on Abortion, issuing its final report in 1939, confirmed these as reasonable estimates.[11] A rising portion of all women seeking abortions were married. In 1899, a report in *Westminster Review* maintained that most abortions in Britain were still obtained by single women.[12] Forty years later, the Inter-Departmental Commission concluded that 'the overwhelming majority of abortions occur among married women ... [and] that abortion is relatively more common in the case of mothers in the higher age groups than in the case of younger mothers.'[13] A parallel rise in the proportion of abortions obtained by married women was detected in Germany.[14] Evidently, a great many abortions conformed to the stopping pattern: they were sought by married women approaching the end of their childbearing years. It seems reasonable to conclude that a rise in the abortion rate made a considerable contribution to the decline of the birth rate prior to the widespread use of contraceptive devices in marriage.[15] But since we have every reason to believe that a great many working-class women in the nineteenth century had also sought abortions, it appears unlikely that rates would have risen sufficiently in the early twentieth century to account for most of the fertility decline at that time.

Turning now to the role of coitus interruptus, abstention and contraceptive devices: changes in any or all of these methods entail a profound alteration in the conduct of conjugal sex. Given the pace of the fertility decline, daughters and sons were evidently breaking radically with the sexual mores of their mothers and fathers. What had brought about this far-reaching revolution in reproductive consciousness and coital behaviour?

To answer this question, consider the personal testimony of working-class women and men from Britain, Germany and Norway recounting their reproductive experiences in the first quarter of the twentieth century. In the case of Britain, vivid accounts are preserved in two collections of letters. The first was sent to the Women's Co-operative Guild in the years just before the First World War in response to an inquiry from the Guild urging its members to recount their childbearing histories.[16] Writing about reproductive experiences that had occurred in the 1880–1910 period, the Women's Guild members were representatives of a largely *pre-limiting population*. A second set of letters was sent in the 1920s to Marie Stopes, the famous (to some, notorious) campaigner for the dissemination of birth-control information and contraceptives to the public at large.[17] In the very act of writing to Stopes to solicit birth-control information, her respondents were moving beyond the wish to restrain fertility into the realm of practical action. Consequently, we should regard them as representatives of a *limiting population,* albeit one that had been largely ineffective thus far.

Ernest Lewis-Faning conducted a survey in 1946 that furnishes a useful check on several themes found in the correspondence.[18] His questionnaire was administered to a quasi-random sample of married female patients found in all departments of general hospitals in England and Scotland. Interviewers inquired as to whether respondents had attempted to limit births at any time in their married lives, and if so, the means used. The strength of the survey for our purposes was that Lewis-Faning divided the sample into three social classes (on the basis of the husband's occupation): class I, professional and middle class; II, skilled manual labour; and III, unskilled manual labour. He tabulated respondents' answers by class and longitudinally by cohort on the basis of the year of marriage, dating back to 1900.

For Norway, we have a source comparable to the British correspondence, an immense archive of 4,300 letters written by women from all over the country and sent to the Office for Maternal Hygiene in Oslo between 1924 and 1929. They have been extensively analysed by Ida Blom; I am relying entirely on her assessments.[19] The German evidence takes a somewhat different form, the results of surveys done by the Berlin doctor and sex researcher Max Marcuse in 1911–13, and by Dr O. Polano of Würzburg in 1914. In these surveys, roughly two-thirds of the working-class respondents reported using some form of birth control, so I shall treat the majority as exemplary of *first-generation limiters*. Here I am utilizing James Woycke's dissertation and R. P. Neuman's analysis of the surveys.[20]

In the early stages of the decline, what means did people use in their efforts to avert conception? In Lewis-Faning's retrospective survey, nine in ten limiters before 1920 had relied on coitus interruptus.[21] More respondents marrying in the 1920s employed contraceptive devices, but the proportion was still less than one-third. The German pattern was very similar. In Marcuse's study, 77 per cent of limiters relied on coitus interruptus, and in Polano's, 83 per cent did.[22] The Stopes correspondence presents a rather different picture. Forty authors in *Mother England* cite abstinence as the method they were currently practising or had attempted to pursue in the past.[23] Withdrawal is mentioned by only thirteen respondents.[24] This may be due to Stopes's disapproval of the latter method, and also to the respondents' reluctance to be too explicit. Data from maternal clinics in Manchester and Salford indicate that both withdrawal and abstinence were widely practised by working-class couples, though the former was used more frequently.[25]

In sum, the weight of evidence points strongly to coitus interruptus as the most popular method in the first phase of the decline, before the widespread use of contraceptive devices.[26] Yet the Stopes correspondence and the clinic data suggest that attempted abstinence was not negligible and may well have been underestimated in the surveys of Marcuse and Lewis-Faning. Demographers generally assume that couples trying to limit births before the widespread use of contraceptive devices would naturally practise coitus interruptus, as a less stressful method than prolonged celibacy.[27] But withdrawal was much less secure, and this generated another kind of stress – the fear of pregnancy – mentioned by several female respondents who favoured abstinence for this reason. Perhaps most women writing to Stopes failed to mention withdrawal because they did not take it seriously as a birth-control option.[28] The technique depends on male commitment and control; it is likely that many women did not have much faith in being able 'to push him out of the way when I think it's near'.[29] As one woman explained in a letter pleading for contraceptive devices:

160

My husband had been withdrawing all the time and the only time I had a suspicion he was not so careful was on his birthday and [nine months later] my second boy was born. ... I make my husband and myself miserable by always worrying in case I have another baby. Please do help us.[30]

The rhythm method was not available to couples practising abstinence or withdrawal in these decades. There was an awareness that the chances of conception were unevenly distributed over the menstrual cycle, but the process and timing of ovulation were not understood. Prevailing medical theory had it exactly backwards, postulating that the 'safe time' was mid-cycle.[31] Couples abandoning a random schedule of intercourse in favour of this advice would have considerably increased their chances of conception; little wonder, then, that the method was disparagingly termed 'Vatican roulette'. In any event, it was not widely practised. The implication of such ignorance is clear: abstainers had to avoid intercourse at all times, and withdrawers had to separate every time. Both methods would have been a great deal easier to employ, particularly in obtaining men's full co-operation, if they could have been observed for a specific week each month and relinquished in favour of normal intercourse the rest of the time.

The determination to 'keep right' in an era before the general use of contraception created an acute dilemma, since the only proper (healthy, natural and moral) avenue for the sex drive was uninterrupted coitus within marriage. Non-coital forms of sex play were clearly beyond the pale for the vast majority of working-class couples, a testament to the rigidity of their sexual socialization. While only a small minority was prepared to experiment, this portion undoubtedly increased as the pressure to call a halt mounted. Woycke detects a rise in oral and anal sex in Germany in the early twentieth century, citing the independent reports of two physicians who were convinced that such practices were 'shockingly frequent' among working-class couples.[32] In her introduction to *Mother England,* Stopes noted that 'in a very few [letters] one or two sentences too intense for publication have been cut out'; these were probably references to non-coital sex. There is one allusion to sodomy in *Dear Doctor Stopes.*[33]

All sources agree that contraceptive devices of any type were infrequently employed by working-class couples before 1920. In Lewis-Faning's survey, fewer than 10 per cent of working-class women marrying before 1920 report any use of mechanical means by either partner. The German findings are similar.[34] Given the widespread desire to limit, why were barrier methods and spermicides not used more often? Respondents wrote bluntly of their own lamentable ignorance concerning the most elementary matters of human reproduction and contraception.[35] Most had heard tell of various 'remedies'; many had tried devices and drugs that 'put you right' offered for sale by charlatans and quacks. Contraceptives were often confused with abortifacients, an impression that was undoubtedly reinforced by unscrupulous advertisements for various products in the penny press.[36] Repeatedly, respondents complained that these commodities were injurious or ineffective, often both.[37] Furthermore, contraceptives were expensive items on a tight working-class budget. In Germany around the turn of the century, rubber condoms cost about five marks per dozen, roughly half a day's pay for a skilled worker.[38] In Britain as well, contraceptives were expensive and often difficult to obtain in working-class districts.[39] Several writers complained to Stopes of the expense of contraceptives, and others were unable to figure out where they could be purchased, indicating that in many neighbourhoods they were not yet sold over the counter in local shops.[40] Finally, some women who thoroughly disliked sex with their husbands (as many did) feared that the regular use of contraceptives would remove a compelling rationale for refusing sex in the face of their husbands' 'lustfulness'. As was noted in another study, 'For such a woman the use of a contraceptive would remove her strongest weapon in the game of sexual politics.'[41]

People's fear of contraception was partly based on a well-founded suspicion of bogus products, but was also due to misconceptions as to the harmful side-effects of 'preventatives'.[42] The advice of doctors was a major source of such misapprehensions.[43] Leaders of the British Medical Association condemned contraceptives as unnatural and warned that all sorts of maladies would befall their users. Espousing semen as a cure-all elixir for women absorbed through the vaginal wall, they opposed anything which interfered with the intermingling of secretions.[44] For many working people, fears of physical injury and mental disorder were blended with deep moral reservations and aesthetic distaste; they regarded contraceptives as 'repulsive and unnatural'.[45] Condoms had an unsavoury reputation, being associated with prostitution, extra-marital liaisons, and the prevention of venereal disease, which *was* the principal context of their use at this time. People's compunction in this regard was buttressed by the major Christian denominations, Catholic and Protestant, which 'viewed with alarm the growing practice of the artificial restriction of the family', urging 'all Christian people to discountenance [such means] … as demoralizing to character and hostile of national welfare'.[46]

Most doctors blocked the dissemination of contraceptive knowledge and devices; they felt that it was their duty to do so. In France, the medical profession was extremely sensitive to the protracted debate on the decline of the nation's birth rate, and doctors were reluctant to advise women to cease childbearing.[47] Doctors elsewhere were more inclined to counsel women to stop while refusing to tell them how. Among the letters of Norwegian women writing to the maternal clinic in Oslo, 'we find examples that a doctor has advised a woman not to get pregnant, due to her health, but has not told the woman anything about what she could do to avoid pregnancy.' In Germany, 'women reported that "thousands of times" doctors would advise them to avoid further pregnancy, yet when asked how to do this responded only with a shrug of the shoulders.'[48] In Britain, married women encountered the same obstinacy: 'When the last baby was born the doctor said can't you finish up but when I asked him how ... he just laughed. What's the use of saying finish up when they won't tell us poor women how to.'[49] Thirty-five respondents in *Mother England* mention such rebuffs, often with a good deal of anger.[50]

The refusal to assist patients in need was not confined to an unrepresentative rearguard of doctors. The editor of the *British Medical Journal,* authoritative organ of the British Medical Association, wrote in 1901: 'The medical profession as a whole has set its face against such [contraceptive] practices which are unnatural and degrading in their mental effect, and oft times injurious to both husband and wife in their physical results.'[51] A prominent doctor speaking at the Leipzig Society for Obstetrics in 1900 insisted that 'the use of contraceptives of any sort can only serve lust, and every doctor, out of concern for public opinion, must not place himself in the position of abetting such behaviour.'[52] By the 1920s, increasing numbers of doctors were becoming uncomfortable with their profession's embargo on prophylactics, and a minority risked their reputations to offer patients practical assistance.[53] In Norway, Blom found a major shift in the late 1920s, with doctors becoming much more helpful thenceforth. But medical schools still taught nothing at all about contraception, and the conviction that all such devices were deleterious to health persisted in the profession.[54] Whenever doctors were swept up in the competitive imperialist maelstrom of the time, portraying the trend to smaller families as a collective act of 'race suicide', their opposition hardened.[55]

While doctors led the resistance, public health nurses, maternity home matrons, pharmacists and government officials also spurned requests for birth-control information.[56] 'The Ministry of Health they would rather learn us how to have them rather than tell us how to avoid them. ... The health visitor said it was very wrong to do anything to stop yourself from having children. ... I don't care if I never see her again. They are no good to us.'[57] One woman commended Stopes on 'your outspoken fearless comments on a government that won't release Birth Control knowledge. ... If only some of the fatheads could come and live here for a while, I am sure out of pure pity for the little ones and the poor harassed mothers, they would soon ... release the Birth Control knowledge.'[58] Several letters reveal class resentment at the withholding of information desperately needed by the poor.[59] 'The rich seem to think a working woman has no right to know anything, at least that has been my own experience', wrote a woman who wanted Stopes to address her reply to 'the lodge' lest her mistress see it and disapprove 'of my trying to prevent being pregnant'. 'I feel that it is a great injustice and unchristian-like that rich women should have this knowledge and a poor woman should live in ignorance of it. ... We absolutely cannot afford any more children and it's a sin to know the poor are to be oppressed because of the wealthier classes. I don't begrudge wealth but I do its value of knowledge.'[60]

Worried by their own sinking birth rates, the propertied classes deplored the 'indiscriminate multiplication of the lower classes'. The increasing disparity in birth rates between the classes stood at the heart of eugenicist agitation on 'the Population Question'. As the Anglican bishops put it in a 1908 conference statement, there was a 'danger of deterioration whenever the race is recruited from the inferior and not from the superior stocks'.[61] While the eugenicists' analysis of the dangers of genetic deterioration achieved broad middle-class assent, their proposed remedy – the mass distribution of birth-control information and devices – was widely spurned. Until the 1920s, when the tide of public opinion finally turned, the major institutions of the propertied classes stood squarely with Malthus against the neo-Malthusians: the answer to the problem of overbreeding among the lower orders was marital prudence and moral restraint. If contraceptives were readily available, the poor would sink into sexual debauchery, marital fidelity would become passé, and the family would disintegrate. As late as 1923 in Britain, the National Council of Public Morals, a bastion of respectability, warned of 'the grave social perils ... of mechanical methods'.[62]

In so far as doctors and clerics actively obstructed the dissemination of contraceptive knowledge and devices in a period of burgeoning proletarian desire to limit births, they slowed the curtailment of working-class fertility. But in another way, their influence was catalytic. An inchoate desire for fewer children could not be transformed into an implacable determination to quit until it was widely known that limitation was a real option. Urban elites with smaller families provided an example of fertility limitation to the labouring classes. This was hardly a matter of moral guidance; it was more a case of rank hypocrisy, as Stopes's respondents indignantly pointed out. While doctors were withholding practical birth-control information from their proletarian patients, they achieved the lowest birth rate of any occupational group in Britain! Clerics were not far behind. The lesson for working-class people, gleaned through observation at a distance, was simply that it was possible to control fertility. Furthermore, they strongly suspected that a great many affluent couples did so without relinquishing marital sex or suffering the needless anxieties of coitus interruptus. This realization undoubtedly undermined a sense that large families were natural and inevitable, and fortified the desire to be free from compulsory childbirth. But access to the requisite knowledge and devices was not readily forthcoming from those who seemed to control 'the means of reproduction' just as surely as they controlled the means of production. 'We women of the working classes only know ... the horrible servitude [and] poverty ... [an] excess of childbearing means. ... The poor people of this land cry out in anguish for this knowledge which the aristocracy and the capitalists would have withheld.'[63]

Most socialist parties, ostensibly leaders of progressive working-class opinion, refused to identify with proletarian anger on this issue or support practical measures of redress. They too opposed the adoption of family limitation and the use of contraceptives in marriage, arguing that 'the Population Question' was a false issue exploited by reactionaries to blame poverty on the poor, diverting attention from the real source of inequality (the capitalist system) and the true solution (class struggle).[64] Overpopulation was dismissed as a Malthusian myth. Good socialists were urged to place their faith in the boundless capacity of humankind to produce wealth for all, irrespective of numbers, in the classless society of the future. When two social-democratic physicians in Berlin, appalled by the poor health of their working-class female patients, publicly proclaimed women's right to control their own bodies, the SPD acted quickly, calling a meeting billed 'Against the Birth Strike'. Before a hall packed with working-class followers, party luminaries such as Klara Zetkin and Rosa Luxemburg rose to denounce the very idea of birth control. In Zetkin's words, it was an individualist indulgence, 'a quackish method for improving the condition of the working classes'. Impervious to the pressing needs of working-class women, Zetkin (long-time editor of *Equality,* the SPD's national women's paper) insisted that 'the proletariat must consider the need for having as many fighters as possible.' Luxemburg, who rarely spoke on personal and family matters, saw fit to weigh in on this occasion. 'The social question can never be resolved by self-help, but only by mass help', she assured her audience. 'As a weapon for the proletariat, child limitation must be rejected categorically.'[65] The huge attendance at the meeting itself, Luxemburg intoned, was indicative of the backwardness of the masses who would not turn out to SPD rallies on the military budget. Despite the undoubted prestige of such speakers, most members of the audience were unswayed. An observer later recalled: 'Every speaker who spoke in favour [of birth control] was greeted with vociferous, long-lasting applause while [opponents] were so hissed that they had difficulty in going on.'[66]

Not all parties of the Left were so impervious to the plight of working-class women. In Norway, the Labour Party addressed their concerns at an early date; in 1886, an issue of the Party's paper *The Social Democrat* was confiscated and the editor taken to court for publishing an article discussing 'marriage without more children than one wants'. Rather than counterposing personal emancipation to the class struggle, as the German SPD did, many Norwegian socialists sought to place the fight for birth control on the political agenda. Augusta Aasen stressed the need for proletarian women to limit childbearing 'to raise their own and the working class's economic and cultural level so they are better equipped for the class struggle being waged.'[67] In France, the syndicalists presented the 'grève de ventre' as a facet of the General Strike which would bring down the capitalist order. A number of CGT unions supported birth control, disseminated neo-Malthusian literature, and held public meetings where the obstinacy of the medical profession was denounced.[68] Many socialist publicists and doctors openly advocated the use of contraceptives and assisted in their dissemination. The two Berlin physicians mentioned above persisted in their efforts, undeterred by police harassment and the censure of the SPD leadership.[69] In Britain, Fabian socialists such as Annie Besant led the campaign for birth-control information, while the major organizations of the British labour movement ignored the issue until the 1920s. Yet as 'the Population Question' was politicized, a number of Labour MPs became outspoken advocates of free dissemination, deploring the party leadership's inaction. Registering the anger and urgency of proletarian women, the National Conference of Labour Women voted overwhelmingly in favour of publicly funded birth-control information in 1924. Despite mounting internal opposition, the Labour government, elected for the first time in the same year, maintained the obstructive policies of its Tory predecessor, forbidding the distribution of contraceptive information through welfare centres and grant-aided clinics.[70]

Given the resistance of most doctors and public health officers, how did working-class people obtain contraceptive information? The main literary vehicle was the penny press, where condoms and abortifacients were increasingly advertised from the 1890s on.[71] Neo-Malthusian propaganda tracts were also widely available, but most were long on condescending rhetoric and short on down-to-earth assistance. Yet several of the more practical birth-control pamphlets became runaway bestsellers, with multiple printings annually, indicating an intense hunger for contraceptive information.[72] Could proletarians, especially females, read this material with adequate comprehension? Working-class literacy had made major strides in the second half of the nineteenth century. In England, one bride in two was unable to sign her name in the marriage register in 1850; by 1900, practically all could.[73] It seems reasonable to conclude that most people interested in obtaining contraceptive devices would have been able to read newspaper advertisements and the more practical pamphlets by birth-control advocates that were written with working-class audiences in mind. A semi-literate Frenchwoman explained her interest in neo-Malthusian literature: 'We are our own mistresses! ... In the books that are sold to us it is impossible to understand anything, but it is for the illustrations and for the addresses that are at the back that one buys them.'[74]

Word of mouth was probably the principal means by which working-class people learned of contraceptives. An older woman commented: 'If you hear a knot of young woman talking together, the chances are that the topic will be the means of prevention.'[75] For small-town residents, the influence of accessible cities was noticeable to many observers. In Huddersfield, 'inter-communication with Leeds by tram and train and the influence of that city, where neo-Malthusian literature and appliances abound, has been an important factor in the reduction of the birth-rate in the neighbourhood.'[76] Yet the misinformation about sex and procreation conveyed in modern school playgrounds must give rise to scepticism; where intense curiosity is combined with ignorance, peer networks tend to spread garbled, incoherent and utterly fanciful accounts.[77] 'It's impossible to ask knowledge of one's acquaintances,' a woman explained to Stopes, 'as they either Laugh or give wonderful cures.'[78] The main obstacle in working-class neighbourhoods appears not to have been a reluctance to discuss contraception (at least in homosocial gatherings) but ignorance, misinformation, and a still-strong taboo against the use of 'artificial' devices within marriage.[79]

Lewis-Faning's survey indicates that the decisive shift among working-class controllers from 'natural' to 'appliance' methods occurred in the cohorts marrying in the 1920s, a decade when working people were deluging Marie Stopes with letters pleading for contraceptive information. What devices were they seeking? The great majority of requests in *Mother England* are unspecified, and writers appear to be eager to pursue whatever method Stopes would recommend. Since she had publicly proclaimed that caps and pessaries were her first choice, it seems reasonable to infer that most women respondents were asking for female devices. For those whose husbands were uncooperative or downright hostile to family limitation, this would have been their only recourse short of abortion. In Lewis-Faning's survey, over half the couples using 'appliance' methods relied on female devices entailing vaginal insertion.[80] Since the ratio of male to female contraceptives employed remained stable from one marriage cohort to the next, the spread of mechanical contraception in the 1920s must have involved a sharp increase in female devices, rising from extremely low prewar levels.

This increase is impressive, since there were major obstacles to be surmounted in using diaphragms and cervical caps. In the first place, they were harder to obtain and more expensive than condoms; even if homemakers could figure out where to acquire them, they had very little disposable income for such 'extras' after purchasing family necessities. Secondly, diaphragms and caps required an experienced clinician to select and fit initially, and these were in short supply. Many women tried to select the right size themselves, with very uncertain results. If caps were not properly fitted, they would become dislodged and fail to contracept; such miscues were commonplace in the early years of their popular use.[81] Furthermore, in the absence of indoor plumbing, caps and diaphragms were liable to be agents of vaginal infection. In a 1934 survey of working-class London, water still had to be fetched from outside the residence in half the households.[82] Finally, and perhaps most significantly, women had to overcome an intense and deeply incul-cated aversion to touching their own genitals. The Guild respondents speak eloquently of the unease they felt in this regard, with several deploring what they termed 'mock modesty'.[83] The next generation of women were evident-ly taking the initiative in an area where one might expect to find an over-whelming reluctance to experiment – mute testimony to the intensity of their desire to control childbearing.

Procreative Risks, Conjugal Power, Sexual Passion and Self-Control

In so far as women bear most of the burdens of repeated pregnancy, childbear-ing and childcare, we would expect them to be more highly motivated than men to call a halt. The evidence bears this out. The assessments of McLaren and Berlanstein on working-class couples in France, and Woycke's judgement on the German evidence, concur with my reading of the British material: 'Male determination to avoid pregnancy was seldom as strong as women's desire to do so.'[84] While most men agreed on the need to stop, women were the driving force behind family limitation.[85]

When women grew determined to cease childbearing, were they able to alter the sexual conduct of their husbands to lessen the risk of conception? In marriages where husbands adamantly refused to co-operate, wives had very little influence and were forced to submit to their sexual advances:

> I am sorry to say that my husband is one of those who think we ought to let Nature, as he calls it, have its way and that if I have twenty children it is only my duty as a married woman to put up with it. I am always dreading my husband wanting his wishes fulfilled and I am powerless to prevent him.

> My husband who is a Catholic does not believe in stopping life by any means. When I say I do not want any more he gets very nasty with me and won't try to keep me right.[86]

In these circumstances women often became inured to coital risk, resorting instead to abortions sought on their own initiative to deal with the hazards of repeated pregnancies.

Where husbands were not reported to be coercive, most female respond-ents indicated that they *were* able to reduce coital frequency through dissua-sion, deferral and evasion. Some developed the habit of 'staying up mending', retiring after their husbands had fallen asleep.[87] While they could put off inter-course for a time, the vast majority of female respondents could not steadfastly refuse a cohabiting husband his 'conjugal rights'. Periodic 'connections' were seen as essential in preserving conjugal harmony: 'To maintain the domestic peace, I must nevertheless once in a while let my husband "have his way."' Another woman wrote: 'I cannot always refuse my husband as it only means living a cat and dog life for both of us.' Without the active co-operation of husbands, complete celibacy was thus out of the question. Even with their consent, abstinence and withdrawal racked marital relations with tension, bitterness and alienation: 'Our love seems to bring us more suffering than anything else'; 'the result is our married life is spoiled and we are gradually drifting apart.'[88]

The sex drive was perceived as an implacable pressure which would continue to mount if not periodically released; sooner or later it had to be satisfied. 'I don't think any man and woman that really love each other can resist nature however much they try', thought a woman writing to Stopes: 'we have tryed very hard but still the third baby came.' A man confessed: 'I have seriously tried to hold myself in check but it's impossible ... yet when I fail to keep myself in control well there's more trouble and it has caused me many a restless night, and bad feelings between the wife and I.'[89] Many women who had managed to 'hold out' for several months realized that they could not continue to do so, and wrote to Stopes with urgent requests for contraceptive information:

Since my last baby was born six months ago, my husband and I have not cohabited as I am so afraid of anything happening again. ... We cannot go on like this any longer as we are both only young. ... My husband is getting fed up. Think how hard it is in one room.[90]

My husband says I don't care for him at all now or I would do as he asks but I do care but am afraid of the consequences. It is very hard as I know it is a matter of time with him and he thinks I do not want him.[91]

Many women feared the consequences of marital abstinence, 'knowing there is much unfaithfulness on the part of the husband where families are limited'. 'If you want to keep your husband straight, you must give and take so I have been told', one woman informed Stopes. A Norwegian woman explained to the staff of the Oslo clinic: 'If you deny your husband his desire, the law gives him a right to go to another and *that* is something which a wife who loves her husband will avoid. What should I do?'[92] In some cases, men threatened to seek sexual liaisons elsewhere if denied at home.

Women who were gratified to gain the active co-operation of their spouses often worried about the potentially harmful effects of abstinence. Given the perceived imbalance in the sexual appetites of men and women, it is not surprising that most of the concern was focused on men: 'My husband is one of the finest and studies me in every way ... but I am wondering if it will eventually injure his health that I have to deny him so often his rights.' It was widely believed that abstinent men were more likely to contract tuberculosis than their sexually active counterparts.[93] Some women were concerned that their celibate husbands were 'abusing' themselves, fearing mental degeneration.[94]

The way men approached their wives sexually was immensely important to women; they often characterized men as good or bad husbands on this criterion alone.[95] Selfish or 'lustful' men were roundly condemned, even by wives who did not contest their right to intercourse whenever they felt like it. In no position to assess the sexual disposition of suitors before consenting to marry, women described themselves as being 'blessed' to have ended up with a careful husband, or alternately, to be 'unfortunate' to be saddled with an inconsiderate dolt. In either case, it was the luck of the draw.

A good husband deserved a good wife: the obligation of reciprocity within an unequal relationship generated self-sacrifice on the part of the subordinate partner. Many women felt guilty in denying considerate husbands their marital dues:

> He has been so good and denied Himself all this time and of course I feel I cannot ask Him to wait any longer.

> Since [my last pregnancy] we have never let Nature have her full swing (if I may say so) and I feel for his sake. ... It does not seem right to deny him, but I dread it happening again.

> My husband is very good, but very passionate. ... I don't want to hurt my husband he is very kind.

> I feel mean in refusing, that which as a married woman I have a right to give, for my husband has been so fine, so patient, kindly and considerate, yet there is always the fear [conception] might happen the first time I agreed.

> Thanks due entirely to my husband who never dreams of worrying me more than once or perhaps twice a month. ... I hate to say 'No' in view of my husband's goodness to me.

A woman's empathy could be dangerous in this context: 'I was so afraid of being caught again that I stopped all intercourse, then my husband fell ill and of course I had to humour him a bit, the result was another baby.'[96]

Since women feared pregnancy more than men did, the consequence of differential distress for the ratio of sexual desire is apparent. Several women reported that the dread of another pregnancy had destroyed their passion for 'connections' with their husbands.[97] The widely held belief that females who became highly aroused during intercourse were much more likely to become pregnant, particularly if they had orgasms, must have dampened many women's ardour.[98] Some women were frank enough to admit that they found no pleasure in intercourse, but were nevertheless concerned for their husbands:

> I have never at any time had a desire to be with a man and even with my Husband I never get any sensation or feeling. My Husband on the other Hand is very Lustfull. ... I would like to satisfy his desires yet I am terrified at the thought [of getting pregnant] and it causes unpleasant scenes in the Home.[99]

For a substantial minority of women, however, their own sexual desires, together with their husbands', made prolonged abstinence untenable. The prevailing view of feminist historians is that working-class women in the past disliked sex and wished for as few encounters with their husbands as possible. Elizabeth Roberts, in her oral history interviews with working-class women in Preston and Barrow, reports:

> Sexual intercourse was regarded as necessary for procreation or as an activity indulged in by men for their own pleasure, but it was never discussed in the evidence as something which could give mutual happiness. No hint was ever made that women might have enjoyed sex.[100]

The Stopes correspondence is not nearly so bleak in this regard. While several respondents confirm the conventional stereotype, others present a more balanced and mutual picture, with female passion apparent.[101] The following authors are all women:

> I have a lot of 'Spanish blood' too in my veins which doesn't help any; living as we do is wearing my nerves to pieces.

> When two people are so fond of one another as we are, as I have one of the best, you like to get the best out of life.

> At certain times of the Month we nearly get beyond control ... it is strange for us to go four years without proper connections.

> My husband tells me to control and hold myself in check, well I can, but we do without kisses, and oh, lots of other little things that help make life pleasant.

> It's impossible to put passion entirely out of our lives, for it's the love I bear my dear husband that makes me yield to him at such times.

> I am very passionate as well as he, and we have been so wonderfully happy and I do so want to make this happiness last.[102]

While most respondents portray men's sexual desire as stronger than women's, wives who receive no pleasure from sex appear to be in a minority.[103]

While for many women sexual consent was motivated by love and affectionate reciprocity, others experienced their 'wifely duty' more as a moral obligation. For these women, 'living as nature and God intended us to do' was a basic tenet of Christian marriage; to withhold sexual consent was selfish and sinful.[104] Perhaps more important than Church doctrine in the strict sense was the pervasive conviction that procreation was natural; one dare not interfere with Mother Nature. A north Lancashire woman interviewed by Elizabeth Roberts recalled visiting her doctor and breaking down when he confirmed that she was pregnant:

> He said, 'It's no good crying now, it's too late!' I felt like saying that it wasn't the woman's fault all the time. You are married and you have got to abide by these things. ... They don't know what I have gone through to try to avoid it, you know. We never would take anything in them days. God had sent them and they had to be there. I'm not a religious person, but that were my idea.[105]

For this woman and many others, the marriage contract entailed 'abiding by these things' – remaining open to the risk of conception while doing her conjugal duty. Wrapped in the ideological mists of procreative naturalism lurked the brute force of men exercising their conjugal rights:

> I thought, like hundreds of women do today, that it was only natural, and you had to bear it. ... My husband being some years my senior, I found that he had not a bit of control over his passions. ... If the woman does not feel well she must not say so, as a man has such a lot of ways of punishing a woman if she does not give in to him.'[106]

Under these circumstances, it was extremely difficult for many women to communicate their most basic wishes to their husbands. Many did not even try. A Guild member confessed: 'I may say here that I did not want any more. ... Of course, I can see now that I was a good bit to blame, because I thought I was only like other women would be, and kept all to myself.' For their part, many men looked the other way. A Berlin journeyman was asked whether his wife practised any form of birth control. He did not know, but thought she 'probably looks after that herself because she didn't want the last two children.'[107]

While women, on balance, were keener to cease childbearing than their husbands, most men were willing to exercise at least some self-restraint in the marriage bed. The prevalence of coitus interruptus as the principal birth-control technique establishes a *prima facie* case for male co-operation. Marie Stopes accused working-class men of being more impervious to their wives' wish to avoid conception than 'better informed' men.[108] Yet in reading *Mother England*, I was impressed by the reported willingness of most husbands to restrain their sexual desires. Ida Blom's reading of the Norwegian correspondence also suggests a substantial degree of male collaboration. In the British correspondence, men who are portrayed as being co-operative outnumber uncooperative males two to one, with the former constituting a clear majority even in the letters of female respondents.[109] These men were praised by their spouses as being careful and considerate; they did not 'worry' their wives by insistent sexual demands, and they kept themselves 'under control'. 'My husband is very good and for three years has not had a real "pleasure" in order to keep me right.'... 'My husband is an Ideal daddy since little Reggie came he has had no connections with me at all he is afraid of my becoming pregnant again.'[110]

Where spouses found themselves in dispute over reproductive priorities, what was the nature of their discord? Hypothetically, disagreements concerning the risks of unintended conception might arise for three reasons: couples could differ on the desirability of having another child; they could disagree over coital frequency and other aspects of sexual conduct; or they might have conflicting approaches to birth control. The correspondence indicates that the latter two were the primary bones of contention. Simmering tension arose from men's sexual impulsiveness or indiscipline, based on the reckless assertion of their conjugal prerogatives rather than deriving from their desire to have more children than their spouses wished.

There were a variety of attitudes among uncooperative men. A minority were intensely hostile to the use of contraceptives of any sort and resigned to accept the number of children that Nature, or God, provided. A Frenchwoman reported:

> My husband saw that I wanted to cheat nature. He flew into an awful rage; I was afraid that he would kill me; I resigned myself to the ordeal and now I am going to live with the continual fear of a fifth child.[111]

Some men were ambivalent or simply indifferent to the prospects of another pregnancy: 'My husband doesn't care if we have a dozen, so long as he satisfies his own selfish desires.'[112] A third group of uncooperative men shared their wives' desire to avoid conception, often feeling very intensely on the matter, but were adamant that it was a woman's responsibility to 'look after herself'; after all, they reasoned, it was women who got pregnant. Evidently feeling that their virility and conjugal rights were at stake, they refused to alter their own sexual conduct in the slightest:[113]

> My Husband is inclined to get angry each time there are signs of another arrival and thinks I ought to take all expense and blame on my shoulders, although I do my level best to keep right.[114]

> He was so angry [to discover that she was pregnant] he never came into my room again for two months ... since then he has been very cruel to me because I will not submit to his embrace.[115]

Eleanor Rathbone perceived the connection between women's economic dependency in marriage and men's conjugal prerogatives. Men's sexual access was 'still enforced on their wives as part of the price they are expected to pay for being kept by them'.[116]

Reasons for Wanting to Stop

What reasons did respondents give for wishing to cease childbearing? The outstanding response in the surveys of Lewis-Faning and Polano was that they could not afford any more children. Stopes's respondents concurred, referring most frequently to the husband's wage or irregular employment, implying that his was the primary and often sole income.[117] Breadwinner responsibilities weighed heavily on men's minds as they contemplated the arrival of another child. 'I don't want to be the cause of bringing children into this world and not being able to keep them.' ... 'I am only a working man it take all my time to feed and cloth them if there should be any more I don't know what we should do.'[118] Women frequently cited financial worries too; several mentioned employment opportunities forgone in the event of pregnancy.[119] Overcrowded households impressed many respondents who insisted they had no room for any more.[120]

Concern about the mother's health was the second reason, cited by one woman in four in Lewis-Faning's survey and slightly more frequently in Polano's.[121] Women's dread of future pregnancies and their fierce determination to bear no more children is an especially prominent theme in the Stopes correspondence:[122]

> I have tryed many Pills But Have not seen the desired effect. Please Help me! I have Had my share, ... but I am frighten to death, with what I have gone through, My life is only a living Hell, Yours truly. ...[123]

Similar passages could be cited at length: pleas for help – urgent, fearful, on the brink of despair – by women who recount horrendous experiences 'in confinement', and whose own pain and disabilities were often highlighted by the ominous warnings of attending doctors and midwives that another birth could kill them.[124] The fear of pregnancy under such circumstances can easily be envisioned: the authors do not leave it to our imagination. They speak of sleepless nights, worrying themselves sick, moments of terrible anguish when their 'courses' were overdue, and bitter regret and recrimination at a 'slip in a moment of weakness' after years of total abstinence. Most women recounted difficulties in previous pregnancies, frequently of an acute nature. Some of them would have wanted another child if their previous pregnancies had been relatively easy, but in the circumstances, they decided that they could not abide further births.[125]

Another familiar theme is deteriorating health after the last birth, often in conjunction with a sick or restless infant. While the major concern was the condition of the mother, the illness or disability of other family members (children, husband and elderly parents) also demanded a homemaker's attention, draining her energy and making it imperative not to have any more children.[126] Recognizing the economic importance of their own toil even when most of it was unpaid, many women tied the family's living standards directly to the status of their own health. Combining productive and reproductive tasks was extremely problematic when the timing and frequency of childbirth were not under women's control. The extra burden of another unplanned infant, just as the youngest was toilet-trained, appears to have been the proverbial straw that broke many a woman's back. Several respondents mentioned the acute strains of having to do arduous housework close to term, or rising too quickly from confinement after a difficult birth to meet the demands of the household, suffering injury or debilitating exhaustion in the process. While economic worries were foremost in men's minds, many empathized with their wives' fear of pregnancy and were evidently willing to waive their conjugal rights when there was a serious risk of conception:

> After this child is born I feel I will have to leave her alone as we are both frightened that we may have another and I don't know what we would do if there was.

> I love my wife very dearly and I am worried out of my life because I really think another baby would kill her.[127]

Demographers conventionally present the desire to cease childbearing as arising from the cultural formation of an ideal family size, with couples striving to stop once they have successfully borne the planned number of children.[128] There is no doubt that the two-child family became a common target for middle-class couples after the Second World War; but was such a goal prevalent among the first generation of proletarian limiters? It does not appear to have been. In the Lewis-Faning survey, 84 per cent of working-class women marrying between 1910 and 1924 report that they did not plan to have a definite number of children at marriage. Family-planning norms strengthened over time, with 43 per cent of the 1940–45 cohort indicating that they did plan in this way.[129] The Stopes correspondence corroborates this impression. While a planned ideal was not a factor in the motivation to limit, there is no doubt that the cultural norm was shifting towards smaller families. As one man told Marcuse, 'Four are enough already. We're already laughed at for having four.'[130] Middle-class reformers felt that the functionality of proletarian families hinged on the capacity to control their numbers. A German observer noted:

> In families that are childless or blessed with one or two children, conditions are usually simple, but orderly, and marital harmony prevails. Where there are a lot of children, there is usually strife, distress, filth, and misery.[131]

Perennial Reasons and the Timing of the Decline

Economic constraints and endangered health are compelling reasons in their own right for seeking ways to prevent (or terminate) further pregnancies. Shall we accept the respondents' stated motives at face value? We should, while recognizing that they do not explain the timing of the fertility decline, nor the rapidity of its spread. The stopping pattern was new; the reasons given for adopting it were not. Victorian women had borne more children than women in the Edwardian era would. The former's health was also poor, their pregnancies were just as dangerous and debilitating; their families' incomes were lower, and domestic labour burdens even more onerous. If these conditions were sufficient to induce a change in coital behaviour, why had it not taken place much earlier?

To engender family limitation, both spouses must have a strong *desire* to cease childbearing and the *capacity to take effective action* towards that end. Which factor had been absent before the onset of the decline, and what changed to bring it into being? On the part of women, it seems certain that the wish to limit was present for several decades at least before they were able to achieve this objective. The best index of their feelings in this regard is the high and rising rate of attempted abortions among married women which so alarmed contemporaries. A substantial minority of pregnancies had always been greeted with a sinking heart and feelings of trepidation for the future, but in the first quarter of the twentieth century this proportion was rising. Abortifacients were expensive, injurious, and ineffective more times than not; yet women went to great lengths to obtain them.[132] Who can doubt that many more women would have joined them if these 'remedies' had been cheaper, less dangerous and more effective?

If women were already keen to shorten their childbearing careers, what brought husbands round to their way of thinking? The major impetus, in my view, was the underlying shift in the family economy, inducing a convergence in the reproductive interests of men and women.[133] In the traditional family wage economy, children worked from an early age and their contribution was obvious to parents. A French miner's wife was asked why she had seven children. 'They come naturally', she replied, 'and then, when they grow up, they contribute their wages to the family; it helps balance the household budget.'[134]

A Shoreditch matchmaker told Lady Dilke in 1893, 'Of course, we cheat the School Board. It's hard on the little ones, but their fingers is so quick – they that has the most of 'em is best off.'[135] The next generation of parents would arrive at the opposite conclusion. When referring to children in economic terms, they treated them as a net cost.[136]

The contrast between the Victorian and Edwardian generations can best be appreciated by looking at the difference in the dependency ratio at that point in the family cycle when the question of stopping first arose: when parents were in their mid to late thirties and their eldest children were becoming teenagers. Throughout most of the nineteenth century, working-class youth took paid jobs from the age of ten or eleven, if not earlier, earning more than enough to cover the costs of their own upkeep. As mothers entered the final phase of childbearing, the income of the eldest would ease their families' economic pinch. In the Edwardian era, the eldest children were still in school, attending fairly regularly, when a mother reached her mid thirties and had to determine whether to go on conceiving or try to call a halt.[137] Parents could not anticipate any substantial income supplements from children for another two or three years. Furthermore, the tradition of youth remitting their full wages to their parents had weakened by this time, particularly for boys in their late teens; even when they did go out to work, their income was not as secure from the parents' standpoint. Older daughters were not as likely to be available to mind the younger children, freeing mothers to seek employment. The delay and dissipation of children's economic contribution was accompanied by higher costs associated with prolonged schooling and regular year-round attendance.[138] At the same time, the potential supply of surviving children was increasing, as infant and child mortality declined sharply. This development widened the disparity between the desire for smaller families and the old procreative regime. Facing these prospects, the family's primary breadwinner was increasingly inclined to share his wife's view of the need to quit childbearing.

It was not poverty per se but the prospects of a lower living standard that gave proletarian couples pause for thought. The blunt admission by so many that they 'could not afford any more' ought to be interpreted in this way – as a matter of relative well-being, not absolute dearth. In the words of German workers: 'With children you can't amount to anything these days. We're still young and we want to have life a little better.' ... 'We want to get ahead, and our daughter should have things better than my wife and sister did.'[139] It was the upper layers of the working class that first began to limit. In 1907, Sidney Webb noted that the birth rate had declined far more among the members of the Hearts of Oak Friendly Society (the largest benefit society in Britain at the time, with 272,000 men as members) than in the general proletarian populace. He argued that it 'gave proof of thrift and foresight ... [among] the artisan and skilled mechanic class', the primary base of the association.[140] Seven years later,

Ethel Elderton arrived at the same verdict:

> Among the working classes, people who desire to 'get on' are house-proud and like to be well-dressed and enjoy pleasure; small families are the rule. Young wives will not be tied down by small children; they wish to dress, walk out and amuse themselves more than of old. The reduction has not occurred among the lowest and poorest class, who can neither afford to buy, or will not trouble to use, preventatives. To the lowest classes ... children are a good investment as they cost little to rear and become a source of income at thirteen years of age. To the better class of people children are an anxiety and expense and it is this class that resorts freely to preventative measures.[141]

By the early twentieth century, the continued prosperity of families in the upper strata of the working class became increasingly dependent on limiting conception and terminating unwanted pregnancies. Taking control of one's fertility became a mark of self-reliance and respectability, while the prolific poor were pitied or ridiculed. Formerly, fecundity had been associated with masculine virility; now, uncontrolled childbearing was considered to be reckless imprudence, a self-inflicted source of poverty.

Together with underlying shifts in the value of additional children, changes in reproductive consciousness, especially women's, galvanized the fertility decline. Let us examine the subjective transformation more closely. The dominant recollection of the older Guild women who had not limited was of stoic resignation; they would have liked fewer children, but they had felt that it was beyond their control:

> At the time it was much more usual to trust Providence, and if a woman died it only proved her weakness and unfitness for motherhood.

> In my early motherhood I took for granted that women had to suffer at these times, and that it was best to be brave and not to make a fuss.[142]

In the midst of such resignation, women 'got caught', babies 'just came', and kept coming. A consoling faith that the Lord would provide for all those He sent was extremely common among pre-limiters.[143] A Catholic factory worker from the Rhineland, married twenty years with five living and three dead children, hoped that no more would come, but comforted himself with the thought that 'if there are too many, then the dear Lord, who puts them in this world, will also feed them.'[144]

The Guild correspondents deeply regretted their mothers' prudish reluctance to provide them with sexual or reproductive information, vowing that this silence would not be repeated with their own daughters:[145]

> I was married at twenty-eight in utter ignorance of the things that most vitally affect a wife and mother. My mother, a dear, pious soul, thought ignorance was

innocence, and the only thing I remember her saying on the subject of childbirth was 'God never sends a babe without bread to feed it.' Dame Experience long ago knocked the bottom out of that argument for me.[146]

Among the daughters of procreative fatalists, stoicism finally crumbled. They began to take an instrumental attitude to their own health, considering repeated and uncontrolled pregnancy a preventable malady. Increasingly, they perceived the relationship between sex and procreation as a matter of probability and risk, rather than blind fate or God's will. Even though mechanical devices were still widely rejected as harmful and repugnant, contraception had finally come 'within the calculus of conscious choice' (to use Ansley Coale's felicitous phrase).[147] What had brought about this transformation in women's consciousness?

The rapid increase in the routine intervention of doctors in working-class pregnancy and birthing in the early twentieth century seems to have been a catalyst. In the second half of the nineteenth century, about 70 per cent of all babies were delivered by midwives without doctors in attendance; in the poorer districts of England, the proportion was undoubtedly higher.[148] By the interwar years, the pattern had changed dramatically: all but the poorest families could afford their services at confinement. The majority of correspondents who refer to the matter at all indicate that doctors attended their home births.[149] In these same decades, working-class homes were invaded by a burgeoning army of middle-class charity visitors and state officials. The home visits of public health nurses would have augmented the doctors' influence in turning pregnancy from a natural event into a medical problem.[150]

While refusing to help women obtain contraceptive devices, doctors did legitimate their fears concerning abnormal and protracted childbirth.[151] The doctors' solemn advice fills the Stopes correspondence, their most common instruction being to avoid further pregnancy, complete with terrifying warnings of the dire consequences of failing to do so. Their admonitions must have buttressed many a woman's resolve not to sacrifice her own health on the altar of her 'wifely duty' to her husband. Medical talk provided working-class women with a vocabulary of scientific authority better to envisage and describe the inner workings of their bodies and to assign terms to their maladies. The letters are full of such borrowed terminology – prolapses, embolisms, glycosuria, sciatica.[152] Imported into working-class speech, this alien discourse had its uses. It helped to erode the mysteries of the female body, shrouded in ignorance, shame and 'mock modesty'.[153] Medical discourse made it increasingly difficult to regard the maladies associated with childbirth as natural, a manifestation of God's will. Certainly infant deaths, formerly regarded as inevitable, were now considered preventable. Perhaps most importantly, 'the doctor's orders' were a powerful tool in convincing husbands that they ought to restrain themselves, or terrible afflictions (with impressive Latin titles) would befall the missus. Several male respondents reveal the deep impression that a man-to-man talk with the doctor made in persuading them to elevate concern for their wives' health above their own sexual desires: 'The doctor attending my wife "forbade" any more children.' ... 'I must not forget what the doctor says. My considerations are for my wife and my four children.'[154]

Feminism, predominantly a middle-class movement, also seems to have had a diffuse impact on working-class women, fortifying their resolve to stop. Victorian feminists had attacked the notion that a man had the God-given right to have sex with his wife whenever he felt like it, regardless of her wishes.[155] John Stuart Mill denounced the prerogative of spousal rape as a 'most disgusting barbarism, to enforce the lowest degradation of a human being, that of being made the instrument of an animal function contrary to her inclinations'.[156] This argument seems to have made ideological headway. In the matrimonial law reforms of the late-Victorian era, men's 'conjugal rights', traditionally sanctioned through the wedding vows, were tempered and relativized.[157] As the Guild women set down their thoughts two decades later, many expressed a feminist position:

> We must let the men know we are human beings and aspire to something more than to be mere objects on which they can satisfy themselves.[158]

> The wife's body belongs to herself ... it's the men who need to be educated ... no animal will submit to [sex on demand]. Why should the woman?[159]

Recognizably feminist insights were expressed by respondents on closely related issues. Several complained about the standard marital division of labour which permitted the breadwinner to abstain from childcare: 'Men should be more helpful and thoughtful. It is all very well for them to pop in and see [the children] for a few minutes and [go] out of the evenings alone.'[160] A woman writing to Stopes in 1923 presented a lengthy thought-experiment in gender reversal:

> To the men who would condemn you, I would like to give one month as a mother in a working man's home. ... They would have to feed that family, wash for it, bake for it, clean for it, make a good big dinner ... make old clothes into new. This would be fairly hard but 'God Help Them' what would they do if they were handicapped by pregnancy. You wouldn't have one enemy.[161]

Against the traditional pro-natalist morality of the Church, several of Stopes's respondents articulated a feminist counter-morality, anticipating the modern pro-choice slogan: 'Every child a wanted child'. Taking dead aim at the traditional Christian belief that God would provide for all, they insisted that it was 'wicked to bring children into the world to practically starve'.[162]

They redefined the maternal ideal: 'What real mother is going to bring a life into the world to be pushed into the drudgery of the world ... because of the strain on the family exchequer.'[163] Many argued that it would be unfair to their present children to have any more.[164]

Recalling their own reproductive experience before family limitation, Guild members were generally encouraged that the times were changing:

> I now see that a great deal of this agony ought never to have been, with proper attention. It is good to see some of our women waking up to this fact.

> Working-class women are ... far more self-respecting and less humble than their predecessors.[165]

A more insistent attitude by women accounts in part for men's increased willingness to exercise self-restraint. In her *Report on the English Birth Rate,* written in 1914, Ethel Elderton noted that contraception was fairly widely practised by working-class couples in the northern textile districts: 'The married women have frankly told our correspondent that they make their husbands take precautions to prevent conception, the two methods of prevention in use being the sheath and coitus interruptus.'[166]

Even if men's determination to stop was not as intense as their spouses', all that was necessary to avoid numerous conceptions was that husbands be willing to accede to their wives' wishes and not override them in bed. Spousal co-operation did not make withdrawal and abstinence secure methods; 'moments of weakness' and 'slips' were commonplace, as the letters attest. But a very considerable reduction in births was none the less achieved through a determined application of methods that remained notoriously haphazard on a personal level. To continue the descent, reaching the low birth rates that have prevailed in the industrialized world since the collapse of the postwar baby boom, it has been necessary for the great majority of reproductive couples to replace 'natural' methods with the regular use of contraceptives. But in the first phase of the transition, withdrawal and abstention were sufficient to produce a dramatic reduction in the birth rate. What changed in the first quarter of the twentieth century was not the means of birth control but the recognition by masses of women and men that sexual 'restraint' was possible and necessary. From that time on, the desire to avoid pregnancy took precedence over the desire for uninterrupted coitus in increasing numbers of working-class bedrooms.

In Chapter 1, we discussed the peculiarly loose equilibration between labour-power's consumption and its demographic replacement under capitalism. The fertility decline may be seen in this context as the final revolution in transfor-

181

ming the replacement cycle of labour-power. In the course of the second Industrial Revolution, employers gradually converted from an extensive to an intensive mode of consuming labour-power. Domestic commodity production declined, leaving women with fewer ways to earn money at home; young children were withdrawn from factories and sent to school in the face of mass campaigns against their exploitation in industry. The labour movement fought to define a 'living wage' as a wage sufficient to sustain a working man's family, and proletarian families came to rely more than ever before on his income to survive. These shifts in the family economy (occurring first among the upper layers of the working class) raised the costs, and curtailed the eventual benefits, of bearing additional children. In response, working-class families eventually brought their fertility into line with the new production regime. Breaking with an extensive mode of procreation (whereby women had continued to bear children until menopause), proletarian parents intensified the investment of time, energy and resources devoted to each child.

Since it has been a major purpose of this study to establish these links in the reproduction cycle of labour-power, I do not shrink from highlighting them here. But I must insist that they be understood as *culturally mediated connections* within a loose equilibration. The fertility decline cannot be understood adequately as a direct outcome of pragmatic rationality in the struggle to raise living standards. As well as being an economic adjustment, the widespread adoption of a new mode of fertility regulation was a cultural revolution arising from a breakthrough in reproductive consciousness. Demographers have long debated whether the fertility decline is best understood as an economic adjustment or a cultural innovation; this appears to be a spurious dichotomy. When we distinguish the reproductive interests of husbands and wives and see the declining birth rate as a result of both struggle and co-operation between spouses, it is no longer necessary to choose between economic and cultural accounts. We shall explore these theoretical issues more fully below, but first let us briefly recognize the gradual but profound impact of the fertility decline on working-class family life in three areas:

1. By shortening women's childbearing career from roughly fifteen to five years, the fertility decline improved their health, and (together with increasing longevity) created a life-phase after the children had grown up and left home when women could resume employment outside the home. This is the breach where the floodgate eventually opened, as masses of married women re-entered paid work, dissolving the male-breadwinner norm and lessening women's economic dependency in marriage.

2. The dawning realization that it was indeed possible to cease childbearing eroded procreative fatalism. The first phase of the fertility decline was thus

marked by a heightened anxiety about coital risk, as contraception was brought within the realm of conscious choice. When 'preventatives' became more widely available, acceptable and effective, however, it became possible for increasing numbers of couples to enjoy intercourse without the constant dread of unwanted pregnancy. The increasing dissociation of sex from procreative risk had far-reaching consequences. In Christianity, traditionally, marriage was negatively motivated as a necessary container for lust; but now, in a positive sense, sexual pleasure became a realistic objective, and eventually a major factor defining marital happiness and compatibility. Women have always had much more to lose by unwanted pregnancy than men, and hence more to worry about in bed; consequently, the impact of effective contraception on sexual self-expression and a sense of personal mastery over one's life-circumstances was ultimately much greater for females. The advent of 'the Pill' was the decisive turning point in this regard, beginning a new stage in the fertility decline.

3. The fertility decline both reflected and accelerated a transformation in the way children were valued – no longer for their economic contribution, but now for the intangible ways they might enrich the quality of their parents' lives. The more expensive children became in financial terms, the more priceless they were in emotional terms. One does not need six children to have this irreplaceable experience; it is much less draining to have two. The resources devoted to invaluable children varied inversely with their numbers; the fewer parents had, the more care was taken with their upbringing. Formerly devalued, maternal performance came to be regarded as the key to the child's future happiness. As such, it could no longer be left to women's nurturing instincts but had to be educated by health-care professionals and psychologists who knew what was best for the child. Eventually, the child-centred family emerged.

Explaining the Fertility Decline:
Towards an Un-Immaculate Reconception

To this point in the chapter, I have been primarily concerned to develop an empirical account of far-reaching changes in working-class conjugal relations in the course of the fertility decline. A number of criticisms of mainstream demographic research have been raised in passing, but the underlying theoretical issues have remained largely implicit. Let us now address them in a more sustained fashion.

There is an extensive literature on fertility regulation and on factors inducing a transition to smaller family size; most of it derives from contemporary fertility surveys conducted in Third World countries. The conceptual apparatus brought to bear in these studies generally has two components: a macro- and a micro-theory. The former is designed to clarify how societal developments transform the domestic context within which couples make fertility decisions. The objective is to identify changes in extra-domestic social structures correlated with the onset of fertility limitation and subsequently associated with the spread of the stopping pattern throughout the entire population. The prevailing macro-paradigm in mainstream demography goes under the rubric of modernization theory, directing our attention to three processes – industrialization, urbanization and secularization – which are themselves poorly conceived ahistorical abstractions. As social classes are ciphers in modernization theory, the class-specific linkage between these processes and the family economy remains unspecified. Instead, we are presented with a descriptive model of sequential change in a set of disembodied 'factors' whose correlation with the decline in marital fertility, submitted to various measures of statistical significance, is somehow presumed to explain itself. The persistent substitution of description for explanation is a hallmark of the modernization paradigm.

But in many cases, even the correlations are statistically insignificant. In a summary evaluation of the massive body of research undertaken by the Princeton European Fertility Project over the past twenty-five years, co-investigator Susan Watkins candidly admits that the Emperor has no clothes: 'The measures of modernization used in the European Fertility Project do not well predict provincial differences in marital fertility at any time during the late nineteenth and early twentieth centuries.'[167] The relative absence of correlation in the Princeton Group's research is symptomatic of the underlying problem with their study's design: the complete absence of the household level in the dataset, where the smallest unit of analysis is the province (county, department, deanery, or whatever). The ways in which the processes of industrialization, urbanization and secularization transform the couple's mode of subsistence, shifting procreative incentives, lies beyond their purview.

The only viable alternative to modernization theory as a macro-paradigm is some variant of a mode-of-production framework; there are no other competitors in the field. Significantly, two of the most suggestive recent attempts to develop a general model of the fertility decline have adopted a mode-of-production terminology, though neither proceeds within the recognized parameters of historical materialism.[168] We can hardly fault their authors for failing to embrace the full marxist conceptual apparatus, for whatever the potential strengths of a mode-of-production analysis, the fact remains that orthodox marxists have shown no interest in stretching the concept to take inclusive account of family forms and demographic dynamics. Typically, the domestic sphere is left as a black box. To illuminate fertility dynamics within its interior, we need theoretical specification concerning the reproductive couple. Let us turn, then, to the plane of micro-analysis.

Demographers have proposed numerous theories of fertility regulation and procreative outcome, conceived, almost always, at the level of the household or reproductive couple. Their paradigms are typically some variant of the new home economics: the neo-classical micro-economics of constrained choice, premissed on a unitary household utility function, where children entail variable costs and benefits (objective and subjective), trading off against other goods the family seeks. Because I cannot do justice to the diversity of micro-theories here, I have selected for consideration one prominent framework, presented by Richard Easterlin and Eileen Crimmins in *The Fertility Revolution: A Supply–Demand Analysis.*[169] The book has aroused considerable interest among demographers; I take it to be state-of-the-art theorizing in the mainstream of the discipline. The authors situate 'the demand for children' in relation to the prospective 'supply' of surviving offspring. The motivation to restrain fertility arises when supply exceeds demand: that is, when the number of children likely to be conceived by a couple under their existing mode of coital conduct threatens to exceed the number they would like to have. In this model, demand is a rational response to the existing incentive structure for childbearing, balancing the costs of childraising against the prospective benefits of having another child. The greater the excess of supply over demand, the stronger the desire to adopt new methods of birth control or attempt a more rigorous application of familiar means. The capacity to translate this desire into effective fertility restriction varies positively with the strength of the motivation and negatively with the costs (financial, cultural and psychological) associated with employing more effective contraceptive methods.[170]

To produce a sustained decline in marital fertility, two conditions must be present, one or both of which had been lacking in the pre-decline era: a widespread motivation to prevent further conceptions and to terminate unintended pregnancies; and the capacity to take effective action to this end. Very different models of the fertility decline are generated depending on which of these conditions is emphasized; but their relative importance is an empirical question and should not be subject to a priori bias in conceptualization.[171] Both preconditions are represented in Easterlin and Crimmins's model (though appearing in the peculiarly stunted discourse employed by neo-classical economists): *motivation* is theorized in direct proportion to the excess of supply over demand; *capacity to act* in inverse relation to the costs of contraception. The model remains flexible as to how these conditions will be combined. A given fertility decline might be explicable in terms of a rising child surplus, with low and stable contraceptive costs; or alternately, in a situation where supply and demand were fairly stable and there had long been a surfeit of unwanted children, it might be triggered by a cultural breakthrough, a rapid lowering of prohibitive barriers to effective contraceptive practice.

185

This is precisely what historical demographers have debated in the case of the European decline: whether it was declining demand for children or an increasing availability and acceptability of contraceptive measures that precipitated the fertility transition.[172] Demand theorists argue that in the pre-decline era most couples wanted to have at least as many children as survived and that there were overriding benefits, economic and cultural, in bearing large families. Since continuous childbearing until menopause is held to be rational, marital coitus may be treated as intentional behaviour. If intercourse serves other needs, these do not conflict with its procreative objective. The model assumes that motivation is able to induce the desired fertility outcome fairly readily, that there are no major obstacles to obtaining and applying effective means of birth control. Presumably, however, when the demand for children declines or the potential supply rises, contraceptive costs will increase, and the possibility arises that a very substantial proportion of pregnancies will be unwanted.[173] At this point, sex for non-procreative purposes – the modes and conditions of its expression – becomes an independent variable worthy of consideration. Yet sexuality is neglected in most theories of fertility behaviour.

Within a demand-driven model, an adequate account of the fertility decline hinges on explaining why parents begin to want fewer children. An economic thesis argues for a rise in the costs and a decrease in the benefits of having more children, altering the couple's incentive structure for childbearing. As we have seen, there is evidence of such shifts in the period immediately preceding the working-class decline in Western Europe – the curtailment of child labour and the extension of compulsory schooling, delaying children's financial contribution and increasing their costs by enforcing middle-class childcare standards on working-class parents. Furthermore, with improved life expectancy, not as many children were needed to ensure a modicum of security for parents in old age, and state-regulated pension provisions were beginning to appear. In perhaps the boldest conceptualization of the position, Caldwell has presented these changes as reversing wealth flows between the generations, so that additional children, for the first time, cease to be a form of familial wealth and become instead a net drain on their parents over the life-course.[174] Once wealth flows are reversed, the demand for children drops precipitously (which might explain the plummeting nature of the decline once it got under way). The basic conundrum for demand-driven accounts is the rapidity of the generalization of stopping behaviour across extremely heterogeneous socioeconomic formations. Surely this unevenness would preclude a roughly simultaneous shift in household-level incentives for childbearing? How does one account for the 'bunched' nature of the change in coital behaviour within nations especially, but also internationally?

The anomaly has led many demographers to favour a 'cultural' explanation of the transition which emphasizes the prohibitive obstacles (subjective as well as objective) to effective contraception in the pre-decline period.[175] On this side of the debate as well, there is ample corroborative evidence: the difficulty of obtaining knowledge and contraceptive devices; the expense involved in the repeated purchase of condoms on a tight working-class budget; pervasive fears and moral repugnance associated with their use, buttressed by the medical profession and the Christian churches, both Catholic and Protestant; the enduring strength of procreative naturalism. A high-cost model would suggest that the desire to limit had been present at least latently for some time before stopping occurred.[176] If this is true, it might account for the rapidity of the spread of a good idea whose time had come – a mass value shift, diffusing downward from urban elites in response to the dawning realization that family limitation was both possible and advantageous. The major analytical task for the proponents of the cultural account is to explain the timing of the decline. Why was there a rapid increase in the availability and acceptability of contraceptive means in this period and not before? In this regard, they too are faced with an anomaly: the age-old practices of abortion, withdrawal and abstinence were the major means of prevention employed in the first phase of the decline, while contraceptive devices were not widely used within marriage until the 1930s and 1940s. How, then, do we explain a rapid decline in the 'costs' of utilizing means that had not got any cheaper (in the case of abortion) or were monetarily free and had been available within the cultural repertoire of these societies for centuries?

These, then, are the polarized contours of the current debate between those who see the move to smaller families as an *adjustment* to changed socioeconomic circumstances and those who perceive it as a cultural *innovation* rooted in a transformation of reproductive consciousness.[177] I have adduced evidence that can be construed to buttress both positions, while noting that each has a weakness in making sense of the empirical record. Consequently, we are still far from being able to offer a persuasive general explanation for the European fertility decline.

There are those who argue that no such explanation is possible – that the phenomenon is more correctly understood as a myriad of disparate and historically contingent transitions; they would limit the scope for valid generalization, terming the attempt 'an illusory quest'.[178] I am not persuaded that we ought to abandon the search for broad transnational explanations, although it would be illusory to imagine that a single model, or configuration of variables, will ever 'fit' all cases. The rapidity of the decline's international spread, once under way; the steep and uninterrupted nature of the contraction – these well-documented trends cry out for theorizing on a broad scale. This, of course, does not negate the validity and cumulative importance of closely grained studies of specific transitions. But local studies inevitably draw from a repertoire of general theory; it is much better to do so deliberately than unconsciously. The two levels of analysis are complementary, at least potentially. One key to advancing theories of the broad sweep is to rework the prevailing paradigm of fertility regulation in the light of feminist first principles.

Before turning to a feminist critique, let us note that the third factor in Easterlin and Crimmins's model, a rising supply of children, is potentially in play but has not figured in recent debate. In my view, this reflects regression from an earlier consensus. Reviewing fertility studies in 1961, Ronald Freeman noted that 'most sociologists and demographers would probably agree ... that [one of two] basic causes of the general decline [was] ... a sharp reduction in mortality which reduced the number of births necessary to have the desired number of children.'[179] By the 1980s, the consensus had collapsed. The current dismissal stems from studies that have shown that the onset of the decline in marital fertility was not consistently preceded by a drop in infant mortality; the two declined concomitantly in Northwestern Europe from about 1890 on.[180] *Ergo*, mortality change could not have played a causal role in the fertility decline.

This is fallacious reasoning on several grounds. In the first place, no one is seriously contending that the drop in infant death is sufficient in itself to induce a fertility decline, nor is it even a necessary condition universally. In thinking about general models of the decline, it is more fruitful to consider an array of potentially contributing factors, each of which tends to induce stopping behaviour, and to look for the presence of a 'critical mass' of such factors operating in each case. This would preclude the unnecessary rejection of changes, such as a fall in infant death, when they are not universal *antecedents* of the decline but are almost always found to be *concomitant* with it. The entire statistical exercise (correlating the timing of an initial 10 per cent drop in the two indices) engenders a narrow fixation with the moment of the decline's onset. It is thus exclusively concerned with the small segments of the population that pioneered the decline and the specific triggering mechanisms of their inaugural limitation.

It is probable that very different forces spread stopping behaviour throughout the labouring population. For proletarians, life-chances at birth improved dramatically from the turn of the century, more rapidly than the life expectancy of elites (there being much more room for improvement in the lower classes). It would be a mistake to discount this amelioration as a contributing factor in the spread of family limitation among working-class couples. The broad simultaneity of the downturns in infant mortality and fertility suggests that there were causal influences operating in both directions. Furthermore, *child* mortality (from age one on) abated very substantially in the nineteenth century before the onset of the fertility decline. This improvement would probably have been more significant to parental confidence in the survival prospects of existing offspring than changes in infant death rates.[181] It

188

therefore seems reasonable to consider a rising supply of offspring (existing and potential) as a contributory factor in the adoption of the stopping pattern among the proletarian populace. Since either a rising supply or a declining demand is sufficient to generate a condition of involuntary surplus, the postulated contribution of improved life expectancy to the fertility decline is aligned in the debate with the declining-demand position. If supply is increasing and demand contracting simultaneously, the impact on motivation would be compounded.

The fundamental problem with Easterlin and Crimmins's model of fertility regulation (shared by other theories) is that it is conceived at the level of the reproductive couple, as if the procreative interests and sexual needs of husbands and wives were harmoniously aligned. This assumption is unwarranted. Since the burdens of childbearing and childcare are not shared equally, it is reasonable to expect that spouses will frequently operate at cross-purposes. This is not to say that coital conflict will be universal or inevitably of a zero-sum character, but an adequate theoretical framework must allow for spousal differences in procreative objectives and the means used to achieve them. Even highly empathetic husbands did not regard the prospect of another conception with the depth of feeling their wives brought to the experience, and most men were not nearly as attuned to their spouses' needs. In the words of one beleaguered woman writing to Stopes:

> I have ten here to do for and I never leave the house ... yet he can put his hat and coat on and get out as much as he likes. Therefore, a house full of children makes no difference to him at all ... so who got the worry and struggle if not the woman for the sake of her children.[182]

A difference in the desire to halt childbearing is not necessarily manifest as a divergence on optimal family size. As mentioned, working-class women and men in the past did not plan to have a set number of children; the targeting conception is a modernist and middle-class projection on proletarian couples in the past. Rather, the real decision-making problematic was: Do I want another? If not, should I accept the risk of having another or take steps to avert it? And if the latter, what steps do I, or we, take? It is important that a choice-theoretic paradigm of this nature represent realistically the situation people actually confront. Demographic theories of fertility regulation are often vitiated by radical abstractions of the 'ideal family size' type. When women and men are asked how many children they would like to have in contemporary surveys, their answers frequently do not differ much.[183] My impression from the correspondence is that this would have been the case for British working-class women and men in the first quarter of the twentieth century. But they did differ, often dramatically, in the intensity of their desire to stop. This suggests that the degree of motivation is not a linear reflection of the size of the potential child surplus (as Easterlin and Crimmins postulated) because the anticipated costs of the excess will not be evenly borne.

There is more at stake than the motivation to limit; women and men are likely to have divergent attitudes to intercourse and contraceptive responsibility as well; these factors also influence the fertility outcome. Sexuality merits serious consideration in models of fertility decision-making; its absence in most is inexcusable. In Western Europe, it appears that men wished for a higher level of coital frequency than their spouses and were thus in greater conflict with the desire to limit conception, since abstinence and withdrawal (the usual means of control) placed severe restraints on their normal sexual expression. Furthermore, most men considered it to be the missus's job to 'keep herself right', and many were not prepared to share responsibility for contraception even when they shared the desire to cease childbearing.

Once men's and women's interests and objectives are distinguished, it makes sense to pay close attention to the means of contraception employed. Some (such as diaphragms) may be used by women without the knowledge or co-operation of their partners; others (such as abstention and withdrawal) require consent and a minimal degree of joint action to be effective. If it is possible to develop reasonable estimates of the prevalence of various means and their variance from one cohort to the next (as Lewis-Faning did in his survey), we can infer something about the respective intensity of women's and men's desire to call a halt, and the allocation of contraceptive responsibility between spouses, shifting in the course of the decline. Since conventional analysis proceeds at the level of the couple acting jointly, attention to the specific means used has not played a prominent role in the literature on the fertility transition.

Whenever spouses have divergent objectives with regard to childbearing, coital frequency or contraceptive use, the question of conjugal power is immediately posed: Who gets their way in the event of conflict? This is where feminist work on the concept of patriarchy is invaluable; mainstream demography has been impoverished by ignoring it.[184] The two axes of authority relations within families, along the lines of gender and generation, are integrated in the concept of domestic patriarchy. With very few exceptions, demographers have foregrounded the intergenerational dimension, while ignoring the axis of spousal power. Yet both are required for an adequate theorization of fertility regulation, since it is within this power matrix that reproductive incentives and interests are set, and rights and responsibilities allocated. One of the patriarch's most fundamental prerogatives is his right of sexual access to his wife's body whenever he feels like it. The strength of men's 'conjugal rights' and women's 'wifely duties' is evident in the correspondence. The importance of the issue to conjugal relations was apparent; women were prepared to characterize their husbands as kind and considerate or lustful and selfish according to how they handled this prerogative. Shifts in the normative dimension of marital sexual relations ought to figure much more prominently in studies of the fertility decline.

Why do economic demographers have such difficulty in fitting sex into the fertility equation? In treating children as a 'normal good', they create an excessively rational model of fertility behaviour. The premiss of normal goods production is that if people freely work to produce or acquire a good, they self-evidently have a demand for it. This assumption is based on the postulate of a 'leisure preference' in human nature: that in comparison with playing or resting, most work is noxious, so that people must want something to work for it. The problem with treating babies as a normal good is that they are produced by an activity that is not work, but is normally pleasurable, and for most people, periodically at least, something that becomes intensely preferable to doing anything else. Consequently, in the majority of cases it is more difficult (that is, it requires more work) to avoid conception than to produce babies. We cannot then assume that the number of babies produced simply fulfils demand for them, and that couples stop at that point. As soon as we take the sex drive seriously, we must assume the opposite: that due to the 'leisure preference' in coitus, the number of babies produced will be in excess of the number desired unless the costs of reliable birth control approach zero. The more difficult it is to use birth control, the greater this excess will be, all else being equal. The assumption that there is a rough equilibrium between the supply of and demand for children in most historical periods is dubious; it seems far more likely that the chronic tendency is to generate a surplus (especially in relation to women's desires) due to contraceptive failure and sexual recklessness (primarily on men's part). Of course, there are many couples who are unable to have any children, or as many as they would wish, and this deficit must also be taken into account. But overall, it seems reasonable to postulate a frequent, if not inevitable, tendency towards surplus, exacerbated in circumstances where there are no viable agencies for redistributing unwanted babies to families with an involuntary shortfall.

In the polar terms in which it has been couched, the debate assumes that the desire to limit and the capacity to do so vary independently of one another, so that people can become very keen to quit childbearing while lacking the capacity to do so. It is more likely that the two variables will be intimately related, potentiating one another's development. The evidence from the correspondence would suggest that the desire to stop was present among the masses before the minority practice of stopping became widely known, but only in a limited form (being manifest primarily in attempts to induce abortion). The inclination of women to complain in the face of prolonged and ill-prepared childbearing was suppressed beneath profound resignation and a sense of inevitable – hence natural – female burden. Coital inaction persisted until such time as the alternative of contraceptive limitation was seen as possible and worth the risks. These pre-decline cultural and psychological realities are obscured by the economists' choice-theoretic terminology. For a population steeped in procreative naturalism, it makes little sense to speak of repeated pregnancy as fulfilling a 'high demand for children', in the sense of a desired outcome capable of galvanizing determined action. Babies 'just came' and couples received the number 'God sent'. To what extent could people even form strong preferences in this context, beyond the manifest desire of practically everyone to have children? As the investment mothers made in their children's welfare was considerable, initial regrets at the discovery of another pregnancy normally gave way to a degree of maternal bonding that precluded a hard-headed evaluation of whether one would have been better off without the now-beloved child. In high-fertility settings where the practice of deliberate contraception is taboo, retrospective (and indeed proactive) rationalization tends to raise the apparent 'demand for children' to meet the actual supply. Similarly, when the acquisition of such devices for use in marriage is beyond the pale, how can one speak cogently of 'the perceived costs of contraception'? Both terms become misleading as they approach their upper limit in pre-decline settings.

At the outset of the fertility decline, we are striving to explain a cultural revolution that erodes this fatalist passivity and brings the possibility of preventive action within the realm of conscious choice. Paradoxically, it is this transformation that renders the choice-theoretic paradigm relevant, enabling the costs and benefits of bearing additional children to be consciously weighed. I am not saying that we are barred from estimating shifts in the incentive structure of childbearing before such time as they become amenable to deliberate fertility limitation – in fact I would maintain that incentives had probably been shifting against large families at least since the middle of the nineteenth century, especially among relatively prosperous working-class families. The invisible progress of this sea-change accounts in part for the rapidity of the spread of the stopping pattern when working people eventually realized that it was possible to limit. The costs and benefits of having children had deteriorated to such an extent that smaller families were decisively rewarded with a higher living standard, making the reason for their relative advantage over their neighbours with similar incomes and larger families immediately apparent to observant members of the community, as soon as a significant number of couples in a locale were limiting.

Finally, we return to the two explanations of the fertility decline discussed earlier, to see how the theoretical initiatives just proposed might reconcile the polarized accounts, drawing strength from both. The dilemma for working-class couples in the early twentieth century was that the two necessary conditions of deliberate limitation were disjoined. Women were motivated but lacked the power to avoid coitus and the means to avert conception. Men had it in their power, but their motivation was not yet sufficiently strong to restrain their sexuality with any consistency. The evidence we have considered indicates that the desire to limit arose first, and most strongly, in women; but at the same time, the responsibilities of abstinence, coitus interruptus, or condom use were primarily men's. Until such time as men came to fear the prospect of another child strongly enough to exercise sexual self-discipline, there was bound to be simmering tension, if not open conflict, between spouses over the terms and conditions of intercourse. The rate of abortion for married women – rising very considerably from the turn of the century – is an indirect measure of this conflict, representing, as it does, women's fierce determination to terminate pregnancies that their husbands had not been conscientious enough to prevent.

Gender struggle over the terms and conditions of sex in marriage is thus very likely to be a hidden dimension of movement towards the modern form of family limitation. If women are keener on limitation than men, whatever strengthens women's capacity for self-assertion and undermines men's traditional conjugal rights will tend to hasten and deepen the fertility decline. Yet in so far as the means of contraception available necessitate male action in ways which contravene men's traditional sexual behaviour in marriage, then anything that brings their perceived interests in preventing conception into line with those of their wives will operate to overcome their resistance to making the necessary changes in coital behaviour. The decisive down-swing in proletarian birth rates, after decades of gradual descent, was due to a convergence of men's and women's interests in limitation, and to women's increasing capacity to obtain some male co-operation to this end. The two processes were intimately related; in recognizing the urgent need to curtail fertility, husbands were prepared to temper, if not to surrender entirely, their right to incautious intercourse; and wives were better able to insist on restraint when they could appeal to a mutual interest.

When the interests and objectives of husbands and wives are theoretically distinguished and conjugal power is posed, the former polarity between the economic and cultural accounts can be reconciled; a base/superstructure model is rejected, and both forces are accorded their due. There is no doubt that this initiative complicates the conceptual terrain (particularly for purely quantitative studies), but it is far better to paint on a messy canvas than on an immaculate one with a vacant centre.

6

Conclusion

Because family forms are embedded in socioeconomic structures, family life is bound to be altered in close association with transformations in prevailing modes of production. Such a perspective has been central to the conduct of this inquiry and its predecessor. In *A Millennium of Family Change,* I endeavoured to show how family forms changed in the transition from feudalism to capitalism. The same approach has been pursued in this text, correlating changes in working-class family life with transformations in the capitalist mode of production during the first and second Industrial Revolutions. If this perspective is valid, then we would expect to find that the maturation of capitalism's third Industrial Revolution would have fostered deep mutations in family forms once again. This has indeed occurred. Since the 1960s, throughout the developed capitalist world, family forms have changed in several far-reaching ways:

■ With a sustained rise in the employment rates of married women, the traditional family economy, based on the male breadwinner and the full-time homemaker, has been replaced by a two-earner family norm. In the 1950s, only 10 to 15 per cent of married woman worked for pay; now, roughly half do. While rates vary by country, the increase has occurred right across the board. Neither recessions nor the upsurge of 'pro-family' traditionalism have forced women's retreat from a deepening involvement in the paid labour force. The decline of the male-breadwinner norm has profoundly unsettled conjugal relations, reducing women's economic dependency upon their husbands, dissolving an entrenched sense of the natural division of labour between spouses, and undercutting men's customary prerogatives as breadwinners (above all, the right to treat the home as a leisure centre, abstaining from housework and childcare).

- The institution of marriage has been transformed. Its contract has been secularized and is now regulated almost exclusively by family law. The legal grounds of marital dissolution have been broadened, the court rigmarole has been simplified and its costs have been reduced. No-fault options have made it possible to end a legal union without submitting to the ordeal of a nasty courtroom fight. Divorce rates have soared as a result. In England and Wales before 1914, fewer than 1,000 divorce decrees were granted annually; in practical terms, divorce was not available to proletarians. By the 1980s, about 150,000 decrees were granted per year, and roughly four marriages in ten ended in divorce. The bulk of the increase, with rates quadrupling, has occurred since the 1960s. The greatest increase has been among working-class petitioners. By 1984, women initiated 73 per cent of divorce proceedings.[1]

- Rising divorce rates reveal a flight from oppressive and unhappy relationships, not from marriage per se. In the same decades when divorce rates burgeoned, almost all adults married. In 1950, 17 per cent of British women reaching the age of forty-five had never been married; by 1975, this proportion had dipped to 7 per cent.[2] Rather than endure a bad marriage, most people are now inclined to end it and to search for another partner; shortly after finding one, they remarry. The majority of divorcees remarry within six years of becoming single, and the median age of remarriage is a very young thirty-five. Four unions in ten now involve a remarriage for one or both partners. Among those remarrying, divorcees outnumber the widowed by more than five to one, reversing the traditional ratio. While the marital ideal remains a lifelong union, the reality is that conjugal relations in Western societies are rapidly approaching a new norm of serial monogamy.

- As family forms and marital norms changed, so did co-residence patterns. Mean household size has dipped below three persons, a level without historical precedent. Until recently, the major cause of the shrinkage was the declining birth rate. In Western Europe, women now bear on average only 1.7 children, well below the replacement rate of 2.1. There has also been a sharp rise in one-person households, doubling in the last two decades. The big factor here is an ageing population, with rising numbers of widowed persons living alone in the 'empty nest' phase of the family cycle.

- Even as Western households shrink in size, their composition becomes more varied. While most people still live in nuclear family groups, a rising portion do not. Unmarried couples are much more inclined to live together informally, as the stigma of doing so dissipates. In England and Wales, only 1 per cent of women marrying for the first time in the 1950s reported cohabiting with their husbands before marriage; by 1980, 20 per cent did so. Over the same period, births outside marriage became commonplace. One birth in four took place out of wedlock in 1988, four times the rate of 1961.[3] With divorce and illegitimacy rates soaring, more and more children live with only one parent, usually the mother. In 1981, one-eighth of British households with dependent children were headed by single parents (with mothers outnumbering fathers seven to one). In the United States (where these trends are most advanced) it has been estimated that 40 to 50 per cent of children live apart from their fathers at some time before their eighteenth birthdays, the majority for at least five years.[4]

We may become aware of how pervasive these trends are by reading newspapers or watching television, but such accounts tend to corroborate personal experience. We wrestle with familial change in our own lives and observe how the families of our friends cope. Comparing our own family norms with those of our parents, we draw upon and rework childhood memories. Relations with primary kin fill our deepest emotional reservoirs of belonging and devotion; they also give rise to our most distressing experiences of loss and betrayal. Since the feelings which stem from our own familial experiences have such a powerful impact on our thinking about 'the family', the delusion of a value-neutral epistemology is especially pernicious in family studies. The historical sociology of family forms is deeply immersed in popular culture, myth and folk wisdom – more so than other social-science disciplines.[5]

During the past two decades, people have become increasingly concerned about the trends outlined above. While liberals have greeted them with deep disquiet, conservatives have denounced them outright. Especially among the middle-aged and elderly, there is a pervasive sense of malaise and an intense foreboding about the family's future. As the clouds on our horizons darken, the past brightens in retrospect; the current pessimism has elicited a wave of nostalgia for 'the traditional family'. Superficially, sociologists and social-work professionals discuss these changes in a more objective fashion, yet the views of most are not at odds with popular sentiment, but rather could be said to lead it. While stressing family resilience in the past, they picture families today as under unprecedented stress, with ever-growing numbers failing to fulfil their most basic functions. In *The Shaking of the Foundations,* for example, Ronald Fletcher fears that parental childrearing has been profoundly disrupted by television, age-stratified consumerism and the pervasive impact of youth culture:

Basic sentiments – conjugal and parental sentiments among them – are failing to become established in the young at all, resulting in a situation in which

197

individual character no longer possesses any firm ... ground at all for the inward self-regulation of conduct.[6]

Complaints of this kind have been raised repeatedly in the past. In Chapter 2, we examined the alarmist discourse of middle-class reformers in the middle of the nineteenth century. Their panic also arose from a conviction that the lower classes were in the throes of a deep moral crisis which had corroded, perhaps irretrievably, 'family feeling' among them. Now, as then, a healthy dose of scepticism is warranted in the face of public consternation. Time and again in periods of flux, families have displayed an unexpected resilience (as Fletcher himself stressed in his earlier work). While a dominant form of family life declines and its successor gradually emerges, the great mass of families living the transition are much more likely to bend than to break down altogether. This is due, above all, to the deep commitment the vast majority of people make to preserving their closest kin ties.

Such tenacious devotion does not imply an uncritical attachment to 'the family' in its prevailing form. The changes outlined above reflect a deep-seated dissatisfaction with, and repudiation of, specific features of 'the traditional family' *as a lived experience*. Yet the nuclear family *as an abstract ideal* remains overwhelmingly dominant. The vast majority of respondents in surveys insist that the nuclear family is the best of all possible domestic groups in which to raise children and preserve a fulfilling love relationship. In imagining a future society of their dreams, they can conceive of no other family form that might satisfy human needs for intimacy in a durable fashion.[7] This refusal makes it almost inevitable that contemporary changes will be interpreted as instances of 'family breakdown'. Our collective failure of imagination stems from the extreme difficulty of forging stable alternatives to the nuclear family, lacking, as they do, any basis of support in Western societies; in consequence, they seem deviant and inferior. The present situation is thus paradoxical. Even as 'the traditional family' declines and other living arrangements proliferate, there has been a general retreat from the committed experimentation with communal forms of cohabitation and childrearing that were notable features of the youth radicalization two decades ago.

Neo-conservatives have based no small part of their appeal on amplifying popular anxieties concerning the perceived degeneration of family life. The axiomatic starting-point for the conservative account is that 'the traditional family' is a natural group. If it is currently undergoing rapid change, then this must be an unnatural process, portending the family's terminal collapse unless 'family values' are reinstated. *Is* familial change, of the scope and rapidity witnessed in the past three decades, historically unprecedented? Or is there a collective act of forgetting, of myth-making, involved in the prevailing account of the family, then and now?

The dominant view among family historians since the publication of *Household and Family in Past Time* has stressed elements of continuity over those of change.[8] A stripped-down version of the continuity thesis, first propounded by Peter Laslett and his associates in the Cambridge Group, is routinely reiterated in sociology texts on '*the* family' (note the singular, suppressing diversity), as well as being widely aired in university courses where the history of '*the* Western family' is discussed. The professor's introductory lecture goes something like this: 'It was formerly believed that in pre-industrial times the Western family was large and extended. Based on reconstitution studies by family historians, we now know that household groups were really small and nuclear during the early modern era. Hence, the family underwent no basic structural change in the course of industrialization.' This is the confident voice of academic discernment, disseminating the view of recognized experts in the field. Assertions of this pedigree rank high in the hierarchy of modern knowledge. The claim is registered as a new consensus, formed around a set of empirical studies revising an earlier view which is now held to be obviously mistaken. To confess and rectify past ignorance is deeply satisfying, marking the progress of knowledge; the new orthodoxy is thus imbued with extraordinary certitude. If this text and its companion volume succeed in shaking this consensus to some degree, I shall consider the whole exercise to have been worthwhile.[9]

The continuity thesis presents us with an image of familial reproduction that is deeply endogenous – as if the nuclear family had an internal gyroscope that had kept it on course as it weathered the storms of the Industrial Revolution and the development of the modern state, sailing forth into the twentieth century intact and unaltered. Against the apparent backdrop of a millennium of reproductive stasis, familial change in the last quarter-century looks like an aberrant departure. Considered in its entirety, the work of the Cambridge scholars conveys a much richer picture. While failing to appreciate the historical novelty of modern family forms, they have not been entirely impervious to the familial changes wrought by the Industrial Revolution and the formation of the modern state. In fairness to them, the selective assimilation of the nuclear continuity thesis to a popularly conveyed image of a stable family in the recent past is not their doing. The real problem has been the way the Cambridge Group's work has been used as a political foil by family sociologists seeking to defend 'the traditional family' against its contemporary critics.[10]

Strictly speaking, the nuclear family continuity thesis pertains only to Northwestern Europe from the seventeenth through the nineteenth century. But its popular rendition opens the door to a far more sweeping assertion: that the nuclear family stands at the heart of *all* family systems.[11] Ronald Fletcher projects this domestic form back on to the whole of human evolution:

Far from being a domestic group brought into being very recently by 'exploita-
tive capitalism' ... there are firm grounds for supposing that the nuclear family
– within all the complexities of modern society – might well be that small
remaining group which has been the most natural for human beings from their
very first emergence as *homo sapiens* onwards. To destroy this group would therefore be to destroy what has been the most basic and abiding context for the
making and realisation of human nature from time immemorial – from
mankind's very beginning.[12]

This inflation is achieved by referring to 'the ancient trinity of father,
mother and child' in abstraction from familial context, as a universal essence of
the family, 'the bedrock of all other family structures'.[13] If a domestic group is
extended beyond this nucleus, then the broader ensemble is treated as an outer
layer surrounding the nuclear family (conveniently sidestepping the Cambridge Group's co-residence criterion). Our bilateral kinship system, reckoned
from ego's standpoint, fosters this way of looking at family forms: as a series of
concentric rings radiating outward from the nuclear core. Universalists often
cite the work of anthropologists, noting passages where Lowie, Murdock,
Malinowski and others assert the ubiquity of pair bonding, paternal assistance
to mother and suckling child, plus the social recognition of fatherhood. But
even if we were to grant universality in these respects (which is to concede a
great deal, since such claims have been hotly contested by other anthropologists) this would not suffice to warrant characterizing the nuclear family as the
predominant form of the family everywhere and at all times.[14] Sociologists and
historians who use the claims of anthropologists to this end almost invariably
abuse their sources. While the universality of kinship and domesticity is indeed
remarkable, the *variety* of family forms that human communities have fashioned to secure these life-supports is equally impressive. Surveying Northwestern Europe from the early Middle Ages to the twentieth century, we have
examined but a small patch of the global canvas; yet even here, far greater
diversity and change have been found than the nuclear straitjacket admits.

Since interpretations of the past condition our views of the future, it is
inevitable that the former will be mobilized to sway public opinion in the
present context. It is not the fact that this is done but *the way* it has been done
that I find objectionable. What *can* a deeper appreciation of family history
contribute to the present discussion? At the outset, one ought to eschew the
temptation to rummage through the shelves of historical scholarship in search
of 'lessons', as if the Truth were set out somewhere in a Book of Revelations.
The past does not speak of its own accord, nor serve up timely verities to
those who care to listen. The social patterns of the past, like those of the
present, need to be ascertained and interpreted; the two processes are insepar-
able. Furthermore, there is no foreordained relationship between past trends

and present action; nor may we assume a common standpoint through which people act today upon their reading of the past.

We can, however, offer *perspectives,* subverting operative myths about the past, so that people are freer to assess recent trends and to gauge more accurately realistic possibilities emergent in the present conjuncture. Historical perspectives of this nature develop in the cut and thrust of contention between differing views of the past. In this spirit, I join the debate with the Cambridge scholars. Laslett explicates the connection between family history and the discussion of contemporary prospects in this way:

> [The duty of family historians to] our own generation [is] ... particularly urgent because of the widespread conviction that the family is in decline, or in the process of being replaced by other institutions, ... which may or may not fulfil its traditional functions. It is for familial historians to decide how far these essentially historical statements are correct, whether for example the functions of the family have indeed been such as to justify such deep disquiet if they are being weakened. ... Under these circumstances, it behooves us to get things right.[15]

Here Laslett correctly highlights the pivotal relationship between perceptions of the contemporary family in decline and interpretations of the past; but I am not persuaded that he has 'got things right'.

In so far as historical knowledge deepens our awareness of how present social structures were formed, it enables us to recognize that they were humanly shaped and did not just come to pass. They were determined negatively by opportunities foreclosed and roads not taken, as well as positively by the expansive reproduction of dominant forms. Since the field of family relations is the most deeply naturalized of all social terrains, it is difficult to see deliberate human agency at work, both in preserving family forms through the generations and in breaking with the ways of earlier generations. At best, we envisage family forms being altered inadvertently by changes in surrounding social structures.

In political or military history, a contingent sense of the past is preserved through the identification of turning-points where the entire course of history was decisively altered by the outcomes of great struggles. The counterfactual element in historical thought comes into play: 'What would have happened if ... ?' Down below, in the study of more enduring structures such as modes of production and family forms, it is harder to sustain a sense of historical contingency and deliberate social agency. In the first place, the pace of lasting infrastructural change is much slower. Consequently, it is more difficult to distinguish cyclical fluctuations and conjunctural vicissitudes from fundamental watersheds when underlying social structures are altered irreversibly. To achieve this discrimination, essential to the discipline of historical sociology, infrastructural trends must be analysed in the long run. Second, because families are decisive in the formation of human character, there is a constant temptation to invert the explanatory equation, portraying a particular family form – in this case, 'the nuclear family' – as the ubiquitous product of human nature. Since biology changes much more slowly than the most enduring facets of social structure, this projection conveniently accounts for the persistence of family forms through the millennia. Thus, while familial change is attributed to external pressures, continuity is held to be internally generated.

Historical accounts that underestimate familial change over time and downplay cross-cultural variety foster 'naturalist' explanations; they dehistoricize causal reasoning in family history. For the proponents of the nuclear continuity thesis, change requires explanation; consistent reiteration, generation after generation, presumably does not. Since we lack our colleagues' serenity, the vexed question occurs: 'If it were true that the Western family had, until recently, persisted essentially unchanged for centuries, what could possibly account for such constancy through periods of massive change in the surrounding social order?' The silence is deafening.

Origins of the Traditional Family

How do recent changes stand in relation to the history of Western family forms? It is essential at the outset to distinguish between 'the nuclear family' and what is called, in retrospect, 'the traditional family'. The latter is a particular form of the nuclear family based on a sharply segmented division of labour between spouses, wherein men go out to work in order to earn the family's principal income, while women remain at home caring for husbands and children. One problem with the contemporary discussion is the conflation of these referents. Those who decry recent changes typically lament the passing of the traditional family. Due to the dominance of this familial ideal, people are inclined to speak of its decline as if it portended the passing of 'the family' per se. This elision imparts an apocalyptic tenor to discussions of family change.

The discourse of the past two decades has been reminiscent in many ways of public tempests in earlier periods; the spectre of the family's imminent demise was also raised by restorationists in the imbroglio in the middle of the nineteenth century. Now, as then, the reasoning is as consistent as it is fallacious: (a) 'The family' is reduced to what the pundits consider to be its only proper form, representing the familial ideal hitherto dominant. (b) Its historical longevity and cross-cultural ubiquity are greatly exaggerated. (c) On the basis of its imputed universality, the preferred form is presumed to accord most fully with human nature. (d) The decline of this form is therefore held to foreshadow the dissolution of the family. (e) People's capacity to devise alternative forms to meet their domestic needs is grossly underestimated, while the proliferation of new arrangements is interpreted as a sign of decadence. (f) Critics of the traditional form are accused of being 'anti-family', of advocating the family's abolition or applauding its decay.[16]

Perspectives which highlight familial change in history and convey the variety of family forms found in human societies may serve to counter such short-circuited reasoning. What we think of today as 'the traditional family' is actually of quite recent vintage. Its material foundations were laid with the rise of capitalism and the removal of commodity production from domestic space. Its ideological contours were forged initially by the ascendant bourgeoisie, where 'the family' came to be venerated as a moral counterweight to the market. The home was idealized as a private sanctuary wherein the nobler sentiments of family feeling (kin loyalty, parental devotion and conjugal love) could be nurtured in a tranquil domain secluded from the bustling, impersonal world of industry and commerce. Even the fulsome celebrants of laissez-faire capitalism feared that the market's freedoms would be taken to excess if the sanctity of the family home were not preserved. If a man's prospects for personal gain were not harnessed to the obligation to provide for his family, a healthy interest in self-advancement would turn into ruthless avarice. If commodity relations invaded every sphere of private life, all sense of personal responsibility to the community would dissolve. This concern with the corrosive effects of the cash nexus is as compelling today as it was then: 'The symbolic opposition between The Family and market relations renders our strong attachment to The Family understandable.'[17]

Only with the divorce of households from the means of production and the spread of market relations could this familial ideal come into its own. Its historical novelty must be appreciated. The allocation of family responsibilities between spouses was defined by the separation of spheres. A man went out to work to support his family financially; beyond this, his domestic responsibilities were minimal. His wife's duty was to remain at home, working without remuneration in a 'labour of love', caring for the children and ensuring that her home was a restful place to which her husband could happily return after a hard day's work. The man was still head of the household, but his daily absence from the home left his wife in charge of its practical management; the domestic sphere was hers to fashion as 'a haven in a heartless world'.

The main focus of women's reproductive responsibility shifted from procreation to mothering. Amidst rising public concern about the nurture of infants, domestic hygiene and the proper upbringing of young children, maternal duties now assumed an inordinate importance in 'the century of the child'.[18] In a departure from the Christian doctrine of original sin, children were thought to be innocent and innately good. Childhood was a precious phase of life, a period of grace before shouldering the cares of the world; as such, it ought to be extended at least until puberty. Young children were now thought to require undivided parental attention. These increasingly onerous responsibilities devolved upon mothers almost exclusively. The novel idea that intensive mothering ought to be a full-time vocation for women, and was indeed their highest calling, became widespread in the Victorian era. Obversely, the daily absence of fathers from the home sanctioned their withdrawal from close involvement with their children's upbringing.

The intensification of maternal work went hand in hand with the transformation of children's role in the family economy and the reversal of wealth flows between the generations. Whereas children formerly made a valuable economic contribution to their parents' households from adolescence on, now they constituted a net drain throughout the entire time they lived at home. Once formal education became pivotal in determining a child's future, parents felt obliged to scrimp and save to keep their children in school. As child mortality fell, parents increasingly revalued their children. Worthless in a productive sense, their emotional value became inestimable. Children were priceless assets; without them, family life was inevitably barren. Yet a couple needed only a few children to enjoy this irreplaceable experience; additional ones became an intolerable burden. Increasingly, women sought to halt childbearing well before menopause.

Working-class families could never hope to fully realize the bourgeois family ideal. (Few bourgeois families could either, but that is another story.) Yet for most facets of the design, a proletarian analogue was fashioned. The distinctive features of the traditional family in its proletarian version took shape in the late nineteenth and early twentieth centuries, as the modern working class was consolidated around its urban, industrial core. This was a nuclear family, to be sure, but it was much more than that. Just as the ripening of capitalist relations was necessary to elevate the bourgeois family as a paramount standard, the consolidation of its subordinate version was based upon the maturation of a fully proletarian condition. By the latter decades of the nineteenth century, most wage-earning households were entirely separated from the means of production. With the decline of opportunities to gain income while working at home, working-class families became completely reliant upon generating a year-round flow of wage income. As men's real wages rose and employment became less seasonal, families with a steady male income shifted from a multi-earner strategy to one based more narrowly on maximizing the primary breadwinner's earning power. Child labour was curtailed and public attitudes became increasingly hostile to married women working outside the home. A 'living wage' was redefined as an income which would enable a man to 'keep' his wife and young children in respectable circumstances.

With the individuation of the wage form, family income ceased to include any value that could be directly attributed to the wife's labour. Conjugal inter-dependency now assumed the asymmetrical form of the homemaker's econ-omic dependency upon her husband. Male househeadship had formerly been based on the ownership and control of family property; as households were divorced from the means of production, this source of domestic power was lost. With the construction of the male-breadwinner wage norm in the second half of the nineteenth century, patriarchal power was replanted in the soil of the wage system, where it took root and flourished for the better part of a century. The domestic prerogatives of working men were now based upon their possession and control of the family's primary wage. While this was a form of conjugal power distinct to the class of wage-earners, it paralleled men's control of profits, salaries and other forms of income among the propertied and professional classes.

The triumph of the breadwinner/housewife standard placed proletarian family ideals within the general ambit of the family model that had become dominant among the urban middle class earlier in the century. Even as these classes grew apart residentially, living in increasingly stratified neighbour-hoods, their familial ideologies converged, under bourgeois hegemony. Both versions: (a) projected the distribution of family responsibilities between spouses on to the separation of spheres, configuring this binary map with gender polarity; (b) idealized the home as a leisure centre to which men could retreat after work, sanctioning their abstention from domestic labour; (c) fetishized women's domestic duties by insisting on their segregation from productive and remunerated work; (d) intensified maternal care for each child, as their life-chances improved dramatically; (e) made children's formal schooling the paramount form of preparation for employment, delaying their entry into the world of work and their exit from home.

With living standards rising, the demographic security of families improved substantially. By the 1920s, the great majority of proletarian infants survived to adulthood, permitting the emotional intensification of mothering. Infant aban-donment and mercenary wet-nursing, pervasive practices in earlier phases of industrialization, abated; residual instances were scandalized and prosecuted in well-publicized trials. With fewer adult deaths (and divorce still extremely rare), the average marriage lasted longer than ever before. Not only could parents reasonably expect almost all infants to live to adulthood, but children could count on their parents surviving and remaining together until they moved out and became financially independent. As rates of family break-up and orphanhood subsided (though the down trend was twice breached by the ravages of war), male-breadwinner families furnished a degree of security without precedent in the history of labouring classes. Where primary bread-winners were steadily employed and decently paid, where women could con-centrate on their domestic duties without having to hold down an external job, family households provided their members with better living conditions than their predecessors had ever been able to achieve. The reasons for this success were only obliquely due to the form itself, and might well have been achieved under different arrangements. But for the majority of working-class families who were able to conform to the male-breadwinner norm, it is hardly surprising that they came to credit the model for their relative success. Families at the bottom of the proletarian heap, living in primary poverty and domestic squalor, typically lacked the steady income of a male breadwinner. This deficiency was very generally identified as the main cause of their poverty, with devastating consequences.

If the primary reason for the traditional family's triumph was its economic and demographic stability, forces of cultural restoration were also at work. The strictures of legal marriage were reasserted in the late-Victorian period, inaugurating a new era of marital conformity. The practice of living together informally before marriage (widespread in the first half of the nineteenth century) was now condemned in proletarian communities and became increasingly rare. Young couples sought parental approval for their choice of partners and hastened to legalize their unions. The rate of childbirth out of wedlock declined as parents, backed by the vociferous stalwarts of community respectability, became more effective in pressing suitors to marry pregnant daughters. Pre-marital sex was thus forced back within the norms of betrothal commitment, while childbearing was once again confined to wedlock. As the practice of taking in boarders or widowed parents declined, all remaining discrepancies between the nuclear family cycle and normal patterns of household cohabitation were eliminated. This streamlining facilitated the conflation of family with household, a major deficiency in modern family studies.

As cities became more settled residentially and their generational depth increased, the density of kin networks in working-class communities thickened. With steady year-round employment increasingly available, it became commonplace to pass one's entire life in the same 'urban village'. Neighbourhoods grew intensely local, territorially bounded and street-oriented. While community networks were based on forms of mutuality and assistance in times of need, working-class families none the less took great pride in being self-reliant. A family's respectability hinged, above all, on being able to provide for its members without having to ask for a hand-out from government welfare agencies or private charities. Closely allied with a sense of pride in preserving family autonomy was a feeling of dignity sustained by 'keeping to ourselves', entailing a firmer enforcement of family privacy against the prying eyes and wagging tongues of the neighbourhood. The family's capacity to preserve its sovereignty in these respects was based on the steadiness and reliability of the primary breadwinner and the financial self-discipline and domestic competence of the homemaker. Both partners needed to fulfil their duties if a family was to live 'decently'.

The subsequent development of working-class families through the inter-war years and down to the 1960s entailed a purification of this basic form, with the furtherance of trends described above: (a) working-class couples eventually brought their family size into line with middle-class couples, adopting a two-child ideal after the Second World War; (b) children remained in school longer, further curtailing their financial contribution to their family of birth and increasing a family's dependency on the breadwinner's income.

These trends engendered a dual confluence. In the first place, working-class families were in many respects more homologous with the families of the propertied classes than ever before. This is reflected in the convergence of family size and in married women's economic dependency, now almost total. Secondly, the familial practices of all classes were in fuller conformity with prevailing ideals than ever before. Studies of the sequence and timing of steps to adulthood – the order and the age at which men and women leave home, set up a household, get married and have their first child – indicate that the socially approved sequence became more universal with each passing decade, and that the dispersion of ages at which these moves were undertaken diminished over time.[19] 'The traditional family' thus had its heyday in the 1950s, prevailing as an ideal without serious challenge, while possibly enjoying a higher level of conformity than any familial standard in history. This 'golden age' supplies the backdrop against which all subsequent changes are judged. It furnishes a virtually inexhaustible reservoir of imagery for the retrospective construction of 'the family as we have known it' in the era of its decline.[20] The impressions formed in the mind's eye are derived from many sources – from childhood recollection, the reminiscences of the elderly, family heirlooms and old photographs, and from mass-media notions of recent history. For many, these images are coloured by a visceral yearning to return to simpler times: when children obeyed their parents, women knew their place, partners remained faithful, and domestic tranquillity prevailed. That, at least, is how the story gets told.

Immediately before the era of living memory, we find ourselves operating in 'a twilight zone', as Eric Hobsbawm has called it:

> between history and memory; between the past as a generalized record which is open to relatively dispassionate inspection and the past as a remembered part of, or background to, one's own life. ... It is by far the hardest part of history for historians, or anyone else, to grasp.[21]

In this zone, dating roughly from the 1870s to the 1950s, the nuclear continuity thesis is fused with the second-hand memories we harbour of our grandparents' families; the resulting alloy is 'the traditional family', a compelling construct. On the basis of untutored common sense, we may initially be inclined to believe that the global triumph of industrial capitalism *must* have transformed family relations, since it transformed everything else. And yet, according to the family historians, we have got it all wrong. Our native intelligence is thus effectively suppressed, and a more visceral claim is lodged. The stable family of recent memory is apparently continuous with 'the Western family' as far back as we can discern (scholars have recently discovered 'the nuclear family' in Ancient Rome).[22] The historical novelty of the bourgeois family form, and of its proletarian counterpart, is effaced. In this light, recent changes seem like a complete historical anomaly.

Against this formidable consensus, I have argued that the traditional family is a recent invention, rising to pre-eminence in the nineteenth century. It is a mistake to suppose that this family model is essentially continuous with the prevailing family form of our ancestors dating right back to the Middle Ages, and in this sense to think of it as a natural destination of all that had gone before. The golden age of the male-breadwinner form of the nuclear family, culminating in the 1950s, is an unusual era in family history. Its present decline leaves families today in a transitional state which is, in significant respects, more typical of family life in the past than the period of stability and conformity of recent memory.

■ Before the rise of the bourgeois family and its working-class counterpart, married women were not excluded from the field of commodity production and restricted to the production of family labour-power. The breadwinner/homemaker family generated an extreme segmentation of conjugal responsibilities, cloistering married women as reproductive specialists; this was exceptional in Western history. The mass entry of married women into paid work returns them to the field of commodity production, where their contribution to the family economy is undeniable.

■ Due to high rates of adult mortality, the duration of marriages in the past was highly unpredictable; many were cut short prematurely. In pre-industrial England, the average marriage lasted only about twenty years; in almost a third of marriages, at least one partner had been married before.[23] By the 1950s, the average duration of marriages was about forty-five years, and remarriage represented a very small proportion of all legal unions. In these respects as well, the golden age of the traditional family was exceptional. Although the means of marital dissolution have changed in the current period (in this respect, high divorce rates have created a genuinely novel situation), the shortening of marital duration and the rise in conjugal uncertainty return modern populations to a more familiar instability. The incidence of children living with single mothers and stepfathers has returned to levels which were normal in the past, after an interlude of exceptional stability.

■ The new trend towards informal cohabitation and subsequent marriage has many features in common with old betrothal customs, where conjugal compatibility was tested before the union was legalized.[24] A moderate increase in the proportion of adults who never marry returns Western populations to the their previous pattern of non-universal marriage.

I am not, of course, suggesting that families today have come to resemble those in the distant past more closely than their immediate predecessors. In fact, they have many genuinely novel features. Yet conjugal instability and high rates of family break-up – the preoccupations of contemporary analysts – are not new but are, rather, the historical norm. When familial change is viewed in a longer-term perspective, the recent past need not be taken as the standard against which current changes and future prospects are assessed. This standpoint requires a break with the continuity thesis.

Putting Recent Trends in Perspective

The rapid proliferation of domestic arrangements that do not correspond to the normal family as traditionally conceived makes it easier today to see familial norms as social constructs – arbitrary, biased and transitory. As the male-breadwinner norm loses its predominance, it becomes apparent that it was not natural or eternal but had a limited lifespan, coming to prominence in the latter half of the nineteenth century and decaying a century later. By taking the long view of family history, we can make a distinction between venerable familial ideals (in this case, the provisioning onus, legitimating male house-headship through the ages) and the specific social relations that come to express them in a given period (the male-breadwinner norm). The prevailing discourse in family studies based on a continuity paradigm tends to occlude distinctions of this type.

In a balanced framework, elements of continuity and change ought to command our attention in *all* historical conjunctures. Admittedly, this is easier said than done. We can begin, however, by distinguishing periods of unusual stasis from others of exceptional flux, and shifting our explanatory emphasis accordingly. The present period is very clearly one of considerable change in family relations. 'History is never more needed than in such moments of apparent liberation from the past'.[25] In such periods of flux, family ideals cease to be entrenched in a set of fixed arrangements which almost everyone emulates. At these times, the struggle for alternatives may be joined. This study has been conducted with the hope that cogent analyses of earlier transitions might serve to illuminate the current conjuncture.

Families change in response to changes in the surrounding society – above all, shifts in the prevailing mode of production and the structures of state authority and provision. These alterations exert pressure on families and also provide their members with opportunities. The mass influx of married women into employment, for example, was pressed by the gradual removal of all other means of supplementing the primary breadwinner's income, while the vast growth of the service sector created a demand for labour in jobs that had traditionally been typed as 'women's work'.

It is not sufficient, however, to explain family change of this order simply by reference to external forces. The internal impetus to change arises from pervasive dissatisfaction with the prevailing family form by those who find it oppressive and are determined to change it. The women who sought external employment in their millions were frustrated by economic dependency and 'being cooped up at home all day'. Defying the patriarchal norm that 'a woman's place is in the home', they ventured forth despite the objections of husbands – often vehemently expressed, particularly in the early stages of the transition. Women were undeniably the instigators of this sea change in family relations. Nor is this exceptional. Most of the major changes in modern family life have been driven by women.[26]

- As we have seen, the fertility decline was instigated by married women who refused to carry pregnancies to term and became increasingly insistent that husbands exercise sexual restraint.

- Legal reforms in the late nineteenth century that entitled women to hold property in marriage were instituted in response to vigorous public campaigns by the women's movement. Recent changes in family law have also been undertaken in response to women's discontent, with the new legislation clearly being influenced by feminist pressure and argument.

- The rapid rise of divorce has been driven primarily by women (almost three-quarters of petitioners) who are intensely dissatisfied with their present marriages.

Time and again, women's drive for equal rights in a male-dominated world has breached the norms of a family form that required them to sacrifice their interests 'for the sake of the family'. The traditional family is intractably at odds with the struggle for gender equality.[27] Many pundits are inclined to blame women, especially feminists, for this conflict. Brigitte Berger and Peter Berger, for instance, write:

The recent rise of feminism is particularly important in this connection. The individual woman is now emphasized over against every communal context in which she may find herself – a redefinition of her situation that breaks not only the community between spouses but (more fundamentally) the mother–child dyad … the most basic human community of all.[28]

In short, women are being accused of acting just like men – of neglecting their family duties while pursuing career employment opportunities. Ironically, the charge serves to confirm the feminist critique: that prevailing family arrangements have worked to women's disadvantage and are not based on genuine equality between spouses. As Carl Degler has pointed out, 'The central values of the modern family stand in opposition to these that underlie women's emancipation. Where the women's movement has stood for equality, the family historically has denied or repudiated equality.'[29]

How much equality between the sexes can modern families withstand? The answer is by no means clear, but depends, ultimately, on the willingness of women and men to renegotiate the terms of conjugal partnership. Certainly, high rates of remarriage indicate that neither sex, in their vast majority, wants out. Widespread disaffection with the traditional family, far from engendering a desire to dispense with families, has left millions of people feeling deeply disappointed that their own experience falls short of the ideal. Instead of confronting the oppressive reality that lies at the heart of this contradiction, family sociologists too often obfuscate it. They write glibly of 'egalitarian marriage', 'the symmetrical family' and 'the democratic household', as if they were describing the prevailing reality of modern family life. In effect, they imply that people whose families fail to measure up to these standards are personal failures.

Since I do not hold 'the traditional family' dear, I am not inclined to lament its passing. Overall, the changes that fill conservative hearts with fear leave me cautiously optimistic: it seems that a greater variety of domestic arrangements are gaining public legitimacy, leaving adults with more alternatives and women with more bargaining power in marriage. Yet this is hardly the occasion for euphoric predictions of the future. We have barely begun to grapple with the fundamental imbalance in traditional childraising. And after two decades of campaigns, commissions and pay equality legislation, the wage gap between the sexes has narrowed very little. The economic inequality that substructures conjugal power still prevails, though the primary breadwinner's domestic prerogatives have undoubtedly been undermined. As well as providing an independent income, employment outside the home has saddled women with the burdens of 'the double day' of labour. Since husbands have resisted increasing their own domestic exertions as their wives go out to work, the overall division of labour between spouses is probably more unequal now than in the 1950s. Obviously, it is insufficient to conduct a struggle for pay equality in the labour market that ignores the foundation of gender inequality in the lopsided allocation of family responsibilities between spouses. If the analytical preoccupation of this study has been to overcome the separation of 'family' from 'economy', the political importance of doing so is manifest. The struggle for gender equality continues on both fronts; the strategic imperative remains to combine them more effectively.

Notes

Chapter 1

1. There has been a unfortunate tendency among marxist-feminists to accept the family/economy dichotomy. Marxism is presumed to furnish an insightful analysis of the capitalist economy, while feminism sheds a penetrating light on family relations. The conceptual tension of the encounter is thus 'resolved' by a division of labour – different theories and expertise for distinct spheres. This strategy is a theoretical cul-de-sac, reinforcing the breach which the separation of households from workplaces fosters under capitalism, instead of disclosing their underlying connections. A fuller discussion of this point is offered in my 'Reflections on the Domestic Labour Debate and Prospects for Marxist-Feminist Synthesis', in Roberta Hamilton and Michèle Barrett, eds, *The Politics of Diversity* (London, 1986).

2. C. B. Macpherson, *The Political Theory of Possessive Individualism: Hobbes to Locke* (London, 1962).

3. State subsidization of the lower end of the housing market normally guarantees a residual housing stock that cannot be profitably produced by private capital without subsidy. The fundamental reason for this deficiency, endemic to rental accommodation under capitalism, is that the builders' profits are realized only after a number of unproductive parasites – real-estate agents, speculators, landlords and bankers – have taken their cut. This dilutes the incentive to build unless the prospective tenants can afford to pay very substantial rents, or state agencies offer financial incentives and underwrite the builders' risks.

4. This fixation with workplace relations must surely be one of marxism's great paradoxes. For here is a body of thought based on aspirations of proletarian independence mired in a tunnel vision of the realm of labour's unfreedom. As for the vistas of idle pleasure beyond the factory gates, orthodox marxists have been decidedly uninterested – almost as if they were a diversion from the class struggle. For their part, most workers find the relations of production that fascinate marxist intellectuals 'boring' – so stultifying in daily life that they are difficult to think about in a creative fashion. Paying only as much attention to their workplace surroundings as is necessary to do the job, they prefer to pass the time daydreaming about what they will do when the shift is over and they are finally 'free'. This is not to say that alienated labour is subjectively meaningless simply because so much of it is 'mindless'. But a programme of emancipation that fails to pay close attention to the daydreams of its constituents and to their lives beyond the stifling confines of their unfreedom is surely doomed to failure.

5. Volume 1 (New York, 1977), pp. 163–77.

6. Ibid., pp. 279–80.

7. Eleanor Rathbone, *The Disinherited Family* (Bristol, 1986 [1924]), p. 178. She recognized this irrationality long ago: 'Any system of wages ... must inevitably be either wasteful or socially disastrous so long as it is the only means of providing for families yet does not adjust itself to their varying sizes': ibid., p. 142. On this point, see also Joan Acker, 'Class, Gender, and the Relations of Distribution', *Signs,* vol. 13 (1988), p. 486.

8. Claude Meillassoux writes of the French state's minimum wage (*smic*): 'The smicard is a celibate labourer in that he has neither wife nor children. He is an employee who labours without interruption for all the working hours of the year. That is, he never falls ill and he is never unemployed. And he dies at the age of retirement. He is really an ideal wage labourer for the employer. Under these conditions, of course, the hourly wage covers the

minimum needs of the labourer. But which needs? Those of the daily reconstitution of labour-power and no more': 'Historical Modalities of the Exploitation and Over-Exploitation of Labour', *Critique of Anthropology,* nos 13/14 (1979), p. 14.

9. Eleanor Leacock, 'Introduction to Frederick Engels's *The Origin of the Family, Private Property and the State*' (New York, 1972), p. 40.

10. Laura Oren, 'The Welfare of Women in Labouring Families: England, 1860–1950', in Mary Hartman and Lois W. Banner, eds, *Clio's Consciousness Raised: New Perspectives on the History of Women* (New York, 1974), p. 228.

11. Ellen Ross, '"Fierce Questions and Taunts": Married Life in Working-Class London, 1870–1914', *Feminist Studies,* vol. 8 (1983), pp. 582–91; Louise Tilly and Joan Wallach Scott, *Women, Work and Family* (New York, 1978), p. 139.

12. Michèle Barrett, *Women's Oppression Today* (London, 1980), ch. 5.

13. Patricia A. Roos, *Gender and Work: A Comparative Analysis of Industrial Societies* (New York, 1985).

14. While the sexist attitudes of employers make discrimination seem natural and proper, the argument is based not upon blind prejudice but upon the rational conduct of profit-maximizers. Employer discrimination pays in so far as management's sexist policies are broadly held to be reasonable and fair in society. If, however, feminist consciousness becomes sufficiently pervasive to undermine this sense of natural order, female employees are likely to become enraged and potential customers alienated. At this point (which has recently been reached in many Western countries), the employer's interest in maximizing profit warrants an effort to lessen discrimination in order to reduce tensions (or at least to render discrimination less visible and more defensible). Firms that are responsive in this regard will be competitively rewarded. In the entire history of capitalism, however, relations of gender hierarchy have been sufficiently naturalized to render discrimination profitable under most circumstances. On this basis, the above generalizations seem warranted.

15. The disjointed relationship between labour-power's consumption and its demographic replacement has not been seriously examined by marxists. Marx provided a few insights in *Capital,* identifying the tendency of capitalism to generate a labour surplus independently of the population growth rate, calling this 'the law of relative surplus population' (vol. 1, pp. 781–802). The subsequent history of capitalism has borne him out; the imbalance became grotesque in the early 1980s, where youth unemployment in the developed capitalist states reached the staggering level of 15–20 per cent, while birth rates dipped well beneath replacement levels. Note that 'the law of relative surplus population' is not a demographic theory per se, but refers to the broad autonomy of the labour market from variance in population growth rates. Marx himself had very little to say about the determination of the latter. Notwithstanding his assertion that 'every ... mode of production has its own special laws of population', one searches Marx's work in vain for a theory of capitalist demography: *Capital,* vol. 1, p. 784.

16. What, then, of Japanese capitalists? They have certainly been successful accumulators, yet they are reputed to have assumed responsibility for their employees' lifetime financial security. Does their commitment vitiate the general argument being advanced here? Not at all. In the first place, the commitment to retain and retrain loyal, long-term employees has been undertaken only by the top companies, and even in these firms has not been extended to the lowest strata of the workforce. Overall, Japan's rates of labour turnover are not much lower than those of other OECD states: David Plath, *Work and Lifecourse in Japan* (Albany, N.Y., 1983). Secondly, where this type of employer commitment does prevail, it takes the form of an informal pact between managers and employees. Managers extend to specific workers certain assurances concerning their continued employment, provided the employees in question devote themselves unstintingly to the company's welfare. It is precisely because capitalism does not require employers to make this undertaking that those who do so are perceived to be caring and generous, gaining in return the loyalty and diligence of favoured employees without enshrining job security as a legal right. The precondition of effective paternalist *privilege* remains the absence of labour's *right* to job security.

17. *Capital,* vol. 1, pp. 455–70. The actual process of rendering labour 'abstract' (i.e.,

interchangeable and malleable) should not be confused with the theoretical category of 'abstract labour'. The latter was a term conceived by Marx for expository purposes in distinguishing labour-value rendered commensurate through the exchange of commodities from the use-value of particular products to their consumers. For Marx, however, the terms are related since he held that the process of generalized commodity exchange would lead inexorably to the abstraction of labour under conditions of 'Modern Industry'.

18.   It is the central flaw of Braverman's great work *Labour and Monopoly Capital* (New York, 1974) that he accepts a traditional craft definition of skill, thus perceiving a unilateral deskilling trend at work under capitalism, failing to recognize the positive side of workers' response to labour mobility, occupational fluidity and technological change. Marx marvelled at the aggressive versatility displayed by sections of the industrial proletariat, in contrast to the defensive occupational rigidity of traditional artisans: 'Large-scale industry, through its very catastrophes, makes the recognition of variation of labour and hence the fitness of the worker for the maximum number of different kinds of labour into a question of life and death.': *Capital,* vol. 1, p. 618. He saw this tendency as potentially offsetting the loss of traditional craft skills.

19.   Beyond securing the family's future subsistence, savings may also be used to set up a family business and shed the proletarian compulsion to sell one's labour-power. Since it is a ubiquitous ambition to work for oneself under capitalism (a testament to the pervasive alienation of wage labour), a minority of proletarians do save their pennies, striving to ascend into the ranks of the petty bourgeoisie. We can therefore postulate a wage ceiling above which capital accumulation occurs and the proletariat evaporates. This level varies with the market space available for small businesses and the start-up costs of their viable creation.

20.   These funds are allocated by means of legislated eligibility criteria and dispensed through state agencies. There is nothing comparable here to the proletarian prerogative of employer choice, which may explain why the form of their dispensation is deeply resented, although the benefits themselves continue to receive solid popular support despite the intense efforts of neo-conservative ideologues to discredit them.

21.   In the OECD states, public expenditure rose from 29 per cent of GDP in 1960 to 39 per cent in 1990. It is revealing, in this regard, that neither the Reagan nor Thatcher administrations were successful in effecting deep cuts in public expenditure, despite swingeing attacks on particular welfare programmes. Elsewhere in the OECD bloc, the relative growth of state social expenditure was slowed or halted in the 1980s, but has not been reversed. If the current recession is a deep one, this portion will rise again to unprecedented levels.

22.   *Capital,* vol. 1, pp. 772–94. Marxists have hotly debated the connection, postulated by Marx, between a rising organic composition of capital and a falling rate of profit. This has been one facet of a larger controversy concerning the validity and relevance of the labour theory of value. It is not necessary to uphold Marx's value theory in its original form to grant the merit of his argument concerning the labour-saving bias of technological change, and the role of this tendency in reconstituting the reserve army of labour in conjunctures of nearly full employment and rising real wages.

23.   Christopher Lasch, 'Reagan's Victims', *New York Review of Books,* vol. 35, no. 12, (1988), pp. 7–8.

24.   Jonas Frykman and Ovar Löfgren, *Culture Builders: A Historical Anthropology of Middle-Class Life* (New Brunswick, N.J., 1987), p. 151.

25.   In a fulsome critique of the Reagan administration from his inimitable red Tory vantage point, Christopher Lasch observes: 'There is a fundamental contradiction between Reagan's rhetorical defense of "family and neighborhood" and his championship of the unregulated business enterprise. ... A society dominated by the free market, in which the "American dream" means making a bundle, has small place for "family values"': 'Reagan's Victims', p. 7.

Chapter 2

1. The term 'rural' here must be used cautiously. Many proto-industrial zones had reached levels of density more akin to the outskirts of modern Third World cities, with loosely configured shantytowns of huddled shacks.

2. Whether they were successful in obtaining such work is another matter: a great many were not. Periodic bouts of unemployment were commonplace, and by no means confined to the bottom layers of the working class.

3. N. J. G. Pounds, *An Historical Geography of Europe* (Cambridge, 1985), p. 303.

4. C. Knick-Harley, 'British Industrialization before 1841: Evidence of Slower Growth during the Industrial Revolution', *Journal of Economic History,* vol. 42 (1982); N. F. R. Crafts, 'British Economic Growth, 1700–1831: A Review of the Evidence', *Economic History Review,* vol. 36 (1983).

5. Rondo Cameron, 'A New View of European Industrialization', *Economic History Review,* vol. 38 (1985), pp. 1–23.

6. The earlier view of exponential growth arose from concentrating on the specific industries that led the Industrial Revolution – coal, iron and cotton. Downward revisions in national income estimates (the stock in trade of the reappraisers) do not alter the fact that the growth of product outputs in these sectors was both unprecedented and explosive. Iron and steel production, for example, increased seventyfold between 1815 and 1913: Pounds, *Historical Geography of Europe,* p. 338. Against those who would now revise the Industrial Revolution out of existence, a brief reminder of the undeniable strengths of the older viewpoint is apposite. For our purposes, however, seeking to illuminate the typical experiences of the bulk of proletarian families, the lead sector fixation is deceptive, and the gradualist revision has undoubted merit.

7. Since this text concentrates on the processes of capitalist industrialization endogenous to Europe, it may be misread as implying the self-sufficiency of that development. I disavow such an interpretation. From the sixteenth century on, capitalist accumulation in Europe advanced by means of imperialist plunder, primary-resource extraction, and the exploitation of labour-power in subordinate modes of production throughout the colonial world. It is doubtful that the Industrial Revolution would ever have occurred in Western Europe without the accumulated wealth and economic advantages of colonialism.

8. While *Capital* contains a superb initial dissection of this particular mode of capitalist exploitation (which Marx termed the extraction of relative surplus-value), he did not adequately distinguish its specific growth dynamics from those of other modes of accumulation within the field of global capitalism; nor has this distinction since been elaborated satisfactorily. The classical marxist discussion of imperialism (by Lenin, Hilferding, Luxemburg and Bukharin) was superficially based on the corporate configuration of different types of capital (banking, industrial and financial) rather than on the inner dynamics of distinct forms of capital accumulation. More recently, an essentially similar and unduly homogeneous conception of global capitalism generated far too sweeping assessments of the obstacles to capitalist industrialization in Third World formations. The analysis of peripheral capitalist formations would especially benefit from a greater attention to distinctions between different forms of surplus-value extraction, profit realization and capital reinvestment.

9. Marx's analysis in *Capital* is nuanced through detailed descriptions of specific sectors where domestic outwork still flourished: 'Besides the factory worker, the workers engaged in manufacture, and the handicraftsmen, whom it concentrates in large masses at one spot, and directly commands, capital also sets another army in motion, by means of invisible threads: the outworkers in the domestic industries, who live in the large towns and are also scattered over the countryside': *Capital,* vol. 1 (New York, 1977), p. 591. In the popularization of Marx's thought after his death, however, a vulgar and unilineal version of his perspective was disseminated, stressing the centralizing dynamics of capitalist industrialization while neglecting the cross-currents. The result has been a lopsided picture: an unduly advanced and inexorable impression of the pace of capitalist maturation, a typically apocalyptic appreciation of capitalist crises, and a profoundly disorienting sense of temporal

horizon within the bourgeois epoch. The stubborn maintenance of this abbreviated calendar has much more to do with the wishful thinking of those who long for capitalism's 'death agony' than with a clear-headed assessment of the system's historically well-demonstrated capacity for renewal. In 'late capitalism', it is evidently much earlier than we had supposed.

10. Pounds, *Historical Geography of Europe*, pp. 302–5.

11. Eric Hopkins, *A Social History of the English Working Classes, 1815–1945* (London, 1979), p. 3; J. F. Bergier, 'The Industrial Bourgeoisie and the Rise of the Working Class 1700–1914', in C. M. Cipolla, ed., *The Fontana Economic History of Europe*, vol. 3 (New York, 1973), p. 426; Jürgen Kocka, 'Problems of Working-Class Formation in Germany: The Early Years, 1800–1875', in Ira Katznelson and Aristide Zolberg, eds, *Working-Class Formation: Nineteenth-Century Patterns in Western Europe and the United States* (Princeton, N.J. 1986), p. 296.

12. Raphael Samuel, 'The Workshop of the World: Steam Power and Hand Technology in Mid-Victorian Britain', *History Workshop Journal*, no. 3 (1977), pp. 17–20.

13. J. J. Lee, 'Labour in German Industrialization', in P. Mathias and M. M. Postan, eds, *Cambridge Economic History of Europe*, vol. 7 (Cambridge, 1978), p. 454.

14. Peter Mathias, *The First Industrial Nation* (London, 1983), p. 240.

15. E. J. Hunt, *British Labour History, 1815–1914* (London, 1981), p. 77.

16. David Landes, *The Unbound Prometheus* (London, 1969), p. 121. Marx underlined the basic difference between industrial capitalist outwork and traditional forms of domestic industry: 'This modern "domestic industry" has nothing, except the name, in common with the old-fashioned domestic industry. ... [The latter] has now been converted into an extension of the factory, the manufacturing workshop, or the warehouse': *Capital*, vol. 1, p. 590–91.

17. Kocka, 'Problems of Working-Class Formation in Germany', p. 312.

18. E. P. Thompson, 'Time, Work-Discipline, and Industrial Capitalism', *Past & Present*, no. 38 (1967), pp. 56–97; William Reddy, *The Rise of Market Culture: The Textile Trade and French Society, 1750–1900* (Cambridge, 1984).

19. *Capital*, vol. 1, pp. 1019–38.

20. Lee, 'Labour in German Industrialization', pp. 483–4; Peter Stearns, *Paths to Authority: The Middle Class and the Industrial Labor Force in France, 1820–1848* (Urbana, Ill., 1978), p. 59; M. A. Bienefeld, *Working Hours in British Industry: An Economic History* (London, 1972).

21. Douglas A. Reid, 'The Decline of Saint Monday, 1766–1876', *Past & Present, no.* 71 (1976), pp. 76–101; Michelle Perrot, 'On the Formation of the French Working Class', in Katznelson and Zolberg, eds, *Working-Class Formation*, p. 75; Stearns, *Paths to Authority*, p. 86.

22. Sidney Pollard, 'Labour in Great Britain', in P. Mathias and M. M. Postan, eds, *Cambridge Economic History of Europe*, vol. 7, pt 1, p. 157.

23. N. L. Tranter, 'The Labour Supply, 1780–1860', in Roderick Floud and Donald McCloskey, eds, *The Economic History of Britain Since 1700*, vol. 1 (Cambridge, 1981); Michael Young and Peter Willmott, *The Symmetrical Family* (New York, 1973), p. 132.

24. Dorothy Marshall, *Industrial England, 1776–1851* (London, 1973), p. 99.

25. Sidney Pollard, *The Genesis of Modern Management* (London, 1965), p. 163.

26. Colin Heywood, *Childhood in Nineteenth-Century France* (Cambridge, 1988), pp. 121–3; Eric J. Hobsbawm, *Labouring Men: Studies in the History of Labour* (London, 1964), p. 352.

27. Richard Price, *Labour in British Society* (London, 1986), pp. 73–83.

28. Jürgen Kocka, 'Craft Traditions and the Labour Movement in Nineteenth-Century Germany', in Pat Thane, Geoffrey Crossick and Roderick Floud, eds, *The Power of the Past: Essays for Eric Hobsbawm* (Cambridge, 1984), p. 104.

29. Kocka, 'Problems of Working-Class Formation in Germany', p. 319.

30. George Sheridan, 'Household and Craft in an Industrializing Economy: The Case of the Silk Weavers of Lyons', in J. M. Merriman, ed., *Consciousness and Class Experience in Nineteenth-Century Europe* (New York, 1979); Perrot, 'On the Formation of the French Working Class'; Ron Aminzade, 'Reinterpreting Capitalist Industrialization: A Study of

Nineteenth-Century France', in S. L. Kaplan and C. J. Koepp, eds, *Work in France: Representations, Meanings, Organization and Practice* (Ithaca, N.Y., 1986), pp. 403–4.

31. Duncan Bythell, *The Sweated Trades: Outwork in Nineteenth-Century Britain* (London, 1978), p. 168.

32. Perrot, 'On the Formation of the French Working Class', p. 77.

33. Joan Wallach Scott, 'Men and Women in the Parisian Garment Trades: Discussions of Family and Work in the 1830s and 1840s', in Thane, Crossick and Floud, eds, *The Power of the Past: Essays for Eric Hobsbawm,* (Cambridge, 1984), p. 85.

34. Kocka, 'Problems of Working-Class Formation in Germany', p. 305.

35. While foregrounding the revolutionary novelty and discontinuity of modern industry, Marx nevertheless understood that industrialists had taken over and refashioned pre-existing family-based production forms in the early factories: 'Capital subsumes the labour process as it finds it, that is to say, it takes over an existing labour process developed by different and more archaic modes of production. ... If changes occur in these traditional established labour processes after their takeover by capital, they are nothing but the gradual consequences of that subsumption': *Capital,* vol. 1 (1976), p. 1021.

36. Louise Tilly and Joan Wallach Scott, *Women, Work and Family* (New York, 1978).

37. William Coleman, *Death Is a Social Disease* (Madison, Wis., 1982), p. 233.

38. To speak, then, of 'working-class living standards' without reference to this characteristic variance between phases is to discuss an abstraction. Yet in the long-standing controversy over proletarian living standards in England during the Industrial Revolution, the demographic realities of varying dependency ratios, and the particular mix of incomes sustaining families at different stages of the domestic cycle, have scarcely been recognized. This matter is discussed further in Chapter 3.

39. Standish Meacham, *A Life Apart: The English Working Class, 1890–1914* (Cambridge, Mass., 1977), p. 73; Lady Bell, *At the Works: A Study of a Manufacturing Town* (London, 1985 [1907]), p. 184.

40. Michael R. Haines, *Fertility and Occupation: Population Patterns in Industrialization* (New York, 1979), p. 224; Adrian Rifkin and Roger Thomas, *Voices of the People: The Social Life of 'La société' at the End of the Second Empire* (London, 1988), p. 123.

41. Since children constitute a fixed cost for parents, the incentive to set them to work arises as soon as they can generate family income or be useful around the house; it does not await the invisible crossing of the break-even threshold. Certainly industrialization lowered the entry-level threshold for young children, most notably in textile production. Only parents who were themselves making a relatively high and steady income could afford to ignore this inducement for the sake of their children's health and education.

42. Heywood, *Childhood in Nineteenth-Century France,* p. 104; Mathias, *The First Industrial Nation,* p. 239; Gerhard Bry, *Wages in Germany, 1871–1945* (Princeton, N.J., 1960), p. 25.

43. Derived from Mathias, *The First Industrial Nation,* p. 239.

44. Since in France this remains very large in the nineteenth century (over half until the 1870s), and women working on family farms were included in the 'active population', the female labour-force participation rate for the country as a whole appears to be somewhat higher than for Britain and Germany. In industry, however, it was no greater. France's census-takers also seem to have counted domestic workers more adequately than did those in other states. In 1906, 28 per cent of industrial workers were toiling at home; 86 per cent of them were female: Roger Price, *A Social History of Nineteenth-Century France* (New York, 1987), pp. 199, 202.

45. Jane Humphries, '"The Most Free from Objection": The Sexual Division of Labor and Women's Work in Nineteenth-Century England', *Journal of Economic History,* vol. 47 (1987), pp. 932–3.

46. Lee, 'Labour in German Industrialization', p. 481.

47. John Gillis, *For Better, For Worse: British Marriages, 1600 to the Present* (New York, 1985), p. 184. See also Nancy G. Osterud, 'Gender Divisions and the Organization of Work in the Leicester Hosiery Industry', in A. V. John, ed., *Unequal Opportunities: Women's Employment in England, 1800–1918* (Oxford, 1986), p. 53; Ivy Pinchbeck, *Women Workers and the*

Industrial Revolution, 1750–1850 (London, 1981 [1930]), pp. 1–2; Margaret Hewitt, *Wives and Mothers in Victorian Industry* (London, 1958), p. 3; and John Gillis, 'Peasant, Plebeian and Proletarian Marriage in Britain, 1600–1900', in David Levine, ed., *Proletarianization and Family History* (New York, 1984), p. 139.

48. Pinchbeck, *Women Workers and the Industrial Revolution,* p. 122.

49. The same shift in the United States (from a positive, indeed insistent, attitude to women's work in industry in the eighteenth century to a negative, stigmatizing one by the late nineteenth century) is documented by Edith Abbott in her classic *Women in Industry: A Study in American Economic History* (New York, 1969 [1910]), ch. 13. See also Alice Kessler-Harris, *Out to Work: A History of Wage-Earning Women in the United States* (New York, 1982), chs 2–4.

50. Sally Alexander, Anna Davin and Eve Hostettler, 'Labouring Women: A Reply to Eric Hobsbawm', *History Workshop Journal,* no. 8 (1979), pp. 174–82.

51. 1881 is the earliest census for which these breakdowns have been done. The rate of women aged 25–64 was 27.6 per cent in 1881 and 25.2 per cent in 1921: R. C. O. Mathews, C. H. Feinstein and J. C. Odling-Smee, *British Economic Growth, 1865–1973* (Oxford, 1982), p. 564. Married women's extra-domestic employment rates were evidently highest in the Lancashire textile districts. Drawing a random sample from the 1851 census, Hewitt has calculated that 30 per cent of married women in the main Lancashire cotton districts were employed at that time. Overall rates for England and Wales were bound to be much lower: *Wives and Mothers in Victorian Industry,* p. 29.

52. Haines, *Fertility and Occupation: Population Patterns in Industrialization,* p. 230.

53. Barbara Franzoi, *At the Very Least She Pays the Rent: Women and German Industrialization, 1871–1914* (Westport, Conn., 1985), p. 33.

54. Women's labour-force participation rates over the life-course were very different in the nineteenth century, when the highest level occurred when they were in their twenties and early thirties, from those of the twentieth century, when (until very recently) female employment rates were at their lowest through the childbearing years and then rose somewhat for women in their forties and fifties who returned to work after their children were grown up. Compare Tilly and Scott, *Women, Work and Family,* p. 135, with Patricia Roos, *Gender and Work: A Comparative Analysis of Industrial Societies* (New York, 1985), pp. 44–5.

55. This seems to have occurred in some feminist accounts: Sonya Rose, 'Gender at Work: Sex, Class and Industrial Capitalism', *History Workshop Journal,* no. 21 (1986), pp. 113–31. At pains to displace simplistic stereotypes by portraying the complexity and variety of women's employment careers, scholars have lost a coherent sense of the mainstream experience, highlighting cross-currents that inevitably coexist with prevailing patterns and trends.

56. J. J. Lee, 'Labour in German Industrialization', p. 490. Trade unionists remarked that young single women were difficult to organize because they saw employment as a short-term life-stage, and looked forward to leaving at marriage or soon after. This was the frequent refrain of labour leaders who had made no genuine attempt to organize women workers and were looking for an excuse to explain their lack of interest or success in this endeavour. But we should not simply reject its veracity on this account. Women trade-union organizers, deeply committed to unionizing working women, frequently made the same point. The fact remains that the great majority of working women in the nineteenth century did view their jobs in a short-term perspective and left them upon marriage.

57. Peter Stearns, *Lives of Labour* (New York, 1975), p. 60.

58. Robyn Dasey, 'Women's Work and the Family: Women Garment Workers in Berlin and Hamburg before the First World War', in R. Evans and W. Lee, eds, *The German Family* (London, 1981), p. 224; Sheila Lewenhak, *Women and Trade Unions: An Outline History of Women in the British Trade-Union Movement* (London, 1977), p. 41; Jane Lewis, 'The Working-Class Wife and Mother and State Intervention, 1870–1918', in Jane Lewis, ed., *Labour and Love: Women's Experience of Home and Family, 1850–1940* (Oxford, 1986), p. 105.

59. John Rule, *The Experience of Labour in Eighteenth-Century Industry* (London, 1981), p. 43.

60.   Jean Neuville, *La Condition ouvrière au XIXe siècle* (Brussels, 1976), p. 11.

61.   Clark Nardinelli, 'Child Labour and the Factory Acts', *Journal of Economic History,* vol. 40 (1980), pp. 739–55; Heywood, *Childhood in Nineteenth-Century France,* p. 104; Katherine Lynch, *Family, Class, and Ideology in Early Industrial France: Social Policy and the Working-Class Family, 1825–1848* (Madison, Wis., 1988), pp. 68–70.

62.   Maxine Berg, *The Age of Manufactures: Industry, Innovation and Work in Britain, 1700–1820* (London, 1985), pp. 259–60.

63.   Nardinelli, 'Child Labour and the Factory Acts', p. 748; J. J. Lee, 'Labour in German Industrialization', p. 467.

64.   John Hurt, *Elementary Schooling and the Working Classes, 1860–1918* (London, 1979), p. 44. By 1851, only 42,000 children under ten years old were recorded as employed in Britain: F. M. L. Thompson, *The Rise of Respectable Society: A Social History of Victorian Britain, 1830–1900* (London, 1988), p. 81.

65.   David Vincent, *Bread, Knowledge and Freedom: A Study of Nineteenth-Century Working-Class Autobiography* (London, 1981), p. 67.

66.   Alfred Kelly, *The German Worker: Working-Class Autobiographies from the Age of Industrialization* (Berkeley, Calif., 1987), pp. 22–3.

67.   Vincent, *Bread, Knowledge and Freedom,* p. 73.

68.   Heywood, *Childhood in Nineteenth-Century France,* p. 196.

69.   Mixing insight with rhetorical exaggeration, Helen Bosanquet concluded in 1906: 'Wherever we find an industry of any degree of specialization, as distinct from unskilled and unspecialized labour, there we may find to a greater or lesser extent a continuity of work binding the generations together, and affording a basis for continuous family life as real and firm, if not as tangible, as landed property itself': *The Family* (London, 1906), p. 217.

70.   Perrot, 'On the Formation of the French Working Class', p. 82; Louise Tilly, 'Coping with Company Paternalism: Family Strategies of Coal Miners in Nineteenth-Century France', *Theory and Society,* vol. 14 (1985), p. 407; John Foster, *Class Struggle and the Industrial Revolution* (London, 1974), pp. 262–9.

71.   Vincent, *Bread, Knowledge and Freedom,* p. 74.

72.   Stearns, *Lives of Labour,* p. 74.

73.   Alain Cottereau, 'The Distinctiveness of Working-Class Cultures in France, 1848–1900', in Katznelson and Zolberg, eds, *Working-Class Formation,* p. 117; Michelle Perrot, 'The Three Ages of Industrial Discipline in Nineteenth-Century France', in John M. Merriman, ed., *Consciousness and Class Experience in Nineteenth-Century Europe* (New York, 1979), p. 155.

74.   Lynch, *Family, Class, and Ideology in Early Industrial France,* p. 186. See also Frances Collier, *The Family Economy of the Working Classes in the Cotton Industry, 1784–1833* (Manchester, 1964); Patrick Joyce, *Work, Society and Politics: The Culture of the Factory in Later Victorian England* (London, 1980), p. 113.

75.   Pollard, *The Genesis of Modern Management,* p. 43.

76.   William Reddy, 'Family and Factory: French Linen Weavers in the Belle Epoque', *Journal of Social History,* vol. 8 (1975), p. 102; Tilly and Scott, *Women, Work and Family,* p. 113.

77.   Pollard, *The Genesis of Modern Management,* pp. 40–47; J. Humphries, 'Protective Legislation: The Capitalist State, and Working-Class Men: The Case of the 1842 Mines Regulation Act', *Feminist Review,* vol. 7 (1981), pp. 1–33; Angela John, *By the Sweat of Their Brow: Women Workers at Victorian Coal Mines* (London, 1980).

78.   Hobsbawm, *Labouring Men,* p. 297.

79.   Michael Anderson, 'Sociological History and the Working-Class Family: Smelser Revisited', *Social History,* vol. 3 (1976), p. 325; M. M. Edwards and R. Lloyd-Jones, 'N. J. Smelser and the Cotton Family: A Reassessment', in N. B. Harte and K. G. Ponting, eds, *Textile History and Economic History* (Manchester, 1973), pp. 304–19; Heywood, *Childhood in Nineteenth-Century France,* p. 188.

80.   Lynch, *Family, Class, and Ideology in Early Industrial France,* p. 185.

81.   Reddy, 'Family and Factory', p. 107; Kocka, 'Problems of Working-Class For-

mation in Germany', p. 318; Edwards and Lloyd-Jones, 'N. J. Smelser', in Harte and Ponting, eds, *Textile History and Economic History*.

82. Lee, 'Labour in German Industrialization', pp. 451–2.

83. William Lazonick, 'The Subjugation of Labour to Capital: The Rise of the Capitalist System', *Review of Radical Political Economics,* vol. 10 (1978), p. 8; Marx, *Capital,* vol. 1 (1977), p. 519; Perrot, 'Three Ages of Industrial Discipline', p. 153; Joyce, *Work, Society and Politics,* p. 112.

84. Humphries, 'Protective Legislation', p. 13; Perrot, 'On the Formation of the French Working Class', pp. 74–7, 86–7.

85. Dennis, *English Industrial Cities,* p. 22.

86. By 1911 only 44 per cent of the French population lived in cities (centres of over 10,000 people), while 79 per cent of Britons and 60 per cent of Germans did. France, as mentioned, had a much slower population growth rate, so that although its pace of urbanization was not as quick, the French countryside suffered depopulation in the nineteenth century, while elsewhere, rural populations maintained their numbers or even grew slightly.

87. Wohl, *Endangered Lives,* p. 290.

88. Catherina Lis, *Social Change and the Labouring Poor: Antwerp, 1770–1860* (New Haven, Conn., 1986), p. 64; Louis Chevalier, *Laboring Classes and Dangerous Classes in Paris during the First Half of the Nineteenth Century* (Princeton, N.J., 1973), p. 187; Nicholas Bullock and James Read, *The Movement for Housing Reform in Germany and France 1840–1914* (Cambridge, 1985), p. 22.

89. Bullock and Read, *The Movement for Housing Reform in Germany and France,* pp. 299–303.

90. A. S. Wohl, 'The Housing of the Working Classes in London, 1815–1914', in S. D. Chapman, ed., *The History of Working-Class Housing* (Newton Abbot, 1971), p. 17.

91. Lis, *Social Change and the Labouring Poor,* p. 202; Bullock and Read, *The Movement for Housing Reform in Germany and France,* p. 23.

92. Helmut Kaelble, *Industrialization and Social Inequality in Nineteenth-Century Europe* (Leamington Spa, 1986), p. 112; Wohl, 'The Housing of the Working Classes in London, 1815–1914', in Chapman, ed., *The History of Working-Class Housing,* p. 26; Lis, *Social Change and the Labouring Poor,* p. 81; Hans Chr. Johansen and Per Boje, 'Working-Class Housing in Odense, 1750–1914', *Scandinavian Economic History Review,* vol. 34 (1986), pp. 150–51.

93. Michael Anderson, *Family Structure in Nineteenth-Century Lancashire* (Cambridge, 1971), p.48; Bullock and Read, *The Movement for Housing Reform in Germany and France,* p. 57; T. C. Smout, *A Century of the Scottish People, 1830–1950* (London, 1986), p. 33.

94. Wohl, *Endangered Lives,* p. 293.

95. Lis, *Social Change and the Labouring Poor,* pp. 75, 78; James Treble, 'Liverpool Working-class Housing, 1801–51', in Chapman, ed., *The History of Working-Class Housing,* p. 211.

96. Treble, 'Liverpool Working-Class Housing', p. 211.

97. John Butt, 'Working-Class Housing in Glasgow, 1851–1914', in Chapman, ed., *The History of Working-Class Housing,* p. 81; Lis, *Social Change and the Labouring Poor,* p. 78; Ashok Desai, *Real Wages in Germany* (Oxford, 1968), p. 123.

98. Ellen Ross, 'Survival Networks: Women's Neighbourhood Sharing in London before World War I', *History Workshop Journal,* no. 15 (1983), p. 10.

99. Samuel Preston and Etienne Van de Walle, 'Urban French Mortality in the Nineteenth Century', *Population Studies,* vol. 32 (1978), pp. 275–97.

100. E. A. Wrigley, *Population and History* (New York, 1969), p. 173.

101. Wohl, *Endangered Lives,* p. 287. See also Anne-Louise Shapiro, *Housing the Poor of Paris, 1850–1902* (London, 1985), p. 85; Bullock and Read, *The Movement for Housing Reform in Germany and France,* pp. 40–41.

102. Anthony S. Wohl, 'Sex and the Single Room: Incest among the Victorian Working Classes', in Anthony S. Wohl, ed., *The Victorian Family* (London, 1978), p. 206.

103. Cited in Wohl, *Endangered Lives,* p. 292.

104. Cited in Wohl, 'The Housing of the Working Classes in London', p. 35.

105. Caroline Davidson, *A Woman's Work Is Never Done: A History of Housework in the*

British Isles, 1650–1950 (London, 1986), p. 190.

106. Louise Tilly, 'Linen Was Their Life: Family Survival Strategies and Parent–Child Relations in Nineteenth-Century France', in Hans Medick and David Sabean, eds, *Interest and Emotion* (Cambridge, 1984), p. 305.

107. The big breakthrough was electricity, but its spread occurred after the First World War. In 1914, only 6 per cent of homes in Britain were wired; by 1938, 65 per cent were: Davidson, *A Woman's Work Is Never Done*, p. 38.

108. Ibid., p. 102.

109. Ibid., pp. 63–8.

110. Wohl, *Endangered Lives*, p. 62.

111. Davidson, *A Woman's Work Is Never Done*, pp. 141–5.

112. Susan Strasser, *Never Done: A History of American Homework* (New York, 1982), p. 105.

113. Davidson, *A Woman's Work Is Never Done*, pp. 151–2.

114. Ibid., p. 152.

115. In working-class districts of London in 1934, running water in houses was the exception rather than the rule: Davidson, *A Woman's Work Is Never Done*, p. 31.

116. Ross, '"Not the Sort That Would Sit on the Doorstep": Respectability in Pre–World War I London Neighbourhoods', *International Labor and Working Class History*, vol. 27 (Spring 1985), p. 42; Smout, *A Century of the Scottish People*, p. 178.

117. Jill Liddington and Jill Norris, *One Hand Tied behind Us: The Rise of the Women's Suffrage Movement* (London, 1978), p. 30.

118. Davidson, *A Woman's Work Is Never Done*, p. 136.

119. John Burnett, *Destiny Obscure: Autobiographies of Childhood, Education and Family from the 1820s to the 1920s* (Harmondsworth, 1984), pp. 220–21.

120. *From Their Point of View* (London, 1908), p. 181.

121. Ross, 'Survival Networks', pp. 12–13.

122. Davidson, *A Woman's Work Is Never Done*, p. 187.

123. Gareth Stedman Jones, 'Working-Class Culture and Working-Class Politics in London, 1870–1900: Notes on the Remaking of the Working-Class', *Journal of Social History*, vol. 7 (1974), pp. 460–508; Ellen Ross, '"Fierce Questions and Taunts": Married Life in Working-Class London, 1870–1914', *Feminist Studies*, vol. 8 (1982), p. 578.

124. Davidson, *A Woman's Work Is Never Done*, pp. 187–8.

125. See the preceding study, *A Millennium of Family Change: Feudalism to Capitalism in Northwestern Europe* (London, 1992), pp. 207–8.

126. Cissie Fairchilds, 'Female Sexual Attitudes and the Rise of Illegitimacy', *Journal of Interdisciplinary History*, vol. 8 (1978), pp. 627–67. In David Levine's words, illegitimacy was evidently 'marriage frustrated, not promiscuity rampant': *Family Formation in an Age of Nascent Capitalism* (New York, 1977), p. 127.

127. Segalen, *Historical Anthropology of the Family*, p. 135.

128. Knodel, *Demographic Behaviour in the Past*, p. 125.

129. Gillis, *For Better, For Worse*, pp. 192–4.

130. In eighteenth-century Lyons, seven men in ten deemed responsible for the pregnancy of single women had left the city before the birth: Shorter, *The Making of the Modern Family*, p. 137.

131. Knodel, *Demographic Behaviour in the Past*, p. 221.

132. Many social historians refer to this as 'concubinage', but I shall eschew the term on the grounds that it conflates two phenomena with profoundly disparate cultural parameters and moral significance: the cohabitation of a couple who are not legally married; and the keeping of a concubine for sexual services by a man who remains legally married to, and living with, another woman. This confusion is particularly insidious in so far as these patterns place women in entirely different circumstances, and are typically found at the extremes of wealth. Informal cohabitation is most common amongst the poor, while mistress-keeping is a rich man's game.

133. Gillis, *For Better, For Worse*, p. 219.

134. Louis Chevalier, *Laboring Classes and Dangerous Classes*, pp. 311–13.

135. Gillis, *For Better, For Worse*, p. 206.

136. Lynch, *Family, Class, and Ideology in Early Industrial France*, p. 82; Lenard Berlanstein, 'Illegitimacy, Concubinage, and Proletarianization in a French Town, 1760–1914', *Journal of Family History*, vol. 5, no. 3 (1980), p. 368.

137. Rule, *The Labouring Classes in Early Industrial England*, p. 201–2.

138. Berlanstein, 'Illegitimacy, Concubinage, and Proletarianization in a French Town', p. 370; Ross, 'Survival Networks', p. 27.

139. Lynch, *Family, Class, and Ideology in Early Industrial France*, p. 108; see also John Gillis, *For Better, For Worse*, p. 190.

140. Lynch, *Family, Class, and Ideology in Early Industrial France*, p. 101; Knodel, *Demographic Behaviour in the Past*, p. 221–2.

141. Gillis, *For Better, For Worse*, pp. 192–4.

142. Ibid., pp. 196–219.

143. Ibid., p. 192.

144. Ibid., p. 197. See also Lynch, *Family, Class, and Ideology in Early Industrial France*, pp. 88–113; Berlanstein, 'Illegitimacy, Concubinage, and Proletarianization in a French Town', p. 371; and G. P. Thompson and Eileen Yeo, *The Unknown Mayhew* (Harmondsworth, 1984 [1971]), pp. 203–10.

145. Chevalier, *Laboring Classes and Dangerous Classes*, p. 315.

146. Bullock and Read, *The Movement for Housing Reform in Germany and France*, p. 31.

147. Shapiro, *Housing the Poor of Paris*, p. 90.

148. One must be cautious here, since it is not difficult to unearth literary evidence for virtually every historical period demonstrating that the gentle people of the propertied classes harboured deep fears that the 'lower orders' had sunk into such abject depravity that civilized family life among them would soon be at an end: Jonas Frykman and Ovar Löfgren, *Culture Builders: A Historical Anthropology of Middle-Class Life* (New Brunswick, N.J., 1987), p. 151. Against the normal background din of clucking tongues, we can none the less discern those extraordinary conjunctures when the alarm of the prosperous exceeds the threshold of reflexive disdain and is whipped into a full-blown moral panic, catalysing reaction and redress. In this regard, the clamour arising in the midst of the Industrial Revolution had the makings of a grand *fortissimo*.

149. Lynch, *Family, Class, and Ideology in Early Industrial France*, p. 169.

150. Lord Ashley, cited in Pinchbeck, *Women Workers and the Industrial Revolution, 1750–1850* (London, 1981 [1930]), p. 197.

151. Lynch, *Family, Class, and Ideology in Early Industrial France*, pp. 36–7.

152. Shapiro, *Housing the Poor of Paris*, p. 85.

153. Bullock and Read, *The Movement for Housing Reform in Germany and France*, p. 40.

154. Lynch, *Family, Class, and Ideology in Early Industrial France*, pp. 193, 196.

155. Ibid., p. 183.

156. John Rule, *The Labouring Classes in Early Industrial England, 1750–1850* (London, 1986), p. 180.

157. Shapiro, *Housing the Poor of Paris*, p. 89.

158. Frederick Engels, *The Condition of the Working Class in England in 1844* (London, 1969), p. 171.

159. F. M. L. Thompson, *The Rise of Respectable Society*, pp. 85–7.

160. In addition to the sources already cited, see for Britain, Gillis, *For Better, For Worse*, and F. M. L. Thompson, *The Rise of Respectable Society*; for France, see Reddy, *The Rise of Market Culture*, pp. 169–84, and Lynch, *Family, Class, and Ideology in Early Industrial France*, pp. 33–9; for Germany, see Dasey, 'Women's Work and the Family', p. 222, and Frevert 'The Civilizing Tendency of Hygiene: Working-Class Women under Medical Control in Imperial Germany', in J. C. Fout, ed., *German Women in the Nineteenth Century* (New York, 1984), p. 326.

161. J. Wickham, 'Working-Class Movement and Working-Class Life: Frankfurt am Main during the Weimar Republic', *Social History*, vol. 8 (1983), p. 333.

162. 'However terrible and disgusting the dissolution of the old family ties within the capitalist system may appear, large-scale industry, by assigning an important part in socially

organized processes of production, outside the sphere of the domestic economy to women, young persons, and children of both sexes, does nevertheless create a new economic foundation for a higher form of the family and of relations between the sexes': Marx, *Capital*, vol. 1 (New York, 1977), pp. 620–21.

163. Shapiro, *Housing the Poor of Paris*, pp. 87–90.

164. Richard J. Evans, 'Politics and the Family, Social Democracy and the Working-Class Family in Theory and Practice before 1914', in Evans and Lee, eds, *The German Family*, p. 259.

165. Michael Anderson, *Family Structure in Nineteenth Century Lancashire*; Tamara K. Hareven, *Family Time and Industrial Time* (Cambridge, 1982), p. 2; Jane Humphries, 'Class Struggle and the Persistence of the Working-Class Family', *Cambridge Journal of Economics*, vol. 1 (1977), pp. 241–58.

166. The following studies are relevant (places and periods researched are in square brackets). Laslett, *Household and Family in Past Time* (Cambridge, 1972) [six English towns and villages, from the seventeenth or eighteenth century to 1851]; Anderson, *Family Structure in Nineteenth-Century Lancashire* [Preston, England in 1851]; W. A. Armstrong, 'A Note on the Household Structure of Mid–Nineteenth Century York in Comparative Perspective', in Laslett, ed., *Household and Family in Past Time* [York, England, 1851]; Richard Wall, 'The Household: Demographic and Economic Change in England, 1650–1970', in Wall, ed., *Family Forms in Historic Europe* (Cambridge, 1984) [England, 1750–1821, 1851]; Louise Tilly, 'Individual Lives and Family Strategies in the French Proletariat', in Robert Wheaton and Tamara K. Hareven, eds, *Family and Sexuality in French History* (Philadelphia, 1980) [Roubaix, France in 1861]; Paul Spagnoli, 'Industrialization, Proletarianization and Marriage: A Reconsideration', *Journal of Family History*, vol. 8 (1983), pp. 230–47 [four industrializing towns in the Lille district of northern France in 1861]; Angelique Janssens, 'Industrialization without Family Change? The Extended Family and the Industrial Life Cycle in a Dutch Industrial Town, 1880–1920', *Journal of Family History*, vol. 11 (1986), pp. 25–42 [Tilburg, the Netherlands, 1880–1920]; P. Schmidtbauer, 'The Changing Household: Austrian Household Structure from the Seventeenth to the Early Twentieth Century', in Wall, ed., *Family Forms in Historic Europe* [Austria, various towns in the nineteenth century]. For a review of the North American evidence, indicating the same tendency to augmentation in the midst of nineteenth-century industrialization, see Steven Ruggles, *Prolonged Connections* (Madison, Wis., 1987), pp. 3–12.

167. Hareven, *Family Time and Industrial Time*, p. 160; Rosemary Orthmann, 'Labour Force Participation, Life Cycle and Expenditure Patterns', in R. B. Joeres and M. J. Maynes, eds, *German Women in the Eighteenth and Nineteenth Centuries* (Bloomington, Ind., 1986), p. 30.

168. Y. Talmon, 'Social Change and Kinship Ties', in R. Hill and R. Konig, eds, *Families in East and West* (Paris, 1970), p. 511.

169. Frykman and Löfgren, *Culture Builders*, p. 152.

170. Critiques of the biases of middle-class observers of working-class family life have proliferated in the new social history: c.f. F. M. L. Thompson, *The Rise of Respectable Society*, p. 129; Frykman and Löfgren, *Culture Builders*, p. 148.

171. In *A Millennium of Family Change*, I addressed this argument at length and presented a counterthesis. The debate is summarized in the concluding chapter of that text.

172. Lynch, *Family, Class, and Ideology in Early Industrial France*, pp. 31–64; Frykman and Löfgren, *Culture Builders*, p. 142.

173. In this, Marx and Engels shared a view that was common in the nineteenth century. It may appear obtuse in retrospect, but it is not difficult to fathom how contemporaries arrived at this conclusion. With their attention riveted on textiles, the vanguard sector of the Industrial Revolution, observers tended to generalize from trends occurring there, extrapolating across the entire economy in the future. In the cotton mills, women and children were typically employed to operate the most advanced machines; at a stroke, mechanization had obviated the need for both specialized artisanal training and brute strength – the two capacities that had been the traditional preserves of men. Correctly predicting that mechanization would soon spread through one industry after another, they

could see no reason why capitalists would not continue to recruit women and children to work on the leading edge of technological innovation, paying them a fraction of men's wages. The specific need for male labour-power seemed to be headed for extinction. Under these circumstances, speculation concerning the future of the working-class family was legion.

174. William J. Goode, *World Revolution and Family Patterns* (New York, 1963); Talcott Parsons, 'The American Family, Its Relation to Personality and the Social Structure', in Parsons and R. F. Bales, eds, *Family, Socialization and Interaction Process* (New York, 1965).

175. Those familiar with the recent history of Western marxism will recognize a striking parallel in the Althusserian response to the problem of economism in historical materialism. By the 1970s, there was a broad consensus that the base–superstructure relationship had been reductively conceived. Althusser's remedy was to loosen the proposed connections between them – hence 'the relative autonomy of superstructures' (fostering an irruption of idealism in the field of cultural studies). Unless one is prepared to abandon the analysis of society as a complex multicausal *unity*, it is far preferable to respond to this sort of empirical challenge by rethinking one's *entire* paradigm. Proceeding in this way, we retain the premiss that there are causal connections between the disparate regions of a social formation, and assume that they have been obscured or misspecified in the inherited model. The immediate task is to propose theoretical revisions in order to take more adequate account of them. The supreme objective of a holistic analysis ought to be to identify and explain underlying causal connections between superficially disparate phenomena, however complex and mediated these relationships are. The relative autonomy thesis can at best serve to discredit causal models that are misconstrued and insufficiently mediated. Despite its apparent sophistication, the point is entirely negative; it explains nothing, while frequently being used to salvage faulty paradigms in need of more basic revision.

176. Anderson, *Family Structure in Nineteenth-Century Lancashire*, p. 85. While reworking Anderson's data, Richard Wall corroborated this finding. 'The conditions of life in large towns did give rise to situations in which children would remain longer in the parental home than they had either in pre-industrial England or in rural areas in the mid-nineteenth century': Wall, 'The Age at Leaving Home', *Journal of Family History*, vol. 3 (1978), p. 193.

177. Spagnoli, 'Industrialization, Proletarianization and Marriage: A Reconsideration', p. 240; Tilly, 'Individual Lives and Family Strategies in the French Proletariat', p. 215.

178. In addition to the accounts cited below, see Ellen Ross, 'Labour and Love: Rediscovering London's Working-Class Mothers, 1870–1918', in Jane Lewis, ed., *Labour and Love: Women's Experience of Home and Family, 1850–1940* (Oxford, 1986) p. 87; Lynn Jamieson, 'Limited Resources and Limiting Conventions: Working-Class Mothers and Daughters in Urban Scotland, c.1890–1925', in Lewis, ed., *Labour and Love*, p. 58; Barbara Franzoi, *At the Very Least She Pays the Rent*, p. 90; and Peter Stearns, 'Working-Class Women in Britain, 1890–1914', in Martha Vicinus, ed., *Suffer and Be Still: Women in the Victorian Age* (Bloomington, Ind., 1972), p. 111. These bonds of familial solidarity are missing from Michael Anderson's excessively atomistic model of the family as a contractual nexus of individuals calculating the manifold benefits and disadvantages of various courses of action in their relations with one another: *Family Structure in Nineteenth-Century Lancashire*, ch. 2. It is not that people's distinct interests in family groups are completely submerged in a culture of domestic altruism (as Gary Becker would have it), but they are constrained by powerful obligations for the care of dependants (above all young children), which are not contractual in nature, but are based on indelible 'blood' relations. Furthermore, women are under greater pressure and are more inclined to submerge their interests 'for the sake of the family' than are men. These lifelong bonds, in turn, foster a sense of duty to care for one's parents in their old age. The evident willingness of adults (however much they resent the burden) to care for elderly parents as their dependency increases cannot be explained within a calculus of self-interest, narrowly conceived: Ruggles, *Prolonged Connections*, pp. 20–29.

179. Vincent, *Bread, Knowledge and Freedom*, p. 82.

180. John Shaffer, 'Family, Class, and Young Women: Occupational Expectations in Nineteenth-Century Paris', *Journal of Family History*, vol. 3 (1978), p. 73.

181. In an early-twentieth-century survey, the US Bureau of Labor reported that sons

gave over 83 per cent, and daughters 95 per cent, of their earnings. There is no reason to suppose that the rate of remission would be any lower in Western European countries; it may well have been slightly higher: Tamara Hareven, 'Family Time and Industrial Time: Family and Work in a Planned Corporation Town, 1900–1924', in Hareven, ed., *Family and Kin in Urban Communities, 1700–1930* (New York, 1977), p. 198.

182. Tilly and Scott, *Women, Work and Family*, p. 120; F. M. L. Thompson, *The Rise of Respectable Society*, p. 114.

183. The percentage of households in a given city with lodgers at various dates: Preston 23 per cent and York 21 per cent in 1851; Glasgow 23 per cent in 1871; Frankfurt 12 per cent, Berlin 11 per cent, and Hamburg 10 per cent in 1864–7; Bochum 14 per cent, Dortmund 15 per cent, and Dusseldorf 14 per cent in 1910; 15 per cent in a working-class sample drawn from several European cities in 1890. For these sources, see Michael Anderson, 'Household Structure and the Industrial Revolution: Mid–Nineteenth Century Preston in Comparative Perspective', in Laslett, ed., *Household and Family in Past Time*, p. 220; Butt, 'Working-Class Housing in Glasgow', p. 80; Wickham, 'Working-Class Movement and Working-Class Life', p. 333; Hans J. Teuteberg and Clemens Wischermann, *Wohnalltag in Deutschland, 1850–1914* (Berlin, 1985), p. 317; David Crew, *Town in the Ruhr* (New York, 1979), p. 235; Haines, *Fertility and Occupation*, p. 226. The overall German estimate of 10 to 20 per cent is from Brüggemeier and Niethammer, 'Lodgers, Schnapps-Casinos and Working-Class Colonies in a Heavy-Industrial Region', in Georg Iggers, ed., *The Social History of Politics* (Leamington Spa, 1985), p. 235. The proportion of households with lodgers was roughly similar in North American cities from 1850 to 1914.

184. Bullock and Read, *The Movement for Housing Reform in Germany and France*, p. 58.

185. Haines, *Fertility and Occupation*, p. 235.

186. Tilly and Scott, *Women, Work and Family*, p. 125; Brüggemeier and Niethammer, 'Lodgers, Schnapps-Casinos and Working-Class Colonies', p. 235.

187. Haines, *Fertility and Occupation*, p. 295.

188. Wall, 'The Household, Demographic and Economic Change in England, 1650–1970', p. 500.

189. Laslett, *Household and Family in Past Time*, p. 154; Wall, 'The Household, Demographic and Economic Change', p. 509.

190. Wall, 'The Household, Demographic and Economic Change', p. 500.

191. The decisive difference between the stem and the nuclear family cycle lies here, in the generational continuity of the former and severance in the latter case. See *A Millennium of Family Change* for a discussion of this point and a critique of the way the Cambridge Group approach the issue.

192. Michael Katz, Mark Stern and Michael Doucet, *The Social Organization of Early Industrial Capitalism* (Cambridge, Mass., 1980), p. 290.

193. Anderson, 'Household Structure and the Industrial Revolution: Mid-Nineteenth Century Preston in Comparative Perspective', p. 43.

194. M. Tebbutt, *Making Ends Meet: Pawnbroking and Working-Class Credit* (New York, 1983), pp. 35–6.

195. Anderson, *Family Structure in Nineteenth-Century Lancashire*, p. 56.

196. *Prolonged Connections*, pp. 110–19.

197. Gillis, *For Better, For Worse*, p. 255.

198. Anderson, *Family Structure in Nineteenth-Century Lancashire*, p. 59.

199. Franzoi, *At the Very Least She Pays the Rent*, p. 88.

200. Janssens, 'Industrialization without Family Change?' p. 31.

201. Ruggles, *Prolonged Connections*, p. 42.

202. Brüggemeier and Niethammer, 'Lodgers, Schnapps-Casinos and Working-Class Colonies', p. 241; Anderson, *Family Structure in Nineteenth-Century Lancashire*.

203. 'The meaning and use of domestic space are not instrinsic to a set of physical characteristics': R. J. Lawrence, 'Domestic Space and Society: A Cross-Cultural Study', *Comparative Studies in Society and History*, vol. 34 (1982), p. 104.

204. Janssens, 'Industrialization without Family Change?', pp. 29–31; Standish Meacham, *A Life Apart: The English Working Class, 1890–1914* (London, 1977), pp. 57–8.

Chapter 3

1. Peter H. Lindert and Jeffrey G. Williamson, 'English Workers' Living Standards during the Industrial Revolution: A New Look', *Economic History Review,* vol. 36 (1983), pp. 1–25; N. F. R. Crafts, *British Economic Growth during the Industrial Revolution* (Oxford, 1985), ch. 5.

2. Jeffrey Williamson, 'Was the Industrial Revolution Worth It? Disamenities and Death in Nineteenth-Century Towns', *Explorations in Economic History,* vol. 19 (1982), pp. 221–45.

3. See Taylor for an introduction to the debate and a compilation of major contributions to it: *The Standard of Living in Britain in the Industrial Revolution* (London, 1975). The discussion has been marred throughout by the exasperating tendency of antagonists to talk past one another. This is in part a function of the lack of intimate familiarity with – and even respect for – the forms of evidence and verification deployed by opponents. The principal 'pessimists' have been historians of labour, presenting a rich array of descriptive materials and combining simple numerical series (on wages and death rates, for example) with the qualitative reports of contemporaries. The 'optimists' have been mainly economists. Eschewing qualitative evidence, they have relied for the most part on continuous wage series adjusted for cost of living components, crunching the results in standard statistical modes of hypothesis testing. Now that the cliometric bandwagon has lost some of its faddish lustre, one can only hope that it will be possible for economic historians to engage in a more fruitful dialogue with social and labour historians than has heretofore occurred in this debate.

4. Admitting that his consumer price index is weak as he massages a fragile set of real-wage estimates, Jeffrey Williamson blithely informs us that 'the workers themselves reveal their preferences' through his assumption-laden statistical procedures: 'Was the Industrial Revolution Worth It?', p. 222. What a revelation, then, to learn that the English workers of the early nineteenth century agree with the author – they, too, were optimists. The ventriloquist exults: 'So much for the pessimist's view that early nineteenth century urban-industrial development produced a "significant" deterioration in the workers' quality of life. Certainly the workers did not see it that way' (ibid., p. 237). It is ironic that Williamson should appeal to the workers' own perceptions, since he and his colleagues have never taken the least account of the testimonial evidence of contemporaries in any form, and have discounted its use by pessimists as subjective and unrepresentative. See E. P. Thompson's classic account of impressions of regression in *The Making of the English Working Class* (Harmondsworth, 1968 [1963]), pp. 207–32.

5. Peter H. Lindert and Jeffrey G. Williamson, 'Growth, Equality and History', *Explorations in Economic History,* vol. 22 (1985), pp. 341–77.

6. The argument harks back to Marx in *Capital*: 'In its blind and measureless drive, its insatiable appetite for surplus labour, capital oversteps not only the moral, but even the merely physical limits of the working day. It usurps the time for growth, development and healthy maintenance of the body. It steals the time required for the consumption of fresh air and sunlight. … It reduces the sound sleep needed for the restoration, renewal and refreshment of the vital forces to the exact amount of torpor essential to the revival of an absolutely exhausted organism. … It attains this objective by shortening the life of labour-power, in the same way as a greedy farmer snatches more produce from the soil by robbing it of its fertility': vol. 1 (New York, 1977), pp. 376–7. While Marx concentrated on the voracious consumption of labour-power by capital, I wish to emphasize the grossly inadequate conditions of labour-power's domestic (re)production.

7. Michael R. Haines, 'Industrial Work and the Family Life Cycle, 1889–1890' in P. Uselding, ed., *Research in Economic History,* vol. 4 (Greenwich, Conn., 1979).

8. The deleterious effect of women's heavy manual labour on the prospects of neonate survival was not confined to urban working-class women. In seeking to explain rising rates of infant mortality in the Prussian provinces of eastern Germany from 1820 to 1870, W. R. Lee came to the conclusion that 'the increased exploitation of female peasant labour' was

the primary factor: 'The Impact of Agrarian Change on Women's Work and Child Care in Early Nineteenth Century Prussia', in J. C. Fout, ed., *German Women in the Nineteenth Century* (New York, 1984), p. 242. This intensification was a facet of early German industrialization.

9. Ute Frevert, 'The Civilizing Tendency of Hygiene: Working-Class Women under Medical Control in Imperial Germany', in Fout, ed., *German Women in the Nineteenth Century*, p. 326.

10. Peter Ward, 'Birth Weight and Standards of Living in Vienna, 1865–1930', *Journal of Interdisciplinary History*, vol. 19 (1988), pp. 227–9.

11. Lynch, *Family, Class, and Ideology in Early Industrial France*, p. 72. See also Frevert, 'The Civilizing Tendency of Hygiene', p. 332; A. E. Lesaege-Duguid, 'La Mortalité infantile dans le Département du Nord de 1815 à 1914', in M. Gillet, ed., *L'Homme, la vie et la mort dans le Nord au 19ᵉ siècle* (Lille, 1972); Patricia Hilden, *Working Women and Socialist Policies in France, 1880–1914* (Oxford, 1986), p. 38; F. B. Smith, *The People's Health, 1830–1910* (London, 1979), p. 123.

12. Dominique Tabutin, 'La Surmortalité féminine en Europe avant 1940', *Population*, vol. 33 (1978), pp. 125–6; A. E. Imhof, 'Women, Family and Death: Excess Mortality of Women in Childbearing Age in Four Communities in Nineteenth-Century Germany', in R. J. Evans and W. R. Lee, eds, *The German Family* (London, 1981).

13. *Life and Labour of the People* (London, 1891), p. 553.

14. A. S. Wohl, *Endangered Lives: Public Health in Victorian Britain (London, 1983), p. 262.*

15. William Coleman, *Death Is a Social Disease* (Madison, Wis., 1982), pp. 221, 230.

16. E. P. Thompson, *The Making of the English Working Class* (Harmondsworth, 1968 [1963]), p. 364.

17. Michael R. Haines, 'Inequality and Childhood Mortality: A Comparison of England and Wales in 1911 and the US in 1900', *Journal of Economic History*, vol. 45 (1985), p. 886.

18. Samuel Preston and Etienne Van de Walle, 'Urban French Mortality in the Nineteenth Century', *Population Studies*, vol. 32 (1978), p. 277; M. W. Flinn, *Scottish Population History* (Cambridge, 1977).

19. R. I. Woods and P. R. A. Hinde, 'Mortality in Victorian England: Models and Patterns', *Journal of Interdisciplinary History*, vol. 18 (1987), p. 42.

20. Adna Weber, *The Growth of Cities in the Nineteenth Century* (Ithaca, N.Y., 1899), p. 237.

21. Stephen J. Kunitz, 'Mortality Since Malthus', in D. Coleman and R. Schofield, eds, *The State of Population Theory: Forward from Malthus* (Oxford, 1986), p. 282.

22. William J. Sewell, *Structure and Mobility: The Men and Women of Marseille, 1820–1870* (Cambridge, 1985), p. 152.

23. Yves Lequin, 'Les Citadins et leur vie quotidienne', in M. Agulhon, ed., *Histoire de la France urbaine*, vol. 4 (Paris, 1983), p. 292; Leslie P. Moch, *Paths to the City: Regional Migration in Nineteenth-Century France* (Beverley Hills, Calif., 1983), pp. 47, 57, 64.

24. De Vries, *European Urbanization, 1500–1800*, pp. 233–7; Weber, *The Growth of Cities*, pp. 236–7.

25. Lynch, *Family, Class, and Ideology in Early Industrial France*, p. 72.

26. Woods and Hinde, 'Mortality in Victorian England: Models and Patterns', pp. 27–54.

27. Chevalier, *Laboring Classes and Dangerous Classes in Paris*, pp. 193–9.

28. Dennis, *English Industrial Cities of the Nineteenth Century*, p. 61.

29. Coleman, *Death Is a Social Disease*, p. 178; Smith, *The People's Health*, p. 231.

30. Woods and Hinde, 'Mortality in Victorian England', pp. 42–4; R. I. Woods, P. A. Watterson and J. H. Woodward, 'The Causes of Rapid Infant Mortality Decline in England and Wales, 1861–1921' [pt 1], *Population Studies*, vol. 42 (1988), p. 353; Thompson, *The Making of the English Working Class*, p. 361.

31. Flinn, *The European Demographic System, 1500–1800*, pp. 130–31.

32. Wohl, *Endangered Lives*, p. 5; Woods and Woodward, *Urban Disease and Mortality in Nineteenth-Century England*, p. 28.

33.   Coleman, *Death Is a Social Disease,* p. 162; Kaelble, *Industrialization and Social Inequality in Nineteenth-Century Europe,* pp. 133, 135.

34.   James Walvin, *English Urban Life, 1776–1851* (London, 1984), pp. 24.

35.   Coleman, *Death Is a Social Disease,* p. 225.

36.   Brian Mitchell, *European Historical Statistics* (London, 1975), pp. 39–44; Woods, Watterson and Woodward, 'The Causes of Rapid Infant Mortality Decline in England and Wales', p. 350.

37.   Consequently, a good deal of research has been done in the past decade to recover height data on various historical populations. For a report on work in progress, see Robert Fogel et al., 'Secular Changes in American and British Stature and Nutrition', in R. I. Rotberg and T. K. Rabb, eds, *Hunger and History* (Cambridge, 1983).

38.   Roderick Floud, 'Measuring the Transformation of the European Economies: Income, Health and Welfare', unpublished paper presented at the Conference on the Transformation of the European Economy, Bellagio, Italy, 1984, p. 19.

39.   D. J. Oddy, 'The Health of the People', in Michael Drake and Theo Barker, eds, *Population and Society in Britain 1850–1950* (London, 1982), p. 123. One slim reed of evidence on height trends over time lends support to the optimists' case for rising English living standards in the early nineteenth century. If we can place any credence in a series that has been 'corrected' for various deficiencies in several different ways, the mean height of lads recruited to the Marine Society from the poor districts of London increased from 1815 on. Their height curve corresponds closely to Tucker's index of real wages for London artisans over the period from 1790 to 1830: Fogel et al., 'Secular Changes in American and British Stature and Nutrition', p. 280.

40.   Fogel et al., 'Secular Changes in American and British Stature and Nutrition', p. 278.

41.   Lee, 'Labour in German Industrialization', p. 478.

42.   Hobsbawm, *Labouring Men,* p. 355.

43.   H. Marvel, 'Factory Regulation: A Reinterpretation of the English Experience', *Journal of Law and Economics,* vol. 20 (1977), pp. 379–402.

44.   Hobsbawm, *Labouring Men,* p. 124.

Chapter 4

1.   David Landes, *The Unbound Prometheus* (London, 1969), p. 194.

2.   E. J. Hobsbawm, *Industry and Empire,* (Harmondsworth, 1968), p. 110.

3.   N. J. G. Pounds, *An Historical Geography of Europe* (Cambridge, 1985), p. 451.

4.   Landes, *The Unbound Prometheus,* pp. 326–58.

5.   Pounds, *Historical Geography of Europe,* p. 452.

6.   Landes, *The Unbound Prometheus,* p. 230.

7.   Ibid., pp. 323–4.

8.   Ibid., p. 322; Hobsbawm, *Labouring Men,* p. 362.

9.   Duncan Bythell, *The Sweated Trades: Outwork in Nineteenth-Century Britain* (London, 1978), p. 147.

10.   Barbara Franzoi, *At the Very Least She Pays the Rent,* (Westport, Conn., 1985), pp. 127–8.

11.   Landes, *The Unbound Prometheus,* p. 300; E. J. Hobsbawm, *The Age of Capital: 1848–1875* (New York, 1975), pp. 233–4; Jürgen Kocka, 'Problems of Working-Class Formation in Germany', in I. Katznelson and A. Zolberg, eds, *Working-Class Formation* (Princeton, N.J., p. 298. While we associate factories with large workforces, they should not be distinguished from workshops by size alone. A factory is a dedicated production facility, standing apart from domestic and leisure space, utilizing powered machinery in at least some parts of the production process, and divorcing labour from capital. None of these features, on its own, distinguishes factories from workshops; taken together, they do.

12. Peter Stearns, *Lives of Labour* (New York, 1975), p. 156.

13. Pounds, *Historical Geography of Europe*, p. 405.

14. Kocka, 'Problems of Working-Class Formation in Germany', p. 317.

15. Landes, *The Unbound Prometheus*, p. 314.

16. Richard Price, *Labour in British Society* (London, 1986), p. 105.

17. M. A. Bienfeld, *Working Hours in British Industry: An Economic History* (London, 1972), pp. 82–142.

18. It was the first time that a reduction had been achieved by universal legislation applying to all industries and to all employees, to men as well as to women and children.

19. Employers tried to compensate for the reduction of the regular work-day by pressing workers to do more overtime, which proved a divisive issue. Most union leaders and a great many members opposed overtime. They were particularly adamant that everyone should be free to refuse it without being subject to management pressure or subsequent reprisal. They also made the point that overtime hurt unemployed members who would otherwise be rehired if extra work had not been taken up by the currently employed. On the other hand, there was rarely any lack of workers who jumped at the chance to make some extra money. On the motives of these workers, see my comment below on rate-busters.

20. Stearns, *Lives of Labour*, p. 193.

21. Patrick Joyce, *Work, Society and Politics: The Culture of the Factory in Later Victorian England* (London, 1980), pp. 90–133; Michelle Perrot, 'On the Formation of the French Working Class', in Katznelson and Zolberg, eds, *Working-Class Formation*, p. 89.

22. Hobsbawm, *The Age of Capital*, pp. 237–8.

23. Price, *Labour in British Society*, pp. 99–102.

24. Craig Littler, *The Development of the Labour Process in Capitalist Societies* (London, 1982), p. 93.

25. Alain Cottereau, 'The Distinctiveness of Working-Class Cultures in France, 1848–1900', in Katznelson and Zolberg, eds, *Working-Class Formation*, p. 132.

26. Landes, *The Unbound Prometheus*, pp. 306–7.

27. Yves Lequin, 'Apprenticeship in Nineteenth-Century France: A Continuing Tradition or Break with the Past?', in Steven Kaplan and Cynthia Koepp, eds, *Work in France: Representations, Meanings, Organization and Practice* (Ithaca, N.Y., 1986), p. 471; Charles More, *Skill and the English Working Class, 1870–1914* (London, 1980), p. 187.

28. Stearns, *Lives of Labour*, p. 67.

29. Price, *Labour in British Society*, p. 108.

30. Mary Nolan, 'Economic Crisis, State Policy, and Working-Class Formation in Germany', in Katznelson and Zolberg, eds *Working-Class Formation*, p. 365.

31. Stearns, *Lives of Labour*, p. 177.

32. J. J. Lee, 'Labour in German Industrialization', p. 464.

33. Stearns, *Lives of Labour*, p. 182.

34. Michelle Perrot, 'The Three Ages of Industrial Discipline in Nineteenth-Century France', in J. M. Merriman, ed., *Consciousness and Class Experience in Nineteenth-Century Europe* (New York, 1979), p. 161.

35. Stearns, *Lives of Labour*, p. 169.

36. Lee, 'Labour in German Industrialization', p. 182.

37. Littler, *The Development of the Labour Process*, p. 87.

38. Ibid., p. 80.

39. Lynch, *Family, Class, and Ideology in Early Industrial France*, p. 188.

40. Ron Aminzade, 'Reinterpreting Capitalist Industrialization: A Study of Nineteenth-Century France', in Kaplan and Koepp, eds, *Work in France: Representations, Meanings, Organization and Practice*, p. 413.

41. Littler, *The Development of the Labour Process*, p. 77.

42. Lenard Berlanstein, *The Working People of Paris, 1871–1914* (Baltimore, 1984), p. 75.

43. More, *Skill and the English Working Class, 1870–1914*, p. 67.

44. Lawrence Schofer, *The Formation of a Modern Labour Force: Upper Silesia, 1865–*

1914 (Berkeley, Calif., 1975), p. 83.

45. Littler, *The Development of the Labour Process*, p. 88.

46. Price, *Labour in British Society*, p. 20.

47. Stearns, *Lives of Labour*, p. 85; Kocka, 'Problems of Working-Class Formation in Germany', p. 310.

48. J. F. C. Harrison, *Early Victorian Britain, 1832–51* (London, 1979), p. 95.

49. Adrian Rifkin and Roger Thomas, *Voices of the People: The Social Life of 'La société' at the End of the Second Empire* (London, 1988), p. 41.

50. Hobsbawm, *Labouring Men*, p. 356.

51. Hobsbawm's brilliant pioneering investigation of this subject placed the initial watershed at mid century, but this may be too late, depicting an overly sharp traverse: 'Custom, Wages and Workload in Nineteenth-Century Industry', in *Labouring Men*. A century earlier, Josiah Tucker had complained about the degeneration of traditional class relations in strikingly similar terms: 'The Master ... considers his People as the scum of the earth whom he has a right to squeeze whenever he can. ... The Journeymen ... think it is no crime to get as much Wages, and to do as little for it as they possibly can': Maxine Berg, *The Age of Manufactures: Industry, Innovation and Work in Britain, 1700–1820* (London, 1985), p. 163.

52. Rifkin and Thomas, *Voices of the People*, p. 149.

53. Hobsbawm, *Labouring Men*, pp. 355–7; Littler, *The Development of the Labour Process*, pp. 82–4, 94.

54. Price, *Labour in British Society*, p. 204; Stearns, *Lives of Labour*, pp. 203–11; Hobsbawm, *The Age of Capital*, pp. 240–41.

55. Stearns, *Lives of Labour*, pp. 244–5.

56. Schofer, *The Formation of a Modern Labour Force*, p. 127; Franz Brüggemeier and Lutz Niethammer, 'Lodgers, Schnapps-Casinos and Working-Class Colonies in a Heavy-Industrial Region', in Georg Iggers, ed., *The Social History of Politics* (Leamington Spa, 1985), p. 234.

57. Schofer, *The Formation of a Modern Labour Force*, pp. 123–31.

58. Dennis, *English Industrial Cities*, p. 133.

59. Lee, 'Labour in German Industrialization', p. 461.

60. Schofer, *The Formation of a Modern Labour Force*, p. 127; Lee, 'Labour in German Industrialization', p. 460.

61. Stearns, *Lives of Labour*, pp. 173–4.

62. In France, the declining birth rate slowed population growth, with the result that there were often labour scarcities. The paternalist response of French employers in the first stage of industrialization is examined in Stearns's *Paths to Authority: The Middle Class and the Industrial Labor Force in France, 1820–1848* (Urbana, Ill., 1978).

63. Stearns, *Lives of Labour*, p. 247.

64. Jürgen Kocka, 'Craft Traditions and the Labour Movement in Nineteenth-Century Germany', in Pat Thane, Geoffrey Crossick and Roderick Floud, eds, *The Power of the Past: Essays for Eric Hobsbawm* (Cambridge, 1984), p. 104.

65. Kocka, 'Problems of Working-Class Formation in Germany', p. 308.

66. Stearns, *Lives of Labour*, p. 163.

67. Ibid., p. 162.

68. Lequin, 'Apprenticeship in Nineteenth-Century France', pp. 458, 467; Colin Heywood, *Childhood in Nineteenth-Century France* (Cambridge, 1988), pp. 198, 202.

69. More, *Skill and the English Working Class*, p. 49; Stearns, *Lives of Labour*, p. 49; John Gillis, *Youth and History: Tradition and Change in European Age Relations, 1770–Present* (New York, 1981), pp. 118–31; Keith McClelland, 'Time to Work, Time to Live: Some Aspects of Work and the Re-formation of Class in Britain, 1850–1880', in Patrick Joyce, ed., *The Historical Meanings of Work* (Cambridge, 1987), p. 191.

70. Stearns, *Lives of Labour*, p. 51.

71. Lynch, *Family, Class, and Ideology in Early Industrial France*, p. 169.

72. Berlanstein, *The Working People of Paris*, p. 76.

73. Lequin, 'Apprenticeship in Nineteenth-Century France', p. 460.

74. My thanks to Pavla Miller and Ian Davey for many stimulating discussions over the years on the rise of compulsory schooling. Though neither is implicated in the deficiencies of this account, their suggestions have undoubtedly improved it immeasurably.

75. Mary Jo Maynes, *Schooling in Western Europe: A Social History* (Albany, N.Y., 1985), p. 134. The proportion of girls is not available, but would have been somewhat lower; the gap closed, however, in the era of compulsory schooling.

76. Prussian legislation had made schooling universal and compulsory for a minimum of eight years (ages six to fourteen) in the eighteenth century, but these regulations were not vigorously or uniformly enforced until the middle decades of the nineteenth. While the provision of elementary schooling in Prussia and Bavaria in the late eighteenth century ran far in advance of England and France, the difference was largely made up by the end of the nineteenth.

77. Maynes, *Schooling in Western Europe,* p. 134.

78. This is not simply the perspective of those who consider the imposition of universal schooling to have been an unmitigated blessing. Radical scholars often portray working-class obduracy in heroic terms, with parents resisting the institutionalization of middle-class indoctrination while their children were rounded up and forcibly corralled into classrooms by inspectors and courts – repressive agents of the bourgeois state. There is an important element of truth in this account, particularly as it applies to the utterly destitute, but too often it obscures the larger picture – that is, the pervasive and growing enthusiasm for education displayed by the vast majority of wage-earning parents in the nineteenth century.

79. From this top–down perspective, the growth of mass schooling is explained as an outgrowth of the drive by competing elites for hegemony and social control. In Britain, Lawrence Stone claims, 'The rise of popular elementary education was very largely an incidental by-product of the struggle between Anglicans and Dissenters for the allegiance of the lower classes': 'Literacy and Education in England, 1500–1900', *Past & Present,* no. 42 (1969), p. 81. Harold Perkin concurs: '[The founding of the British and Foreign School] provoked into existence the rival National Society, and by their competition and constant agitation for State education [they] stimulated the main expansion of elementary education': *Origins of Modern English Society, 1780–1880* (London, 1969), p. 295. A similar supply-side account of schooling in France would highlight the race for schooling hegemony between the republican state bureaucracy and the Catholic Church. For a critique of this perspective and an apposite emphasis on the demand side of the schooling equation, see Thomas Laqueur's 'Working-Class Demand and the Growth of English Elementary Education, 1750–1850', in Lawrence Stone, ed., *Schooling and Society: Studies in the History of Education* (Baltimore, 1976).

80. Vincent, *Bread, Knowledge and Freedom,* p. 102.

81. Phil Gardner, *The Lost Elementary Schools of Victorian England* (London, 1984), p. 85.

82. The terms 'private' and 'public' school may be confusing here, since in the twentieth century they have come to be applied in Britain to institutions that are virtually mirror inversions of their referents elsewhere. Before the era of universal schooling, I shall use the terms 'public' and 'private' to signify the main *funding source* of the institution. The school's *class constituency* is not inherent in these adjectives, but requires further designation: i.e., a 'working-class private school' is filled with working-class children and funded mainly by the fees of their parents. Once universal state schooling is established, class designations are normally used to identify the predominant *socializing influence* of the school: hence, we speak of 'middle-class schools' instructing working-class children.

83. François Furet and Jacques Ozouf, *Reading and Writing: Literacy in France from Calvin to Jules Ferry* (Cambridge, 1982), p. 108.

84. Ibid., p. 108.

85. Ibid., p. 109.

86. Maynes, *Schooling in Western Europe,* p. 112.

87. Laqueur, 'Working-Class Demand', p. 197.

88. Gardner, *The Lost Elementary Schools,* p. 161.

89. Laqueur, 'Working-Class Demand', pp. 196–7.

90. Gardner, *The Lost Elementary Schools*, p. 83.

91. J. S. Hurt, *Elementary Schooling and the Working Classes, 1860–1918* (London, 1979), p. 34.

92. Maynes, *Schooling in Western Europe*, p. 91.

93. Colin Heywood, *Childhood in Nineteenth-Century France* (Cambridge, 1988), p. 209.

94. Gardner, *The Lost Elementary Schools*, p. 95; Laqueur, 'Working-Class Demand', p. 199.

95. Maynes, *Schooling in Western Europe*, p. 93.

96. Gardner, *The Lost Elementary Schools*, p. 96.

97. Laqueur, 'Working-Class Demand', p. 199.

98. Simon Frith, 'Socialization and Rational Schooling: Elementary Education in Leeds before 1870', in Phillip McCann, ed., *Popular Education and Socialization in the Nineteenth Century* (London, 1977), p. 85.

99. Gardner, *The Lost Elementary Schools*, p. 93.

100. Hurt, *Elementary Schooling and the Working Classes*, p. 29.

101. Gardner, *The Lost Elementary Schools*, p. 165.

102. Furet and Ozouf, *Reading and Writing*, p. 123. See also Heywood, *Childhood in Nineteenth-Century France*, p. 195.

103. Hurt, *Elementary Schooling and the Working Classes*, p. 64.

104. Roger Price, *A Social History of Nineteenth-Century France* (New York, 1987), p. 308; Maynes, *Schooling in Western Europe*, p. 111. H. W. Hobart, the Social-Democratic Federation's candidate for the London School Board, levelled a similar charge against British elementary schools. See Brian Simon, *Education and the Labour Movement, 1870–1920* (London, 1965) p. 145.

105. Frith, 'Socialization and Rational Schooling', p. 70.

106. Gardner, *The Lost Elementary Schools*, p. 159.

107. Ibid., p. 92.

108. Ibid., pp. 159–60; Hurt, *Elementary Schooling and the Working Classes*, pp. 30–31.

109. Maynes, *Schooling in Western Europe*, p. 94; Patrick Harrigan, *Mobility, Elites, and Education in French Society of the Second Empire* (Waterloo, 1980); H. van Dijk and C. A. Mandemakers, 'Secondary Education and Social Mobility at the Turn of the Century', *History of Education Quarterly*, vol. 14 (1985), p. 224.

110. Frith, 'Socialization and Rational Schooling', p. 68.

111. Yves Lequin, 'Apprenticeship in Nineteenth-Century France: A Continuing Tradition or Break with the Past?', in S. L. Kaplan and C. J. Koepp, eds, *Work in France: Representations, Meanings, Organization and Practice* (Ithaca, N.Y., 1986), p. 466.

112. Hurt, *Elementary Schooling and the Working Classes*, p. 33. The distinction between class and generational mobility permits us to reconcile two apparently contradictory themes in the sociology of education literature: (a) that school systems stream students, helping to perpetuate the pre-existing class structure and income distribution; and (b) that education makes a material difference – how far children go in school, and how well they do, becomes a major factor in determining their eventual life-earnings and living standards, all else being equal.

113. Harvey Graff, *The Literacy Myth: Literacy and Social Structure in the Nineteenth Century City* (New York, 1979).

114. Vincent, *Bread, Knowledge and Freedom*, p. 90. A German worker has a similar recollection: 'From my school days, I especially loved and valued books and I still have today almost all the books from my last three school years': Alfred Kelly, ed., *The German Worker: Working-Class Autobiographies from the Age of Industrialization* (Berkeley, Calif., 1987), p. 234.

115. Maynes, *Schooling in Western Europe*, p. 84.

116. Vincent, *Bread, Knowledge and Freedom*, p. 91.

117. Furet and Ozouf, *Reading and Writing*, p. 127. The wife of a quarryman 'wishes to procure for her children the education that she herself and her husband lack, and she is eager for them to go to school without really having much idea of what they will learn there.'

118. Ibid., p. 128.

119. Maynes, *Schooling in Western Europe*, pp. 145–6.

120. Colin Heywood, *Childhood in Nineteenth-Century France* (Cambridge, 1988), p. 111.

121. Meg Gomersall, 'Ideals and Realities: The Education of Working-Class Girls, 1800–1870', *History of Education*, vol. 17 (1988), pp. 37–53.

122. Heywood, *Childhood in Nineteenth-Century France*, p. 211.

123. Gomersall, 'Ideals and Realities: The Education of Working-Class Girls', p. 43.

124. Heywood, *Childhood in Nineteenth-Century France*, p. 111.

125. Fiona Paterson, 'Schooling the Family', *Sociology*, vol. 22 (1988), p. 78.

126. Maynes, *Schooling in Western Europe*, p. 148.

127. Laqueur, 'Working-Class Demand', p. 192.

128. Heywood, *Childhood in Nineteenth-Century France*, pp. 192–3; Hurt, *Elementary Schooling and the Working Classes*, pp. 59–70.

129. Hurt, *Elementary Schooling and the Working Classes*, p. 60.

130. Ibid., pp. 62–3, 71.

131. Ellen Ross, 'Response to Harold Benenson's "Victorian Sexual Ideology"', *International Labor and Working Class History*, vol. 25 (1984), pp. 32–3.

132. Anna Davin, 'Child Labour, the Working-Class Family and Domestic Ideology in Nineteenth Century Britain', *Development and Change*, vol. 13 (1982), p. 647.

133. David Rubinstein, *School Attendance in London, 1870–1904* (New York, 1969), pp. 56–89.

134. David Rubinstein, 'Socialization and the London School Board, 1870–1904', in Phillip McCann, ed., *Popular Education and Socialization in the Nineteenth Century* (London, 1977), p. 247.

135. Hurt, *Elementary Schooling and the Working Classes*, p. 62.

136. John Caldwell, *Theory of Fertility Decline* (New York, 1982).

137. *Economy and Society*, vol. 1 (Berkeley, Calif., 1978 [1968]), p. 375.

138. The term 'family wage' is often used in reference to a male breadwinner's wage, supposedly sufficient for family maintenance: Michèle Barrett and Mary McIntosh, 'The "Family Wage": Some Problems for Socialists and Feminists', *Capital & Class*, no. 11 (1980), pp. 51–72. Others, following Tilly and Scott's lead, speak of a 'family wage economy', designating the opposite condition, where the wages of other family members are indispensable to subsistence: *Women, Work and Family* (New York, 1978). An older generation of labour historians referred to the family wage as the lump sum paid to the househead for the use of his family's labour-power. Given the propensity for confusion, I shall steer clear of the term altogether.

139. Elizabeth Roberts, *A Woman's Place: An Oral History of Working-Class Women, 1890–1940* (Oxford, 1984), pp. 136–7; Jane Lewis, 'The Working-Class Wife and Mother and State Intervention, 1870–1918', in Jane Lewis, ed., *Labour and Love: Women's Experience of Home and Family, 1850–1940* (Oxford, 1986), p. 102; Robyn Dasey, 'Women's Work and the Family: Women Garment Workers in Berlin and Hamburg before the First World War', in Richard Evans and William Lee, eds, *The German Family* (London, 1981), p. 224; Tilly and Scott, *Women, Work and Family*, p. 133.

140. Franzoi, *At the Very Least She Pays the Rent*, p. 111; Sheila Lewenhak, *Women and Trade Unions: An Outline History of Women in the British Trade Union Movement* (London, 1977, p. 41; Peter Stearns, 'Working-Class Women in Britain, 1890–1914', in Martha Vicinus, ed., *Suffer and Be Still: Women in the Victorian Age* (Bloomington, Ind., 1972), p. 113.

141. Quataert has identified a crucial watershed in Imperial Germany in the 1880s: 'A Source Analysis in German Women's History: Factory Inspectors' Reports and the Shaping of Working-Class Lives, 1878–1914', *Central European History*, vol. 16, no. 2 (1983), pp. 112–13.

142. In legal codes, the relation of onus and entitlement was reversed: husbands were granted possession of their wives' property at marriage, so that they might act as family providers. This common-law right was not terminated in Britain until the Married Women's Property Acts of 1870 and 1882; in France, comparable changes in the French Civil Code

were finally introduced in 1907.

143.   Eleanor Rathbone mounted a devastating critique of the private wage system and the male-breadwinner norm in her 1924 study *The Disinherited Family* (Bristol, 1986 [1924]). All subsequent students of these matters owe a great debt to her pioneering analysis.

144.   The persistence of this same set of minimal expectations among working-class couples in the twentieth century is depicted in excruciating detail in Norman Dennis, Fernando Henriques and Clifford Slaughter, *Coal Is Our Life: An Analysis of a Yorkshire Mining Community* (London, 1956); and in Lillian Rubin's *Worlds of Pain: Life in the Working-Class Family* (New York, 1976).

145.   Ivy Pinchbeck, *Women Workers and the Industrial Revolution, 1750–1850* (London, 1981), pp. 1–2, 121; Quataert, 'A Source Analysis in German Women's History', p. 112; Rathbone, *The Disinherited Family*, pp. 128–9.

146.   In this respect the labourer was in the same position as the peasant, whose wife also made a palpable contribution to family subsistence without negating his role as househead.

147.   The ideological consolation for the economic devaluation of domestic work was the glorification of motherhood and the sacred duties of the wife in the care of her family. The triumph of this ideological complex amongst the business and professional classes in the Victorian era has been well studied by feminist social historians, and needs no reiteration here. Various elements of this ideology (the notion of a woman's proper sphere, the duty to fashion her home as a haven in a heartless world, the drive for family privacy) were influential in the upper stratum of the working class, where they were incorporated into its own conception of domestic respectability. Other elements (the Cult of True Womanhood and the lady of leisure) were so alien to artisanal family experience as to find little resonance there.

148.   Sonya Rose, 'Gender Segregation in the Transition to the Factory: The English Hosiery Industry, 1850–1910', *Feminist Studies*, vol. 13, no. 1 (1987), pp. 178–9. Alice Clark and Ivy Pinchbeck, great historians of women's labour, recognized that the individuation of the wage form was a decisive change for women. Their appraisals of its implications were, however, strikingly different. Clark underlined the negative consequences: '[In the seventeenth century,] the notion that it could be to a man's advantage to debar women from well-paid work would have seemed ridiculous [since] the idea of individual property in wages had hardly arisen. ... Capitalism, however, broke away from families and dealt directly with individuals, the first fruits of individualism being shown by the exclusion of women from the journeymen's associations': *Working Life of Women in the Seventeenth Century* (London, 1968 [1919]), pp. 299–301. Pinchbeck saw the development primarily in a positive light: 'In industries in which a family wage prevailed, women scarcely knew the extent of, or had the opportunity of handling, their own earnings. ... Under the new regime every woman received her own earnings as a matter of course. The significance of this change was at once seen in the new sense of freedom which prompted so many young women to retain control of their own wage and to leave home at an early age "to become their own mistresses"': *Women Workers and the Industrial Revolution*, p. 313. The individuated wage undoubtedly strengthened the hand of many women who earned it, while at the same time undermining housewives who did not. Is the glass half empty or half full? Given the consolidation of the male-breadwinner norm and the overwhelming reality of married women's economic dependency in the past century, I find Clark's analysis more cogent. In the contemporary era, however, as married women's employment rates rise and the male-breadwinner norm breaks down, Pinchbeck's argument becomes apposite.

149.   Johanna Brenner and Maria Ramas, 'Rethinking Women's Oppression', *New Left Review*, no. 144 (1984), pp. 42–4.

150.   In recent discussions of 'the family wage', this distinction (between payment form and subsistence norm) has not been clearly drawn; the contribution of each to changes in working-class family life has thus been impossible to assess.

151.   Thompson, *The Making of the English Working Class*, p. 335; Pinchbeck, *Women Workers and the Industrial Revolution*, p. 199.

152.   Barbara Taylor, *Eve and the New Jerusalem* (London, 1983), pp. 83–117. Even

though Chartist bodies had an ambiguous position at best, and at worst were openly hostile, their stance had by no means hardened in the 1830s and 1840s. Dorothy Thompson has documented the strong presence of women in the great Chartist marches and demonstrations of these decades, and their subsequent absence from labour movement meetings and demonstrations from around 1848 on: 'Working-class women seem to have retreated into the home at some time around, or a little before, the middle of the century': 'Women and Nineteenth Century Radical Politics: A Lost Dimension', in Juliet Mitchell and Ann Oakley, eds, *The Rights and Wrongs of Women* (Harmondsworth, 1976), p. 115; Patrick Joyce, *Work, Society and Politics: The Culture of the Factory in Later Victorian England* (London, 1980), pp. 114–15.

153.   E. P. Thompson and Eileen Yeo, *The Unknown Mayhew: Selections from the Morning Chronicle* (Harmondsworth, 1984 [1971]), p. 565.

154.   Sarah Boston, *Women Workers and the Trade-Union Movement* (London, 1980), p. 16.

155.   Charles Sowerwine, 'Workers and Women in France before 1914: The Debate over the Couriau Affair', *Journal of Modern History*, vol. 55 (1983), pp. 413–14; Joan Wallach Scott, 'Men and Women in the Parisian Garment Trades: Discussions of Family and Work in the 1830s and 1840s', in Pat Thane, Geoffrey Crossick and Roderick Floud, eds, *The Power of the Past: Essays for Eric Hobsbawm* (Cambridge, 1984), p. 86.

156.   Patricia Hilden, *Working Women and Socialist Policies in France, 1880–1914* (Oxford, 1986), p. 34.

157.   Burnett, *Destiny Obscure*, p. 219.

158.   John Holley, 'The Two Family Economies of Industrialism: Factory Workers in Victorian Scotland', *Journal of Family History*, vol. 6, no. 1 (1981), pp. 57–69; Jane Lewis, *Women in England, 1870–1950* (Sussex, 1984), p. 49.

159.   Ute Frevert, 'The Civilizing Tendency of Hygiene: Working-Class Women under Medical Control in Imperial Germany', in J. C. Fout, ed., *German Women in the Nineteenth Century* (New York, 1984), p. 326.

160.   Gillis, *For Better, For Worse*, p. 252. Sheila Lewenhak, *Women and Trade Unions: An Outline History of Women in the British Trade-Union Movement* (London, 1977), p. 41.

161.   Rathbone, *The Disinherited Family*, p. 137; Michael Hannigan, 'Proletarian Families and Social Protest: Production and Reproduction as Issues of Social Conflict in Nineteenth-Century France', in Steven Kaplan and Cynthia Koepp, eds, *Work in France: Representations, Meanings, Organization and Practice* (Ithaca, N.Y., 1986), pp. 450–51.

162.   I argued this case for Britain in 'Patriarchy Stabilized: The Construction of the Male Breadwinner Wage Norm in Nineteenth-Century Britain', *Social History*, vol. 11, no. 1 (1986), pp. 53–76. For Germany (in addition to sources already cited), see Franzoi, 'Domestic Industry: Work Options and Women's Choices', in Fout, ed., *German Women in the Nineteenth Century*, pp. 18, 42; and for France, Sowerwine, 'Workers and Women in France before 1914', and James McMillan, *Housewife or Harlot: The Place of Women in French Society, 1870–1940* (Brighton, 1981), pp. 13, 160.

163.   Franzoi, 'Domestic Industry, Work Options and Women's Choices', p. 110; E. J. Hunt, *Regional Wage Variations in Britain, 1850–1914* (Oxford, 1973), p. 119; Peter Stearns, 'The Adaptation of Workers', in Stearns, ed., *The Other Side of Western Civilization*, vol. 2 (New York, 1973), p. 182.

164.   In the latter half of the nineteenth century, 'the symbols of the working class … became more and more masculine: … represented by the barrel-chested male worker with broad shoulders, swollen biceps, and powerful muscles': Perrot, 'On the Formation of the French Working Class', p. 99. Contrast this image with the reports of the health inspectors in the early Victorian period who depict anaemic, emaciated specimens emerging from the factories and mines with bent backs and stooped shoulders. The manly representation required a considerable improvement in working-class health to have become prominent at all, yet it was still far from the actual physique of most workers in heavy industry. At the time of the Boer War, up to 40 per cent of the enlistees from large industrial towns were deemed by the British army too physically unfit to fight.

165.   McClelland, 'Time to Work, Time to Live', in P. Joyce, *The Historical Meanings*

236

of Work (Cambridge, 1987), p. 199.

166. Hannigan, 'Proletarian Families and Social Protest', p. 433.

167. Joanna Bornat, 'Lost Leaders: Women, Trade Unionism and the Case of General Union of Textile Workers, 1875–1914', in Angela V. John, ed., *Unequal Opportunities: Women's Employment in England, 1800–1918* (Oxford, 1986), p. 223.

168. John Rule, *The Labouring Classes in Early Industrial England, 1750–1850* (London, 1986), p. 186.

169. Barbara Taylor, *Eve and the New Jerusalem* (London, 1983), p. 112. The Owenite freethinkers were a notable exception, but they were voices in the wilderness. 'I do not like the doctrine of women keeping at home and minding the house and family', Richard Carlile argued. 'It is as much the proper business of the man as the woman's, and the woman, who is so confined, is not the proper companion of the public useful man': Taylor, ibid., p. 81.

170. Pinchbeck, *Women Workers and the Industrial Revolution*, pp. 199–200.

171. Taylor, *Eve and the New Jerusalem*, p. 112.

172. Lewis, *Women in England*, p. 50; Bornat, 'Lost Leaders', p. 225.

173. Dasey, 'Women's Work and the Family: Women Garment Workers in Berlin and Hamburg before the First World War', p. 224; Lewenhak, *Women and Trade Unions*, p. 41; Jane Lewis, 'The Working-Class Wife and Mother and State Intervention, 1870–1918', in Lewis, ed., *Labour and Love: Women's Experience of Home and Family, 1850–1940* (Oxford, 1986), p. 105.

174. Nancy Osterud, 'Gender Divisions and the Organization of Work in the Leicester Hosiery Industry', in Angela John, ed., *Unequal Opportunities: Women's Employment in England*, p. 53.

175. Jane Humphries,'"The Most Free from Objection": The Sexual Division of Labor and Women's Work in Nineteenth-Century England', *Journal of Economic History*, vol. 47, no. 4 (1987), p. 939. Jane Mark-Lawson and Anne Witz have disputed Humphries's claim that 'male colliers almost universally wanted state intervention to regulate the labour of women and children and the overwhelming majority of hewers believed that women should be prohibited from working below ground': 'Protective Legislation, the Capitalist State, and Working-Class Men: The Case of the 1842 Mines Regulation Act', *Feminist Review*, no. 7 (1981), pp. 15–16. They show that this was certainly not the case in the coal fields of east Scotland, where many colliers used their own daughters as assistants. If women were barred underground, where they then worked, the men threatened to move to pits where they were permitted: Mark-Lawson and Witz, 'From "Family Labour" to "Family Wage"? The Case of Women's Labour in Nineteenth-Century Coalmining', *Social History*, vol. 13, no. 2 (1988), p. 163. Beyond east Scotland, I would question how widespread such opposition was. The authors underestimate the degree to which female labour had been phased out and replaced by pony haulage in most English coal fields before the commission hearings of 1842.

176. Scott, 'Men and Women in the Parisian Garment Trades', p. 82.

177. Where the exclusion of women from a trade proved impossible, all-male unions tended to revert to more pragmatic solutions, calling for the organization of women workers (often in a separate union) and equal pay legislation. This appears to be a progressive move, but motives and effects were mixed. The exclusionists' reasoning was often that the enforcement of equal pay (without adequate training for female novices) would eliminate the employers' incentive to hire women in the first place, and men's superior strength, skills and experience would soon drive the remaining females from industry: McMillan, *Housewife or Harlot*, p. 14. So long as women were systematically disadvantaged, this was a real danger. Working women worried that they would lose their jobs under equal pay provisions.

178. Sonya Rose, 'Gender Segregation in the Transition to the Factory: The English Hosiery Industry, 1850–1910', *Feminist Studies*, vol. 13, no. 1 (1987), pp. 163–84. Male unionists' drive to segregate the sexes in industry was complemented by the intervention of factory inspectors who sought segregation to protect girls from the moral perils of 'unregulated sex-mixing'. This latter concern will be discussed below.

179. One must recognize, however, that the capacity of craft unions to restrict the labour supply varied greatly, and hence the tenacity with which they fought to do so.

Exclusionary strategies were pursued more relentlessly and successfully in Britain than on the continent; the drive was relatively weak in Germany: c.f. Jürgen Kocka, 'Craft Traditions and the Labour Movement in Nineteenth-Century Germany', in Thane, Crossick and Floud, eds, *The Power of the Past: Essays for Eric Hobsbawm,* p. 100.

180.   'The Unhappy Marriage of Marxism and Feminism: Towards a More Progressive Union', in Lydia Sargent, ed., *Women and Revolution: A Discussion of the Unhappy Marriage of Marxism and Feminism* (London, 1981), p. 20.

181.   Osterud, 'Gender Divisions and the Organization of Work in the Leicester Hosiery Industry', p. 53; Mark-Lawson and Witz, 'From "Family Labour" to "Family Wage"?', p. 162; Taylor, *Eve and the New Jerusalem,* p. 108; M. L. Davies, ed., *Maternity: Letters from Working Women* (London, 1978 [1915]), p. 30.

182.   Lewis, 'The Working-Class Wife and Mother and State Intervention', p. 104.

183.   Sowerwine, 'Workers and Women in France before 1914', p. 438.

184.   Ibid., p. 438; Alain Cottereau, 'The Distinctiveness of Working-Class Cultures in France, 1848–1900', in Ira Katznelson and Aristide Zolberg, eds, *Working-Class Formation* (Princeton, N.J., 1986), p. 153.

185.   James Schmiechen, *Sweated Industries and Sweated Labour: The London Clothing Trades, 1860–1914* (Chicago, 1984), p. 87.

186.   Bornat, 'Lost Leaders', p. 207.

187.   Schmiechen, *Sweated Industries and Sweated Labour,* pp. 88, 93, 99–101.

188.   Margaret Hewitt, *Wives and Mothers in Victorian Industry* (London, 1958), pp. 48–61; Humphries, 'Protective Legislation, the Capitalist State, and Working-Class Men', pp. 16–18; Bornat, 'Lost Leaders', p. 223.

189.   The accusation that working wives and slovenly homemakers drove men into the pubs was a common one. For a German example, see James Jackson, 'Overcrowding and Family Life: Working-Class Families and the Housing Crisis in Later Nineteenth-Century Duisburg', in Richard Evans and W. R. Lee, eds, *The German Family* (London, 1981), p. 95; for France, see William Reddy, *The Rise of Market Culture: The Textile Trade and French Society, 1750–1900* (Cambridge, 1984), p. 266. Even home visitors who were empathetic to working-class women's burdens blamed poor homemakers for driving their husbands to drink: Lady Bell, *At the Works: A Study of a Manufacturing Town* (London, 1985 [1907]), p. 188.

190.   Humphries, 'Protective Legislation, the Capitalist State, and Working-Class Men', p. 17; Engels, *The Condition of the Working Class in England* (London, 1969 [1845]), pp. 175–6; Quataert, 'A Source Analysis in German Women's History', p. 111; Franzoi, *At the Very Least She Pays the Rent,* p. 94.

191.   Marianna Valverde, '"Giving the Female a Turn": The Social, Legal and Moral Regulation of Women's Work in British Cotton Mills, 1820–1850', *Journal of Social History,* vol. 21, no. 4 (1988), p. 628.

192.   Humphries, '"The Most Free from Objection"', p. 937; Kocka, 'Problems of Working-Class Formation in Germany', p. 320; Valverde, '"Giving the Female a Turn"', pp. 620–21.

193.   Quataert, 'A Source Analysis in German Women's History', pp. 106–8.

194.   William Coleman, *Death Is a Social Disease* (Madison, Wis., 1982), p. 235.

195.   Thompson, *The Making of the English Working Class,* p. 339.

196.   Valverde, '"Giving the Female a Turn"', pp. 627–9.

197.   Derek Linton, 'Between School and Marriage, Workshop and Household: Young Working Women as a Social Problem in Late Imperial Germany', *European History Quarterly,* no. 18 (1988), p. 391.

198.   Ibid., p. 390.

199.   Pinchbeck, *Women Workers and the Industrial Revolution,* p. 237.

200.   Jeffrey Weeks, *Sex, Politics and Society: The Regulation of Sexuality since 1800* (London, 1981), pp. 57–8; Linton, 'Between School and Marriage, Workshop and Household', p. 392.

201.   Karen Hausen, 'Family and Role-Division', in Evans and Lee, eds, *The German Family,* p. 65.

202. Scott, 'Men and Women in the Parisian Garment Trades', p. 83.

203. Anthony Wohl, *Endangered Lives: Public Health in Victorian Britain* (London, 1983), p. 27; Lewis, 'The Working-Class Wife and Mother and State Intervention', p. 100; Taylor, *Eve and the New Jerusalem*, pp. 109, 111; Adrian Rifkin and Roger Thomas, *Voices of the People: The Social Life of 'La société' at the End of the Second Empire* (London, 1988), p. 38; Hannigan 'Proletarian Families and Social Protest', pp. 418-19; Clementina Black, ed., *Married Women's Work* (London, 1983), p. 14.

204. *The Family* (London, 1906), p. 222.

205. Lewis, *Women in England*, p. 51.

206. *The Family*, p. 203.

207. Ibid., p. 199.

208. Ibid., pp. 200-202.

209. Standish Meacham, *A Life Apart: The English Working Class, 1890-1914* (London, 1977), p. 152.

210. Lewis, *Women in England*, p. 47.

211. Cited in Pinchbeck, *Women Workers and the Industrial Revolution*, p. 200.

212. K. D. M. Snell, *Annals of the Labouring Poor: Social Change and Agrarian England, 1600-1900* (Cambridge, 1985), p. 313.

213. *The Condition of the Working Class in England*, p. 173.

214. Lewenhak, *Women and Trade Unions*, pp. 54-5.

215. *The Condition of the Working Class in England*, p. 173.

216. Ibid., p. 173.

217. Pinchbeck, *Women Workers and the Industrial Revolution*; Frevert, 'The Civilizing Tendency of Hygiene', p. 326.

218. Hausen, 'Family and Role-Division'; Caroline Davidson, *A Woman's Work Is Never Done: A History of Housework in the British Isles, 1650-1950* (London, 1986), p. 187; Burnett, *Destiny Obscure*, p. 219.

219. Davidson, *A Woman's Work Is Never Done*, p. 187; Clark, *Working Life of Women in the Seventeenth Century*, p. 5.

220. Perrot, 'On the Formation of the French Working Class', p. 98.

221. Bullock and Read, *The Movement for Housing Reform in Germany and France*, p. 304; Christian Topalov, *Le Logement en France: Histoire d'une marchandise impossible* (Paris, 1987), p. 131; Hartmut Kaelble, *Industrialization and Social Inequality in Nineteenth-Century Europe* (Leamington Spa, 1986), pp. 112, 117.

222. Dennis, *English Industrial Cities of the Nineteenth Century*, p. 201.

223. Hans Jurgen Teuteberg and Clemens Wischermann, *Wohnalltag in Deutschland, 1850-1914*, (Berlin, 1985), p. 132; Smout, *A Century of the Scottish People*, pp. 33-4; James Jackson, 'Overcrowding and Family Life: Working-Class Families and the Housing Crisis in Later Nineteenth-Century Duisburg', in Richard Evans and W. R. Lee, eds, *The German Family* (London, 1981), p. 207.

224. Bullock and Read, *The Movement for Housing Reform in Germany and France*, p. 56; Shapiro, *Housing the Poor of Paris*, p. 58.

225. M. J. Daunton, *House and Home in the Victorian City: Working-Class Housing, 1850-1914* (London, 1983), p. 81; Teuteberg and Wischermann, *Wohnalltag in Deutschland*, p. 152.

226. Brown, 'Public Health Crises and Public Response', pp. 2-3; Teuteberg and Wischermann, *Wohnalltag in Deutschland*, p. 138.

227. Berlanstein, *The Working People of Paris*, pp. 56-60.

228. J. A. Hassan, 'The Growth and Impact of the British Water Industry in the Nineteenth Century', *Economic History Review*, vol. 38 (1985), pp. 531-3; Wohl, *Endangered Lives*, pp. 108-16.

229. Coleman, *Death Is a Social Disease*, pp. 149-80; John Brown, 'Public Health Crises and Public Response: The Role of Investments in Sanitary Infrastructure in German Cities, 1871-1910', (unpubl. MS, 1988), p. 6.

230. Wohl, *Endangered Lives*, pp. 308-21.

231. Hassan, 'The Growth and Impact of the British Water Industry', p. 538.

232. Daunton, *House and Home in the Victorian City*, pp. 246–55.

233. Robert Woods and P. R. Andrew Hinde, 'Mortality in Victorian England: Models and Patterns', *Journal of Interdisciplinary History*, vol. 18 (1987), p. 39; Samuel Preston and Etienne Van de Walle, 'Urban French Mortality in the Nineteenth Century', *Population Studies*, vol. 32 (1978), p. 277.

234. Stephen Kunitz, 'Mortality since Malthus', in David Coleman and Roger Schofield, eds, *The State of Population Theory: Forward from Malthus* (Oxford, 1986), p. 283; Preston and Van de Walle, 'Urban French Mortality in the Nineteenth Century', p. 283.

235. Preston and Van de Walle, 'Urban French Mortality in the Nineteenth Century', p. 288.

236. D. J. Oddy, 'Working-Class Diets in Late Nineteenth-Century Britain', *Economic History Review*, vol. 23 (1970), p. 319; Oddy, 'The Health of the People', in Michael Drake and Theo Barker, eds, *Population and Society in Britain, 1850–1950* (London, 1982), p. 123.

237. Berlanstein, *The Working People of Paris*, p. 54.

238. Reinhard Spree, *Health and Social Class in Imperial Germany* (Oxford, 1988), p. 65.

239. Teuteberg and Wischermann, *Wohnalltag in Deutschland*, p. 141.

240. Daunton, *House and Home in the Victorian City*, pp. 237–46.

241. Caroline Davidson, *A Woman's Work Is Never Done: A History of Housework in the British Isles, 1650–1950* (London, 1986), pp. 33–43.

242. Ruth S. Cowan, *More Work for Mother: The Ironies of Household Technology from the Open Hearth to the Microwave* (New York, 1983).

243. *Fair Sex: Family Size and Structure, 1900–39* (London, 1982), p. 59.

244. Ute Frevert, 'The Civilizing Tendency of Hygiene: Working-Class Women under Medical Control in Imperial Germany', in J. C. Fout, ed., *German Women in the Nineteenth Century* (New York, 1984), p. 333; Jane Lewis, *The Politics of Motherhood* (London, 1980), pp. 61–88. See also Ellen Ross, 'Labour and Love: Rediscovering London's Working-Class Mothers, 1870–1918', in Jane Lewis, ed., *Labour and Love: Women's Experience of Home and Family, 1850–1940* (Oxford, 1986).

245. Berlanstein, *The Working People of Paris*, p. 61.

246. Frevert, 'The Civilizing Tendency of Hygiene', p. 335.

247. Jane Lewis, 'The Working-Class Wife and Mother and State Intervention, 1870–1918', in Lewis, ed., *Labour and Love*, pp. 109–15.

248. Gareth Stedman Jones, 'Working-Class Culture and Working-Class Politics in London, 1870–1900: Notes on the Remaking of the Working-Class', *Journal of Social History*, vol. 7 (1974), pp. 460–508.

249. Maud Pember Reeves, *Round About a Pound a Week* (London, 1979 [1913]), pp. 159–75.

250. Ellen Ross, 'Survival Networks: Women's Neighbourhood Sharing in London before World War I', *History Workshop Journal*, no. 15 (1983), pp. 10–11.

251. Richard Dennis, *English Industrial Cities of the Nineteenth Century: A Social Geography* (Cambridge, 1984), p. 113–25; John McKay, *Tramways and Trolleys: The Rise of Urban Mass Transport in Europe* (Princeton, N.J., 1976), pp. 192–7.

252. Making a number of heroic assumptions, we can develop a very rough estimate of journey-to-work usage for regularly employed workers. Take a working-class city with an extensive tram service registering 240 rides per capita per annum; reserve 120 rides for journeys to and from work, and give 20 to occasional users; 100 remain. For regular users, assume 2 rides a day, 250 days a year, generating 500 work-related rides per year. At this rate, a fifth of the city's population would consume the 100 available rides. But how many people might need to take the tram to work? Assume that all regular workers are between the ages fifteen and sixty-four, that 60 per cent of the city's population is in this group, and that half of the group is employed outside their homes. This would mean that only 30 per cent of the city's population might need to be twice-daily users if they lived too far away from their work. On these assumptions, two-thirds of those working year-round outside their homes would avail themselves of the opportunity to do so. If the same assumptions are applied to a more typical city rating 160 rides per capita per year, then only 44.6 per cent of the regularly employed would ride twice daily on working days.

253. Dennis, *English Industrial Cities of the Nineteenth Century*, pp. 136–40.

254. John Holley portrays the family economy of the labouring poor in Scottish textile towns operating on a different basis in the era before compulsory schooling. Given the low pay of the male head, the employment prospects of the children as a group predominated, and families resided close to the mill where the children were employed. Fathers who were unable to obtain work in the mill took whatever jobs they could find in the district: 'The Two Family Economies of Industrialism: Factory Workers in Victorian Scotland', *Journal of Family History*, vol. 6 (1981), pp. 62–6. I have argued that the prevalence of this type of family economy diminished greatly in the latter decades of the nineteenth century. As families became increasingly reliant upon the primary breadwinner's income, it seems likely that the residential constraint operated more strongly through his place of employment.

255. Robert Roberts, *The Classic Slum: Salford Life in the First Quarter of the Century* (Harmondsworth, 1973), p. 116.

256. Dennis, *English Industrial Cities of the Nineteenth Century*, pp. 119–24.

257. Ibid., pp. 256–7; Anderson, *Family Structure in Nineteenth-Century Lancashire* (Cambridge, 1971), p. 41.

258. Dennis, *English Industrial Cities of the Nineteenth Century*, p. 34; Shapiro, *Housing the Poor of Paris*, p. 55; Roger Price, *A Social History of Nineteenth-Century France* (New York, 1987), p. 221.

259. Dennis, *English Industrial Cities of the Nineteenth Century*, pp. 256–7; Brüggemeier and Niethammer, 'Lodgers, Schnapps-Casinos and Working-Class Colonies in a Heavy-Industrial Region', p. 233.

260. Dennis, *English Industrial Cities of the Nineteenth Century*, pp. 258–62.

261. Standish Meacham, *A Life Apart: The English Working Class, 1890–1914* (London, 1977), pp. 42–3.

262. A. S. Wohl, 'The Housing of the Working Classes in London, 1815–1914', in S. D. Chapman, ed., *The History of Working-Class Housing* (Newton Abbot, 1971), p. 19.

263. Dennis, *English Industrial Cities of the Nineteenth Century*, p. 261.

264. Wohl, 'The Housing of the Working Classes in London', p. 17.

265. Teuteberg and Wischermann, *Wohnalltag in Deutschland*, p. 117; Dennis, *English Industrial Cities of the Nineteenth Century*, p. 256. See also Stearns, *Lives of Labour*, pp. 246–7; Lequin, 'Apprenticeship in Nineteenth-Century France', p. 462; Martine Segalen, *Historical Anthropology of the Family* (Cambridge, 1986), p. 136; and Berlanstein, *The Working People of Paris*, pp. 43, 106–7.

266. Roberts, *The Classic Slum*; Michael Young and Peter Wilmott, *Family and Kinship in East London* (Harmondsworth, 1962 [1957]); Meacham, *A Life Apart*, p. 47.

267. *Round About a Pound a Week*, p. 39.

268. 'Survival Networks', p. 5.

269. Dennis, *English Industrial Cities of the Nineteenth Century*, p. 273; Anderson, *Family Structure in Nineteenth-Century Lancashire*, pp. 56–67. These proportions do not appear to have changed appreciably from 1850 to 1880.

270. Tyler Stovall, '"Friends, Neighbours and Communists": Community Formation in Suburban Paris during the Early Twentieth Century', *Journal of Social History*, vol. 22 (1988), p. 240.

271. Gillis, *For Better, For Worse*, p. 255; Anderson, *Family Structure in Nineteenth-Century Lancashire*, pp. 56–67. Readers of *A Millennium of Family Change*, this study's precursor, will note how the settling of working-class family life in the late Victorian era recalls many features of the weak-stem variant which typified peasant settlements across Northwestern Europe in the early modern period. It is as if the process of forging 'urban villages' had enabled people to re-create the kin and community structures of their village ancestors, after the Industrial Revolution had torn them apart.

272. Bell, *At the Works*, p. 115.

273. Young and Wilmott, *Family and Kinship in East London*, pp. 104–7.

274. Dennis, *English Industrial Cities of the Nineteenth Century*, p. 286.

275. Meacham, *A Life Apart*, p. 17.

276. Lis, *Social Change and the Labouring Poor*, p. 159; Ross, 'Survival Networks', p. 6;

Reinhard Sieder, 'Childhood Experiences in Viennese Working-Class Families around 1900', *Continuity and Change,* vol. 1 (1986), p. 77; Kerr, *The People of Ship Street* (London, 1958), pp. 102–3.

277.   Frykman and Löfgren, *Culture Builders,* p. 147; Ross, 'Survival Networks', p. 6.

278.   Ross, 'Survival Networks', p. 7; M. Tebbutt, *Making Ends Meet: Pawnbroking and Working-Class Credit* (New York, 1983), pp. 49–50.

279.   Ross, 'Survival Networks', p. 11.

280.   Sieder, 'Childhood Experiences in Viennese Working-Class Families', p. 77.

281.   Ross, 'Survival Networks', pp. 14–19; Ellen Ross, '"Not the Sort That Would Sit on the Doorstep": Respectability in Pre–World War I London Neighbourhoods', *International Labor and Working-Class History,* no. 27, 1985, pp. 39–59; Meacham, *A Life Apart,* p. 50.

282.   Gillis, *For Better, For Worse,* p. 265.

283.   Ibid., pp. 256–7, 264–5. John Burnett, ed., *Destiny Obscure: Autobiographies of Childhood, Education and Family from the 1820s to the 1920s* (Harmondsworth, 1984), pp. 253–5.

284.   Edward Shorter, John Knodel and Etienne van de Walle, 'The Decline of Non-Marital Fertility in Europe, 1880–1940', *Population Studies,* vol. 25 (1971), pp. 375–93.

285.   Gillis, *For Better, For Worse,* pp. 258–9.

286.   *Culture Builders,* p. 147.

287.   Burnett, *Destiny Obscure,* pp. 224–8.

288.   Sieder, 'Childhood Experiences in Viennese Working-Class Families', p. 62.

289.   Meacham, *A Life Apart,* p. 55.

290.   Daunton, *House and Home in the Victorian City,* p. 269.

291.   Ruggles, *Prolonged Connections,* pp. 5–6.

292.   While roughly 11 per cent of households in major German cities contained lodgers in 1871, by 1905 only 8 per cent did: Teuteberg and Wischermann, *Wohnalltag in Deutschland,* p. 317.

293.   Jonas Frykman and Ovar Löfgren, *Culture Builders: A Historical Anthropology of Middle-Class Life* (New Brunswick, N.J., 1987), p. 145.

294.   John Butt, 'Working-Class Housing in Glasgow, 1851–1914', in S. D. Chapman, ed., *The History of Working-Class Housing* (Newton Abbot, 1971), pp. 64–6.

295.   For Germany, see James Jackson, 'Overcrowding and Family Life: Working-Class Families and the Housing Crisis in Later Nineteenth-Century Duisburg', in R. J. Evans and W. R. Lee, eds, *The German Family* (London, 1981) p. 195; for England, Leonore Davidoff, 'The Separation of Home and Work? Landladies and Lodgers in Nineteenth and Twen-tieth-Century England', in Sandra Burman, ed., *Fit Work for Women* (New York, 1979), pp. 68–74; for the United States, John Modell and Tamara Hareven, 'Urbanization and the Malleable Household: An Examination of Boarding and Lodging in American Families', *Journal of Marriage and the Family,* vol. 35 (1973), pp. 467–79.

296.   F. M. L. Thompson, *The Rise of Respectable Society,* p. 128.

297.   Ibid., p. 131.

298.   Reinhard Sieder, 'Childhood Experiences in Viennese Working-Class Families around 1900', *Continuity and Change,* vol. 1 (1986), pp. 69–74.

299.   Kelly, *The German Worker,* p. 29.

300.   Daunton, *House and Home in the Victorian City,* pp. 277–9; Thompson, *The Rise of Respectable Society,* pp. 193–5. Lest the front parlour be thought of as an English idiosyncrasy, see Frykman and Löfgren's discussion of the Swedish version: 'The parlour with its plants, mantlepiece clock, and lace-decorated sofa was not a pathetic attempt to imitate bourgeois life-styles; instead, the room had its own symbolic meaning in working-class culture. It was a cultural space separated from the drudgeries of everyday life, and to enter it meant being ritually transformed. It had an atmosphere all its own. ...': *Culture Builders,* p. 149.

301.   Burnett, *Destiny Obscure,* p. 225.

302.   Thompson, *The Rise of Respectable Society,* p. 194.

303.   *The Queen's Poor* (London, 1910), pp. 22–3.

304. Michael Haines, *Fertility and Occupation: Population Patterns in Industrialization* (New York, 1979); L. B. More, *Wage Earners' Budgets: A Study of Standards and Costs of Living in New York City* (New York, 1971 [1907]), pp. 254, 258–9; Alfred Kelly, *The German Worker: Working-Class Autobiographies from the Age of Industrialization* (Berkeley, Calif., 1987), p. 18.

305. Thomas Wright, *The Great Unwashed* (New York, 1970 [1868]), p. 203.

306. Tilly and Scott, *Women, Work and Family*, p. 206.

307. Dorothy Marshall, *Industrial England, 1776–1851* (London, 1973), p. 102.

308. John Benson, *British Coalminers in the Nineteenth Century: A Social History* (Dublin, 1980), p. 110.

309. Thompson and Yeo, *The Unknown Mayhew: Selections from the Morning Chronicle* (Harmondsworth, 1984 [1971]), p. 394.

310. T. C. Smout, *A Century of the Scottish People, 1830–1950* (London, 1986), pp. 138–44.

311. Marshall, *Industrial England*, p. 102; E. J. Hobsbawm, *Workers: Worlds of Labour* (New York, 1984), p. 186.

312. Thomas Wright, *The Great Unwashed*, p. 167.

313. Jan Pahl, 'Patterns of Money Management within Marriage', *Journal of Social Policy*, vol. 9, no. 3 (1980), pp. 313–35. These patterns varied interregionally. In an English survey conducted in the late 1960s, 23 per cent of married women from the northwest reported that they and their spouses employed the whole-wage system, while only 6 per cent of couples in the southeast did so: ibid., p. 318.

314. Rathbone, *The Disinherited Family*, p. 168.

315. Ibid., p. 168.

316. Reeves, *Round About a Pound a Week*, p. 10.

317. *At the Works*, p. 79.

318. Lewis, *Women in England*, p. 26; Rathbone, *The Disinherited Family*, p. 169.

319. Roberts, *A Woman's Place*, p. 83; John Fout, 'The Women's Role in the German Working-Class Family in the 1890s', in Fout, ed., *German Women in the Nineteenth Century* (New York, 1984), p. 306.

320. Ellen Ross, '"Fierce Questions and Taunts": Married Life in Working-Class London, 1870–1914', *Feminist Studies*, vol. 8, no. 3 (1982), p. 582.

321. Meacham, *A Life Apart*, p. 72.

322. Gillis, *For Better, For Worse*, p. 185; Thomas Wright, *Some Habits and Customs of the Working Classes* (New York, 1967 [1867]), p. 74; Ross, '"Fierce Questions and Taunts"', p. 577; Burnett, *Destiny Obscure*, p. 230; Fout, 'The Woman's Role in the German Working-Class Family', p. 306.

323. G. R. Porter, 'On the Self-Imposed Taxation of the Working-Classes in the United Kingdom', *Journal of the Royal Statistical Society*, vol. 13 (1850), p. 364.

324. Reeves, *Round About a Pound a Week*, pp. 9–10, 153. This type of calculus is complicated by the fact that men paid for essential items such as their own work boots and Benefit Society dues with the money they retained; it did not all go for drink, bets and tobacco.

325. Bell, *At the Works*, p. 78; Elizabeth Roberts, *A Woman's Place: An Oral History of Working-Class Women, 1890–1940* (Oxford, 1984), p. 110; Davies, *Maternity: Letters from Working Women*, pp. 18, 38, 88; Maud Reeves, *Round About a Pound a Week*, p. 17.

326. Reeves, *Round About a Pound a Week*, p. 14.

327. Rathbone, *The Disinherited Family*, p. 205.

328. The participation of young bachelors in the rituals of masculine leisure in pubs, betting shops and clubs was poor training for their subsequent marital responsibilities. Men 'who have been wont in their gay young days to spend 50 to 75 per cent. of their earnings on their *menus plaisirs*, fail to see why they should deprive themselves when, after all, "a man's money is his own" and "other fellows' wives have to manage on less"': Rathbone, *The Disinherited Family*, p. 167.

329. Katherine Lynch, *Family, Class, and Ideology in Early Industrial France* (Madison, Wis., 1988), p. 77.

330.   William Lucas Sargant, *Economy of the Labouring Classes* (London, 1857), p. 118.

331.   A middle-class meddler, rebuffed at a proletarian doorstep, perceptively noted: 'If she gets a black eye she answers any questions by saying "Oh, it's nothing, we just had a bit of a fight last night, that's all." It is obvious that "oh, it's nothing" is intended to tell people to mind their own business, more precisely, is it not also a way for workers' wives to establish their right to resolve their quarrels without being treated like souls "in distress" by bosses, policemen and social workers?': Rifkin and Thomas, *Voices of the People,* p. 120.

332.   Hans Medick, 'Plebeian Culture in the Transition to Capitalism', in Raphael Samuel and Gareth Stedman Jones, eds, *Culture, Ideology and Politics* (London, 1982); John Rule, *The Labouring Classes in Early Industrial England, 1750–1850* (London, 1986), p. 213.

333.   Peter Stearns, 'Working-Class Women in Britain, 1890–1914', in Martha Vicinus, ed., *Suffer and Be Still: Women in the Victorian Age* (Bloomington, Ind., 1972), p. 108.

334.   As Rathbone pointed out: 'Middle-class parents whose incomes are low in proportion to the standard of their class have to forgo many pleasures which their fellows enjoy – foreign travel, entertaining, theatre-going, motoring. But they seldom have to choose ... between going short themselves of nourishing food and warm clothing or seeing their children go short': *The Disinherited Family,* p. 169.

335.   Meacham, *A Life Apart,* p. 61; Fout, 'The Women's Role in the German Working-Class Family', p. 305; Burnett, *Destiny Obscure,* p. 229; Kelly, *The German Worker,* p. 32.

336.   *At the Works,* p. 182.

337.   Lewis, *Women in England,* p. 45; see also Rule, *The Labouring Classes in Early Industrial England,* p. 182.

338.   Quataert, 'A Source Analysis in German Women's History', p. 112.

339.   The full recognition of this reality, and the question of its adequate theoretical incorporation, were the key points at issue in 'the domestic labour debate' conducted by marxist–feminists in the 1970s.

340.   Dennis, Henriques and Slaughter provide an excellent introduction to this arrangement in *Coal Is Our Life* (pp. 171–245), although they minimize the extent of patriarchal dominance inherent in it.

341.   Pat Ayers and Jan Lambertz, 'Marriage Relations, Money and Domestic Violence in Working-Class Liverpool, 1919–39', in Jane Lewis, ed., *Labour and Love: Women's Experience of Home and Family, 1850–1940* (Oxford, 1986), p. 203.

342.   Loane, *An Englishman's Castle* (London, 1909), p. 183.

343.   Meacham, *A Life Apart,* p. 72.

344.   Ayers and Lambertz, 'Marriage Relations, Money and Domestic Violence in Working-Class Liverpool', pp. 197–8.

345.   Ellen Ross, 'Survival Networks: Women's Neighbourhood Sharing in London before World War I', *History Workshop Journal,* no. 15 (1983), p. 5; Ovar Löfgren, 'Family and Household: Images and Realities, Cultural Change in Swedish Society', in Robert Netting, Richard Wilk and Eric Arnould, eds, *Households: Comparative and Historical Studies of the Domestic Group* (Berkeley, Calif., 1984), p. 466.

346.   Ross, 'Survival Networks', p. 1. See also Lenard Berlanstein, *The Working People of Paris,* p. 140.

347.   Bell, *At the Works,* p. 234.

348.   *Round About a Pound a Week,* p. 155.

349.   M. Tebbutt, *Making Ends Meet: Pawnbroking and Working-Class Credit* (New York, 1983), p. 40.

350.   *An Englishman's Castle,* p. 178; Burnett, *Destiny Obscure,* p. 229; See also Gillis's assessment: 'Children belonged to the female sphere, and their care and discipline was entirely the mother's responsibility': *For Better, For Worse,* p. 248.

351.   Berlanstein, *The Working People of Paris,* pp. 140–41.

352.   Roberts, *A Woman's Place,* pp. 110–21.

353.   Black, *Married Women's Work,* p. 10; Pinchbeck, *Women Workers and the Industrial Revolution,* p. 104; Laura Oren, 'The Welfare of Women in Labouring Families: England, 1860–1950', in Mary Hartman and Lois Banner, eds, *Clio's Consciousness Raised* (New York,

1974), p. 228; Marx, *Capital,* vol. 1 (New York, 1977), p. 809. While these authors refer to Britain, see also Roger Price, *A Social History of Nineteenth-Century France* (New York, 1987), p. 217; and Reinhard Sieder, 'Childhood Experiences in Viennese Working-Class Families around 1900', *Continuity and Change* , vol. 1 (1986), pp. 66–7.

354.   Reeves, *Round About a Pound a Week,* p. 156. See also Rathbone, *The Disinherited Family,* pp. 169–70.

355.   Sieder, 'Childhood Experiences in Viennese Working-Class Families', p. 63.

356.   Ibid., pp. 62–6.

Chapter 5

1.   The *Princeton European Fertility Project* has amassed an impressive body of data tracking the fertility decline at the provincial level from 1870 on. The summary findings of the Project have been published as a collection of essays in Ansley Coale and Susan Watkins, eds, *The Decline of Fertility in Europe* (Princeton, N.J., 1986) providing a statistical overview of the decline in 700 European provinces. On the Princeton Project's achievements and shortcomings, see the reflections of Charles Tilly, Rudolf Andorka and David Levine in *Population and Development Review,* vol. 12 (1986), pp. 323–40. My own views are elaborated in *Sociological Forum,* vol. 1, no. 4 (1986).

2.   Ansley Coale and Roy Treadway, 'A Summary of the Changing Distribution of Overall Fertility, Marital Fertility, and the Proportion Married in the Provinces of Europe', in Coale and Watkins, eds, *The Decline of Fertility in Europe,* p. 37.

3.   In France, the onset of deliberate family limitation was coincident with, and shaped by, the Revolution: David Weir, 'Fertility Transition in Rural France, 1740–1829', thesis synopsis, *Journal of Economic History,* vol. 44 (1984). Proletarian limitation, however, probably did not get under way much before it did elsewhere. In the heavily industrialized Nord and Pas-de-Calais region, marital fertility remained very high until at least 1871, when it stood 34 per cent above the national average: E. A. Wrigley, 'The Fall of Marital Fertility in Nineteenth-Century France: Exemplar or Exception?' *European Journal of Population,* vol. 1 (1985), p. 152. In the working-class suburbs of Paris, fertility peaked in the early 1880s, falling off steeply thereafter: Lenard Berlanstein, *The Working People of Paris, 1871–1914* (Baltimore, 1984), pp. 141–3.

4.   Michael Haines, *Fertility and Occupation: Population Patterns in Industrialization* (New York, 1979); Diana Gittins, *Fair Sex: Family Size and Structure, 1900–39* (London, 1982); Peter Stearns, *Lives of Labour* (New York, 1975), p. 274. F. M. L. Thompson has recently examined the temporal sequence in which the occupational groups of England and Wales began to limit births within marriage. While stressing that the pattern was anything but neat, he summarized it among working-class strata in these terms: 'The one thread linking the great majority of these occupational groups was the extent, and timing, of their exposure to the processes of industrialization. Thus, machine technologies, large-scale organization, or factory methods, came earliest to textiles, railways, or printing [early limiters]; much later to furniture and shoemaking [intermediate]; and not at all to building, dock, and farm work [late]; and in the sense that coal mining remained essentially a labour-intensive industry using traditional methods, not to that industry either [latest]': *The Rise of Respectable Society: A Social History of Victorian Britain, 1830–1900* (London, 1988), p. 72 [my insertions in square brackets].

5.   The pattern of dispersion and subsequent reconvergence is evident on a provincial basis in most European states, as the Princeton studies have shown: Coale and Treadway, pp. 42–3; Michael Teitelbaum, *The British Fertility Decline: Demographic Transition in the Crucible of the Industrial Revolution* (Princeton, N.J., 1984), pp. 120–26. Evidence of class disparities in marital fertility is not as easily established, although the overall pattern is clear enough. For France, see Wesley Camp, *Marriage and the Family in France since the Revolution* (New York, 1961), p. 118; for Italy, Massimo Livi-Bacci, *A History of Italian Fertility* (Prin-

ceton, N.J., 1977), pp. 284–7; for Germany, Reinhard Spree, *Health and Social Class in Imperial Germany* (Oxford, 1988), p. 204, and R. P. Neuman, 'Working-Class Birth Control in Wilhelmine Germany', in *Comparative Studies in Society and History*, vol. 20, no. 3 (1978), p. 408; for England, John W. Innes, *Class Fertility Trends in England and Wales, 1876–1934* (Princeton, N.J., 1938); and R. Woods and C. W. Smith, 'The Decline of Marital Fertility in the Late Nineteenth Century: The Case of England and Wales', *Population Studies*, vol. 37, no. 2 (1983), pp. 207–25; and for Scotland, T. C. Smout, *A Century of the Scottish People, 1830–1950* (London, 1986), p. 174. Since census occupational codes differ, precise comparisons are impossible, but I have found no evidence that contradicts the broad class sequence described above.

6. Coale and Treadway, 'A Summary of the Changing Distribution of Overall Fertility', p. 52.

7. John Knodel, 'Family Limitation and the Fertility Transition: Evidence from the Age Patterns of Fertility in Europe and Asia', *Population Studies*, vol. 31, no. 2 (1977).

8. The possibility that deliberate limitation by means of stopping had been present long before the fertility decline was originally aroused by Wrigley's work on Colyton, but this now appears to have been an exceptional parish. On England, see Chris Wilson, 'The Proximate Determinants of Marital Fertility in England, 1600–1799', in Lloyd Bonfield, Richard Smith and Keith Wrightson, eds, *The World We Have Gained* (Oxford, 1986); on Germany, John Knodel, 'Natural Fertility in Pre-industrial Germany', *Population Studies*, vol. 32 (1978), pp. 481–510. Neither finds any indication that stopping was prevalent before the decline.

9. Sauer has made the case for an increase in Britain, Woycke has done the same for Germany, Blom finds evidence of an increase after the First World War in Norway, Treffers for the Netherlands, and Shorter presents a range of evidence for several regions of Northwestern Europe: R. Sauer, 'Infanticide and Abortion in Nineteenth-Century Britain', *Population Studies* vol. 32, no. 1 (1978), p. 91; James Woycke, *The Diffusion of Birth Control in Germany, 1871–1933*, doctoral thesis, University of Toronto, 1984, pp. 125–6; Ida Blom, *Barnebegrensning-synd eller sunn fornuft* (Bergen, 1980); P. E. Treffers, 'Abortion in Amsterdam', *Population Studies*, vol. 20, no. 3 (1967), pp. 299–300; Edward Shorter, *A History of Women's Bodies* (New York, 1982), pp. 191–7. Blom has suggested that the high rate of adult female mortality in the early twentieth century, persisting for decades after the rate of infant mortality began to fall, may well have been due to complications arising from botched abortions. In Norway, maternal death in childbirth actually increased in the twenties and thirties, as abortions peaked.

10. Woycke, *The Diffusion of Birth Control in Germany*, p. 126.

11. Gittins, *Fair Sex*, p. 164.

12. Sauer, 'Infanticide and Abortion in Nineteenth-Century Britain', p. 91.

13. Gittins, *Fair Sex*, p. 164.

14. Woycke, *The Diffusion of Birth Control in Germany*, pp. 130–33.

15. Why was the resort to abortion so frequent, particularly for married women? Despite its danger, expense and uncertainty, abortion had two great advantages over preventive measures as far as women were concerned. In the first place, it was reactive, and hence occasional. If women were lucky enough to avoid pregnancy, they did not have to do anything. Given the rate of sterility at the time, a surprising number of women escaped the ordeal. Secondly, women could act on their own initiative. Coitus interruptus, celibacy or the use of condoms required male cooperation; those women who found that this was not readily forthcoming became inured to coital risk. Provided abortion occurred before 'quickening' (in the third month), it was not regarded by most women as a grave sin, but rather as a necessary evil. A woman was not ostracized for seeking an abortion; her network of friends and kin typically lent comfort and assistance in 'putting her right': Jane Lewis, *Women in England, 1870–1950* (Sussex, 1984), pp. 17–18; Brookes, 'Women and Reproduction', pp. 159–60.

16. *Maternity: Letters from Working Women* (London, 1978 [1915]). Replies were received from 386 members, covering 460 cases; of these, 160 were printed. The book, edited by the Guild's General Secretary, Margaret Davies, created an immediate sensation

when it was published in 1915.

17. Written in the 1920s, these letters are found in a chapter of *Dear Dr Stopes* (Harmondsworth, 1981) entitled 'The Lower Classes', and in a more extensive collection published as *Mother England: A Contemporary History*, 2nd edn (London, 1930). For the latter text, Stopes drew some 200 letters from her private files received in 1926 from working-class people with surnames beginning with A to H.

18. 'Report on an Enquiry into Family Limitation and Its Influence on Human Fertility during the Past Fifty Years', *Papers of the Royal Commission on Population*, vol. 1 (London, 1949).

19. Blom, *Barnebegrensning-synd eller sunn fornuft* (Bergen, 1980). I am most grateful to Ida Blom for her patient correspondence with me in English, and to Kari Dehli for translating key passages from Blom's work.

20. Woycke, *Birth Control in Germany, 1871–1933* (London, 1988); Neuman, 'Working-Class Birth Control in Wilhelmine Germany', *Comparative Studies in Society and History*, vol. 20 (1978), pp. 408–28. Woycke's text was originally a doctoral dissertation completed at the University of Toronto in 1984, and it is this version that I have cited below. Thanks to Ned Shorter for drawing my attention to his student's thesis.

21. Lewis-Faning, 'Report on an Enquiry into Family Limitation', p. 56. Lewis-Faning groups all birth-control practices into two categories: 'appliance' and 'non-appliance' methods. Strictly speaking, abstinence and the rhythm method were included with coitus interruptus in the latter category, but the author reports that the combined incidence of celibacy and cyclical abstinence was negligible, so that 'non-appliance methods may be taken throughout to refer to Coitus Interruptus' (p. 8).

22. Woycke, *Birth Control in Germany*, p. 39.

23. See Stopes, ed., *Mother England*, pp. 9, 11, 16, 17, 22, 28, 31, 35, 36–7, 39, 40, 41, 43, 47, 52, 54, 58, 59, 63, 66, 68, 70, 74, 91, 104, 113, 114, 117, 120, 124, 130, 138, 139, 147, 153, 159, 161, 164–5, 166, 177.

24. See ibid., pp. 3, 8, 36, 47, 50, 61, 74, 84, 98, 101, 130, 144, 160. In some letters, it is not clear whether references such as 'my husband holds himself in check' refer to abstinence or withdrawal, and of course both methods might be tried at different times by the same couple. I have assigned all such vague references to one or other category on the basis of my best guess as to the primary means used.

25. Gittins, *Fair Sex*, pp. 165–9.

26. Many women mention prolonged breastfeeding as a means of limiting fertility: *Mother England*, pp. 8, 16, 55, 62, 64, 73, 77, 99, 148, 155, 170. The suggestion was often raised by nurses who were not prepared to recommend contraceptives. Delayed weaning is a spacing technique; it is practically useless to women attempting to stop. Respondents rejected it outright for their purposes, agreeing with the popular adage: 'If women want from children to be freed, to trust nursing's but a broken reed': Angus McLaren, *Reproductive Rituals* (London, 1984), p. 67.

27. Etienne van de Walle, 'Motivations and Technology in the Decline of French Fertility', in Robert Wheaton and Tamara Hareven, eds, *Family and Sexuality in French History* (Philadelphia, 1980); John Knodel and Etienne van de Walle, 'Lessons from the Past: Policy Implications of Historical Fertility Studies', in Coale and Watkins, eds, *The Decline of Fertility in Europe*, p. 403.

28. Gittins, *Fair Sex*, p. 162.

29. Jane Lewis, *Women in England, 1870–1950* (Sussex, 1984), p. 18.

30. Stopes, ed., *Mother England*, pp. 84–5.

31. Angus McLaren, *Sexuality and Social Order: The Debate over the Fertility of Women and Workers in France, 1770–1920* (New York, 1983), p. 51.

32. Woycke, *Birth Control in Germany*, p. 37.

33. Stopes, ed., *Mother England*, p. vi; *Dear Dr Stopes*, p. 15.

34. Lewis-Faning, 'Report on an Enquiry into Family Limitation', p. 52; Neuman, 'Working-Class Birth Control in Wilhelmine Germany', p. 418; Woycke, *Birth Control in Germany*, pp. 33–9. The mass distribution of condoms to soldiers during the First World War undoubtedly increased their postwar use: John Peel, 'The Manufacture and Retailing

of Contraceptives in England', *Population Studies,* vol. 17 (1963), p. 120. However, in so far as their wartime purpose reinforced the close association of 'French Letters' with prostitution and the prevention of venereal disease, it is doubtful that their dissemination had much of an impact on conjugal use immediately after the war.

35. The blight of ignorance is an especially prominent theme in the *Maternity* correspondence, owing primarily to the self-improvement ethos of the Women's Guild. While bourgeois accusations of ignorance effectively blamed the wretched for their own poverty and misery, working-class admissions did not necessarily connote a self-deprecating and submissive mentality. More often, the recognition of their own sorry lack of knowledge aroused the righteous indignation of respondents against doctors, parsons, public health officials and the rich for keeping them in the dark. See the discussion of class resentment below.

36. Stopes, ed., *Mother England,* pp. 19, 75; Hall, ed., *Dear Dr Stopes,* p. 36; Blom, *Barnebegrensning-synd eller sunn fornuft,* p. 51.

37. Stopes, ed, *Mother England,* pp. 4, 47, 57, 75, 110, 128, 146, 153, 155, 157, 166; Hall, ed., *Dear Dr Stopes,* p. 29.

38. Neuman, 'Working-Class Birth Control in Wilhelmine Germany', p. 419.

39. Barbara Brookes, 'Women and Reproduction, 1860–1939', in Jane Lewis, ed., *Labour and Love: Women's Experience of Home and Family, 1850–1940* (Oxford, 1986), p. 159.

40. Stopes, ed., *Mother England,* pp. 77, 86, 99, 103, 105, 124, 148, 155, 170.

41. Mirjana Morokvasic, 'Sexuality and Control of Procreation' in Kate Young, Carol Wolkowitz and Roslyn McCullagh, eds, *Of Marriage and the Market* (London, 1981), pp. 136–7. Many Victorian feminists opposed birth-control devices for the same reason. See Lucy Bland, 'Marriage Laid Bare: Middle-Class Women and Marital Sex, c.1880–1914', in Lewis, ed., *Labour and Love,* p. 129.

42. Stopes, ed., *Mother England,* pp. 128, 147.

43. Woycke, *Birth Control in Germany,* p. 110.

44. Richard Soloway, *Birth Control and the Population Question in England, 1877–1930* (Chapel Hill, N.C., 1982), pp. 111–32. Similar misconceptions were propounded by German and French doctors. See Woycke, *Birth Control in Germany,* pp. 110–21; and McLaren, *Sexuality and Social Order,* pp. 44–64.

45. Davies, ed., *Maternity,* p. 94; Stopes, ed., *Mother England,* pp. 3, 21, 42, 58, 84, 98, 119.

46. Soloway, *Birth Control and the Population Question in England,* p. 99. The Church of England did not condone the use of birth control until the Lambeth Conference of 1930.

47. French doctors, like their colleagues elsewhere, deplored the increasing resort to coitus interruptus, arguing that 'semen losses constituted one of the greatest dangers to the nation's health': McLaren, *Sexuality and Social Order,* pp. 52–62. The regular transmission of 'the seminal liquor' was critical to women's health and sanity; 'conjugal onanism' held a myriad of dangers for men, too – from back pains and 'gonorrhoeal running' to nervous disorders and a dissipation of 'the sentiment of pleasure': McLaren, p. 57.

48. Blom, *Barnebegrensning-synd eller sunn fornuft,* p. 52; Woycke, *Birth Control in Germany,* p. 110.

49. Stopes, ed., *Mother England,* p. 134.

50. Ibid., pp. 5, 17, 20, 24, 49, 63, 68, 69, 79, 80, 83, 94, 100, 101, 108, 111, 113, 115, 124, 125, 131, 132, 134, 137, 141, 142, 150, 153, 154, 157, 170, 171, 172, 173.

51. Soloway, *Birth Control and the Population Question in England,* p. 117.

52. Woycke, *Birth Control in Germany,* p. 111.

53. Ibid., p. 112.

54. Blom, *Barnebegrensning-synd eller sunn fornuft,* p. 52.

55. Woycke, *Birth Control in Germany,* p. 134.

56. Stopes, ed., *Mother England,* pp. 37, 48, 94.

57. Ibid., p. 81.

58. Ibid., p. 51.

59. Ibid., pp. 107, 115, 133, 154; for France, see McLaren, *Sexuality and Social Order,* p. 130.

60. Hall, ed., *Dear Dr Stopes*, p. 17; Stopes, ed., *Mother England*, pp. 99, 115.

61. Soloway, *Birth Control and the Population Question in England*, p. 101.

62. Ibid., p. 223.

63. Hall, ed., *Dear Dr Stopes*, p. 19.

64. McLaren, *Sexuality and Social Order*, pp. 79–89; Neuman, 'Working-Class Birth Control in Wilhelmine Germany', pp. 412–14; Soloway, *Birth Control and the Population Question in England*, pp. 70–90.

65. Neuman, 'Working-Class Birth Control in Wilhelmine Germany', pp. 413–14.

66. Rathbone, *The Disinherited Family*, p. 30.

67. Blom, *Barnebegrensning-synd eller sunn fornuft*, pp. 126–44.

68. McLaren, *Sexuality and Social Order*, pp. 128–9.

69. Neuman, 'Working-Class Birth Control in Wilhelmine Germany', p. 414.

70. Soloway, *Birth Control and the Population Question in England*, pp. 284–5.

71. Peel, 'The Manufacture and Retailing of Contraceptives in England'; McLaren, *Birth Control in Nineteenth-Century England*, p. 238; Neuman, 'Working-Class Birth Control in Wilhelmine Germany', p. 417.

72. McLaren, *Birth Control in Nineteenth-Century England*, p. 224.

73. R. I. Woods, 'Approaches to the Fertility Transition in Victorian England', *Population Studies*, vol. 41 (1987), p. 296.

74. McLaren, *Sexuality and Social Order*, p. 135.

75. Ethel Elderton, *Report on the English Birth Rate* (London, 1914), p. 135. See also Rathbone, *The Disinherited Family*, p. 195.

76. Elderton, *Report on the English Birth Rate*, p. 107.

77. Stopes, ed., *Mother England*, pp. 62, 84–5.

78. Ibid., p. 97.

79. The Stopes correspondence is replete with examples of ignorance and misinformation on the most elementary matters of human anatomy and biology. See also Ellen Ross, who recounts the eureka of a woman to her husband attending her first birth: 'It's come from the same place as you put it in!': 'Survival Networks: Women's Neighbourhood Sharing in London before World War I', *History Workshop Journal*, no. 15 (1983), p. 51.

80. Lewis-Faning, *Report on an Enquiry into Family Limitation*, p. 134.

81. Enid Charles, *The Practice of Birth Control: An Analysis of the Birth-Control Experiences of Nine Hundred Women* (London, 1932), pp. 40–42.

82. Caroline Davidson, *A Woman's Work Is Never Done: A History of Housework in the British Isles, 1650–1950* (London, 1986), p. 31.

83. Davies, ed., *Maternity*, pp. 64, 70, 72. See also Ellen Ross's account of the punitive repression of girls' sexual curiosity by their mothers in Edwardian London: '"Not the Sort That Would Sit on the Doorstep": Respectability in Pre–World War I London Neighbourhoods', *International Labor and Working Class History*, vol. 27 (1985), pp. 49–51.

84. Woycke, *Birth Control in Germany*, p. 88; McLaren, *Sexuality and Social Order*, pp. 132–3; Berlanstein, *The Working People of Paris*, p. 144.

85. I found only one instance in *Mother England* in which a husband was keener to quit than his wife. In two cases, men wanted to use condoms but their wives refused for religious or aesthetic reasons; in the latter, the woman is portrayed as being intensely keen to quit: Stopes, ed., *Mother England*, pp. 42, 58. Roberts cites a woman who wanted a large family while her husband had other ideas: *A Woman's Place: An Oral History of Working-Class Women, 1890–1940*, p. 91. A few such cases can be found, but they appear to be extraordinary.

86. Stopes, ed., *Mother England*, pp. 145, 100.

87. Burnett, *Destiny Obscure*, p. 260.

88. Stopes, ed., *Mother England*, pp. 80, 114. See also pp. 2, 3, 4, 9, 22, 27, 31, 35, 40, 41, 43, 47, 53, 54, 58, 61, 66, 70, 80, 85, 91, 98, 101, 113, 122, 124, 136, 144, 162, 164–5.

89. Ibid., pp. 168, 35, 43.

90. Blom, *Barnebegrensning-synd eller sunn fornuft*, p. 150; Stopes, ed., *Mother England*, pp. 83, 105.

91. Stopes, ed., *Mother England*, pp. 83, 105, 147, 162.
92. Ibid., p. 145; Blom, *Barnebegrensning-synd eller sunn fornuft*, p. 150.
93. McLaren, *Sexuality and Social Order*, pp. 132–3.
94. Stopes, ed., *Mother England*, pp. 101, 168, 35, 43, 101, 3, 144, 91, 106, 145, 166; Hall, ed., *Dear Dr Stopes*, pp. 15–16.
95. 'Much depends on what kind of husband the wife has. ... A woman cannot possibly get on if she has a worrying husband. I think that makes a lot of difference': Davies, ed., *Maternity*, p. 171. See also pp. 27, 48, 66, 99, 99–100; and Stopes, ed., *Mother England*, pp. 148, 158.
96. Stopes, ed., *Mother England*, pp. 41, 53, 59, 120, 161; Blom, *Barnebegrensning-synd eller sunn fornuft*, p. 150.
97. Stopes, ed., *Mother England*, pp. 70, 85, 139, 161, 163, 164.
98. Charles, *The Practice of Birth Control* (London, 1932), p. 26.
99. Stopes, ed., *Mother England*, p. 11.
100. *A Woman's Place*, p. 84. Jane Lewis finds 'copious evidence ... of women who felt no sexual pleasure because of fear of pregnancy, and there is some indication that working-class women may have internalized middle-class ideas of passionlessness and its correlate: male sensuality': *Women in England*, p. 16. Patricia Branca asserts that 'there is no sign of sexual pleasure in [working-class] marriage': *Women in Europe since 1750* (London, 1978), p. 139.
101. Stopes, ed., *Mother England*, pp. 2, 21–2, 40, 58, 70, 105, 114–15, 151, 161, 165, 168, 176.
102. Ibid., pp. 114–15, 4, 53, 61, 156, 136.
103. Since Marie Stopes was widely renowned for her manual *Married Love* (which sold out six printings in its first year of publication), it seems likely that women writing to her were biased towards those who found pleasure in conjugal sex. Even so, the correspondence indicates that at least a substantial minority of working-class women did enjoy sex with their husbands. The picture Roberts presents of universal dislike strikes me as unrepresentative.
104. Stopes, ed., *Mother England*, p. 40.
105. Roberts, *A Woman's Place*, p. 88.
106. Davies, *Maternity*, pp. 48–9.
107. Ibid., p. 43; Neuman, 'Working-Class Birth Control in Wilhelmine Germany', p. 423.
108. Stopes, ed., *Mother England*, p. 60; Eleanor Barton of the Woman's Co-operative Guild held the same view: Lewis, *Women in England*, p. 16.
109. Women vouch for the willingness of their husbands to co-operate through abstinence or withdrawal on the following pages of *Mother England*: 4, 17, 19, 20, 41, 54, 65, 68, 70, 84, 91, 112, 114, 117, 124, 125, 130, 132, 135, 141, 144, 147, 153, 159, 177. Men declare their willingness to co-operate on pages 14, 22, 31, 42–3, 47, 58, 74, 161. Since men would not have been writing to Stopes if they were not keenly interested in avoiding conception, these male respondents must reflect the more co-operative end of the spectrum. I am not inclined to infer a similar bias in the husbands of women respondents, since there were compelling reasons for wives who wished to limit, but whose husbands were indifferent or hostile to this objective, to write Stopes for information about female contraceptives. However, there are a great many letters from women who describe themselves as being at risk of conception without ever mentioning their husbands. It is impossible to tell whether these women: (a) were being taken against their will (i.e., raped); (b) felt that it was wrong to refuse to do their 'wifely duty'; or (c) had themselves sufficiently intense sex drives to rule out abstinence or withdrawal as options. If we add some of these respondents in as inferred cases of male uncooperativeness, the correspondence as a whole would be more nearly balanced.
110. Stopes, ed., *Mother England*, pp. 20, 91.
111. McLaren, *Sexuality and Social Order*, p. 133.
112. Stopes, ed., *Mother England*, p. 121.
113. Ibid., p. 72; Neuman, 'Working-Class Birth Control in Wilhelmine Germany', pp. 421–4.

114. Stopes, ed., *Mother England*, p. 72.

115. Hall, ed., *Dear Dr Stopes*, p. 15.

116. *The Disinherited Family*, p. 197.

117. In the Lewis-Faning survey, 49 per cent of skilled labourers' wives and 67 per cent of the unskilled answered in this fashion: 'Report on an Enquiry into Family Limitation', p. 178. In Polano's Würzburg survey, economic constraints were cited by 45 per cent of all respondents: Neuman, 'Working-Class Birth Control in Wilhelmine Germany', p. 424. A full citation of the references in Stopes's *Mother England* would be so copious as to include almost every page. The following exemplify the range of issues involved in the respondents' concern to halt childbearing in order to make ends meet: pp. 8–9, 39, 48, 91, 92, 110, 132. Male unemployment was frequently mentioned: pp. 12, 14, 23, 28, 41, 79, 88, 92, 103, 118, 124, 159, 166.

118. Stopes, ed., *Mother England*, pp. 14, 17. See also pp. 57, 59, 66, 93, 103, 173; Neuman, 'Working-Class Birth Control in Wilhelmine Germany', pp. 424–6.

119. Stopes, ed., *Mother England*, pp. 13, 89, 99; Neuman, 'Working-Class Birth Control in Wilhelmine Germany', 425.

120. Stopes, ed., *Mother England*, pp. 4, 21, 23, 33, 41, 52, 79, 104, 105, 168; Hall, ed., *Dear Dr Stopes*, p. 25.

121. Neuman, 'Working-Class Birth Control in Wilhelmine Germany', p. 424.

122. A complete citation on this point would again be too lengthy. Readers will need to scan only a few pages in *Mother England* to be impressed by the pervasive concern with women's health in pregnancy and throughout the breastfeeding period. The following provide a typical cross-section: pp. 8, 26, 34, 36, 38, 45, 78, 92–3, 102, 136–7.

123. Ibid., p. 123.

124. Ibid., pp. 44, 75, 79, 86, 131, 153.

125. The fear of childbirth complications in curtailing women's 'demand for children' is underestimated by demographers. In most models of fertility behaviour, the perceived cost of another pregnancy is never explicitly registered, but is implicitly assumed to detract from the desire for additional children. In reality, a woman or couple may genuinely wish for more children but be unwilling to undergo the anticipated perils of further childbirth, and thus call a halt before achieving their desired family size.

126. Blom, *Barnebegrensning-synd eller sunn fornuft*.

127. Stopes, ed., *Mother England*, pp. 14, 42.

128. Ansley Coale, 'The Decline of Fertility in Europe since the Eighteenth Century', in Coale and Watkins, eds, *The Decline of Fertility in Europe* (Princeton, N.J., 1986), p. 29; Knodel, 'Family Limitation and the Fertility Transition', p. 220.

129. Lewis-Faning, 'Report on an Enquiry into Family Limitation', p. 149. Middle-class women were only moderately in advance of proletarians on this score: 22 per cent planned in the 1910–24 cohorts. This raises strong doubts that family size was a prominent motive for stopping among urban professional couples who began limiting childbearing in the second half of the nineteenth century.

130. Neuman, 'Working-Class Birth Control in Wilhelmine Germany', p. 425.

131. Kelly, *The German Worker*, p. 32.

132. Brookes, 'Women and Reproduction',p. 156–63.

133. N. F. R. Crafts, 'A Time Series Study of Fertility in England and Wales, 1877–1938', *Journal of European Economic History*, vol. 13 (1984); David Levine, *Reproducing Families: The Political Economy of English Population History* (Cambridge, 1987), pp. 160–76.

134. Louise Tilly, 'Coping with Company Paternalism: Family Strategies of Coal Miners in Nineteenth-Century France', *Theory and Society*, vol. 14, no. 4 (1985), p. 404.

135. David Rubinstein, *School Attendance in London, 1870–1904* (New York, 1969), p. 61.

136. Neuman, 'Working-Class Birth Control in Wilhelmine Germany', pp. 424–6.

137. John Caldwell, 'Mass Education as a Determinant of the Timing of Fertility Decline', *Population and Development Review*, vol. 6, no. 2 (1980), pp. 225–55.

138. Ross, 'Survival Networks', p. 20.

139. Neuman, 'Working-Class Birth Control in Wilhelmine Germany', pp. 425–6.

140. *The Decline of the Birth-Rate*, Fabian Tract no. 131 (London, 1907), pp. 6–7.

141. *Report on the English Birth Rate*, pp. 43, 50, 62.

142. Davies, ed., *Maternity*, pp. 33, 39.

143. Roberts, *A Woman's Place*, pp. 87–8.

144. Neuman, 'Working-Class Birth Control in Wilhelmine Germany', p. 423.

145. Davies, ed., *Maternity*, pp. 50, 64, 70, 72, 116, 118, 156.

146. Ibid., p. 44.

147. Coale, 'The Demographic Transition Reconsidered', *International Population Conference, Liège 1973*, vol. 1 (Liège, 1973).

148. A. S. Wohl, *Endangered Lives: Public Health in Victorian Britain* (London, 1983), p. 14.

149. The routine hospitalization of births was a later development. In 1927, 15 per cent of all births in Britain occurred in hospitals; by 1946, 54 per cent did: Jane Lewis, *The Politics of Motherhood* (London, 1980), p. 120.

150. Lewis, *Women in England*, pp. 36–7. See also Jane Lewis, 'The Working-Class Wife and Mother and State Intervention, 1870–1918', in Lewis, ed., *Labour and Love*, p. 101.

151. Feminists have undertaken a vigorous critique of the takeover of birthing by male doctors, the competitive displacement and professional denigration of midwives in the process, the subsequent hospitalization of routine births, and the conversion of pregnancy from a natural condition into a pathology routinely requiring high-powered medical intervention. This expropriation was, on balance, a significant defeat for women's reproductive autonomy. But important gains were made in the same transition – a sharp decline in infant death and a subsequent fall in maternal injury and mortality – which must account for women's acceptance of the change. In retrospect, one can see that the advances could have been made in the same period without the male takeover of the birth process, with all its oppressive consequences. But the mixed nature of the changeover needs to be squarely confronted in the form in which it occurred. It is facile either to denounce the conversion *tout court*, as radical feminists are inclined to do, or to celebrate it, as Shorter has done, attributing its blessings to the presence of doctors, women's true allies: *A History of Women's Bodies* (New York, 1982).

152. Stopes, ed., *Mother England*, pp. 24, 40, 56, 76, 78, 84, 92, 96, 98, 101–2, 113, 115–16, 160, 163, 167; Hall, ed., *Dear Dr Stopes*, p. 30.

153. Davies, ed., *Maternity*, pp. 64, 70, 72.

154. Stopes, ed., *Mother England*, pp. 57, 17, 31, 46, 65, 108, 171.

155. Bland, 'Marriage Laid Bare'. The Christian condemnation of all who sought 'to cheat nature' by dissociating sex from procreation included women who 'selfishly' refused to have intercourse with their husbands in order to avoid repeated pregnancies: Etienne van de Walle, 'Motivations and Technology in the Decline of French Fertility', in R. Wheaton and T. Hareven, eds, *Family and Sexuality in French History* (Philadelphia, 1980), pp. 140–43. But even theologians, lending moral sanction to the husband's prerogative of sexual access, sought exemption for women under special circumstances: 'To those who in their pregnancy suffer extreme pains and ailments ... God never intended to obligate women ... for that would truly be an oppression. ... This is therefore far removed from the fantasy and frenzy of those sensual men who desire that without exception or demur their wives should be obliged to ... submit to their sexual passions. No, this is an error, an act of impiety and a tyrannical abuse': Jean-Louis Flandrin, *Families in Former Times* (New York, 1979), p. 218.

156. *On the Subjection of Women* (London, 1929 [1869]), p. 59.

157. Lee Holcombe, *Wives and Property: Reform of the Married Women's Property Law in Nineteenth-Century England* (Toronto, 1983); Ira Minor, 'Working-Class Women and Matrimonial Law Reform, 1890–1914', in D. E. Martin and D. Rubinstein, eds, *Ideology and the Labour Movement* (London, 1979).

158. Davies, ed., *Maternity*, p. 68.

159. Ibid., pp. 27–8.

160. Stopes, ed., *Mother England*, p. 106.

161. Hall, ed., *Dear Dr Stopes*, p. 18.

162. Ibid., pp. 16, 22; Stopes, ed., *Mother England*, pp. 111, 120, 61.

163. Davies, ed., *Maternity*, p. 90.

164. Stopes, ed., *Mother England*, pp. 25, 64, 72, 73, 89, 92, 93, 102, 106, 110, 118, 120, 130, 142, 167, 168.

165. Davies, ed., *Maternity*, pp. 62, 46.

166. *Report on the English Birth-Rate*, p. 61.

167. 'Conclusions', in Ansley Coale and Susan Watkins, eds, *The Decline of Fertility in Europe* (Princeton, N.J., 1986), p. 440.

168. John Caldwell, *Theory of Fertility Decline* (New York, 1982); Ron Lesthaeghe and Chris Wilson, 'Modes of Production, Secularization, and the Pace of the Fertility Decline in Western Europe, 1870–1930', in Ansley Coale and Susan Watkins, eds, *The Decline of Fertility in Europe* (Princeton, N.J., 1986).

169. Chicago, 1985. I find their supply-demand terminology problematic, for reasons I shall explain further on, but use it here to present the paradigm in the terms in which its authors (and indeed most demographers) would discuss it.

170. *The Fertility Revolution*, p. 10.

171. Judith Blake and Prithwis Das Gupta, 'Reproductive Motivation Versus Contraceptive Technology: Is Recent American Experience an Exception?' *Population and Development Review*, vol. 1 (1975), pp. 229–49.

172. John Cleland and Christopher Wilson, 'Demand Theories of the Fertility Transition: An Iconoclastic View', *Population Studies*, vol. 41 (1987), pp. 5–30.

173. Preoccupied as he was with sex, not demography, Freud none the less saw the connection between them: 'What is the use of reducing infant mortality [he wondered in *Civilization and Its Discontents*] when it is precisely that reduction which imposes the greatest restraint on us in the begetting of children. ... [We] have created difficult conditions for our sexual life in marriage' (New York, 1961), p. 35.

174. *Theory of Fertility Decline* (New York, 1982).

175. John Knodel and Etienne van de Walle, 'Lessons from the Past: Policy Implications of Historical Fertility Studies', in Ansley Coale and Susan Watkins, eds, *The Decline of Fertility in Europe*.

176. Ibid., pp. 404–7.

177. Gosta Carlsson, 'The Decline of Fertility: Innovation or Adjustment Process?', *Population Studies*, vol. 20 (1966), pp. 149–74.

178. Allan Sharlin, 'Urban–Rural Differences in Fertility in Europe during the Demographic Transition', in Ansley Coale and Susan Watkins, eds, *The Decline of Fertility in Europe*, p. 257.

179. 'The Sociology of Human Fertility: A Trend Report and Bibiography', *Current Sociology/La Sociologie contemporaine*, vols 10–11 (1981), pp. 35–119.

180. Samuel Preston, ed., *The Effects of Infant and Child Mortality on Fertility* (New York, 1978); Francine van de Walle, 'Infant Mortality and the European Demographic Transition' in Coale and Watkins, eds, *The Decline of Fertility in Europe*.

181. Poul Matthiessan and James McCann, 'The Effects of Infant and Child Mortality on Fertility', in Samuel Preston, ed., *The Effects of Infant and Child Mortality on Fertility* (New York, 1978).

182. Stopes, ed., *Mother England*, pp. 144–5.

183. Karen Mason and Anju Taj, 'Differences between Women's and Men's Reproductive Goals in Developing Countries', *Population and Development Review*, vol. 13 (1987), pp. 611–38.

184. Nancy Folbre has cogently argued this position. Her work has been extremely important in the development of my own thinking on the fertility transition. See 'Of Patriarchy Born: The Political Economy of Fertility Decisions', *Feminist Studies*, vol. 9 (1983), pp. 261–84; and 'Cleaning House: New Perspectives on Households and Economic Development', *Journal of Development Economics*, vol. 22 (1986), pp. 5–40.

Chapter 6

1. Ronald Fletcher, *The Shaking of the Foundations: Family and Society,* (London, 1988), pp. 49–50; J. E. Goldthorpe, *Family Life in Western Societies* (Cambridge, 1987), p. 43.

2. Goldthorpe, *Family Life in Western Societies,* p. 137.

3. John Gillis, *For Better, For Worse: British Marriages, 1600 to the Present* (New York, 1985), p. 307; *Time,* 2 Dec. 1985; *The Guardian,* 29 June 1989.

4. Goldthorpe, *Family Life in Western Societies,* p. 229.

5. Renate Bridenthal, 'The Family: The View from a Room of Her Own', in Barrie Thorne, ed., *Rethinking the Family: Some Feminist Questions* (New York, 1982), p. 225.

6. *The Shaking of the Foundations: Family and Society* (London, 1988), p. 203.

7. In a study of steelworker families in Hamilton, Ontario (conducted by June Corman, David Livingstone, Meg Luxton, and the author) 91 per cent of male steelworkers and 85 per cent of their female partners agreed that the nuclear family was 'the best possible arrangement for raising children [and] one area of the present social order we should preserve'.

8. Peter Laslett, ed., *Household and Family in Past Time* (Cambridge, 1972)

9. Substantive objections to the continuity thesis were discussed in some detail in *A Millennium of Family Change,* and are summarized in its concluding chapter. They will not be repeated here.

10. See, for example, the work of Brigitte Berger and Peter Berger: *The War over the Family: Capturing the Middle Ground* (New York, 1984), p. 87; and Ronald Fletcher, *The Abolitionists: The Family and Marriage under Attack* (London, 1988), pp. 19–21. The fact that the Group's interpretation of the past is used to bolster what I regard as a pernicious view of the present situation has no direct bearing on the veracity of the historical arguments under dispute.

11. The door was initially set ajar by Laslett who, in his introduction to *Household and Family in Past Time,* mooted what he termed a null hypothesis: that historians ought to assume that simple household groups predominated in the past in lieu of strong evidence to the contrary. He has recently acknowledged that this notion was an expository disaster, although he blames the statistical illiteracy of his readers for their failure to understand what he meant: 'The Character of Familial History, Its Limitations and the Conditions for Its Proper Pursuit', in Tamara Hareven and Andrejs Plakans, eds, *Family History at the Crossroads* (Princeton, N.J., 1987), p. 278.

12. Ronald Fletcher, *The Abolitionists,* p. 193.

13. Ralph Linton, 'The Natural History of the Family', in Ruth N. Anshen, ed., *The Family: Its Function and Destiny* (New York, 1949). Significantly, Fletcher cites this passage on the opening page of *The Shaking of the Foundations.*

14. Jane Collier, Michelle Rosaldo and Sylvia Yanagisako, 'Is There a Family? New Anthropological Views', in Thorne, ed., *Rethinking the Family: Some Feminist Questions.*

15. 'The Character of Familial History, Its Limitations and the Conditions for Its Proper Pursuit', in Hareven and Plakans, eds, *Family History at the Crossroads* p. 264.

16. Fletcher exemplifies this reasoning in *The Shaking of the Foundations* and *The Abolitionists.*

17. Jane Collier, Michelle Rosaldo and Sylvia Yanagisako, 'Is There a Family? New Anthropological Views', in Thorne, ed., *Rethinking the Family,* pp.34–5.

18. Carl Degler, *At Odds: Women and the Family in America from the Revolution to the Present* (New York, 1980), p. 72. The synopsis of this paragraph draws on Degler's survey, especially Chapter 4. The objections of late-Victorian feminists to women's domestic relegation and to the sharp segmentation of public and private spheres is also discussed in Carol Dyhouse's superb study, *Feminism and the Family in England, 1880–1939* (Oxford, 1989). On the making of the bourgeois family in the first half of the nineteenth century, see the magisterial reconstruction of Leonore Davidoff and Catherine Hall, *Family Fortunes: Men and Women of the English Middle Class, 1780–1850* (London, 1987), and in the Scandinavian context, Jonas Frykman and Ovar Löfgren, *Culture Builders: A Historical Anthropology of*

Middle-Class Life (New Brunswick, N.J., 1987).

19. Michael Anderson, 'The Emergence of the Modern Life Cycle in Britain', *Social History*, vol. 10 (1985), pp. 69–87; Theodore Hershberg, ed., *Philadelphia: Work, Space, Family and Group Experience in the Nineteenth Century* (New York).

20. Goldthorpe, *Family Life in Western Societies*, p. 42.

21. E. J. Hobsbawm, *The Age of Empire: 1875–1914* (London, 1987), p. 3.

22. Richard P. Saller and Brent D. Shaw, 'Tombstones and Roman Family Relations in the Principate: Civilians, Soldiers and Slaves', *Journal of Roman Studies*, vol. 74 (1984), pp. 124–56.

23. Peter Laslett, *Family Life and Illicit Love in Earlier Generations* (Cambridge, 1977), pp. 58, 184.

24. John Gillis, *For Better, For Worse: British Marriages, 1600 to the Present* (New York, 1985), p. 307.

25. David Brion Davis, 'The Rebel', *New York Review of Books*, vol. 37, no. 8 (1990), p. 33.

26. Fletcher agrees: 'The liberation of women and their progress towards equality has been, without doubt, the most marked feature in changing the nature of marriage, the family, the household, the domestic group, and the having and caring for children': *The Shaking of the Foundations: Family and Society*, p. 149.

27. This is the title of Carl Degler's analysis of women's long-standing conflict with established family norms in the United States: *At Odds: Women and the Family in America from the Revolution to the Present* (New York, 1950). He concludes: 'After two hundred years of development, both the future of the family and the fulfillment of women as persons are at odds as never before' (p. 473).

28. *The War over the Family*, p. 120.

29. *At Odds*, p. 471.

Bibliography

Abbott, E. *Women in Industry: A Study in American Economic History*. New York: Arno Press, 1969 [1910].

Abelson, A. 'Inheritance and Population Control in a Basque Valley before 1900'. *Peasant Studies*, vol. 7, no. 1, 1978, pp. 11–27.

Acker, J. 'Class, Gender, and the Relations of Distribution'. *Signs*, vol. 13, no. 3, 1988, pp. 473–97.

Alexander, S. 'Women's Work in Nineteenth-Century London: A Study of the Years 1820–50'. In J. Mitchell and A. Oakley, eds, *The Rights and Wrongs of Women*. Harmondsworth: Penguin, 1976.

Alexander, S., Davin, A. and Hostettler, E. 'Labouring Women: A Reply to Eric Hobsbawm'. *History Workshop Journal*, no. 8, 1979, pp. 174–82.

Alter, G. *Family and the Female Life Course: The Women of Verviers, Belgium, 1849–1880*. Madison, Wis.: University of Wisconsin Press, 1988.

Althusser, L. and Balibar, E. *Reading Capital*. London: New Left Books, 1970.

Aminzade, R. 'Reinterpreting Capitalist Industrialization: A Study of Nineteenth-Century France'. In S. L. Kaplan and C. J. Koepp, eds, *Work in France: Representations, Meanings, Organization and Practice*. Ithaca, N.Y.: Cornell University Press, 1986.

Anderson, M. *Family Structure in Nineteenth-Century Lancashire*. Cambridge: Cambridge University Press, 1971.

———. 'Household Structure and the Industrial Revolution: Mid-Nineteenth Century Preston in Comparative Perspective'. In P. Laslett, ed., *Household and Family in Past Time*. Cambridge: Cambridge University Press, 1972.

———. 'Marriage Patterns in Victorian Britain'. *Journal of Family History*, vol. 1, no. 1, 1976, pp. 55–78.

———. 'Sociological History and the Working-Class Family: Smelser Revisited'. *Social History*, vol. 3, 1976, pp. 317–34.

———. 'The Emergence of the Modern Life Cycle in Britain'. *Social History*, vol. 10, no. 1, 1985, pp. 69–85.

Andorka, R. *Determinants of Fertility in Advanced Societies*. London: Methuen, 1978.

Ankarloo, B. 'Marriage and Family Formation in Transition'. In T. K. Hareven, ed., *The Family and the Life Course in Historical Perspective*. New York: Academic Press, 1978.

Armstrong, W. A. 'A Note on the Household Structure of Mid–Nineteenth Century York in Comparative Perspective'. In P. Laslett, ed., *Household and Family in Past Time*. Cambridge: Cambridge University Press, 1972.

Ayers, P. and Lambertz, J. 'Marriage Relations, Money and Domestic Violence in Working-Class Liverpool, 1919–39'. In J. Lewis, ed., *Labour and Love: Women's Experience of Home and Family, 1850–1940*. Oxford: Basil Blackwell, 1986.

Bairoch, P. 'Agriculture and the Industrial Revolution: 1700–1914'. In C. M. Cipolla, ed., *The Fontana Economic History of Europe*, vol. 3. London: Fontana, 1974.

Banks, J. A. *Victorian Values: Secularism and the Size of Families*. London: Routledge & Kegan Paul, 1981.

Barrett, M. *Women's Oppression Today*. London: Verso, 1980.

Barrett, M. and McIntosh, M. 'The "Family Wage": Some Problems for Socialists and

Feminists'. *Capital & Class*, vol. 11, 1980, pp. 51–72.

———. *The Anti-social Family*. London: Verso, 1982.

Beechey, V. 'Some Notes on Female Wage Labour in Capitalist Production'. *Capital & Class*, vol. 3, 1977, pp. 45–67.

Bell, L. *At the Works: A Study of a Manufacturing Town*. London: Virago, 1985 [1907].

Belmont, N. 'The Symbolic Function of the Wedding Procession in the Popular Rituals of Marriage'. In R. Forster and O. Ranum, eds, *Ritual, Religion and the Sacred*. Baltimore: Johns Hopkins University Press, 1982.

Benson, J. *British Coalminers in the Nineteenth Century: A Social History*. Dublin: Gill & Macmillan, 1980.

Berg, M. *The Age of Manufactures: Industry, Innovation and Work in Britain, 1700–1820*. London: Fontana, 1985.

Berger, B. and Berger, P. *The War over the Family: Capturing the Middle Ground*. New York: Anchor Doubleday, 1984.

Bergier, J. F. 'The Industrial Bourgeoisie and the Rise of the Working Class 1700–1914'. In C. M. Cipolla, ed., *The Fontana Economic History of Europe*, vol. 3. London: Fontana, 1973.

Berlanstein, L. 'Illegitimacy, Concubinage and Proletarianization in a French Town, 1760–1914'. *Journal of Family History*, vol. 5, no. 3, 1980, pp. 360–74.

———. *The Working People of Paris, 1871–1914*. Baltimore: Johns Hopkins University Press, 1984.

Berman, H. J. *Law and Revolution: The Formation of the Western Legal Tradition*. Cambridge, Mass.: Harvard University Press, 1983.

Bienefeld, M. A. *Working Hours in British Industry: An Economic History*. London: Weidenfeld & Nicolson, 1972.

Birdsall, N. 'Fertility and Economic Change in Eighteenth- and Nineteenth-Century Europe: A Comment'. *Population and Development Review*, vol. 9, no. 1, 1983, pp. 111–23.

Black, C., ed. *Married Women's Work*. London: Virago, 1983 [1915].

Blake, J. and Das Gupta, P. 'Reproductive Motivation Versus Contraceptive Technology: Is Recent American Experience an Exception?' *Population and Development Review*, vol. 1, no. 2, 1975, pp. 229–49.

Bland, L. 'Marriage Laid Bare: Middle-Class Women and Marital Sex, c.1880–1914'. In J. Lewis, ed., *Labour and Love: Women's Experience of Home and Family, 1850–1940*. Oxford: Basil Blackwell, 1986.

Blom, I. *Barnebegrensning-synd eller sunn fornuft*. Bergen: Universitetsforlaget, 1980.

Booth, C. *Life and Labour of the People in London*. London: Macmillan, 1902.

Bornat, J. 'Lost Leaders: Women, Trade Unionism and the Case of the General Union of Textile Workers, 1875–1914'. In A. V. John, ed., *Unequal Opportunities: Women's Employment in England, 1800–1918*. Oxford: Basil Blackwell, 1986.

Bosanquet, H. *The Family*. London: Macmillan, 1906.

Boston, S. *Women Workers and the Trade-Union Movement*. London: Davis-Poynter, 1980.

Bourgeois-Pichat, J. 'Social and Biological Determinants of Human Fertility in Non-industrial Societies'. *Proceedings of the American Philosophical Society*, vol. 3, no. 3, 1967, pp. 160–63.

Bradley, B. P. and Mendels, F. F. 'Can the Hypothesis of a Nuclear Family Organization Be Tested Statistically?' *Population Studies*, vol. 2, no. 2, 1978, pp. 381–94.

Branca, P. 'A New Perspective on Women's Work: A Comparative Typology'. *Journal of Social History*, vol. 9, 1975, pp. 129–53.

———. *Women in Europe since 1750*. London: Croom Helm, 1978.

Braverman, H. *Labour and Monopoly Capital: The Degradation of Work in the Twentieth Century*. New York: Monthly Review Press, 1974.

Brenner, J. and Ramas, M. 'Rethinking Women's Oppression'. *New Left Review*, no. 144, 1984, pp. 33–71.

Bridenthal. R. 'The Family: The View from a Room of Her Own'. In B. Thorne, ed., *Rethinking the Family: Some Feminist Questions*. New York: Longman, 1982.

Brookes, B. 'Women and Reproduction, 1860–1939'. In J. Lewis, ed., *Labour and Love: Women's Experience of Home and Family, 1850–1940*. Oxford: Basil Blackwell, 1986.

Brown, E. H. P. and Browne, M. *A Century of Pay*. New York: St Martin's Press, 1968.

Brown, J. 'Public Health Crises and Public Response: The Role of Investments in Sanitary Infrastructure in German Cities, 1871–1910'. Unpublished MS, 1988.

Brüggemeier, F. J. and Niethammer, L. 'Lodgers, Schnapps-Casinos and Working-Class Colonies in a Heavy-Industrial Region'. In Georg Iggers, ed., *The Social History of Politics*. Leamington Spa: Berg, 1985.

Bry, G. *Wages in Germany, 1871–1945*. Princeton, N.J.: Princeton University Press, 1960.

Bullock, N. and Read, J. *The Movement for Housing Reform in Germany and France, 1840–1914*. Cambridge: Cambridge University Press, 1985.

Burke G. 'The Decline of the Independent Bal Maiden: The Impact of Change in the Cornish Mining Industry'. In A. V. John, ed., *Unequal Opportunities: Women's Employment in England, 1800–1918*. Oxford: Basil Blackwell, 1986.

Burnett, J. *A Social History of Housing, 1815–1970*. Vancouver: David & Charles, 1978.

———, ed. *Destiny Obscure: Autobiographies of Childhood, Education and Family from the 1820s to the 1920s*. Harmondsworth: Penguin, 1982.

Butt, J. 'Working-Class Housing in Glasgow, 1851–1914'. In S. D. Chapman, ed., *The History of Working-Class Housing*. Newton Abbot: David & Charles, 1971.

Bythell, D. *The Handloom Weavers*. Cambridge: Cambridge University Press, 1969.

———. *The Sweated Trades: Outwork in Nineteenth-Century Britain*. London: Batsford, 1978.

Caldwell, J. 'Mass Education as a Determinant of the Timing of Fertility Decline'. *Population and Development Review*, vol. 6, no. 2, 1980, pp. 225–55.

———. *Theory of Fertility Decline*. New York: Academic Press, 1982.

Cameron, R. 'A New View of European Industrializaton'. *Economic History Review*, 2nd ser., vol. 38, no. 1, 1985, pp. 1–23.

Camp, W. D. *Marriage and the Family in France since the Revolution*. New York: Bookman, 1961.

Carlsson, G. 'The Decline of Fertility: Innovation or Adjustment Process?'. *Population Studies*, vol. 20, no. 2, 1966, pp. 149–74.

Carré, J. J., Dubois, P. and Malinvaud, E. *French Economic Growth* (transl.). Stanford, Calif.: Stanford University Press, 1975.

Chapman, S. D., ed. *The History of Working-Class Housing*. Newton Abbot: David & Charles, 1971.

Charles, E. *The Practice of Birth Control: An Analysis of the Birth-Control Experiences of Nine Hundred Women*. London: Williams & Norgate, 1932.

Chevalier, L. *Laboring Classes and Dangerous Classes in Paris during the First Half of the Nineteenth Century*. Princeton, N.J.: Princeton University Press, 1973.

Clark, A. *Working Life of Women in the Seventeenth Century*. London: Routledge & Kegan Paul, 1968 [1919].

Cleland, J. and Wilson, C. 'Demand Theories of the Fertility Transition: An Iconoclastic View'. *Population Studies*, vol. 41, 1987, pp. 5–30.

Coale, A. J. 'The Demographic Transition Reconsidered'. In *International Population Conference, Liège 1973*, vol. 1. Liège: International Union for the Scientific Study of Population, 1973.

———. 'The Decline of Fertility in Europe since the Eighteenth Century as a Chapter in Human Demographic History'. In A. J. Coale and S. C. Watkins, eds, *The Decline of Fertility in Europe*. Princeton, N.J.: Princeton University Press, 1986.

Coale, A. J., Anderson, B. and Harm, E. *Human Fertility in Russia since the Nineteenth Century*. Princeton, N.J.: Princeton University Press, 1979.

Coale, A. J. and Watkins, S. C., eds. *The Decline of Fertility in Europe*. Princeton, N.J.: Princeton University Press, 1986.

Coale, A. J. and Treadway, R. 'A Summary of the Changing Distribution of Overall Fertility,

Marital Fertility, and the Proportion Married in the Provinces of Europe'. In A. J. Coale and S. C. Watkins, eds, *The Decline of Fertility in Europe*. Princeton, N.J.: Princeton University Press, 1986.

Coleman, W. *Death Is a Social Disease*. Madison, Wis.: University of Wisconsin Press, 1982.

Collier, F. *The Family Economy of the Working Classes in the Cotton Industry, 1784–1833*. Manchester: Manchester University Press, 1965.

Collier, J., Rosaldo, M. and Tanagisako, S. 'Is There a Family? New Anthropological Views'. In B. Thorne, ed., *Rethinking the Family: Some Feminist Questions*. New York: Longman, 1982.

Cottereau, A. 'The Distinctiveness of Working-Class Cultures in France, 1848–1900'. In I. Katznelson and A. Zolberg, eds, *Working-Class Formation: Nineteenth-Century Patterns in Western Europe and the United States*. Princeton, N.J.: Princeton University Press, 1986.

Cowan, R. S. *More Work for Mother: The Ironies of Household Technology from the Open Hearth to the Microwave*. New York: Basic Books, 1983.

Crafts, N. F. R. 'British Economic Growth, 1700–1831: A Review of the Evidence'. *Economic History Review*, 2nd ser., vol. 36, 1983, pp. 177–99.

———. 'A Time Series Study of Fertility in England and Wales, 1877–1938'. *Journal of European Economic History*, vol. 13, 1984, pp. 571–90.

———. *British Economic Growth during the Industrial Revolution*. Oxford: Clarendon Press, 1985.

Creighton, C. 'Family, Property and Relations of Production in Western Europe'. *Economy and Society*, vol. 9, no. 2, 1980, pp. 129–67.

Crew, D. *Town in the Ruhr*. New York: Columbia University Press, 1979.

Crossick, G. *An Artisan Elite in Victorian Society: Kentish London, 1840–1880*. London: Croom Helm, 1978.

Dasey, R. 'Women's Work and the Family: Women Garment Workers in Berlin and Hamburg before the First World War'. In R. Evans and W. Lee, eds, *The German Family*. London: Croom Helm, 1981.

Daunton, M. J. *House and Home in the Victorian City: Working-Class Housing, 1850–1914*. London: Edward Arnold, 1983.

Davidoff, L. 'The Separation of Home and Work? Landladies and Lodgers in Nineteenth- and Twentieth-Century England'. In S. Burman, ed., *Fit Work for Women*. New York: St Martin's Press, 1979.

Davidoff, L. and Hall, C. *Family Fortunes: Men and Women of the English Middle Class, 1780–1850*. London: Hutchinson, 1987.

Davidson, C. *A Woman's Work Is Never Done: A History of Housework in the British Isles, 1650–1950*. London: Chatto & Windus, 1986.

Davies, M. L., ed. *Maternity: Letters from Working Women*. London: Virago, 1978 [1915].

Davin, A. 'Imperialism and Motherhood'. *History Workshop Journal*, no. 5, 1978, pp. 9–65.

———. 'Child Labour, the Working-Class Family and Domestic Ideology in Nineteenth-Century Britain'. *Development and Change*, vol. 13, 1982, pp. 633–52.

Davis, D. B. 'The Rebel'. *New York Review of Books*, vol. 37, no. 8, 1990, pp. 30–33.

Deane, P. *The First Industrial Revolution*, 2nd edn. Cambridge: Cambridge University Press, 1979.

Degler, C. *At Odds: Women and the Family in America from the Revolution to the Present*. New York: Oxford University Press, 1980.

Delphy, C. 'Continuities and Discontinuities in Marriage and Divorce'. In D. L. Barker and S. Allen, eds, *Sexual Divisions and Society: Process and Change*. London: Longman, 1976.

Demos, J. and Boocock, S. S., eds. *Turning Points: Historical and Sociological Essays on the Family*. Chicago: University of Chicago Press, 1978.

Dennis, N., Henriques, F. and Slaughter, C. *Coal Is Our Life*. London: Tavistock, 1956.

Dennis, R. *English Industrial Cities of the Nineteenth Century: A Social Geography*. Cambridge: Cambridge University Press, 1984.

Desai, A. *Real Wages in Germany*. Oxford: Oxford University Press, 1968.

De Vries, L. *European Urbanization, 1500–1800*. Cambridge, Mass.: Harvard University Press, 1984.

Dickinson, J. 'From Poor Law to Social Insurance: The Periodization of State Intervention in the Reproduction Process'. In J. Dickinson and B. Russell, eds, *Family, Economy and State*. London: Croom Helm, 1986.

Donnison, J. *Midwives and Medical Men: A History of Inter-professional Rivalries and Women's Rights*. London, Heinemann, 1977.

Dublin, T. *Women at Work: The Transformation of Work and Community in Lowell, Massachusetts, 1826–1860*. New York: Columbia University Press, 1979.

Dyhouse, C. *Feminism and the Family in England, 1880–1939*. Oxford: Basil Blackwell, 1989.

Easterlin, R. and Crimmins, E. *The Fertility Revolution: A Supply–Demand Analysis*. Chicago: University of Chicago Press, 1985.

Edwards, M. M. and Lloyd-Jones, R. 'N. J. Smelser and the Cotton Factory Family: A Reassessment'. In N. B. Harte and K. G. Ponting, eds, *Textile History and Economic History*. Manchester: Manchester University Press, 1973.

Ehmer, J. 'The Artisan Family in Nineteenth-Century Austria: Embourgeoisement of the Petite Bourgeoisie?' In G. Crossick and H. G. Haupt, eds, *Shopkeepers and Master Artisans in Nineteenth-Century Europe*. London: Methuen, 1984.

Ehrenreich, B. and English, D. *Witches, Nurses and Midwives: A History of Women Healers*. London: Writers & Readers, 1973.

Elderton, E. M. *Report on the English Birth Rate*. London: Cambridge University Press, 1914.

Engels, F. 'The Housing Question'. In K. Marx and F. Engels, *Selected Works*. Moscow: Progress Publishers, 1958.

————. *The Condition of the Working Class in England*. London: Panther, 1969.

Esperance, J. 'Doctors and Women in Nineteenth Century Society: Sexuality and Role'. In J. Woodward and D. Richards, eds, *Health Care and Popular Medicine in Nineteenth Century England*. London: Croom Helm, 1977.

Evans, R. J. 'Politics and the Family: Social Democracy and the Working-class Family in Theory and Practice before 1914'. In R. J. Evans and W. R. Lee, eds, *The German Family*. London: Croom Helm, 1981.

Fairchilds, C. 'Female Sexual Attitudes and the Rise of Illegitimacy'. *Journal of Interdisciplinary History*, vol. 8, 1978, pp. 627–67.

Flandrin, J. C. *Families in Former Times: Kinship, Household and Sexuality*. New York: Cambridge University Press, 1979.

Fletcher, R. *The Shaking of the Foundations: Family and Society*. London: Routledge, 1988.

————. *The Abolitionists: The Family and Marriage under Attack*. London: Routledge, 1988.

Flinn, M. W. *Scottish Population History*. Cambridge: Cambridge University Press, 1977.

Floud, R. 'Measuring the Transformation of the European Economies: Income, Health and Welfare'. Unpublished paper presented at the Conference on the Transformation of the European Economy, Bellagio, Italy, 1984.

Floud, R. and Wachter, K. 'Poverty and Physical Stature: Evidence on the Standard of Living of London Boys, 1770–1870'. *Social Science History*, vol. 6, no. 4, 1982, pp. 442–52.

Fogel, R. et al. 'Secular Changes in American and British Stature and Nutrition'. In R. I. Rotberg and T. K. Rabb, eds, *Hunger and History*. Cambridge: Cambridge University Press, 1983.

Folbre, N. 'Of Patriarchy Born: The Political Economy of Fertility Decisions'. *Feminist Studies*, vol. 9, no. 2, 1983, pp. 261–84.

————. 'Cleaning House: New Perspectives on Households and Economic Development'. *Journal of Development Economics*, vol. 22, 1986, pp. 5–40.

————. 'Hearts and Spades: Paradigms of Household Economics'. *World Development*, vol. 14, no. 2, 1986, pp. 245–55.

Foster, J. *Class Struggle and the Industrial Revolution*. London: Weidenfeld & Nicolson, 1974.

Fout, J. C. 'The Woman's Role in the German Working-Class Family in the 1890s'. In J.

C. Fout, ed., *German Women in the Nineteenth Century*. New York: Holmes & Meier, 1984.

Franzoi, B. 'Domestic Industry: Work Options and Women's Choices'. In J. C. Fout, ed., *German Women in the Nineteenth Century*. New York: Holmes & Meier, 1984.

———. *At the Very Least She Pays the Rent: Women and German Industrialization, 1971–1914*. Westport, Conn.: Greenwood, 1985.

Freedman, R. 'The Sociology of Human Fertility: A Trend Report and Bibliography'. *Current Sociology/La Sociologie contemporaine*, vol. 10/11, no. 2, 1981, pp. 35–119.

Freud, S. *Civilization and Its Discontents*. New York: W. W. Norton, 1961.

Freudenberger, H., Mattrer, F. and Nardinelli, C. 'A New Look at the Early Factory Labor Force'. *Journal of Economic History*, vol. 44, no. 4, 1984, pp. 1085–91.

Frevert, U. 'The Civilizing Tendency of Hygiene: Working-Class Women under Medical Control in Imperial Germany'. In J. C. Fout, ed., *German Women in the Nineteenth Century*. New York: Holmes & Meier, 1984.

———. 'Professional Medicine and the Working-Classes in Imperial Germany'. *Journal of Contemporary History*, vol. 20, 1985, pp. 637–58.

Frith, S. 'Socialization and Rational Schooling: Elementary Education in Leeds before 1870'. In P. McCann, ed., *Popular Education and Socialization in the Nineteenth Century*. London: Methuen, 1977.

Frykman J. and Löfgren, O. *Culture Builders: A Historical Anthropology of Middle-Class Life*. New Brunswick, N.J.: Rutgers University Press, 1987.

Furet, F. and Ozouf, J. *Reading and Writing: Literacy in France from Calvin to Jules Ferry*. Cambridge: Cambridge University Press, 1982.

Gardner, P. *The Lost Elementary Schools of Victorian England*. London: Croom Helm, 1984.

Gillis, J. *Youth and History: Tradition and Change in European Age Relations, 1770–Present*. New York, Academic Press: 1981.

———. 'Peasant, Plebeian and Proletarian Marriage in Britain, 1600–1900'. In D. Levine, ed. *Proletarianization and Family History*. New York, Oxford University Press: 1984.

———. *For Better, For Worse: British Marriages, 1600 to the Present*. New York: 1985.

Gittins, D. *Fair Sex: Family Size and Structure, 1900–39*. London: Hutchinson, 1982.

Glass, D. V. 'Some Indicators of Difference between Urban and Rural Mortality in England and Wales and Scotland'. *Population Studies*, vol. 17, 1964, pp. 263–7.

Glass, D. V. and Eversely, D. E. C., eds. *Population in History*. London: Edward Arnold, 1965.

Goldthorpe, J. E. *Family Life in Western Societies*. Cambridge: Cambridge University Press, 1987.

Gomersall, M. 'Ideals and Realities: The Education of Working-Class Girls, 1800–1870'. *History of Education*, vol. 17, no. 1, 1988, pp. 37–53.

Goode, W. J. *World Revolution and Family Patterns*. New York: Macmillan, 1963.

Gordon, M., ed. *The American Family in Social-Historical Perspective*, 2nd edn. New York: St Martin's Press, 1978.

Graff, H. J. *The Literacy Myth: Literacy and Social Structure in the Nineteenth-Century City*. New York: Academic Press, 1979.

Gray, R. 'The Languages of Factory Reform in Britain, c.1830–1860'. In P. Joyce, ed., *The Historical Meanings of Work*. Cambridge: Cambridge University Press, 1987.

Grew, R. and Harrigan, P. J. with Whitney, J. 'The Availability of Schooling in Nineteenth-Century France'. *Journal of Interdisciplinary History*, vol. 14, no. 1, 1983, pp. 25–63.

Haines, M. R. *Fertility and Occupation: Population Patterns in Industrialization*. New York: Academic Press, 1979.

———. 'Industrial Work and the Family Life Cycle, 1889–1890.' In P. Uselding, ed. *Research in Economic History*, vol. 4. Greenwich, Conn.: Jai Press, 1979.

———. 'Inequality and Childhood Mortality: A Comparison of England and Wales in 1911 and the U.S. in 1900'. *Journal of Economic History*, vol. 45, 1985, pp. 885–912.

Hannigan, M. P. 'Agriculture and Industry in the Nineteenth Century Stephanois: Household Employment Patterns and the Rise of a Permanent Proletariat'. In M. Hannigan and C.

Stephenson, eds, *Proletarians and Protest: The Roots of Class Formation in an Industrializing World*. New York: Greenwood Press, 1986.

———. 'Proletarian Families and Social Protest: Production and Reproduction as Issues of Social Conflict in Nineteenth-Century France'. In S. L. Kaplan and C. J. Koepp, eds, *Work in France: Representations: Meanings, Organization and Practice*. Ithaca, N.Y.: Cornell University Press, 1986.

Hareven, T. 'Family Time and Industrial Time: Family and Work in a Planned Corporation Town, 1900–1924'. In T. Hareven, ed., *Family and Kin in Urban Communities, 1700–1930*. New York: Franklin Watts, 1977.

———. *Family Time and Industrial Time*. Cambridge: Cambridge University Press, 1982.

Harrigan, P. J. *Mobility, Elites, and Education in French Society of the Second Empire*. Waterloo: Historical Reflections Press, 1980.

Harrison, J. F. C. *Early Victorian Britain, 1832–51*. London: Fontana, 1979 [1971].

———. *The Common People: A History from the Norman Conquest to the Present*. London: Fontana, 1984.

Harrison, R. and Mort, F. 'Patriarchal Aspects of Nineteenth-Century State Formation: Property Relations, Marriage and Divorce, and Sexuality'. In P. Corrigan, ed., *Capitalism, State Formation and Marxist Theory*. London: Quartet, 1980.

Hartman, H. 'The Unhappy Marriage of Marxism and Feminism: Towards a More Progressive Union'. In L. Sargent, ed., *Women and Revolution: A Discussion of the Unhappy Marriage of Marxism and Feminism*. London: Pluto, 1981.

Hassan, J. A. 'The Growth and Impact of the British Water Industry in the Nineteenth Century'. *Economic History Review*, 2nd ser., vol. 38, 1985, pp. 531–47.

Hausen, K. 'Family and Role-Division'. In R. J. Evans and W. R. Lee, eds, *The German Family*. London: Croom Helm, 1981.

Heckman, J., Hotz, J. and Walker, J. 'New Evidence on the Timing and Spacing of Births'. *American Economic Review*, vol. 75, no. 2, 1985, pp. 179–84.

Hershberg, Theodore. *Philadelphia: Work, Space, Family and Group Experience in the Nineteenth Century*. New York: Oxford University Press, 1981.

Hewitt, M. *Wives and Mothers in Victorian Industry*. London: Rockliff, 1958.

Heywood, C. *Childhood in Nineteenth-Century France*. Cambridge: Cambridge University Press, 1988.

Hilden, P. *Working Women and Socialist Policies in France, 1880–1914*. Oxford: Clarendon Press, 1986.

Hiley, M. *Victorian Working Women: Portraits from Life*. Boston: D. R. Godine, 1980.

Hobsbawm, E. J. *The Age of Revolution: 1789–1848*. New York: Mentor, 1962.

———. *Labouring Men: Studies in the History of Labour*. London: Weidenfeld & Nicolson, 1964.

———. *Industry and Empire*. Harmondsworth: Penguin, 1968.

———. *The Age of Capital: 1848–1875*. New York: Mentor, 1975.

———. *Workers: Worlds of Labour*. New York: Pantheon, 1984.

———. *The Age of Empire: 1875–1914*. London: Sphere Books, 1987 [1962].

Holcombe, L. *Wives and Property: Reform of the Married Women's Property Law in Nineteenth-Century England*. Toronto: University of Toronto Press, 1983.

Holley, J. C. 'The Two Family Economies of Industrialism: Factory Workers in Victorian Scotland'. *Journal of Family History*, vol. 6, no. 1, 1981, pp. 57–69.

Hollis, P., ed. *Class and Conflict in Nineteenth-Century England: 1815–1850*. London: Routledge & Kegan Paul, 1973.

Holtzman, E. M. 'The Pursuit of Married Love: Women's Attitudes Toward Sexuality and Marriage in Great Britain, 1918–1939'. *Journal of Social History*, vol. 16, no. 2, 1982, pp. 39–51.

Hopkins, E. *A Social History of the English Working Classes, 1815–1945*. London: Edward Arnold, 1979.

———. 'Working Hours and Conditions during the Industrial Revolution: A Re-Appraisal'.

Economic History Review, 2nd ser., vol. 35, no. 1, 1982, pp. 52–66.

Hufton, O. *The Poor of Eighteenth-Century France, 1750–1789.* Oxford: Oxford University Press, 1974.

Humphries, J. 'Class Struggle and the Persistence of the Working-Class Family'. *Cambridge Journal of Economics,* vol. 1, no. 3, 1977, pp. 241–58.

——. 'The Working-Class Family, Women's Liberation, and Class Struggle: The Case of Nineteenth-Century British History'. *Review of Radical Political Economics,* vol. 9, no. 3, 1977, pp. 25–41.

——. 'Protective Legislation, the Capitalist State, and Workin-Class Men: The Case of the 1842 Mines Regulation Act'. *Feminist Review,* vol. 7, 1981, pp. 1–33.

——. '"The Most Free from Objection": The Sexual Division of Labor and Women's Work in Nineteenth-Century England'. *Journal of Economic History,* vol. 47, no. 4, 1987, pp. 929–47.

Hunt, E. J. *Regional Wage Variations in Britain, 1850–1914.* Oxford: Clarendon Press, 1973.

——. *British Labour History, 1815–1914.* London: Weidenfeld & Nicolson, 1981.

Hurt, J. S. *Elementary Schooling and the Working Classes, 1860–1918.* London: Routledge & Kegan Paul, 1979.

Imhof, A. E. 'Women, Family and Death: Excess Mortality of Women in Childbearing Age in Four Communities in Nineteenth-Century Germany'. In R. J. Evans and W. R. Lee, eds, *The German Family.* London: Croom Helm, 1981.

Innes, J. W. *Class Fertility Trends in England and Wales, 1876–1934.* Princeton, N.J.: Princeton University Press, 1938.

Jackson, J. H. 'Overcrowding and Family Life: Working-Class Families and the Housing Crisis in Later Nineteenth-Century Duisburg'. In R. J. Evans and W. R. Lee, eds, *The German Family.* London: Croom Helm, 1981.

Jamieson, L. 'Limited Resources and Limiting Conventions: Working-Class Mothers and Daughters in Urban Scotland, c.1890–1925'. In J. Lewis, ed., *Labour and Love: Women's Experience of Home and Family, 1850–1940.* Oxford: Basil Blackwell, 1986.

Janssens, A. 'Industrialization without Family Change? The Extended Family and the Industrial Life Cycle in a Dutch Industrial Town, 1880–1920'. *Journal of Family History,* vol. 11, no. 1, 1986, pp. 25–42.

Joeres, R. B. and Maynes, M. J., eds. *German Women in the Eighteenth and Nineteenth Centuries.* Bloomington, Ind.: Indiana University Press, 1986.

Johansen, H. C. and Boje, P. 'Working-Class Housing in Odense, 1750–1914'. *Scandinavian Economic History Review,* vol. 34, no. 2, 1986, pp. 135–52.

John, A. *By the Sweat of Their Brow: Women Workers at Victorian Coal Mines.* London: Croom Helm, 1980.

Jones, G. S. *Outcast London.* Oxford: Oxford University Press, 1971.

——. 'Working-Class Culture and Working-Class Politics in London, 1870–1900: Notes on the Remaking of the Working-Class'. *Journal of Social History,* vol. 7, 1974, pp. 460–508.

Joyce, P. *Work, Society and Politics: The Culture of the Factory in Later Victorian England.* London: Methuen, 1980.

Kaelble, H. *Industrialization and Social Inequality in Nineteenth-Century Europe.* Leamington Spa: Berg, 1986.

Kalvemark, A. 'Illegitimacy and Marriage in Three Swedish Parishes in the Nineteenth Century'. In P. Laslett, K. Oosterveen and R. M. Smith, eds, *Bastardy and Its Comparative History.* Cambridge, Mass.: Harvard University Press, 1980.

Kanipe, E. S. 'Working-Class Women and the Social Question in Late Nineteenth Century France'. *Proceedings of the Annual Meeting of the Western Society for French History.* vol. 6, 1978.

Katz, M. B. *The People of Hamilton, Canada West: Family and Class in a Mid–Nineteenth Century City.* Cambridge, Mass.: Harvard University Press, 1975.

Katz, M., Stern, M. and Doucet, M. *The Social Organization of Early Industrial Capitalism.*

Cambridge, Mass.: Harvard University Press, 1980.

Katznelson, I. and Zolberg, A. R., eds. *Working-Class Formation: Nineteenth-Century Patterns in Western Europe and the United States.* Princeton, N.J.: Princeton University Press, 1986.

Kelly, A. *The German Worker: Working-Class Autobiographies from the Age of Industrialization.* Berkeley, Calif.: University of California Press, 1987.

Kerr, M. *The People of Ship Street.* London: Routledge & Kegan Paul, 1958.

Kessler-Harris, A. *Out to Work: A History of Wage-Earning Women in the United States.* New York, Oxford University Press, 1982.

Knick-Harley, C. 'British Industrialization before 1841: Evidence of Slower Growth during the Industrial Revolution'. *Journal of Economic History,* vol. 42, no. 2, 1982, pp. 267–89.

Knodel, J. *The Decline of Fertility in Germany, 1871–1939.* Princeton, N.J.: Princeton University Press, 1974.

————. 'Family Limitation and the Fertility Transition: Evidence from the Age Patterns of Fertility in Europe and Asia'. *Population Studies,* vol. 31, no. 2, 1977, pp. 219–49.

————. 'Town and Country in Nineteenth-Century Germany: A Review of Urban–Rural Differentials in Demographic Behaviour'. *Social Science History,* vol. 1, 1977, pp. 356–82.

————. 'Natural Fertility in Pre-industrial Germany'. *Population Studies,* vol. 32, 1978, pp. 481–510.

————. 'From Natural Fertility to Family Limitation: The Onset of Fertility Transition in a Sample of German Villages'. *Demography,* vol. 16, no. 4, 1979, pp. 493–521.

————. 'Child Mortality and Reproductive Behaviour in German Village Populations'. *Population Studies,* vol. 36, no. 2, 1982, pp. 177–200.

————. 'Demographic Transitions in German Villages'. In A. J. Coale and S. C. Watkins, eds, *The Decline of Fertility in Europe.* Princeton, N.J.: Princeton University Press, 1986.

————. *Demographic Behaviour in the Past: A Study of Fourteen German Village Populations in the Eighteenth and Nineteenth Centuries.* Cambridge: Cambridge University Press, 1988.

Knodel, J. and van de Walle, E. 'Lessons from the Past: Policy Implications of Historical Fertility Studies'. In A. J. Coale and S. C. Watkins, eds, *The Decline in Fertility in Europe.* Princeton, N.J.: Princeton University Press, 1986.

Kocka, J. 'Craft Traditions and the Labour Movement in Nineteenth-Century Germany'. In P. Thane, G. Crossick and R. Floud, eds. *The Power of the Past: Essays for Eric Hobsbawm.* Cambridge: Cambridge University Press, 1984.

————. 'Problems of Working-Class Formation in Germany: The Early Years, 1800–1875'. In I. Katznelson and A. Zolberg, eds, *Working-Class Formation: Nineteenth-Century Patterns in Western Europe and the United States.* Princeton, N.J.: Princeton University Press, 1986.

Kunitz, S. J. 'Mortality since Malthus'. In D. Coleman and R. Schofield, eds, *The State of Population Theory: Forward from Malthus.* Oxford: Basil Blackwell, 1986.

Land, H. 'The Family Wage'. *Feminist Review,* vol. 6, 1980, pp. 55–78.

Landes, D. *The Unbound Prometheus.* Cambridge: Cambridge University Press, 1969.

Laqueur, T. W. 'Working-Class Demand and the Growth of English Elementary Education, 1750–1850'. In L. Stone, ed., *Schooling and Society: Studies in the History of Education.* Baltimore: Johns Hopkins University Press, 1976.

Lasch, C. 'Reagan's Victims'. *New York Review of Books,* vol. 35, no. 12, 1988, pp. 7–8.

Laslett, P. *Household and Family in Past Time.* Cambridge: Cambridge University Press, 1972.

————. *Family Life and Illicit Love in Earlier Generations.* Cambridge: Cambridge University Press, 1977.

————. 'The Character of Familial History, Its Limitations and the Conditions for Its Proper Pursuit'. In T. K. Hareven and A. Plakans, eds, *Family History at the Crossroads.* Princeton, N.J.: Princeton University Press, 1987.

Lawrence, R. J. 'Domestic Space and Society: A Cross-Cultural Study'. *Comparative Studies in Society and History,* vol. 24, 1982, pp. 104–30.

Lazonick, W. 'The Subjugation of Labour to Capital: The Rise of the Capitalist System'. *Review of Radical Political Economics,* vol. 10, no. 1, 1978, pp. 1–31.

Leacock, E. Introduction to *The Origin of the Family, Private Property and the State*, by Frederick Engels. New York: International Publishers, 1972.

Leavitt, J. W. *Brought to Bed: Childbearing in America, 1750–1950*. New York: Oxford University Press, 1986.

Lee, J. J. 'Labour in German Industrialization'. In P. Mathias and M. M. Postan, eds, *Cambridge Economic History of Europe*, vol. 7. Cambridge: Cambridge University Press, 1978.

Lee, W. R. 'The Impact of Agrarian Change on Women's Work and Child Care in Early Nineteenth-Century Prussia'. In J. C. Fout, ed., *German Women in the Nineteenth Century*. New York: Holmes & Meier, 1984.

Lees, L. H. 'Getting and Spending: The Family Budgets of English Industrial Workers in 1890'. In J. M. Merriman, ed., *Consciousness and Class Experience in Nineteenth-Century Europe*. New York: Holmes & Meier, 1979.

Lehning, J. R. 'Nuptiality and Rural Industry: Families and Labor in the French Countryside.' *Journal of Family History*, vol. 8, no. 4, 1983, pp. 333–45.

Lequin, Y. 'Labour in the French Economy since the Revolution'. In P. Mathias and M. Postan, eds, *The Cambridge Economic History of Europe*, vol. 7, Cambridge: Cambridge University Press, 1972.

————. 'Les Citodins et leur vie quotidienne'. In M. Agulhon, ed., *Histoire de la France urbaine*, vol. 4. Paris: Seuil, 1983.

————. 'Apprenticeship in Nineteenth-Century France: A Continuing Tradition or Break with the Past?' In S. L. Kaplan and C. J. Koepp, eds, *Work in France: Representations, Meanings, Organization and Practice*. Ithaca, N.Y.: Cornell University Press, 1986.

Lesaege-Duguid, A. E. 'La Mortalité infantile dans le Département du Nord de 1815 à 1914'. In M. Gillet, ed., *L'Homme, la vie et la mort dans le Nord au 19e siècle*. Lille: Université de Lille, 1972.

Lesthaeghe, R. *The Decline of Belgian Fertility, 1800–1970*. Princeton, N.J.: Princeton University Press, 1978.

Lesthaeghe, R. and Wilson, C. 'Modes of Production, Secularization, and the Pace of the Fertility Decline in Western Europe, 1870–1930'. In A. J. Coale and S. C. Watkins, eds. *The Decline of Fertility in Europe*. Princeton, N.J.: Princeton University Press, 1986.

Levine, D. *Family Formation in an Age of Nascent Capitalism*. New York: Academic Press, 1977.

————. *Reproducing Families: The Political Economy of English Population History*. Cambridge: Cambridge University Press, 1987.

Lewenhak, S. *Women and Trade Unions: An Outline History of Women in the British Trade-Union Movement*. London: Ernest Benn, 1977.

Lewis, J. *The Politics of Motherhood*. London: Croom Helm, 1980.

————. 'Parents, Children, School Fees and the London School Board, 1870–1890'. *History of Education Quarterly*, vol. 11, no. 4, 1982, pp. 291–312.

————. *Women in England, 1870–1950*. Sussex: Wheatsheaf, 1984.

————. 'The Working-Class Wife and Mother and State Intervention, 1870–1918'. In J. Lewis, ed., *Labour and Love: Women's Experience of Home and Family, 1850–1940*. Oxford: Basil Blackwell, 1986.

Lewis, J. and Lockridge, K. A. '"Sally Has Been Sick": Pregnancy and Family Limitation among Virginia Gentry Women, 1780–1830'. *Journal of Social History*, vol. 22, no. 1, 1988, pp. 5–19.

Lewis-Faning, E. 'Report on an Enquiry into Family Limitation and Its Influence on Human Fertility during the Past Fifty Years'. *Papers of the Royal Commission on Population*, vol. 1. London: HMSO, 1949.

Liddington, J. and Norris, J. *One Hand Tied behind Us: The Rise of the Women's Suffrage Movement*. London: Virago, 1978.

Lilley, S. 'Technological Progress and the Industrial Revolution, 1700–1914'. In C. M. Cipolla, ed., *The Fontana Economic History of Europe*, vol. 3. London: Fontana, 1974.

Lindert, P. H. and Williamson, J. G. 'English Workers' Living Standards during the Industrial

Revolution: A New Look'. *Economic History Review*, 2nd ser., vol. 36, no. 1, 1983, pp. 1–25.

———. 'Growth, Equality and History'. *Explorations in Economic History*, vol. 22, 1985, pp. 341–77.

Linton, D. S. 'Between School and Marriage, Workshop and Household: Young Working Women as a Social Problem in Late Imperial Germany'. *European History Quarterly*, vol. 18, 1988, pp. 387–408.

Linton, R. 'The Natural History of the Family'. In R. N. Anshen, ed., *The Family: Its Function and Destiny*. New York: Harper, 1949.

Lis, C. *Social Change and the Labouring Poor: Antwerp, 1770–1860*. New Haven, Conn.: Yale University Press, 1986.

Littler, C.R. *The Development of the Labour Process in Capitalist Societies*. London: Heinemann, 1982.

Livi-Bacci, M. *A Century of Portuguese Fertility*. Princeton, N.J.: Princeton University Press, 1971.

———. *A History of Italian Fertility*. Princeton, N.J.: Princeton University Press, 1977.

Loane, M. *From Their Point of View*. London: Edward Arnold, 1908.

———. *An Englishman's Castle*. London: Edward Arnold, 1909.

———. *The Queen's Poor: Life as They Found It*. London: Edward Arnold, 1910.

Löfgren, O. 'Family and Household: Images and Realities, Cultural Change in Swedish Society'. In R. Netting, R. Wilk and E. Arnold, eds, *Households: Comparative and Historical Studies of the Domestic Group*. Berkeley, Calif.: University of California Press, 1984.

Lown, J. 'Not So Much a Factory, More a Form of Patriarchy: Gender and Class during Industrialization'. In E. Gramarnikov, D. Morgan, J. Purvis and D. Taylorson, eds, *Gender, Class and Work*. London: Heinemann, 1983.

Luxton, M. *More Than a Labour of Love: Three Generations of Women's Work in the Home*. Toronto: The Women's Press, 1980.

Lynch, K. A. *Family, Class, and Ideology in Early Industrial France: Social Policy and the Working-Class Family, 1825–1848*. Madison, Wis.: University of Wisconsin Press, 1988.

Macpherson, C. B. *The Political Theory of Possessive Individualism: Hobbes to Locke*. London: Oxford University Press, 1962.

McBride, T. 'The Long Road Home: Women's Work and Industrialization'. In R. Bridenthal and C. Koonz, eds, *Becoming Visible: Women in European History*. Boston: Houghton Mifflin, 1977.

McCann, P. 'Popular Education, Socialization and Social Control: Spitalfields, 1812–1824'. In P. McCann, ed., *Popular Education and Socialization in the Nineteenth Century*. London: Methuen, 1977.

McClelland, K. 'Time to Work, Time to Live: Some Aspects of Work and the Re-formation of Class in Britain, 1850–1880'. In P. Joyce, ed., *The Historical Meanings of Work*. Cambridge: Cambridge University Press, 1987.

McCrone, K. 'The Assertion of Women's Rights in Mid-Victorian England'. *Historical Papers of the Canadian Historical Association, 1972*.

McDonough, R. and Harrison, R. 'Patriarchy and Relations of Production'. In A. Kuhn and A. M. Wolpe, eds, *Feminism and Materialism: Women and Modes of Production*. London: Routledge & Kegan Paul, 1978.

McDougall, M. L. 'Consciousness and Community: The Workers of Lyon, 1830–1850'. *Journal of Social History*, vol. 12, no. 1, 1978, pp. 129–45.

McIntosh, M. 'The State and the Oppression of Women'. In A. Kuhn and A. M. Wolpe, eds, *Feminism and Materialism: Women and Modes of Production*. London: Routledge & Kegan Paul, 1978.

McKay, J. P. *Tramways and Trolleys: The Rise of Urban Mass Transport in Europe*. Princeton, N.J.: Princeton University Press, 1976.

McLaren, A. *Sexuality and Social Order: The Debate over the Fertility of Women and Workers in*

France, 1770–1920. New York: Holmes & Meier, 1983.

———. *Reproductive Rituals: The Perception of Fertility in England from the Sixteenth to the Nineteenth Century*. London: Methuen, 1984.

McMillan, J. F. *Housewife or Harlot: The Place of Women in French Society, 1870–1940*. Brighton: Harvester, 1981.

McQuillan, K. 'Modes of Production and Demographic Patterns in Nineteenth-Century France'. *American Journal of Sociology,* vol. 89, no. 6, 1984, pp. 1324–46.

Madoc-Jones, B. 'Patterns of Attendance and Their Social Significance: Mitcham National School, 1830–39'. In P. McCann, ed., *Popular Education and Socialization in the Nineteenth Century*. London: Methuen, 1977.

Mandel, E. *Late Capitalism*. London: New Left Books, 1975.

Mark-Lawson, J. and Witz, A. 'From "Family Labour" to "Family Wage"? The Case of Women's Labour in Nineteenth-Century Coalmining'. *Social History,* vol. 13, no. 2, 1988, pp. 151–74.

Marsden, W. E. 'Social Environment, School Attendance and Educational Achievement in a Merseyside Town, 1970–1900'. In P. McCann, ed., *Popular Education and Socialization in the Nineteenth Century*. London: Methuen, 1977.

Marshall, D. *Industrial England, 1776–1851*. London: Routledge & Kegan Paul, 1973.

Martin, E. W. *The Standard of Living in 1860*. Chicago: University of Chicago Press, 1942 [Johnson Reprint, 1970].

Marvel, H. 'Factory Regulation: A Reinterpretation of the English Experience'. *Journal of Law and Economics,* vol. 20, no. 2, 1977, pp. 379–402.

Marx, K. *Capital: The Process of Capitalist Production as a Whole,* vol. 3, F. Engels, ed. Moscow: Foreign Languages Publishers, 1959.

———. *Pre-Capitalist Economic Formations*. New York: International Publishers, 1965.

———. *A Contribution to the Critique of Political Economy*. Moscow: Progress Publishers, 1970.

———. *Theories of Surplus Value, Part III*. Moscow: Progress Publishers, 1971.

———. *Grundrisse: Introduction to the Critique of Political Economy*. Harmondsworth: Penguin, 1973.

———. 'The Communist Manifesto'. In *The Revolutions of 1848: Political Writings,* vol. 1. D. Fernbach, trans. New York: Vintage, 1974.

———. *The Revolutions of 1848: Political Writings,* vol. 1. D. Fernbach, trans. New York: Vintage, 1974.

———. *Capital: A Critique of Political Economy,* vol. 1. B. Fowkes, trans. New York: Vintage, 1977.

Marx, K. and Engels, F. *The German Ideology,* C. J. Arthur, ed. and intro., New York: International, 1970.

Mason, K. O. and Taj, A. M. 'Differences between Women's and Men's Reproductive Goals in Developing Countries'. *Population and Development Review,* vol. 13, 1987, pp. 611–38.

Mathias, P. *The First Industrial Nation,* 2nd edn. London: Methuen, 1983.

Mathews, R. C. O., Feinstein, C. H. and Odling-Smee, J. C. *British Economic Growth, 1865–1973*. Oxford: Clarendon Press, 1982.

Matthiessan, P. and McCann, J. 'The Effects of Infant and Child Mortality on Fertility'. In S. Preston, ed., *The Effects of Infant and Child Mortality on Fertility*. New York: Academic Press, 1978.

Maynes, M. J. *Schooling for the People: Comparative Local Studies of Schooling in France and Germany, 1750–1850*. New York, Holmes & Meier, 1985.

———. *Schooling in Western Europe: A Social History*. Albany, N.Y.: SUNY Press, 1985.

———. 'Gender and Class in Working-Class Women's Autobiographies'. In R. B. Joeres and M. J. Maynes, eds, *German Women in the Eighteenth and Nineteenth Centuries*. Bloomington, Ind.: Indiana University Press, 1986.

Meacham, S. *A Life Apart: The English Working Class, 1890–1914*. London: Thames & Hudson, 1977.

Medick, H. 'Plebeian Culture in the Transition to Capitalism'. In R. Samuel and G. Stedman Jones, eds, *Culture, Ideology and Politics*. London: Routledge & Kegan Paul, 1982.

Meillassoux, C. 'Historical Modalities of the Exploitation and Over-Exploitation of Labour'. *Critique of Anthropology*, vols 13/14, 1979, pp. 7–16.

Mill, J. S. *On the Subjection of Women*. London: Everyman, 1929 [1869].

Minor, I. 'Working-Class Women and Matrimonial Law Reform, 1890–1914'. In D. E. Martin and D. Rubinstein, eds, *Ideology and the Labour Movement*. London: Croom Helm, 1979.

Mitchell, B., *European Historical Statistics*. London: MacMillan, 1975.

Mitchell, J. *Psychoanalysis and Feminism*. New York: Random House, 1975.

Moch, L. P. *Paths to the City: Regional Migration in Nineteenth-Century France*. Beverly Hills, Calif.: Sage, 1983.

Modell, J. and Hareven, T. K. 'Urbanization and the Malleable Household: An Examination of Boarding and Lodging in American Families'. *Journal of Marriage and the Family*, vol. 35, 1973, pp. 467–79.

Molyneux, M. 'Beyond the Domestic Labour Debate'. *New Left Review*, no. 116, 1979, pp. 3–28.

More, C. *Skill and the English Working Class, 1870–1914*. London: Croom Helm, 1980.

More, L. B. *Wage Earners' Budgets: A Study of Standards and Costs of Living in New York City*. New York: Arno Press, 1971 [1907].

Morokvasic, M. 'Sexuality and the Control of Procreation'. In K. Young, C. Wolkowitz and R. McCullagh, eds, *Of Marriage and the Market*. London: CSE Books, 1981.

Nardinelli, C. 'Child Labour and the Factory Acts'. *Journal of Economic History*, vol. 40, no. 4, 1980, pp. 739–55.

Nakane, C. 'An Interpretation of the Size and Structure of the Household in Japan over Three Centuries'. In P. Laslett, ed., *Household and Family in Past Time*. Cambridge: Cambridge University Press, 1972.

Neuman, R. P. 'Working-Class Birth Control in Wilhelmine Germany'. *Comparative Studies in Society and History*, vol. 20, no. 3, 1978, pp. 408–28.

Neuville, J. *La Condition ouvrière au XIXᵉ siècle*. Brussels: Editions Vie Ouvrière, 1976.

Nicholson, N. J. *Gender and History: The Limits of Social Theory in the Age of the Family*. New York: Columbia University Press, 1986.

Nolan, M. 'Economic Crisis, State Policy, and Working-Class Formation in Germany'. In I. Katznelson and A. R. Zolberg, eds, *Working-Class Formation: Nineteenth-Century Patterns in Western Europe and the United States*. Princeton, N.J.: Princeton University Press, 1986.

Oakley, A. *Woman's Work: The Housewife, Past and Present*. New York: Pantheon, 1974.

Oddy, D. J. 'Working-Class Diets in Late Nineteenth-Century Britain'. *Economic History Review*, 2nd ser., vol. 23, no. 2, 1970, pp. 314–23.

———. 'The Health of the People'. In M. Drake and T. C. Barker, eds, *Population and Society in Britain 1850–1950*. London: Batsford, 1982.

Oren, L. 'The Welfare of Women in Labouring Families: England, 1860–1950'. In M. Hartman and L. W. Banner, eds, *Clio's Consciousness Raised: New Perspectives on the History of Women*. New York: Harper Colophon, 1974.

Orthmann, R. 'Labour Force Participation, Life Cycle and Expenditure Patterns'. In R. B. Joeres and M. J. Maynes, eds, *German Women in the Eighteenth and Nineteenth Centuries*. Bloomington, Ind.: Indiana University Press, 1986.

Osterud, N. G. 'Gender Divisions and the Organization of Work in the Leicester Hosiery Industry'. In A. V. John, ed., *Unequal Opportunities: Women's Employment in England, 1800–1918*. Oxford: Basil Blackwell, 1986.

Pahl, J. 'Patterns of Money Management within Marriage'. *Journal of Social Policy*, vol. 9, no. 3, 1980, pp. 313–50.

Parsons, T. 'The American Family, Its Relation to Personality and the Social Structure'. In T. Parsons and R. F. Bales, eds, *Family, Socialization and Interaction Process*. London: Routledge & Kegan Paul, 1965.

Paterson, F. 'Schooling the Family'. *Sociology,* vol. 22, no. 1, 1988, pp. 65–86.

Peel, J. 'The Manufacture and Retailing of Contraceptives in England'. *Population Studies,* vol. 17, 1963, pp. 113–25.

Perkin, H. *Origins of Modern English Society, 1780–1880.* London: Routledge & Kegan Paul, 1969.

Perrot, M. 'The Three Ages of Industrial Discipline in Nineteenth-Century France'. In J. M. Merriman, ed., *Consciousness and Class Experience in Nineteenth-Century Europe.* New York: Holmes & Meier, 1979.

———. 'On the Formation of the French Working Class'. In I. Katznelson and A. R. Zolberg, eds, *Working-Class Formation: Nineteenth-Century Patterns in Western Europe and the United States.* Princeton, N.J.: Princeton University Press, 1986.

Phillips, R. *Family Breakdown in Late Eighteenth-Century France.* Oxford: Clarendon Press, 1980.

Pinchbeck, I. *Women Workers and the Industrial Revolution, 1750–1850.* London: Virago, 1981 [1930].

Plath, D. *Work and Lifecourse in Japan.* Albany, N.Y.: SUNY Press, 1983.

Pollard, S. *The Genesis of Modern Management.* London: Edward Arnold, 1965.

———. 'Labour in Great Britain'. In P. Mathias and M. M. Postan, eds, *Cambridge Economic History of Europe,* vol. 7, pt 1. Cambridge: Cambridge University Press, 1978.

———. *Peaceful Conquest: The Industrialization of Europe, 1760–1970.* Oxford: Oxford University Press, 1981.

Porter, G. R. 'On the Self-imposed Taxation of the Working-Classes in the United Kingdom'. *Journal of the Royal Statistical Society of London,* vol. 13, 1850, pp. 358–64.

Poulantzas, N. *Political Power and Social Classes.* London: New Left Books/Sheed & Ward, 1973.

Pounds, N. J. G. *An Historical Geography of Europe.* Cambridge: Cambridge University Press, 1985.

Pred, S. 'Production, Family, and Free-Time Projects: A Time-Geographic Perspective on the Individual and Social Change in Nineteenth-Century U.S. Cities'. *Journal of Historical Geography,* vol. 7, no. 1, 1981, pp. 3–36.

Preston, S., ed. *The Effects of Infant and Child Mortality on Fertility.* New York: Academic Press, 1978.

Preston, S. and van de Walle, E. 'Urban French Mortality in the Nineteenth Century'. *Population Studies,* vol. 32, no. 2, 1978, pp. 275–97.

Price, R. 'Structures of Subordination in Nineteenth-Century British Industry'. In P. Thane, G. Crossick and R. Floud, eds, *The Power of the Past: Essays for Eric Hobsbawm.* Cambridge: Cambridge University Press, 1984.

———. *Labour in British Society.* London: Croom Helm, 1986.

———. *A Social History of Nineteenth-Century France.* New York: Holmes & Meier, 1987.

Quataert, J. H. 'A Source Analysis in German Women's History: Factory Inspectors' Reports and the Shaping of Working-Class Lives, 1878–1914'. *Central European History,* vol. 16, no. 2, 1983, pp. 99–121.

Rathbone, E. *The Disinherited Family,* intro. by S. Fleming. Bristol: Falling Wall Press, 1986 [1924].

Reddy, W. M. 'Family and Factory: French Linen Weavers in the Belle Epoque'. *Journal of Social History,* vol. 8, 1975, pp. 102–12.

———. *The Rise of Market Culture: The Textile Trade and French Society, 1750–1900.* Cambridge: Cambridge University Press, 1984.

Reeves, M. P. *Round About a Pound a Week,* intro. by S. Alexander. London: Virago, 1979 [1913].

Reid, D. A. 'The Decline of Saint Monday, 1766–1876'. *Past & Present,* no. 71, 1976, pp. 76–101.

Rice, M. *Working-Class Wives, Their Health and Conditions*. London: Virago, 1981.

Rifkin, A. and Thomas, R. *Voices of the People: The Social Life of 'La Société' at the End of the Second Empire*. London: Routledge & Kegan Paul, 1988.

Roberts, E. *A Woman's Place: An Oral History of Working-Class Women, 1890–1940*. Oxford: Basil Blackwell, 1984.

Roberts, R. *The Classic Slum: Salford Life in the First Quarter of the Century*. Harmondsworth: Penguin, 1973 [1971].

Roos, P. A. *Gender and Work: A Comparative Analysis of Industrial Societies*. New York: SUNY Press, 1985.

Rose, S. O. 'Gender at Work: Sex, Class and Industrial Capitalism'. *History Workshop Journal*, no. 21, 1986, pp. 113–31.

———. 'Gender Segregation in the Transition to the Factory: The English Hosiery Industry, 1850–1910'. *Feminist Studies*, vol. 13, no. 1, 1987, pp. 163–84.

Ross, E. '"Fierce Questions and Taunts": Married Life in Working-Class London, 1870–1914'. *Feminist Studies*, vol. 8, no. 3, 1982, pp. 575–602.

———. 'Survival Networks: Women's Neighbourhood Sharing in London before World War I'. *History Workshop Journal*, no. 15, 1983, pp. 4–27.

———. 'Response to Harold Benenson's "Victorian Sexual Ideology"'. *International Labor and Working Class History*, no. 25, 1984, pp. 30–36.

———. '"Not the Sort That Would Sit on the Doorstep": Respectability in Pre–World War I London Neighbourhoods'. *International Labor and Working Class History*, no. 27, 1985, pp. 39–59.

———. 'Labour and Love: Rediscovering London's Working-Class Mothers, 1870–1918'. In J. Lewis, ed., *Labour and Love: Women's Experience of Home and Family, 1850–1940*. Oxford: Basil Blackwell, 1986.

Rostow, W. W. *The Stages of Economic Growth: A Non-Communist Manifesto*. Cambridge: Cambridge University Press, 1962.

Rubin, L. *Worlds of Pain: Life in the Working-Class Family*. New York: Basic Books, 1976.

Rubinstein, D. *School Attendance in London, 1870–1904*. New York: Augustus Kelley, 1969.

———. 'Socialization and the London School Board, 1870–1904'. In P. McCann, ed., *Popular Education and Socialization in the Nineteenth Century*. London: Methuen, 1977.

Ruggles, S. *Prolonged Connections: The Rise of the Extended Family in Nineteenth-Century England and America*. Madison, Wis.: University of Wisconsin Press, 1987.

Rule, J. *The Experience of Labour in Eighteenth-Century Industry*. London: Croom Helm, 1981.

———. *The Labouring Classes in Early Industrial England, 1750–1850*. London: Longman, 1986.

Saito, O. 'Labour Supply Behaviour of the Poor in the English Industrial Revolution'. *Journal of European Economic History*, vol. 10, no. 3, 1981, pp. 633–51.

Saller, R. P. and Shaw, B. D. 'Tombstones and Roman Family Relations in the Principate: Civilians. Soldiers and Slaves'. *Journal of Roman Studies*, vol. 74, 1984, pp. 124–66.

Samuel, R. 'The Workshop of the World: Steam Power and Hand Technology in Mid-Victorian Britain'. *History Workshop Journal*, no. 3, 1977, pp. 6–72.

Sargant, W. L. *Economy of the Labouring Classes*. London: Simkin Marshall, 1857.

Sauer , R. 'Infanticide and Abortion in Nineteenth-Century Britain'. *Population Studies*, vol. 32, no. 1, 1978, pp. 81–93.

Schmidtbauer, P. 'The Changing Household: Austrian Household Structure from the Seventeenth to the Early Twentieth Century'. In R. Wall, ed., *Family Forms in Historic Europe*. Cambridge: Cambridge University Press, 1984.

Schmiechen, J. A. *Sweated Industries and Sweated Labour: The London Clothing Trades, 1860–1914*. Chicago: University of Illinois Press, 1984.

Schofer, L. *The Formation of a Modern Labour Force: Upper Silesia, 1865–1914*. Berkeley, Calif.: University of California Press, 1975.

Schomerus, H. 'The Family Life-Cycle: A Study of Factory Workers in Nineteenth-Century

Württemberg'. In R. J. Evans and W. R. Lee, eds, *The German Family*. London: Croom Helm, 1981.

Scott, J. W. 'Men and Women in the Parisian Garment Trades: Discussions of Family and Work in the 1830s and 1840s'. In P. Thane, G. Crossick and R. Floud, eds, *The Power of the Past: Essays for Eric Hobsbawm*. Cambridge: Cambridge University Press, 1984.

———. '"L'Ouvrière! Mot impie, sordide ...": Women Workers in the Discourse of French Political Economy, 1840–1860'. In P. Joyce, ed., *The Historical Meanings of Work*. Cambridge: Cambridge University Press, 1987.

Seccombe, W. 'The Housewife and Her Labour under Capitalism'. *New Left Review*, no. 83, 1973, pp. 3–24.

———. 'Domestic Labour and the Working-Class Household'. In B. Fox, ed., *Hidden in the Household: Women's Domestic Labour under Capitalism*. Toronto: The Women's Press, 1980.

———. 'Patriarchy Stabilized: The Construction of the Male-Breadwinner Wage Norm in Nineteenth-Century Britain'. *Social History*, vol. 11, no. 1, 1986, pp. 53–76.

———. 'Reflections on the Domestic Labour Debate and Prospects for Marxist–Feminist Synthesis'. In R. Hamilton and M. Barrett, eds, *The Politics of Diversity*. London: Verso, 1986.

———. 'Starting to Stop: Working-Class Fertility Decline in Britain'. *Past & Present*, no. 126, 1990, pp. 151–88.

———. *A Millennium of Family Change: Feudalism to Capitalism in Northwestern Europe*. London: Verso, 1992.

Segalen, M. *Historical Anthropology of the Family*. Cambridge: Cambridge University Press, 1986.

Sen, G. 'The Sexual Division of Labour and the Working-Class Family: Towards a Conceptual Synthesis of Class Relations and the Subordination of Women'. *Review of Radical Political Economics*, vol. 12, no. 2, 1980, pp. 76–86.

Sewell, W. J. *Work and Revolution in France: The Language of Labor from the Old Regime to 1848*. Cambridge: Cambridge University Press, 1980.

———. *Structure and Mobility: The Men and Women of Marseille, 1820–1870*. Cambridge: Cambridge University Press, 1985.

———. 'Artisans, Factory Workers, and the Formation of the French Working Class, 1789–1848'. In I. Katznelson and A. Zolberg, eds, *Working-Class Formation: Nineteenth-Century Patterns in Western Europe and the United States*. Princeton, N.J.: Princeton University Press, 1986.

Shaffer, J. F. 'Family, Class, and Young Women: Occupational Expectations in Nineteenth-Century Paris'. *Journal of Family History*, vol. 3, no. 1, 1978, pp. 62–77.

Shapiro, A. L. *Housing the Poor of Paris, 1850–1902*. Madison, Wis.: University of Wisconsin Press, 1985.

Sharlin, A. 'Urban–Rural Differences in Fertility in Europe during the Demographic Transition.' In A. Coale and S. Watkins, eds, *The Decline of Fertility in Europe*. Princeton, N.J.: Princeton University Press, 1986.

Sheridan, G. 'Household and Craft in an Industrializing Economy: The Case of the Silk Weavers of Lyons'. In J. M. Merriman, ed., *Consciousness and Class Experience in Nineteenth-Century Europe*. New York: Holmes & Meier, 1979.

Shorter, E. *The Making of the Modern Family*. New York: Basic Books, 1975.

———. *A History of Women's Bodies*. New York: Basic Books, 1982.

Shorter, E., Knodel, J. and van de Walle, E. 'The Decline of Non-Marital Fertility in Europe, 1880–1940'. *Population Studies*, vol. 25, 1971, pp. 371–93.

Sieder, R. 'Childhood Experiences in Viennese Working-Class Families around 1900'. *Continuity and Change*, vol. 1, 1986, pp. 69–74.

Simon, B. *Education and the Labour Movement, 1870–1920*. London: Lawrence & Wishart, 1965.

Smelser, N. J. *Social Change in the Industrial Revolution*. London: Routledge, 1959.

Smith, A. *The Wealth of Nations*, ed. and introduction by A. Skinner. Harmondsworth: Penguin, 1970.

Smith, D. B. *Inside the Great House*. Ithaca, N.Y.: Cornell University Press, 1980.

Smith, F. B. *The People's Health, 1830–1910*. London: Croom Helm, 1979.

Smout, T. C. *A Century of the Scottish People, 1830–1950*. London: Fontana, 1986.

Smuts, R. W. *Women and Work in America*. New York: Schocken Books, 1971 [1959].

Snell, K. D. M. *Annals of the Labouring Poor: Social Change and Agrarian England 1600–1900*. Cambridge: Cambridge University Press, 1985.

Soloway, R. *Birth Control and the Population Question in England, 1877–1930*. Chapel Hill, N.C.: University of North Carolina Press, 1982.

Sowerwine, C. 'Workers and Women in France before 1914: The Debate over the Couriau Affair'. *Journal of Modern History*, vol. 55, 1983, pp. 411–41.

Spagnoli, P. 'Industrialization, Proletarianization and Marriage: A Reconsideration'. *Journal of Family History*, vol. 8, no. 3, 1983, pp. 230–47.

Spree, R. *Health and Social Class in Imperial Germany*. Leamington Spa: Berg, 1988.

Stark, O. 'Bargaining, Altruism, and Demographic Phenomena'. *Population and Development Review*, vol. 10, 1984, pp. 679–92.

Stearns, P. 'Working-Class Women in Britain, 1890–1914'. In M. Vicinus, ed., *Suffer and Be Still: Women in the Victorian Age*. Bloomington, Ind.: Indiana University Press, 1972.

———. 'The Adaptation of Workers'. In P. Stearns, ed., *The Other Side of Western Civilization*, vol. 2. New York: Harcourt Brace Jovanovich, 1973.

———. *Lives of Labour*. New York: Holmes & Meier, 1975.

———. *Paths to Authority: The Middle Class and the Industrial Labor Force in France, 1820–1848*. Urbana, Ill.: University of Illinois Press, 1978.

Stearns P. N. and Walkowitz, D. J., eds. *Workers in the Industrial Revolution: Recent Studies of Labour in the United States and Europe*. Princeton, N.J.: Transaction, 1974.

Stedman Jones, G. 'Working-Class Culture and Working-Class Politics in London, 1870–1900: Notes on the Remaking of the Working–Class'. *Journal of Social History*, vol. 7, 1974, pp. 460–508.

Stern, M. J. *Society and Family Strategy: Erie County, New York, 1850–1920*. New York: SUNY Press, 1987.

Stone, L. 'Literacy and Education in England, 1640–1900'. *Past & Present*, no. 42, 1969, pp. 69–139.

Stopes, M., ed. *Mother England: A Contemporary History*, 2nd edn. London: Bale & Danielsson, 1930.

———. *Dear Dr Stopes: Sex in the 1920s*, ed. by R. Hall. Harmondsworth: Penguin, 1981 [1978].

Stovall, T. '"Friends, Neighbours and Communists": Community Formation in Suburban Paris during the Early Twentieth Century'. *Journal of Social History*, vol. 22, no. 2, 1988, pp. 237–54.

Strachey, R. *The Cause: A Short History of the Women's Movement in Great Britain*. London: Virago, 1979 [1928].

Strasser, S. M. 'An Enlarged Human Existence? Technology and Household Work in Nineteenth-Century America'. In S. F. Berk, ed., *Women and Household Labor*. Beverly Hills, Calif.: Sage, 1980.

———. *Never Done: A History of American Homework*. New York: Pantheon, 1982.

Tabutin, D. 'La Surmortalité féminine en Europe avant 1940'. *Population*, vol. 33, no. 1, 1978, pp. 121–48.

Talmon, Y. 'Social Change and Kinship Ties'. In R. Hill and R. Konig, eds, *Families in East and West*. Paris: Mouton, 1970.

Taylor, A. J. *The Standard of Living in Britain in the Industrial Revolution*. London: Methuen, 1975.

Taylor, B. *Eve and the New Jerusalem*. London: Virago, 1983.

Tax, M. *The Rising of the Women: Feminist Solidarity and Class Conflict, 1880–1917*. New York: Monthly Review Press, 1980.

Tebbutt, M. *Making Ends Meet: Pawnbroking and Working-class Credit*. New York: St Martin's Press, 1983.

Teitelbaum, M., *The British Fertility Decline: Demographic Transition in the Crucible of the Industrial Revolution*. Princeton, N.J.: Princeton University Press, 1984.

Teuteberg, H. J. and Wischermann, C. *Wohnalltag in Deutschland, 1850–1914*. Berlin: Coppenrath, 1985.

Thompson, D. 'Women and Nineteenth-Century Radical Politics: A Lost Dimension'. In J. Mitchell and A. Oakley, eds, *The Rights and Wrongs of Women*. Harmondsworth: Penguin, 1976.

Thompson, E. P. 'Time, Work-Discipline, and Industrial Capitalism'. *Past & Present*, no. 38, 1967, pp. 56–97.

———. *The Making of the English Working Class*. Harmondsworth: Penguin, 1968 [1963].

———. 'Patrician Society, Plebeian Culture'. *Journal of Social History*, vol. 7, no. 4, 1974, pp. 382–405.

Thompson, E. P. and Yeo, E. *The Unknown Mayhew: Selections from the Morning Chronicle*. Harmondsworth: Penguin, 1984 [1971].

Thompson, F. M. L. *The Rise of Respectable Society: A Social History of Victorian Britain, 1830–1900*. London: Fontana, 1988.

Thompson, P. *The Edwardians: The Remaking of British Society*. London: Weidenfeld & Nicolson, 1975.

Tilly, L. 'The Family Wage Economy of a French Textile City: Roubaix, 1872–1906'. *Journal of Family History*, vol. 4, no. 4, 1979, pp. 381–94.

———. 'Individual Lives and Family Strategies in the French Proletariat'. In R. Wheaton and T. K. Hareven, eds, *Family and Sexuality in French History*. Philadelphia: University of Pennsylvania Press, 1980.

———. 'Linen Was Their Life: Family Survival Strategies and Parent–Child Relations in Nineteenth-Century France'. In H. Medick and D. Sabean, eds, *Interest and Emotion*. Cambridge: Cambridge University Press, 1984.

———. 'Coping with Company Paternalism: Family Strategies of Coal Miners in Nineteenth-Century France'. *Theory and Society*, vol. 14, no. 4, 1985, pp. 403–17.

Tilly, L. A. and Scott, J. W. *Women, Work and Family*. New York: Holt, Rinehart & Winston, 1978.

Toffler, A. *The Third Wave*. New York: Bantam, 1980.

Topalov, C. *Le Logement en France: Histoire d'une marchandise impossible*. Paris: Presses de la Fondation Nationale des Sciences Politiques, 1987.

Tranter, N. L. 'The Labour Supply, 1780–1860'. In R. Floud and D. McCloskey, eds, *The Economic History of Britain since 1700*, vol. 1. Cambridge: Cambridge University Press, 1981.

———. *Population and Society, 1750–1940*. London: Longman, 1985.

Treble, J. H. 'Liverpool Working-Class Housing, 1801–51'. In S. D. Chapman, ed., *The History of Working-Class Housing*. Newton Abbot: David & Charles, 1971.

———. *Urban Poverty in Britain, 1830–1914*. London: Methuen, 1979.

Treffers, P. E. 'Abortion in Amsterdam'. *Population Studies*, vol. 20, no. 3, 1967, pp. 295–309.

Tucker, B. M. 'The Family and Industrial Discipline in Ante-Bellum New England'. *Labour History*, vol. 21, no. 1, 1979–80, pp. 55–75.

Valverde, M. '"Giving the Female a Turn": The Social, Legal and Moral Regulation of Women's Work in British Cotton Mills, 1820–1850'. *Journal of Social History*, vol. 21, no. 4, 1988, pp. 619–34.

van de Walle, E. 'Motivations and Technology in the Decline of French Fertility'. In R. Wheaton and T. K. Hareven, eds, *Family and Sexuality in French History*. Philadelphia: University of Pennsylvania Press, 1980.

van de Walle, F. 'Infant Mortality and the European Demographic Transition'. In A. J. Coale and S. C. Watkins, eds, *The Decline of Fertility in Europe*. Princeton, N.J.: Princeton University Press, 1986.

van Dijk, H. and Mandemakers, C. A. 'Secondary Education and Social Mobility at the Turn of the Century'. *History of Education Quarterly*, vol. 14, no. 3, 1985, pp. 199–226.

van Tunzelmann, G. N. *Steam Power and British Industrialization to 1860*. Oxford: Oxford University Press, 1978.

Vedrenne-Villeneuve, E. 'L'Inégalité sociale devant la mort dans la première moitié du XIXe siècle'. *Population*, vol. 16, 1961, pp. 665–98.

Vincent, D. *Bread, Knowledge and Freedom: A Study of Nineteenth-Century Working-Class Autobiography*. London: Methuen, 1981.

Vogel, L. 'Marxism and Feminism: Unhappy Marriage, Trial Separation or Something Else'. In L. Sargent, ed., *Women and Revolution: A Discussion of the Unhappy Marriage of Marxism and Feminism*. London: Pluto, 1981.

Wachter, K. W. with Hammel, E. A. and Laslett, P. *Statistical Studies of Historical Social Structure*. New York: Academic Press, 1978.

Wall, R. 'Regional and Temporal Variations in English Household Structure from 1650'. In J. Hobcraft and P. Rees, eds, *Regional Demographic Development*. London: Croom Helm, 1977.

———. 'The Age at Leaving Home'. *Journal of Family History*, vol. 3, no. 2, 1978, pp. 181–202.

———. 'Women Alone in English Society'. *Annales de Démographie Historique*. 1981.

———. 'Regional and Temporal Variation in the Structure of the British Household since 1851'. In M. Drake and T. C. Barker, eds, *Population and Society in Britain, 1850–1950*. London: Batsford, 1982.

———. 'The Household: Demographic and Economic Change in England, 1650–1970'. In R. Wall, ed., *Family Forms in Historic Europe*. Cambridge: Cambridge University Press, 1984.

Walvin, J. *English Urban Life, 1776–1851*. London: Hutchinson, 1984.

Ward, P. 'Birth Weight and Standards of Living in Vienna, 1865–1930'. *Journal of Interdisciplinary History*, vol. 19, no. 2, 1980, pp. 203–29.

Wardle, D. *The Rise of the Schooled Society*. London: Routledge & Kegan Paul, 1974.

Webb, S. *The Decline of the Birth-Rate*, Fabian Tract no. 131. London: The Fabian Society, 1907.

Weber, A. *The Growth of Cities*. Ithaca, N.Y.: Cornell University Press, 1899.

Weber, M. *The Theory of Social and Economic Organization*. New York: Oxford University Press, 1947.

———. *Economy and Society*, vol. 1. Berkeley, Calif.: University of California Press, 1978.

Weeks, J. *Sex, Politics and Society: The Regulation of Sexuality since 1800*. London: Longman, 1981.

Weinbaum, B. *The Curious Courtship of Women's Liberation and Socialism*. Boston: South End Press, 1978.

Weir, D. 'Fertility Transition in Rural France, 1740–1829'. *Journal of Economic History*, vol. 44, no. 2, 1984, pp. 612–14.

———. 'Life under Pressure: France and England, 1670–1870'. *Journal of Economic History*, vol. 44, no. 1, 1984, pp. 27–45.

Weissbach, L. S. 'Child Labor Legislation in Nineteenth-Century France'. *Journal of Economic History*, vol. 37, 1977, pp. 268–71.

———. *Assuring the Future Harvest: Child Labor Reform in France, 1827–1885*. Baton Rouge, La.: Louisiana State University Press, 1989.

Wickham, J. 'Working-Class Movement and Working-Class Life: Frankfurt am Main during the Weimar Republic'. *Social History*, vol. 8, no. 3, 1983, pp. 315–43.

Williamson, J. 'Was the Industrial Revolution Worth It? Disamenities and Death in Nineteenth-Century Towns'. *Explorations in Economic History*, vol. 19, 1982, pp. 221–45.

Wilson, C. 'The Proximate Determinants of Marital Fertility in England, 1600–1799'. In L.

Bonfield, R. Smith and K. Wrightson, eds, *The World We Have Gained*. Oxford: Basil Blackwell, 1986.

Wilson, E. *Women and the Welfare State*. London: Tavistock, 1977.

Wohl, A. S. 'The Housing of the Working Classes in London, 1815–1914'. In S. D. Chapman, ed., *The History of Working-Class Housing*. Newton Abbot: David & Charles, 1971.

———. 'Sex and the Single Room: Incest among the Victorian Working Classes'. In A. S. Wohl, ed., *The Victorian Family*. London: Croom Helm, 1978.

———. *Endangered Lives: Public Health in Victorian Britain*. London: J. M. Dent & Sons, 1983.

Woods, R. I. 'Approaches to the Fertility Transition in Victorian England'. *Population Studies,* vol. 41, 1987, pp. 283–311.

Woods, R. I. and Hinde, P. R. A. 'Nuptiality and Age at Marriage in Nineteenth-Century England'. *Journal of Family History,* vol. 10, no. 2, 1985, pp. 119–44.

———. 'Mortality in Victorian England: Models and Patterns'. *Journal of Interdisciplinary History,* vol. 18, no. 1, 1987, pp. 27–54.

Woods, R. I. and Smith, C. W. 'The Decline of Marital Fertility in the Late Nineteenth Century: The Case of England and Wales'. *Population Studies,* vol. 37, no. 2, 1983, pp. 207–25.

Woods, R. I., Watterson, P. A. and Woodward, J. H. 'The Causes of Rapid Infant Mortality Decline in England and Wales, 1861–1921', pt 1. *Population Studies,* vol. 42, 1988, pp. 343–66.

Woods, R. I. and Woodward, J. *Urban Disease and Mortality in Nineteenth-Century England*. New York: St Martin's Press, 1984.

Woodward, J. H. *"To Do the Sick No Harm": A Study of the British Voluntary Hospital System to 1875*. London: Routledge & Kegan Paul, 1974.

Woycke, J. *The Diffusion of Birth Control in Germany, 1871–1933*. Doctoral Thesis, University of Toronto, 1984.

———. *Birth Control in Germany, 1871–1933*. London: Routledge, 1988.

Wright, T. *Some Habits and Customs of the Working Classes*. New York: Kelley Publishers, 1967 [1867].

———. *The Great Unwashed*. New York: Kelley Publishers, 1970 [1868].

Wrigley, E. A. *Population and History*. New York: McGraw-Hill, 1969.

———. 'The Fall of Marital Fertility in Nineteenth-Century France: Exemplar or Exception?' *European Journal of Population,* vol. 1, 1985, pp. .

———. 'Men on the Land and Men in the Countryside: Employment in Agriculture in Early Nineteenth-Century England'. In L. Bonfield, R. M. Smith and K. Wrightson, eds, *The World We Have Gained*. Oxford: Basil Blackwell, 1986.

Young, M. and Willmott, P. *Family and Kinship in East London*. Harmondsworth: Penguin, 1962 [1957].

———. *The Symetrical Family*. New York: Pantheon, 1973.

Yver, J. *Egalité entre héritiers et exclusion des enfants dotés*. Paris: Sirey, 1966.

Index

Aasen, Augusta 165–6
Adams, Francis 107–8
adolescence: *see* youth, youth socialization
alcohol 54; drinking the paycheque, drunkenness 11, 147, 148–9, 150, 151; the social drinker 149
Anderson, Michael 58, 66
apprentices/apprenticeship 29, 35, 37, 103, 117; contract 37; decline of 63, 94–5; living arrangements 62, 94; masters' prerogatives 37; transformation under capitalism 94: *see also* labour–capital relations; labour force; recruitment, kin relations; tenure; trades; youth socialization
Ashley, Lord 57, 120, 123
Austria: Vienna 41, 139, 145

Belgium 35; Antwerp 41, 42, 139; Brussels 41, 42; Ghent 41
Bell, Lady 138, 148, 151
Berger, Brigitte and Peter 210
Berlanstein, Lenard 154, 168
Besant, Annie 166
betrothal 49, 50, 206
birth: *see* childbirth
birth control 183; abortion, abortifacients 158–9, 176, 187, 193, 246 n15; abstinence 158, 159, 160, 161, 169–70, 181, 187, 193; attitudes toward 165, 173, 178; birth spacing 158; and class 163–4; coitus interruptus 158, 159, 160, 161, 172, 181, 187, 193, 248 n47; condoms/sheaths 162, 181, 193; contraceptives 18, 158, 159, 161–4; costs 162, 185, 187, 191, 192; delay of first birth 158; female devices 167; ignorance, misinformation concerning 161, 162, 167, 248 n35; knowledge of 163, 166–7, 178; literature, newspapers 166, 167; male resistance, co-operation 160, 161, 168, 169, 172, 173, 179–80, 181, 189, 190, 193, 250 n109; rhythm method 161; women's views 158–9, 160, 162, 163, 166–8: *see also*

breastfeeding; Church, opposition to birth control; fertility; fertility decline; mortality; sex, conjugal; sexuality
Blom, Ida 160, 163, 172
boarders: *see* lodgers
Booth, Charles 75
Bosanquet, Helen 121–2
boys 36, 37–8, 48, 62, 63, 105, 149: *see also* children; employment, father–son continuity; youth, young men
breadwinner: *see* family wage economy; male breadwinners
breastfeeding 74, 130, 200, 247 n26
British Medical Association 162, 163

Caldwell, John 186
capitalism 5, 6, 77, 78; capital accumulation dynamics 16, 23, 74, 216 n8; centralization of means of production 6, 29, 67–8; class structure; 5–6, 38, 57; conception of freedom 6; enterprise form, 83; first stage of industrial capitalism 21–69, 122; household, private 5–7, 29; labour demand 14–18; and laissez-faire ideology 126; and the nuclear family form 18–20, 55, 58, 59, 103, 122, 203; profit-making 16, 23; second stage of industrial capitalism 81–155, 122; third stage of industrial capitalism 195–7; transition from first to second stage 78–80; and wage form 8–10: *see also* capitalists; family, and capitalism; historical materialism; labour–capital relations; labour market; labour-power; mode of production; patriarchy; proletarianization; technology; unemployment; wage form; workplace
capitalists 6, 14, 74, 89, 127, 214 n14; hiring and firing prerogatives 18, 37, 40, 88; indifference to workers' reproduction 9, 15, 65, 78–80, 214 n16: *see also* capitalism; employment; labour–capital relations
celibacy: *see* birth control, abstinence

277

child 74, 76, 177, 188, 204, 205; differentials: by class 77; by gender 74; by residential district 76–77, 127; rural/urban 75, 127–8; infant 45, 56, 59, 76, 120, 126, 128, 130, 177, 179, 188, 227 n8; maternal 74, 120, 130; sex ratio: *see also* childcare; infanticide; health; housing; population
mothers/mothering/motherhood 10, 45, 74, 99, 151, 203–4, 210; maternal ideal; 180–1; mother–daughter relations 46, 48, 65, 103, 138, 139, 178–9: *see also* parent–child relations

neighborhoods 41, 76; barter exchange 140; networks 45, 67, 142; residential settling 135–43, 206; 'respectable' versus 'rough' 48, 53–4, 135, 140–41; street life 142–3, 206: *see also* community; housing; residence; urbanization
Netherlands: Amsterdam 75, 76
Neuman, R. P. 160
newspapers: *see* literature
Norway: Oslo 160, 162, 169
nuclear family: *see* family, nuclear

old age 19, 32, 64, 66, 68, 74, 186: *see also* family cycle, empty nest phase; parent–child relations, adult children
outwork: *see* homework

parenting/parent–child relations; 49–50, 62, 65, 88, 96, 109, 141, 197; adult children 19, 65, 66, 67, 68; custodial rights 100, 109, 186, 204; wealth flows between generations, 109, 177–8, 186: *see also* child care; child labour; children; employment, father–son continuity; fathers; marriage, parental influence; mothers, mother–daughter relations; patriarchy; schools/schooling; parents' attitude; youth socialization
Parsons, Talcott 61
paternalism: *see* employment, truck system; housing, company; labour–capital relations, paternalism; patriarchs/ patriarchy
patriarchs/patriarchy 10–14, 40, 54–8, 86, 141, 154, 157, 170, 172, 190, 193, 203, 205, 209, 210; husband's dominance 11–13, 190; and proletarianization 32, 33, 57, 59, 121, 205; rule of the father 37, 40, 56, 57, 59, 154–5, 190; weakening paternal control 55–57, 109–10, 111, 120: *see also* family;

fathers/fatherhood; male breadwinners; spousal relations
pawning 66, 140, 147
peasants/peasantry 21, 22, 50, 57, 59, 151
petty commodity production: *see* domestic manufacture
Polano, O. 160, 174
poor/poverty 39, 43, 48, 53, 67, 75, 88, 99, 108–9, 150, 177–8; the labouring poor 33, 47, 73, 114, 117; slum housing 42, 43, 76
population: growth 18; the 'population question' 158, 164, 165, 166; in relation to mode of production 2, 214 n15; rural population supply 22: *see also* fertility; fertility decline; health; labour-power; migration; mortality; urbanization
Princeton European Fertility Project 184
proletarian condition 5–6, 21–2, 215 n19
proletarianization 21–2, 29–30, 54, 55, 63, 71, 73, 84, 103, 137; effects on families 30, 50, 55–6, 58, 59; proletarian versus peasant family structure 57–8, 59, 60, 65; resistance to 30, 33; semi-proletarian 21, 71, 84; see also: capitalism; labour–capital relations; labour market; labour-power; industrial revolution; workers; workplace
proletariat: *see* working class
property 55: *see also* real estate
Proudhon, Pierre Joseph 114, 118

Rathbone, Eleanor 174
real estate 44–5: *see also* housing
Reeves, Maud 132, 136–7, 154, 155
reformers/reform movements 59, 79, 144, 175, 179, 198; moralism 55, 120; and 'the social question' 53: *see also* housing, reforms/reformers; schools/schooling, reformers
rent 124; ground rent 44; portion of income spent on 41–2, 72, 124; relation to overcrowding 41, 68, 124–5; subletting 42, 64; versus homeownership 41, 137: *see also* housing; urbanization
residence: distance from work 41, 64, 134; independent accommodation 6–7, 63; matrilocal preference 65, 67, 138; mobility 64, 67, 135–7; organization of domestic space 64, 68, 144–6; parlour, front room 145–6, 242 n300; proximity to kin 19, 67, 138: *see also* household; housing; migration
Riehl, Wilhelm Heinrich 57